London 2012 Olympic and Paralympic Games

The Official Commemorative Book

London 2012 Olympic and Paralympic Games
The Official Commemorative Book

Tom Knight and Sybil Ruscoe
Foreword by Sebastian Coe KBE

WILEY

This edition first published in 2012
Copyright © 2012 John Wiley & Sons

Registered office
John Wiley & Sons Ltd, The Atrium, Southern Gate,
Chichester, West Sussex, PO19 8SQ,
United Kingdom

An official London 2012 publication.

London 2012 emblem(s) © The London Organising Committee of the Olympic Games and Paralympic Games Ltd (LOCOG) 2007-2012. London 2012 mascots © LOCOG 2009-2010. London 2012 Pictograms © LOCOG 2009. All rights reserved.

For details of our global editorial offices, for customer services and for information about how to apply for permission to reuse the copyright material in this book please see our website at www.wiley.com

A catalogue record for this book is available from the British Library.

FSC
www.fsc.org
MIX
Paper from
responsible sources
FSC® C023561

ISBN 978-1-119-97314-0 (hardback);
ISBN 978-1-119-94154-5 (ebk); 978-1-119-97677-6 (ebk);
ISBN 978-1-119-97678-3 (ebk); 978-1-119-97679-0 (ebk)
Typeset in Futura
Designed by Jason Anscomb (rawshock design)
Printed in the UK by Butler Tanner & Dennis

Contents

Foreword

In Singapore back in 2005, I stood in front of the International Olympic Committee and presented London's vision for the 2012 Olympic and Paralympic Games.

I promised that if our bid was successful, we would stage spectacular sport in iconic settings, and provide a magical experience for athletes, spectators and viewers around the world.

I vowed that our venues would be full of passionate fans, and our streets filled with people celebrating sport, art and culture.

I stated that the construction of the Olympic Park would be the catalyst for the single biggest transformation in London for more than a century, bringing major social and economic benefits to one of the UK's most deprived areas, and I declared that we would use the power of the Games to excite young people and inspire a generation.

Seven years on from that extraordinary moment when the President of the International Olympic Committee, Jacques Rogge, opened an envelope and announced that London had been chosen as Host City, there is little doubt that with the help of so many people across the UK we achieved everything we set out to do – and much, much more.

The London 2012 Games were Games for everyone – for people of all faiths, cultures and backgrounds. From the unforgettable Olympic Opening Ceremony onwards, the greatest ever gathering of countries and territories provided a glimpse of what the world might look like as one nation.

Olympic and Paralympic athletes have a unique power to capture the imagination, and on countless occasions we saw sport connecting the world. People everywhere were transfixed by the joy of sport, with the athletes performing at an awe-inspiring level and almost always with grace and sportsmanship. We had a plethora of world, Olympic and Paralympic records that we could marvel at. Our minds were opened to what people can achieve by sheer talent and determination.

We are immensely proud of our sporting heritage in the UK, and the honour of London becoming the first city to host the Summer Olympic Games for a third occasion. We knew British people would embrace the Games and the demand for tickets was insatiable, creating an extraordinary atmosphere in venues all around the UK right through both Games. To see a packed Olympic Stadium for morning sessions during both the Olympic and Paralympic Games was unprecedented. This was London calling – higher, faster, stronger and louder than ever before.

As well as the best athletes, we also had the best volunteers, our Games Makers, who dedicated themselves to doing something positive for the athletes, for their community, for their country, and for the world.

When our time came, we got it right – and I am incredibly proud to say that all this was made in Britain. I hope the London 2012 Games made you proud too, and that this beautiful book will rekindle memories of an incredible summer and be treasured and shared for many years to come.

Sebastian Coe KBE

Chair, London Organising Committee of the Olympic Games and Paralympic Games

Introduction

The declaration contained just 23 words: 'The International Olympic Committee has the honour of announcing that the Games of the XXX Olympiad are awarded to the city of London.' Yet the wild cheering that greeted the announcement by Jacques Rogge, the President of the International Olympic Committee (IOC), that London had won the right to host the Games in 2012 was an eruption of national fervour – signalling, as it surely did, a new era in British sport.

The initial outburst of joy on 6 July 2005 came from the 100-strong London delegation, led by the Chairman of the London Olympic Bid, Lord Coe, at the Raffles City Convention Centre in Singapore. International superstar footballer David Beckham was among those who leapt from his seat with an enthusiasm mirrored by everyone around him. After the nanosecond it took for the result to be beamed to the other side of the world, the noise was echoed by the thousands gathered in London's Trafalgar Square and Stratford, home of the yet-to-be constructed Olympic Park.

This victory – by just four votes in one of the most hotly contested races in the bidding history of the Games – was a magnificent triumph. It was a triumph for the fresh vision for the Games offered by London, put together with determination and passion, and with attention paid to every detail.

It was also a tribute to the clearsightedness and steely determination of the bid team that their blueprint would go on to deliver Games that would inspire young people all over the world.

At the after-vote party Coe's delegation danced until the early hours to mark the successful end of

'It's not often in this job that you punch the air and do a little jig and embrace the person next to you.'

Prime Minister Tony Blair, on hearing of the success of the London 2012 bid

the campaign. It had been a long road, beginning in 1997 with the determination of the British Olympic Association (BOA) to bring the Games to London. Nothing, it seemed, could quell the excitement as British Olympians, politicians and assembled journalists celebrated through the sultry Singapore night. Yet all that was to change within hours, as news received from London during the afternoon of 7 July 2005 brought festivities to an abrupt end.

That day will always be remembered for the terrorist attack on London's transport system. It was to claim 56 lives, including those of the four suicide bombers, and injure more than 770 people. In Singapore Ken Livingstone, then Mayor of London, captured the mood of the team with an emotional, defiant speech to the media. He declared that London was renowned for its diversity – a place where people from all over the world came to fulfil their ambitions and dreams. That, he vowed, would not stop.

The same message to the IOC about ambitions and dreams, and London's planned legacy for the youth of the world, had lain at the heart of the bid campaign. This vision took London from last place in the early assessments to beat Paris and the rest of the stellar field which also included

Crowds in Trafalgar Square celebrate the news that London has won the 2012 Games on 6 July 2005. The smiles said it all as IOC President Jacques Rogge announced London as the winning Host City.

Opposite page: The Olympic Stadium is the centrepiece of the Olympic Park. Its design sums up the London 2012 design philosophy: adaptability, affordability, sustainability and deliverability.

London 2012 Chair Lord Coe (right) receives the Host City contract from IOC president Jacques Rogge after London won the vote to stage the 2012 Games. London won in the final round of voting, beating long-standing favourites Paris into second place.

Madrid, Moscow and New York City. Ironically the bid's strength was born out of British sport's disappointment at the defeat of Birmingham (bidding for the 1992 Games) and Manchester (bidding for the 1996 and 2000 Games). While both cities benefitted hugely in financial and investment terms from their experience, neither performed well when it came to IOC votes. The London bid emerged from the BOA's conviction that only the capital could offer a realistic chance of victory. Simon Clegg, former chief executive of the BOA, recalled, 'After Sydney was chosen at the IOC session in September 1993, we came home and took stock of why Manchester had not fared better. We said then that we would not bid for 2004, and the clear message from the IOC was that only London would be considered a serious contender.'

As a result, the BOA instigated an investigation into where in London an Olympic bid would be based. In 1997 a 395-page report, produced by David Luckes (goalkeeper in the British men's Hockey team at the Atlanta 1996 Games), identified possible sites in east and west London, and the BOA began lobbying for the bid in parliament, local government and the media.

Support was pledged by Ken Livingstone, the first elected Mayor of London, when he recognised the benefit of a London bid focused on the East End – an area sorely needing investment and regeneration. Also crucial was Team GB's achievement at the Sydney 2000 Games. Craig Reedie, former Chairman of the BOA, explained: 'We needed the London Assembly's support and the Government on board but we also had to do well in Sydney. Those Games, as we know, were a resounding success on all fronts. The team did well, television audiences were huge and the Games captured the public imagination in this country. People were asking, "Why can't we do that here?"'

The question was echoed throughout the country and gradually taken up in the press. The first media organisation to push the case for a London bid was the *Daily Telegraph*, whose sports editor, the late David Welch, had seen the Sydney effect at first hand. One woman convinced of the case for a London bid was Tessa Jowell, then Secretary of State for Culture, Media and Sport, who took on the task of convincing a sceptical cabinet that the project was viable. It was not an easy job, but Jowell persevered, aware of the implications of securing the Games – something far greater than 17 days of sport. 'You host them because of the power of the legacy and the great national moment that hosting a Games creates ... the power of government to back something that was going to be transformational to east London but also to all those kids with unfulfilled potential, up and down the country, who love their sport; and if anything was going to harness that, it was an Olympic Games.'

Jowell was sure that she had positive answers to the issues of affordability, deliverability and 'win-ability' as she set about championing the BOA cause in government. One by one she convinced her cabinet colleagues of the benefits to all their departments of hosting an Olympic and Paralympic Games. Finally she tackled the Prime Minister Tony Blair: 'Tell me what the answer to this question is – we are the fourth largest economy in the world, we are a nation who loves our sport and we think

London is the greatest city in the world, yet we don't dare to bid for the Olympic Games?' When Blair finally agreed that Britain should bid, there was still a wait for a government announcement because of the 2003 invasion of Iraq.

The bid was then led by the London-based American businesswoman Barbara Cassani, and the Candidature File was duly submitted to the IOC. It was officially launched in January 2004 at the Royal Opera House in Covent Garden, with presentations by both Blair and Livingstone. By May, however, when London had been listed as one of five cities to go forward to the crucial IOC vote in 2005, Cassani had decided that she was not the person to take the campaign any further. She gave her decision privately to Tessa Jowell.

'You can win,' she said, 'but not with me.'

Cassani's Vice-Chair, Lord Coe, assumed the leadership as the bid gained momentum following the submission of the official bid book to the IOC, and secured its place in the national consciousness. Early in 2005 the team impressed the IOC evaluation commission on its fact-finding mission to the capital. By the time the London team arrived for the vote in Singapore, there was a feel-good factor surrounding Coe and the British delegation.

When it mattered most, the London team produced one of the finest presentations ever seen at an IOC session. Word perfect, they offered an Olympic and Paralympic Games that promised a lasting legacy for the youth of the world. Jowell and Livingstone were among the speakers, and Lord

How the IOC votes gave London the 2012 Games

First round
London 22
Paris 21
Madrid 20
New York City 19
Moscow 15 (eliminated)

Second round
Madrid 32
London 27
Paris 25
New York City 16 (eliminated)

Third round
London 39
Paris 33
Madrid 31 (eliminated)

Fourth round
London 54
Paris 50 (eliminated)

Note: IOC members from countries with candidate cities were ineligible to vote while their candidates were still in contention

A view of the Lower Lea Valley, the site chosen for the London 2012 Games, prior to development. The east London site had 52 electricity pylons and more than 200 buildings, most of which were industrial sheds.

Doctor, scholar and philanthropist William Penny Brookes, whose 'Olympian Games' in Much Wenlock were to inspire Baron Pierre de Coubertin when he visited Brookes in 1890.

Coe appealed to the IOC delegates in a moving finale: 'Today in Britain's fourth bid in recent years, we offer London's vision of inspiration and legacy. Choose London today and you send a clear message to the youth of the world: more than ever, the Olympic Games are for you.'

So it came to be that after the previous two incarnations in 1908 and 1948, London became the first city to host the Games on three occasions. Its Olympic and Paralympic heritage is deep rooted, intriguingly reflected in the mascots chosen for the London 2012 Games, a striking departure from the usual animal forms. With their metallic finish, camera eyes and a London taxi light on their heads, these two creatures certainly looked different from

anything we've seen before. Children of all ages immediately took to them – and to their story. Written by the noted children's author Michael Morpurgo, the story describes how the mascots were created from the droplets of steel used to build the final girders that went into the Olympic Stadium. What sets Wenlock and Mandeville apart from all their predecessors, however, are their names.

Wenlock gets its name from Much Wenlock, a small town in Shropshire. In the nineteenth century it was the home of the Much Wenlock Games, an annual sporting and artistic event open to 'every grade of man' and featuring athletics, quoits, football and cricket. The first Much Wenlock Games were staged in 1850, the brainchild of the local doctor, scholar and philanthropist William Penny Brookes. They reflected Brookes' belief in sport as a way of addressing petty crime, drunkenness and theft, and his ultimate goal was the revival of an international Olympic competition in Athens. By 1890 the Wenlock Games had become so successful that an intrigued French educationalist, Baron Pierre de Coubertin, decided to travel to Shropshire on a fact-finding mission.

Pierre de Coubertin, celebrated as the founder of the modern Olympic Movement, was a recreational horseman, rower and fencer. His dream of an international sporting festival was inspired by a preoccupation with improving the mental and moral condition of the French in the wake of the country's defeat in the Franco-Prussian war of the 1870s. He began with improving physical education in French schools and went on to travel extensively, seeking to recruit like-minded foreigners in his drive to establish an international sports congress in Paris. Brookes and de Coubertin became great friends, with the Wenlock Games in many ways providing de Coubertin with a blueprint for a modern Olympic Games. The Frenchman's congress first met in 1894 and voted to re-establish the Olympic Games, some 1,500 years after its demise. Penny Brookes, who had been

'I came to pay homage and tribute to Dr Brookes, who really was the founder of the modern Olympic Games.'

Juan Antonio Samaranch, then President of the IOC, when he visited Brookes' grave in 1994

unable through ill health to travel to Paris for the congress, died in 1896, just four months before the first modern Olympic Games took place in Athens. Today his Much Wenlock Games are acknowledged to have been a great inspiration in effecting their return.

Just 10 years later Britain was invited to host the London 1908 Games, following Italy's admission that costs incurred by the eruption of Mount Vesuvius and the near-destruction of Naples would prevent Rome from staging the event. Despite having only two years to prepare, Edwardian Britain and the newly formed BOA, under its dashing chairman Lord Desborough, eagerly took up the challenge to support the fledgling Games.

The other London 2012 mascot, Mandeville,

evokes the Buckinghamshire village of Stoke Mandeville, just an hour's journey north-west from London. Nearby is the hospital of the same name, now famous throughout the world for treating spinal injuries. It is also where the first International Wheelchair Games – the precursor of today's Paralympic Games – were staged for veterans of the Second World War.

It was at Stoke Mandeville Hospital in 1948 that Dr Ludwig Guttmann, a Jewish neurosurgeon who had fled Nazi Germany in 1939, organised the first Stoke Mandeville Games – fittingly held to coincide with the opening of the London Olympic Games at the White City Stadium. The event was conceived by Guttmann to celebrate his belief that sport and exercise were vital in reversing the

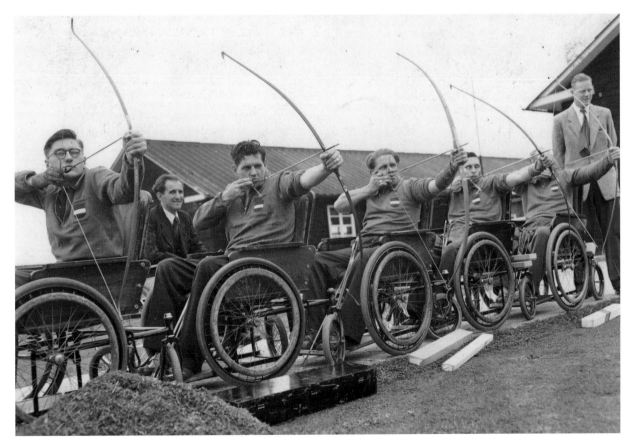

A Dutch archery team takes aim at the second International Stoke Mandeville Games in August 1953. For wheelchair athletes only, these Games were the inspiration of Dr Ludwig Guttmann and were first held in 1948.

The official poster of the London 1948 Olympic Games, opened by King George VI in blazing sunshine on 29 July. The Opening Ceremony was to make a powerful impact on those who saw it, with James Cameron of the *Daily Express* noting, 'You cannot usher 59 nations into an arena, make them mingle in a split minute schedule, give them a common salutation, without something profitable emerging, big or little as it may be'.

OLYMPIC GAMES

29 JULY 1948 14 AUGUST
LONDON

Opposite: John Mark, the final Torchbearer for the 1948 Olympic Games, lights the Cauldron at the Opening Ceremony on 29 July 1948. The 1948 Olympic Flame was a symbol of peace carried through many war-torn countries in the aftermath of the Second World War.

low survival rate among veterans of the Second World War with spinal injuries. Dr Guttmann had previously invented wheelchair polo for patients he had watched pushing a ball around with walking sticks; he also introduced netball and archery as the exercise regime helped the men develop their upper body strength. His popularity led to him being known as 'Poppa' by the patients in his care.

The Games, then for wheelchair athletes only, were staged annually from 1948 at Stoke Mandeville. The event achieved international status in 1952, when Dutch veterans travelled to Buckinghamshire to take part, and subsequently became known as the International Wheelchair Games. Today the pioneering doctor, who died in 1980, is still referred to as the 'Father of Sport for People with Disabilities'. Stoke Mandeville Hospital has a global reputation for excellence,

and Dr Guttmann will always be associated with the work there.

Neither Brookes nor Guttmann could have envisaged how dramatically their events would evolve. When the Olympic Games were first staged in London, for instance, just 2,023 competitors from 22 countries made the trip and only 44 of them were women. By the turn of the twenty-first century, the IOC was struggling with gigantism as the size and cost of the Games threatened to overwhelm potential Host Cities; over 10,600 athletes competed in Sydney in 2000. By then, women were contesting virtually every event and, in Cathy Freeman, could boast the star attraction of the 16 days of competition. Now, of course, as London proved, demand to compete in and see the Games has far outstripped the ability of cities and stadia to cope, and numbers have had to be capped accordingly.

The Paralympic Games, too, have continued to grow from their humble beginnings at Stoke Mandeville. The first global event in Rome in 1960 saw 400 athletes from 23 countries take part; in Beijing in 2008 there were almost 4,000 competitors representing 146 nations in six major classifications of disability. It was not until Seoul in 1988 though that the Paralympic Games were awarded equal billing to the Olympic Games and were staged on the same scale. Almost a quarter of a century later, London 2012 sees both the Olympic and Paralympic Games reach new heights in sophistication, technology, inclusivity and internationalism.

In celebrating the spirit of the London 2012 Games, we are never far from either Wenlock or Mandeville. The genius of these mascots lies in their links with the places and people who brought us the two biggest sporting events in the world. In capturing the imagination of a new generation, they celebrate Britain's association with the very beginning of the modern Olympic and Paralympic Games, which in so many ways were coming home.

Chapter One
Setting the Stage

The Vision for the Games

'We are hiring
the best people
in the world
and you have to
have confidence
in them.'

Tessa Jowell, former
Minister for the Olympics

It is difficult to imagine now that the site of the beautiful and bounteous Olympic Park was, only five years ago, an underdeveloped, polluted corner of east London. To the untrained eye, the job of transforming this patch of land, roughly the size of London's Hyde Park at 2.5 square kilometres, seemed an impossible one. In 2005, when the bid for the Games was won, the future Park held a variety of small businesses in an almost Victorian setting of narrow streets, criss-crossed by a slither of waterways suffocated by car tyres, shopping trolleys, Japanese knotweed and floating pennywort. Ken Livingstone, then the Mayor of London, realised that only an event as big as the Games would attract the level of investment needed to bring this forgotten land into the twenty-first century, and so it was chosen as the setting for this unique festival of sport.

Once the bid was secured, the task of translating the impassioned presentation to IOC members in Singapore into the reality of buildings and roads began in earnest. The London Olympic Games and Paralympic Games Act, which received Royal Assent in March 2006, created the Olympic Delivery Authority (ODA) – a publicly accountable body with the power to buy land and arrange the building of everything required for London 2012. Their remit included all the venues, from the Olympic Stadium to the Lee Valley White Water Centre, as well as infrastructure buildings (such as the Primary Substation) and utilities networks to support the Olympic Park during and after the Games. It was also responsible for increasing capacity on, and improving the accessibility of, transport infrastructure to help ensure London 2012 was a 'public transport Games'.

Making it happen

This was to be the biggest and most diverse construction project seen in the United Kingdom for decades. And unlike virtually any other job, it came with an immovable deadline, which was used to concentrate minds. Dates were non-negotiable, as Sir John Armitt, the chairman of the ODA, observed 'You know you have to do it. The Games were going to start on 27 July 2012 and ... you work backwards from that date. The great thing about it is that it forces you to make decisions more quickly and to a degree it makes things easier because everyone knows that time is of the essence ... the world was turning up in 2012.'

The vision for the Olympic Park was ambitious by any standards. Even Kevin Owens, the architect who became Design Principal of LOCOG in 2006, admitted that the scale of the vision required a 'sharp intake of breath' for him and others. Virtual simulations were one thing, but hands-on engagement was needed to prove the key. 'We'd seen the images on a computer screen,' Owens explains, 'but what clinched it was when, together with the ODA, we returned to old-fashioned methods and created the Park with plasticine models and trees on sticks. That brought it to life. When the earth was finally shaped and sculpted, we saw what it could be.'

Time, such a precious commodity, had to be rationed to each stage. The ODA schedule allowed two years of planning, four years of building and another 12 months for LOCOG to test the venues and infrastructure. The two years of planning saw the London Development Agency draw up the necessary compulsory purchase orders and open negotiations with the hundred or so small businesses that had to relocate – a process that could have

In July 2010, with just two years to go until the Games, workers held a celebration on the Olympic Park. The curving roof of the incredible Aquatics Centre was taking shape, and the Olympic Stadium behind was well underway.

'The Olympic Park was another great British success story: a committed workforce sharing a vision, uniting to build something truly special, on time and under budget.'

Dennis Hone, Chief Executive of the Olympic Delivery Authority

taken years except that the schedule did not allow for excessive red tape. Work began in earnest with the construction of two 6km underground tunnels in December 2006. They were to contain 200km of power cables, allowing the derelict and polluted site to be cleared of 52 pylons.

Burying the power lines was arguably the most crucial aspect of the entire project. With the ODA allocated £8.1 billion when the budget for the entire Games was set at £9.325 billion in March 2007, it was vital that things started well and Tessa Jowell, then the Minister for the Olympics, insisted on as little government interference as possible. She noted that 'When the ODA completed the undergrounding of the power lines, on budget and ahead of time, it was a very good demonstration

of how if you have contingency to work with in something as difficult as that – and it was a difficult, filthy job to do – they could decide whether they were going to lose two days or spend £10 million. That was a breakthrough moment in the early days.'

Sustainability measures set in place from the very start of the project meant that 220 buildings on the site were not simply bulldozed but demolished brick by brick so that materials could be stored and used later. The earth, contaminated with oil, tar, arsenic and lead, then had to be cleaned, and around 1.5 million cubic metres of soil was cleaned by five on-site soil-washing machines with 80 per cent redistributed on the Olympic Park site. The attention to detail was staggering. The ODA worked closely with the

The wetlands in the Olympic Park have helped to create a new habitat for wildlife. Invasive species of plants have been removed and new native species such as reed, iris, and willow will be able to flourish.

Greening the Olympic Park

4,000 trees planted
74,000 plants
60,000 bulbs
350,000 wetlands plants
45 hectares of wildlife habitats (reeds, grasslands, ponds and woods)
675 bat roost and bird boxes

'Thousands of tonnes of soil were cleaned and re-used around the site, in what must have been the fastest and biggest clean-up ever seen in this country.'

David Higgins, then Chief Executive of the ODA

Celia Hammond Animal Trust to rescue more than 160 cats and kittens from the park, seeds were collected for native plants to be reintroduced after construction, over 2,000 newts were relocated and 30,000 tonnes of silt, gravel and rubble removed from the 8.35km of waterways choked after decades of neglect.

Around 5km of temporary roads, 46km of temporary cabling and 1km of temporary water pipes were laid so that work on the so-called 'big build' could begin. Gradually, under the constant glare of television cameras, visiting dignitaries from the IOC and Parliament and journalists, the Olympic Park began to take shape.

As the project evolved, the vision remained constant. 'We were very clear from the start that we focused on delivering the best Games ever, both in physical terms and for people's memories,' notes Owens. 'The question was always "How do we design for six weeks of the summer to last forever in people's memories?" We wanted to

create an Olympic and Paralympic Games that were of the place itself. This was London and, in creating the largest new park in Europe for more than a century, we celebrated the things we were revealing, like waterways and towpaths. It is a park for the Games, but the design always had in mind the intimate nature of a park, somewhere where families would come for picnics in years to come. … The principles of urban planning were applied throughout, even to the temporary venues. It would have been too easy to fall back on the mantra that this was "only for six weeks of 2012".'

At the core of the vision and planning, a vital part of the commitment made to the IOC, remained the legacy of the Olympic Park and all that it involved. Integral to that legacy was the massive investment in, and improvements to, the transport system, so important to a park served by 10 rail lines. Since every spectator was expected to visit the Olympic Park by public transport, cycling or walking, a fast service from the main hub at St Pancras was delivered with the Javelin® train, enabling passengers to travel to and from Stratford International station in only seven minutes. The ODA played its part in this transport refurbishment, working with delivery partners including Network Rail and Transport for London (TfL) to treble the capacity and increase accessibility at Stratford Station, extend two lines of the Docklands Light Railway and increase its rolling stock, not to mention improvements to lines, signal boxes and platforms. Further ODA investment contributed to improvements in the London Underground system and the city's cycling and walking routes, as well as extending the schedules operated by TfL.

The key to this construction project – enabling it to finish on time and on budget – were the collaborative relationships between planners, designers, architects, builders and the myriad companies who supplied materials and personnel. Lessons were learned from previous Games, and both the ODA and LOCOG drew on experts from these Games. Rod Sheard, senior principal at Populous, designed the Olympic Stadium for the

Sydney 2000 Games and did likewise in London.

For Armitt, the finishing line for the Olympic Park build was the Olympic and Paralympic Village. Almost 3,000 apartments in 11 residential blocks provided housing for 16,000 athletes and team officials during the Olympic Games, and another 7,200 athletes and officials at the Paralympic Games. This final build in the Park was officially handed over to LOCOG in January 2012, the ODA returning to the apartments after the Games to prepare the properties for sale as both affordable housing and homes for sale and rent. For the statistically minded, the kitting out of these by LOCOG required 16,000 beds, 28,000 branded duvets and 22,000 pillows.

Venues

Even before the global economic downturn, the organisers of the 2012 Games were conscious that Beijing 2008 probably represented the last truly grandiose Games. Instead, recognising lessons inherent in the approaches of Barcelona 1992 and Sydney 2000 to sustainability and legacy, London 2012 and all its partners set about creating a lasting impression for future generations. That ethos is there in every square metre of the Olympic Park, most notably in the venues and facilities – a heady mixture of the traditional and sensational. LOCOG and the ODA employed imagination and innovation, both in developing spectacular sports venues and in adapting some of the capital's most famous landmarks. Theirs was a new, and impressive, take on the staging of the world's biggest sporting event.

Consider the centrepiece of the Olympic and Paralympic Games, the 80,000-capacity London 2012 Olympic Stadium, which took just three years to complete, on time and on budget. Possibly not as dramatic as the Bird's Nest Stadium in Beijing, it has no pretensions to be anything other than what it is – a beautifully elegant, simple and demountable arena, designed with what those in the computer industry used to call futureproofing. The original plan was that

the structure would shrink after the Olympic and Paralympic Games had finished, to become a 25,000-seater athletics stadium. As a result its steel interior resembles Meccano, with the rest being assembled like a giant Airfix kit. The plan that dominated the bid book in 2005 has changed since, of course, and while the Stadium will still host the 2017 World Athletics Championships, it can be modified and reconfigured for a range of possible future uses, not exclusively sport. Described as the most sustainable Olympic Stadium ever built, the structure used recycled concrete, copper and granite – and even surplus gas pipes in the 800m long ringbeam at the rim.

The Stadium could not grab all the limelight, however. In fact the two venues on the Olympic Park with probably the biggest 'wow' factor were the Aquatics Centre and the Velodrome. The former was the first venue to be commissioned after its architect, Zaha Hadid, won an international design competition for the facility before the result of the bid (and which would have been built whether or not London had been made Host City). The more spectacular of the two buildings, inspired by the fluid geometry of water in motion, Hadid's Aquatics

'We have proved that Britain can deliver a construction and civil engineering project of this size, on time and on budget.'

Sir John Armitt,
Chairman of the ODA

The Aquatics Centre was a dramatic stage for the London 2012 Aquatics events. Its diving platforms are the first entirely bespoke structures ever to be built for an Olympic Games, creating a truly elegant result.

Above: Coloured lighting brought the Basketball Arena to life at night-time. The venue was a celebration of the temporary, holding its own in the north of the Olympic Park.

Games venues in the Olympic Park

Aquatics Centre – Diving, Swimming, Synchronised Swimming, Paralympic Swimming, Modern Pentathlon - swimming

Basketball Arena – Basketball, Wheelchair Basketball, Wheelchair Rugby, Handball

BMX Track – BMX

Copper Box – Handball, Goalball, Modern Pentathlon - fencing

Eton Manor – Wheelchair Tennis

Olympic Stadium – Athletics, Paralympic Athletics

Riverbank Arena – Hockey, 5-a-side Football, 7-a-side Football

Velodrome – Track Cycling, Paralympic Track Cycling

Water Polo Arena – Water Polo

Centre harmonises with the river and rolling parkland of the Olympic Park; its iconic sweeping roof has been likened to a stingray, or even a surfboard. Despite the need to compromise the original design with two demountable, temporary stands at Games-time (to create a capacity of 17,500), the Centre was an immediate hit. When British diver Tom Daley christened the pool in front of a live television audience in 2011, he called it 'awesome'. And the very sight of this compelling structure, with its three shimmering pools, inspired the great Australian swimmer Ian Thorpe to attempt an eventually futile attempt to return to the Games.

As with the Olympic Stadium, the Aquatics Centre was designed for the future. When the temporary wings come down in 2013, they will reveal an affordable and family-friendly public swimming centre, with permanent seating for 2,500. Lord Coe could not hide his pride at how this facility typified the London 2012 mission when he observed, 'Around seven years ago, we were standing on a parcel of land that was contaminated, with rivers that were filthy, an area that had been neglected for far too long. It probably shouldn't have taken the Olympic Games to have done that, to be honest, but it has. Once the Games have gone, we are left with a fantastic community facility that we hope one day will host world swimming championships.'

At the Velodrome, Hopkins Architects called in champion Olympian Sir Chris Hoy to help them create the perfect venue for Olympic and Paralympic Track Cycling – as well as an appealing sports building in legacy for high-performance athletes, not to mention enthusiasts and families. The Velodrome will in later years sit in the middle of an attractive VeloPark, run by the Lee Valley Regional Park Authority. Daylight pours into the building, with natural ventilation through the louvred wooden skin of the building helping to stabilise the temperature inside. On the Ron Webb-designed Siberian pine track, however, the temperature is maintained at 26–28°C – the optimum heat for fast times in competition. Poised on the landscaped slopes of the Olympic Park and topped by the lightest of cable-net roofs, strung like a tennis racket, the Velodrome looks for all the world like a Pringle potato crisp – which is how it earned its early nickname. It was also true to London's vision of building permanent venues only when a legacy use had been identified.

London moved to match Beijing's Water Cube and its illuminated bubble-wrap exterior with the Basketball Arena, the largest temporary structure ever built for the Olympic and Paralympic Games. The simplest of buildings, the Arena is set apart by its cladding and the white recyclable PVC stretched over the apparent coils of scaffold, giving it the appearance of an intricate paper origami sculpture. At the Games the building became a must-see venue, appearing shiny during the day and glowing with an ever-changing light show at night – simple and spectacular.

Among other striking venues are the Copper Box, which hosted Handball, the fencing element of the Modern Pentathlon, and Goalball, and was designed to become a community sports and fitness centre after the Games, and Eton Manor, in the north of the Olympic Park. The Hockey venue, at the temporary Riverbank Arena, featured innovative blue pitches, while the BMX Track and the Lee Valley White Water Centre also attracted much attention.

Previous page: The Velodrome's soaring roof is one of the Olympic Park's great design successes, embodying the poise and drama of the sport. It is topped by a roof weighing only 1,000 tonnes – around half that of any other covered velodrome.

The Equestrian events were held in Greenwich Park, an impressive World Heritage Site full of history. A horseshoe-shaped temporary arena was built there, taking advantage of the historic buildings and impressive London skyline beyond.

At the latter, a gushing mountain stream was replicated in the flattest of Hertfordshire parkland, with pumps forcing water around a closed 300m competition course and 160m intermediate/ training course. All these venues will provide lasting community and elite sporting facilities, managed by the Lee Valley Regional Park Authority.

Around London

Away from the Olympic Park, athletes contested medals at several historic sites across London. These included Archery at Lord's Cricket Ground and Equestrian events at Greenwich Park, home to the Royal Observatory and Greenwich Mean Time. Britain's oldest Royal Park and a UNESCO World Heritage Site, Greenwich proved an inspired choice, offering visitors panoramic Games-time views over the capital.

The Mall leading up to Buckingham Palace became a memorable backdrop for the Olympic and Paralympic Marathons. Hyde Park was the venue for Marathon Swimming, Triathlon and Road Cycling, while The Royal Artillery Barracks in Woolwich hosted the Shooting competitions.

Cycling time trials were held at historic Hampton Court, built by Cardinal Wolsey in 1515 and later one of King Henry VIII's palaces. And right at the heart of official London, Beach Volleyball took place in probably the most extraordinary of temporary venues – on Horse Guards Parade.

Across the UK

The Jurassic coast of Dorset was the setting for the Sailing events, based around the Weymouth and Portland National Sailing Academy. Here a new slipway and moorings were built for London 2012, improving the facilities for local sailors as well as elite, world-class competitors. Weymouth benefitted from a major new trunk road into the town; the Games venue also helped to regenerate the former Naval Air Station at Portland, where new houses, shops and marina facilities continue to be developed.

Football, one sport that needed no new venues, was played at six stadiums around the United Kingdom. They were Hampden Park, Scotland's national football stadium in Glasgow; the Millennium Stadium, Cardiff; Wembley Stadium,

London; St James' Park, Newcastle; the City of Coventry Stadium; and Old Trafford, Manchester.

A Sustainable Games

Considerations of sustainability underpinned every planning and procurement decision at London 2012. A radical ecological vision went way beyond the headline-grabbing concepts of carbon offsetting or recycling. This was a strategy with global impact. It was designed to provide an environmental legacy and a new sustainability knowledge bank to inform decision-makers in sports event planning for decades to come.

At the heart of London 2012's sustainability policy were the ecological passions of two native Londoners: Ken Livingstone, Mayor of London at the time of the Olympic bid, and David Stubbs, Head of Sustainability, LOCOG.

Stubbs grew up in Ealing, west London, where he studied the wildlife, plants and birds of a disused city reservoir as a boy. An environmental adviser for the 1997 Ryder Cup at Valderrama in Spain, he had also spent two months working with the environmental team at the Sydney 2000 Games. Stubbs was convinced that London 2012 could showcase new attitudes, ensuring that sustainability became the starting point for every decision, not merely a part of it, with its principles embedded in both LOCOG and the ODA. 'It would be a once in a lifetime opportunity to … provide the world with a framework of how sustainability could be at the heart of global sporting events,' he reveals.

In construction, LOCOG and the ODA adopted a holistic approach. Over 60 per cent of building materials arrived at the Olympic Park site by rail to minimise the impact on the environment; two million tons of soil was cleansed on site; wood was scrutinised to ensure it came from sustainable sources; and non-essential air-conditioning was significantly cut back. Every unit of every London 2012 venue was assessed for the amount of energy it needed to be heated or cooled, and the Olympic Park boasted its own Energy Centre that provided power, heating and cooling.

Away from the construction site, commitment to a low-carbon Games also ran deep, inspiring plans to strike out the carbon before it even got to London. It was a challenging process, with officials subjecting every procurement decision, from hats and umbrellas, burgers and drinks through to toilets and T-shirts, stadia seating and venue finishes, to five key sustainability questions:

Where does it come from?
Who made it?
What's it made of?
What's it wrapped in?
What happens afterwards – can we hire it, sell it on, donate it or recycle it?

At Olympic and Paralympic Games in the past, large elements of the infrastructure, such as barriers, temporary offices, food outlets, signage and seating, were bespoke items manufactured for a particular venue. After the Games they were often scrapped. In London, by contrast, many of the key pieces of infrastructure were hired, leased, bought back or recycled into a new, post-London 2012 role.

The sustainable ethos driving London 2012 also concentrated on people's health and their quality of life. Much of the produce eaten at Games venues was locally or regionally produced in the UK, food contractors had to commit to supplying certain Fair Trade products, and all food had to comply with high standards of animal welfare. Drinks were not sold in cans at the venues, while recycling bins were colour-coded to ensure the maximum amount

---

The London 2012 sustainability mantra

Sustainability is about making everyday choices that make a positive difference, helping us all to live healthy lifestyles within a fair share of the earth's finite resources. Being sustainable means thinking about people's current and long-term needs, improving quality of life and ensuring a thriving natural environment.

Games venues across the UK

Brands Hatch – Paralympic Road Cycling
City of Coventry Stadium – Football
Eton Dorney – Rowing, Paralympic Rowing, Canoe Sprint
Hadleigh Farm – Cycling - Mountain Bike
Hampden Park, Glasgow – Football
Hampton Court Palace – Road Cycling
Lee Valley White Water Centre – Canoe Slalom
Millennium Stadium, Cardiff – Football
Old Trafford, Manchester – Football
St James' Park, Newcastle – Football
Weymouth and Portland – Sailing, Paralympic Sailing

'I saw what was possible at the Games in Sydney and I wanted to bring that home to London.'

David Stubbs, Head of Sustainability, LOCOG

10 examples of Games Maker roles for London 2012

Catering Team Member
Driver
Multi Faith Team Leader
First Aid Responder
Language Services Team
  Member
Results Team Member
Venue Entry Team Member
Costume Team Leader
Ceremonies Stage Team
  Leader
Web Content Assistant

of waste could be recycled or composted.

Local people living near the Olympic Park were also pivotal to the legacy element of London 2012's sustainability policy. Their importance in the scheme of things was acknowledged from the outset; the whole process of regeneration sought to engage with local communities. Creating local jobs and training opportunities, as well as improving the quality of life for those in the vicinity, were key aims in the ODA's Sustainable Development Strategy. 'We knew that we had to respect those Londoners who live and work in the area,' confirms Stubbs. 'We couldn't just rock up and say we're going to put on a great big event and do nothing for them in the future.' In fact London 2012 has created one of the biggest biodiversity projects in the world. The Games' enduring legacy is an impressive area of parkland, re-profiled and cleansed rivers, new wetland havens and wet woodlands planted with native species designed to encourage the return of the indigenous flora and fauna.

For Stubbs, the planting and regeneration at the Olympic Park represents the closing of a personal ecological circle. 'I'd like to imagine that one day there will be a young Londoner visiting our Olympic Park in a school group who will be inspired to study ecology,' he reflects, 'just like I was all those years ago at that old reservoir in Ealing.'

National Celebration

From the moment the London bid was launched, the key to success was the involvement of the whole UK in a national festival of sport. Planning for this continued through the next seven years, with the UK divided into nine regions, plus the four home countries. This work was overseen by the Nations and Regions Group, chaired by London 2012 Board member Sir Charles Allen, and supported with regular visits around the UK by LOCOG Chair Seb Coe. Volunteers were recruited locally, and training camps across the country brought the reality of the Olympic and Paralympic Games to people nationwide. Thousands of schoolchildren learned about the Games and the Olympic and

Paralympic Movements through their geography and history lessons; some also made contact with youngsters in many of the competing nations.

Get Set, the official London 2012 education programme, drew on the inspiration and excitement of the Games to teach young people about sport, culture, health, communication, enterprise and citizenship. Double Olympic Rowing champion James Cracknell helped promote a series of maths and science challenges, children learned about peace and culture through the Olympic Truce, the Get Set website provided teachers with resources for lessons and The Pod encouraged young people to embrace a sustainable ethos. Paralympic silver medallist Ben Rushgrove, who met children at Mile Oak Primary School, particularly enjoyed seeing 'how passionate they were about making a difference to their environment by reducing their lunchtime and snack waste'.

True to the pledge made to the IOC in 2005, LOCOG teamed up with UK Sport, UNICEF and the British Council to create International Inspiration – the biggest global Olympic legacy project in history. A variety of sports development

A new Games Maker (right) arrives to collect a Games-time uniform and gain accreditation in April 2012. All Games Makers had to attend at least three training events, and many also took part in the London Prepares series to gain valuable experience.

'It has opened my eyes to the fact that sport stands a chance of offering me a bigger and brighter future.'

Chukwu, young leader in Nigeria and member of the International Inspiration programme

schemes aimed to enrich the lives of 12 million children in over 20 countries. In South Africa, for example, children were taught about HIV and AIDS prevention through their engagement with football, netball, rugby and cricket, and children in Bangladesh learned swimming survival skills. In Trinidad and Tobago, the first Paralympic School Day and Sports Festival was organised by young leaders to inspire athletes of all abilities.

Volunteers

The Olympic and Paralympic Games rely on volunteers to make them successful and a quarter of a million people were inspired to apply to become London 2012 Games Makers – a truly impressive response. The chosen 70,000, ranging from students to pensioners, and selected from an impressive 250,000 applicants, became a distinctive sight in their royal purple and poppy red Grenadier Guards-style uniforms as they welcomed the world. They undertook a wide variety of roles from caterers at the venues and

Olympic and Paralympic Village to chaplains and faith leaders helping with spiritual advice. Some volunteered as anti-doping chaperones while athletes underwent post-event drug testing; others served as dressers at the Opening Ceremonies, where they helped with elaborate headdresses and complicated costumes.

The army of volunteers included 2,000 young people, aged between 16 and 18, who distributed competition results for the Technology team and helped out on the field of play at various competitions such as Aquatics, Football and Athletics. Led by scout leaders, sports coaches and community leaders, the teenagers gained unique insight into a global sporting event.

Training camps

In the weeks before the London 2012 Games the UK became a nation of training camps. World-class sporting facilities across the country hosted the world's greatest athletes. In Wales, for example, Cardiff, Newport and Swansea

Who trained where

China – Lisburn, Northern Ireland
Australia – Tonbridge, Kent
Zambia – Glasgow, Scotland
Guinea Bissau – Huntington, Yorkshire
South Africa – Cardiff, Wales
Jamaica – Birmingham, West Midlands
Japan – Weymouth, Dorset
Grenada – Sunderland, Tyne and Wear
Rwanda – Bury St Edmunds, Suffolk
Maldives – Bedford, Bedfordshire

The completion of the Olympic and Paralympic Village was a significant milestone. The architects on the project were free to be creative with the façades. This particular design was taken from an architect's own paintings, which some have said look like beach towels thrown over the balconies.

were used as training bases for over a thousand Olympic and Paralympic athletes from countries such as New Zealand, Great Britain, Liberia, Mexico, South Africa and Trinidad and Tobago.

In Scotland, teams from Namibia and Zambia were based in Glasgow, due to host the 2014 Commonwealth Games, while Team GB swimmers trained in Edinburgh. Northern Ireland welcomed Chinese gymnasts and Australian boxers to training facilities in Lisburn and Belfast. In Birmingham, where teams from Jamaica and the United States were based, athletes were greeted at the city's airport by five giant Olympic rings posted on the new control tower and London 2012 pictograms on the taxiway. Pupils at Tonbridge School in Kent were inspired by Australian track and field athletes who prepared on the athletics track still used by double Olympic gold medal winner Dame Kelly Holmes. Pupils acted as sports coaches in a series of sporting events held by the school for the local community, including a mini-Olympic Games for a thousand primary schoolchildren from West Kent. Holmes paid tribute to the support she had enjoyed as an athlete from the people of her home town, observing 'I'm extremely excited by the potential that the Olympic Games has to inspire children of all ages and abilities to be the best they can be in sport, whether

that's as competitors, volunteers, coaches or leaders … so for Kent and its young people to be involved is fantastic.'

Team GB

And what about the athletes themselves, at the centre of it all and carrying the nation's hopes? It was apparent upon winning the Games that Britain would field its biggest-ever team – more than twice the size of the contingent who paraded in Beijing. Nothing was to be left to chance. Within days of London winning the bid, the British Olympic Association called representatives of all the 35 Olympic sports, from both the Summer and Winter Games, together. At this meeting they established what many considered a ridiculously ambitious target for London 2012 – that of finishing fourth in the medals table at the Olympic Games and second at the Paralympic Games. For the Olympic Games, this meant finishing above the Australians, behind the top three of the USA, China and Russia – from a nation that had been tenth in the medals table at the Athens 2004 Games and had achieved only one gold medal at Atlanta 1996. If these targets were to be achieved, UK Sport, made solely responsible for the Lottery and Exchequer funding of elite sport in 2005, would have to approach the Government with a case for increasing their funding.

Fortunately UK Sport had just the man in Peter Keen, the former university lecturer, cycling international and coach to Chris Boardman who had established the highly successful high-performance programme at British Cycling. He joined UK Sport in 2004 and masterminded the targeting of Lottery funds into the sports and athletes who could benefit most. Throughout the autumn of 2005, Keen perfected the proposal that presented the Government – and in particular the Treasury

'We knew that London 2012 would be a great opportunity to engage and excite young people about sport … to inspire them to continue playing here in west Kent.'

Tim Haynes, headmaster of Tonbridge School

– with five options for funding Britain's sporting future, based on a 'no compromise' approach. Money would go only to sports that showed the commitment, desire and organisation to succeed. The plan worked. In March 2006 Gordon Brown, the Chancellor of the Exchequer, announced that UK Sport would receive the extra money it needed to achieve Olympic and Paralympic Games success.

British sport was now among the best funded of any in the world, with facilities to match, while an underlying attention to detail saw all monies monitored and success measured through UK Sport's Mission 2012 programme. Governing bodies raised their game and imported the best available coaches to accelerate progress. Performances surged, and while investment continued to pour into the nation's emerging talent, ensuring further success at the Rio de Janeiro 2016 Games, one legacy of the London Games emerged four years early. Team GB delivered the result at the Beijing 2008 Games that it had been looking for at London 2012.

As with all Host Cities, the IOC were on hand to supervise and help with all aspects of the preparations. Denis Oswald, the former international rower and IOC member from Switzerland, led the 16-person commission that visited London 10 times between 2005 and 2012. They assessed all the preparations, including the building of the venues, transport links, staging of the Games and plans for the recruitment of volunteers, ticketing, as well as the engagement of the rest of the UK. At times in the past, this commission has had to rectify mistakes and issue warnings over time delays. For London, however, there was never anything but praise.

The big build was completed on schedule in July 2011, with 42 successful test events hosted in 28 venues through the spring of 2012. By May the Olympic and Paralympic Village was furnished and ready, the Opening Ceremony was in rehearsal and final preparations to venues and the Park were under way. The Games were fast approaching and people across the nation, excited and expectant, awaited the arrival of the Olympic Flame.

Delighted fans in Trafalgar Square celebrate the success of Britain's Olympic and Paralympic athletes at Beijing 2008. It was an encouraging sign as London 2012 took guardianship of the Olympic and Paralympic flags, starting the countdown to the London 2012 Games.

'It's fantastic fun. There's a real buzz and energy. Volunteering is the most satisfying and fulfilling thing I've ever done.'

Nicholas Cooke,
Games Maker

On Day One of the Games, the sun rises over the Olympic Rings on the Olympic Park. London was ready to welcome spectators, the media and athletes, as well as countless volunteers and workers.

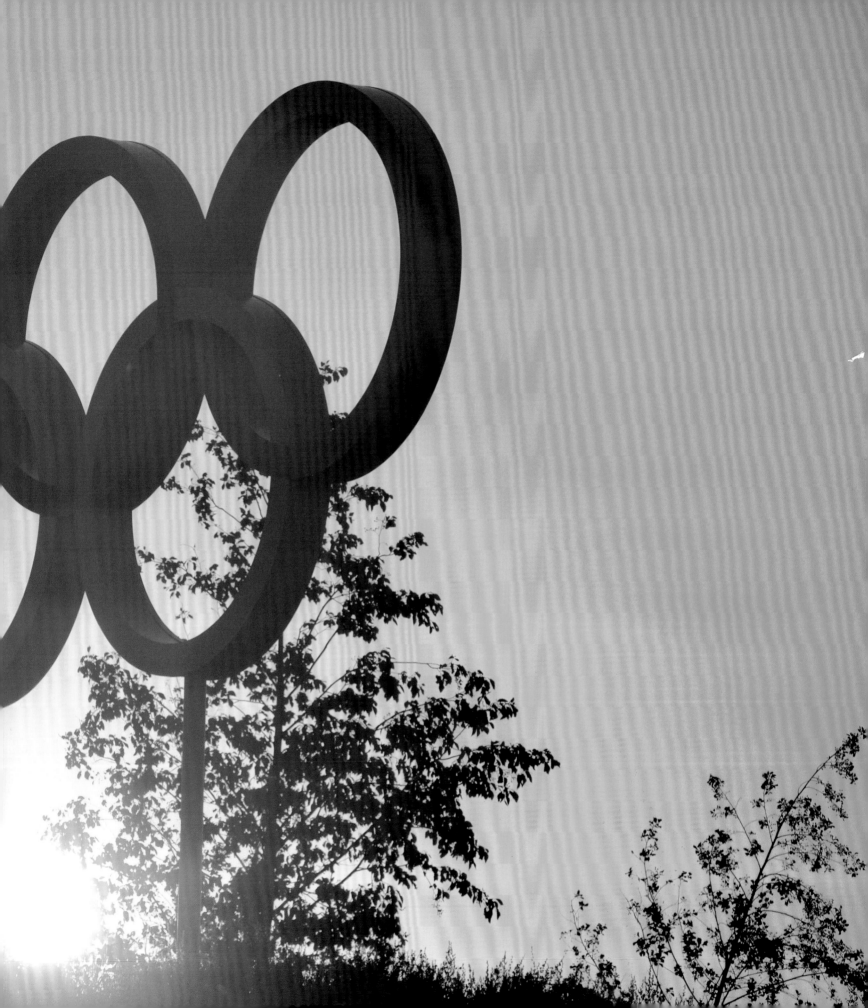

Chapter Two
Welcoming the World

Above: Olympic Torchbearer Christopher Stokes rides on the footplate of a steam engine from the Severn Valley Railway. He acknowledges a trunk salute from elephants Five, aged 20, and Latabe, 19, at West Midlands Safari Park in Bewdley. The Olympic Torch Relay passed within ten miles of 95 per cent of the UK population.

Above right: Huge crowds greet war veteran Ben Parkinson as he carries the Torch through the centre of Doncaster. Ben lost both his legs and suffered brain damage when he stepped on a land mine in Afghanistan. He was determined to walk his 300m stretch, and did so with members of his former regiment cheering him on.

The Olympic Torch Relay

From the moment the Olympic Flame set off on its 8,000-mile journey from Land's End in Cornwall it proved an irresistible attraction wherever it appeared. The gold-coloured Torch, 800mm in height and bearing 8,000 perforations to represent the 8,000 Torchbearers, drew vast crowds and became the focus of the most remarkable, emotionally charged nationwide event ever seen in this country. Excitement grew as the days counted down to the Opening Ceremony, and when the young musician and model Tyler Rix carried the Flame into London's Hyde Park on the eve of the Games, more than 60,000 people were there to greet him. By the time Sir Steve Redgrave brought the Olympic Flame into the Opening Ceremony, LOCOG estimated that some 15 million people had cheered it on its way through more than a thousand communities.

It had been a remarkable journey. The Flame, kindled at the ancient site of Olympia and brought on board The Firefly BA2012 from Greece, had visited the summit of Snowdon in North Wales, the Giant's Causeway in Northern Ireland and the sweeping sands at St Andrews on Scotland's East Coast, the setting for one of the most iconic scenes from the 'Chariots of Fire' film. It experienced very varied forms of transport, from steam trains to cable cars, canal barges to cross-channel ferries, a helium balloon at the Eden Centre in Cornwall and even a zip wire from the Tyne Bridge in Newcastle. The Torch Relay's route went within 10 miles of 95 per cent of the UK population, including stops at Much Wenlock, Stonehenge, Windsor Castle, the White Cliffs of Dover, the Isle of Man, Orkney and the Channel Islands.

Football legend Sir Bobby Charlton carried the Flame from his beloved Old Trafford in Manchester, while the UN Secretary-General Ban Ki-moon donned the white and gold uniform to parade the Torch through crowds 10-deep in Parliament Square in London. There was even a link to the founder of the modern Olympic Movement when Antoine de

Navacelle, great grand-nephew of Baron Pierre de Coubertin, held the Torch aloft at the BBC Television Centre at White City.

Torchbearers who particularly captured the nation's imagination were the extraordinary people nominated because of their service to the community. Among them were ex-servicemen, such as Craig Lundberg, blinded in Afghanistan, who lit the Celebration Cauldron on Liverpool's Pierhead, and Ben Parkinson, the Paratrooper severely injured in Afghanistan in 2006, whose short walk with the Torch through Doncaster took almost half an hour.

The Paralympic Torch Relay

For the Paralympic Games, which began with Dr Ludwig Guttmann's work at Stoke Mandeville Hospital in the 1940s, it was entirely appropriate that the London 2012 Paralympic Flame should come from the very top of the four UK nations' highest peaks. In an inspired piece of organisation, the task of creating the Paralympic Flame was handed to youngsters in England, Northern Ireland, Wales and Scotland.

In England, a group of Scouts was accompanied by mountaineer Karl Hinett, who sustained multiple injuries and burns in Iraq. Local guides led them on the four-hour climb of Scafell Pike in the Lake District. At its summit, 978m above sea level, they nurtured a Flame from sparks created by striking a ferrocerium rod against a steel surface.

In Northern Ireland, a Flame was struck at the top of Slieve Donard, 850m above sea level. Among the intrepid climbers were Scouts and two members of a group of 15 blind and partially sighted climbers training to ascend Ben Nevis, Bernie Sloan from Warrenpoint and Pat Shields from Newry. At 1,085m, Snowdon/Yr Wyddfa was the challenge undertaken by Scouts and mountain guides in Wales; the group also included 50-year-old Elaine Peart, who suffers from bipolar disorder, and Lord Coe. The ascent in Scotland of Ben Nevis in Lochaber, Britain's highest mountain at 1,344m. A team of Scouts struck flint against steel to create the Flame at the summit.

All the Paralympic Flames were brought down in miners' lanterns to feature in Cauldron-lighting ceremonies in London, Belfast, Cardiff and Edinburgh.

From these four corners of the country the National Flames converged on Stoke Mandeville, the spiritual home of the Paralympic Games. They were brought to the grounds of the hospital where Dr Guttmann created the first, Stoke Mandeville Games for the Paralysed in 1948 as part of a rehabilitation programme for veterans of the Second World War. There, on the eve of the Opening Ceremony of the Paralympic Games, Lord Coe, Chair of LOCOG, Sir Philip Craven, President of the International Paralympic Committee and Eva Loeffler, Guttmann's daughter, paid tribute to the work of Stoke Mandeville Hospital as a crowd of more than 3,000 saw the lighting of the Cauldron.

The Flames were then united to create the London 2012 Paralympic Flame, before lighting a silver, mirrored finish Paralympic Torch for a 92-mile journey to the Olympic Stadium in Stratford. Carried in relay by 116 teams of five people, the Flame visited well-known landmarks such as Abbey Road, London Zoo, the Swaminaryan Mandir Temple in Neasden, Piccadilly Circus, Westminster Abbey, City Hall and Hackney Town Hall. As it entered Stratford and the Olympic Park, the Opening Ceremony was already under way and building towards the dramatic entrance of the Paralympic Flame.

A Torchbearer team including Greegan Clarkson, Caroline Baird and Argyle Bird pass through Newham as part of the 92-mile Paralympic Torch Relay.

Historic Greenwich Park is dressed for the London 2012 Equestrian Jumping events. Once the hunting ground of King Henry VIII, it also fittingly hosted the Eventing and Dressage competitions.

Opposite: Historic venues welcome London 2012. 1 Olympic Rings on Tower Bridge; 2 Lord's Cricket Ground dressed for the Archery competitions; 3 St Paul's from the River Thames; 4 Time Trial at Hampton Court Palace; 5 Beach Volleyball at Horse Guards Parade.

Dressing London

As befits any Host City of the Games, London was transformed in the summer of 2012. An explosion of colour brought life to the streets, airports, bus and railway stations as well as the competition venues. The distinctive London 2012 logo adorned banners, street signs, flags and wayfinder markers across the capital. Five giant Olympic Rings floated on the River Thames; others welcomed travellers to Heathrow Airport and the major railway stations. Already buoyed by the success of the Queen's Diamond Jubilee celebrations, the Mayor of London, Boris Johnson, was determined that the city and its constituent boroughs should play their part in celebrating this 'summer like no other'. There were more than 6,000 colourful lamp-post banners, almost 25km of bunting and 638 square metres of building decorations, while a myriad of specially commissioned sporting sculptures and installations sprang up on buildings and in the major tourist thoroughfares.

London's famous bridges were given the lighting treatment as the Thames joined the celebrations, and it was only fitting that the course of this great river featured in a dramatic introduction to the Opening Ceremony. Spectacular Rings, 25 metres wide and 12 metres tall, were lowered into place on a newly lit Tower Bridge, just one month before the Games began. The bridge's lighting display glowed with gold every time a British athlete topped the podium, and the giant Rings on the

River were also lit with gold throughout the night. No less spectacular were the Paralympic Agitos, which replaced the Rings on Tower Bridge in an overnight operation.

The sports venues across the UK glowed with a hot palette of purple, pink and tangerine as they were dressed up for the Games. Banners and flags proclaimed 'Inspire a Generation' and 'Excite', and some of the country's most famous sports stadia were treated to a new outfit for the Games. Just 24 hours after Roger Federer and Andy Murray had walked off the Centre Court after their epic final on 8 July, Wimbledon's makeover was under way. Traditional green and purple was cast aside in favour of London 2012's distinctive colour scheme, while at the Archery venue at Lord's Cricket Ground the famous Pavilion was jazzed up with trendy sofas, plush pink rugs and purple silk cushions.

It was the little touches that made London so different as a Host City. A fine illustration, along with the Long Room at Lord's, was at Hampton Court Palace, where three golden thrones awaited the winners of the men's and women's Time Trial. Far more than a backdrop, the city became an active participant in the Games. At Greenwich Park, site of the Equestrian events, the designs of the jumps intriguingly reflected British heritage from Stonehenge to The Beatles. The historic buildings surrounding Horse Guards Parade blazed with floodlights and even the iconic home of the Reds, Old Trafford, was in the pink as Manchester United's stadium hosted Olympic Football matches.

There was no more special venue than The Mall, accustomed to Royal processions and, latterly, London Marathon finishes. For the Road Cycling and Olympic Marathons, the iconic red tarmac was put in the shade by the vivid new colour scheme, and photographers revelled in the backdrop of Buckingham Palace and the Victoria Memorial. Boris Johnson described the presence of an Olympic podium in The Mall as 'totally magical'. The atmosphere was astonishing, he observed. 'There's a weird glow about people and they're passing it to each other like a benign contagion.'

'I can't think of a better place than London to hold an event that unites the world.'

Nelson Mandela, quoted by Tony Blair in London's bid to host the 2012 Games

What's in the Olympic and Paralympic Village

Social area with:
Computer games
Pool and table football
Cinema
Dry 'bar'
Gymnasium and a team of professional trainers
Multi-faith centre and a team of chaplains
Health clinic
Beauty and grooming salon
Bank
Dry cleaner
Florist
Post office
Tourist information office

The London 2012 Olympic Village Truce Wall, a fixture of the Games since Sydney 2000. Athletes and officials are invited to sign the wall as a symbol of support for peace through sport.

The teams arrive

London always promised a warm welcome to the athletes who would become the Games' stars, and that is exactly what they received on arrival at the Olympic and Paralympic Village. It was not long before the 11 residential plots of five to seven tower blocks of apartments, together with the squares and courtyards, were festooned with the flags of the national teams taking residence. Some competitors came direct from the airport to the Village, situated within walking distance of so many venues in the Olympic Park, while others moved in from their respective training centres around the UK.

The Welcome Ceremony afforded each team was typical of LOCOG's approach. Normally a traditional affair, teams arriving in London were treated to a 30-minute production by the National Youth Theatre, complete with dancers, clowns and jesters. Anthems completed, teams were then invited to sign the Truce Wall, installed as an Olympic tradition since the Sydney Games in 2000 and designed to promote peace through sport. Opening the Wall at the start of the Olympic Games, Jacques Rogge, the IOC President, observed, 'Sport is not immune from and cannot cure all the ills of the world. But sport can help

bridge differences and bring people together. We can see proof of that at these Games.'

Tickets for the Games

The first round of ticket sales for the Olympic Games began in the summer of 2011 and sparked unprecedented interest. There were 6.6 million tickets available for all sports during this round and 1.9 million people applied for 23 million tickets. To no one's surprise, the biggest rush was for a seat in the Olympic Stadium to watch the men's 100m final and organisers were faced with more than one million requests for such prized tickets.

The level of interest inevitably brought disappointment: unprecedented demand was little comfort to those who had missed out. The IOC, however, were delighted because it suggested that every sport would be a sell-out – something very rare even for an Olympic Games. IOC President Jacques Rogge said he was 'amazed' at the demand for tickets, adding 'You are bound to have people who are unhappy. The system put in place by LOCOG was fair.'

Like the Olympic Games, the Paralympic Games proved a massive attraction to the public: in 2011 some 116,000 people applied for the initial 1.5 million tickets put on sale. So great was the demand for seats that ballots had to take place in some price categories for 126 of the 300 ticketed sessions. Sir Philip Craven, the President of the International Paralympic Committee, called it 'unprecedented', adding 'the response has been phenomenal', with most venues sold out. In total, 2.5 million tickets were put on sale for the Paralympic Games.

The rush for tickets underlined what had always been said about London's staging of the Olympic and Paralympic Games: that it would demonstrate Britain's love of sport to the world.

Keeping the Games secure

The biggest event staged in this country meant the deployment of the most extensive security arrangements seen in this country in peacetime, with both the IOC President, Jacques Rogge, and the Prime Minister, David Cameron, stressing that the safety of athletes and the public was the top priority. There was an issue with the ability of private security to provide enough staff and this resulted in the Home Office and Ministry of Defence deploying additional troops, adding to the already tight security around the event.

Soldiers on the ground were supported by weaponry installed on rooftops around the Olympic Park, in Hyde Park and Blackheath and on ships berthed in the River Thames and in the English Channel off Weymouth.

Technology at London 2012

The global scale of the Olympic and Paralympic Games has made the success of both events heavily dependent on the technology involved, both in managing individual competitions and delivering them through diverse routes to spectators and the media. Much of this technology relies on knowledge acquired over several Games, yet the pace of change has become a major challenge. In 2012 LOCOG achieved an unprecedented display of state-of-the-art communications systems provided by sponsors and partners.

The figures were mind-boggling. For example, 350 technologists were employed to keep 950 servers and 16,000 desktops, notebooks and tablets running 24 hours a day, seven days a week,

The London Games use state-of-the-art scoring technology to time and classify events while an army of technical staff monitor the action, ensuring that athletes keep within the rules of their Olympic disciplines. Laser beams tracked trampolinists and mini versions of the Mini car collected hammers and javelins from the Athletics infield.

throughout the Olympic and Paralympic Games. The Atos system, controlled from the Technology Operations Centre in the Olympic Park, ensured the smooth running of a communications network that would have powered a small city. With 34 Olympic venues and 20 Paralympic venues to link, the system needed 16,500 fixed line telephones requiring 4,500km of cabling. Over 14,000 mobile telephones and numbers had to be distributed to the thousands of officials, administrators and technicians, and more than 10,000 radios were used by some 40,000 staff at the Olympic and Paralympic Games.

Such a complex system had to be robust, not just to work when it needed to, but also to be secure against cyberthreats. More than 200,000 hours of testing were carried out, with hundreds of scenarios thrown at the system and its operators – from internet viruses to the more mundane problem of someone inadvertently pulling a plug.

One major innovation in London was the development of the Commentator Information System (CIS). This meant that for the first time the 21,000 accredited broadcasters and 6,500 accredited press could see results of events in real time – so quickly, in fact, that times and places could be confirmed before even the crowd had reacted. Simply transmitting the action to the assembled media and spectators, wherever they were, required in itself a staggering array of technology: 1,000 wireless access points, 80,000 voice and data outlets in all venues, the integration of 65 competition scoreboards and the deployment

---

Food for sport in the Olympic and Paralympic Village

The main dining area has 24-hour service and seating for 5,000.
It serves:
1.2 million meals
60,000 meals a day
1,300 types of dishes

Food includes:
25,000 loaves of bread
232 tons of potatoes
75,000 litres of milk
330 tons of fruit and vegetables
2.7 million bananas

Left: As part of the Welcome Ceremony for each team at the Olympic and Paralympic Village, the National Youth Theatre perform a 30-minute production in the Village Plaza. The 140 performers created a vibrant and quirky welcome for each delegation.

London 2012 undertook the greatest number of doping control tests in Olympic Games history. More than 150 scientists at the brand new laboratory in Harlow, Essex, accredited by the World Anti-Doping Agency, conducted investigations into 6,250 samples throughout the Olympic and Paralympic Games.

of 10,000 television screens with channels dedicated to the Olympic and Paralympic Games. The system also included the management of the London2012.com website, with its estimated 150 million visitors.

All the above systems had to be designed and planned to support the generation of six gigabytes of data a second during the Olympic and Paralympic Games. Approximately 30 per cent more results data was processed in London than at the Beijing 2008 Games, reflecting the rapid advances in technology over the last four years. With the world now boasting 8.5 billion PCs, smart phones and tablets, London had to deliver the smartest of smart Olympic and Paralympic Games – a huge achievement by all concerned.

Keeping it clean

The integrity of the Olympic and Paralympic Games is never tested more severely than by the threat of doping. From the outset the organisers of London 2012 were determined to address the challenge, with Lord Coe, the Chair of LOCOG, declaring the fight against drugs to be one of the 'underpinning

visions' of the bid put to the IOC in 2005. Professor David Cowan, a world-renowned anti-doping expert and Head of the Department of Forensic Science at King's College, London, was put in charge of a new, state-of-the-art laboratory for use at the Games. Provided by GlaxoSmithKline, the lab was located in Harlow, Essex, some 22 miles from the Olympic Park. Its facilities were impressive, enabling around 160 staff to analyse more than 6,000 urine samples and 1,000 blood samples – taken from more than 10,500 athletes during the Games – at a rate of 400 a day.

Cowan issued a pointed warning to any potential user: 'The person who thinks they can beat our drug test, watch out.' John Fahey, the President of the World Anti-Doping Agency (WADA), arrived in London declaring that 107 athletes had been sanctioned following an extensive pre-Olympic programme of more than 71,000 tests and that a new test for Human Growth Hormone had been developed. He said London would be 'the most tested Games in history', adding: 'We're helping to provide an Olympic Games that is as free from doping as is possible.'

In the event LOCOG's doping control programme, which saw more athletes tested than at any previous Games, meant that every competitor came to London with a 50–50 chance of being tested. The programme was, of course, in addition to the normal drug-testing procedures, which call for mandatory analysis of urine samples provided by medallists.

Some athletes were tested more than once, and certain sports and events were targeted because of their doping record at previous championships. The challenge for Professor Cowan and his team was to analyse samples for the more than 200 illicit substances identified on the WADA list of banned compounds and to provide results within 24 hours. The samples were also frozen for eight years, in keeping with recent practice, so that further analysis can be carried out when and if required.

'Isles of Wonder'

The Opening Ceremony of the Olympic Games proved to be a magnificent celebration of Great Britain's history, heritage and humour. Masterminded by the Oscar-winning film director Danny Boyle, its distinctive blend of wit, spectacle and magic created a memorable, occasionally madcap warm-up act for the Olympic Games.

Boyle's own energetic and mischievous character set the tone for a quirky and quintessentially British interpretation of the 'Isles of Wonder' theme. Over one billion people watched the three-hour Ceremony on television around the world. Inside the Stadium 80,000 spectators, including the Royal Family and many heads of state, watched the compelling display unfold.

It began with the tolling of the London 2012 Olympic Bell by Bradley Wiggins, Britain's newly crowned Tour de France winner, due to compete only hours later in the Olympic Road Race. The largest harmonically tuned bell in the world, recently forged by London's Whitechapel Bell Foundry, launched a breathtaking people's history of the British Isles, inspired by the vision of great poets William Shakespeare, William Blake and John Milton. A 'green and pleasant land' came to life in the Stadium, complete with birdsong, wildflower meadows, rolling hills and fields of corn. Sheep and cattle grazed in the fields while men played cricket and women and children danced around maypoles.

Furious drumming, led by Dame Evelyn Glennie, greeted the onset of the Industrial Revolution. In 1709 Abraham Darby's first use of coke to smelt iron ore in Coalbrookdale, Shropshire, set in motion events that transformed people's lives all over the world and made Britain the 'workshop of the world'. Spectators felt the heat of the blast furnace in the 'Pandemonium' tableau, named after the capital of Hell in Milton's *Paradise Lost*. Hundreds of workers swarmed from the land to the mills and factories, as blackened and smoking chimneys rose up through the ground, weaving looms clattered and beam engines throbbed.

Kenneth Branagh strode the stage in the guise of Britain's greatest engineer, Isambard Kingdom Brunel, and five flaming Olympic Rings were forged and gloriously launched into the night sky. The 20th-century wars were poignantly portrayed, while Suffragettes called for votes for women and trade unionists marched on the Jarrow Crusade, the anti-unemployment protest of 1936.

In a moving and spectacular homage to the National Health Service, 600 NHS staff danced around the arena with hospital beds and patients. The Manchester-born Londoner Boyle explained 'Everybody is aware of how important the NHS is in this country … we believe in universal health care … no matter how poor … no matter who you are, you will get treated.' Young people from the Great Ormond Street Children's Hospital, which has benefited since 1929 from the royalties of J.M. Barrie's *Peter Pan,* formed part of a vivid tribute to British children's literature. *Harry Potter* author J.K. Rowling gave a reading from Barrie's masterpiece, while a huge puppet of Harry's arch-enemy

Bradley Wiggins, Team GB Cyclist and winner of the 2012 Tour de France, strikes the 23-ton Olympic Bell to mark the start of the Olympic Opening Ceremony. The Bell, engraved with the words 'Be not afeard, the isle is full of noises' from Shakespeare's *The Tempest*, was forged a few months earlier in Whitechapel, east London.

'...the Olympic Games are coming home tonight. This great, sport-loving country is widely recognised as the birthplace of modern sport.'

Jacques Rogge,
IOC PRESIDENT

'Be not afeard; the isle is full of noises,
Sounds and sweet airs, that give delight and hurt not.
Sometimes a thousand twangling instruments
Will hum about mine ears; and sometime voices,
That, if I then had waked after long sleep,
Will make me sleep again: and then, in dreaming,
The clouds methought would open, and show riches
Ready to drop upon me; that, when I waked,
I cried to dream again.'

Shakespeare, The Tempest,
3.2.148-156, quoted by
Kenneth Branagh in the
Opening Ceremony

Above right: Six hundred NHS staff and young patients from Great Ormond Street Children's Hospital perform in a stunning tribute to British children's literature. Over 300 of the beds used in the sequence will be adapted and donated to hospitals in Tunisia.

Right: On Her Majesty's Olympic Service. Stuntmen dressed as HM Queen Elizabeth II and James Bond parachute into the Olympic Park from a helicopter. In the film that preceded the dramatic entrance, James Bond was shown meeting the Queen in her private study.

Olympic Ceremony numbers

12,956 props
15,000 square metres of staging
500 speakers
1 million watt PA system
80,000 spectators
40 animals
7,346 square metres of turf
34,570 buttons on costumes
600 NHS staff dancers

Voldemort towered in the arena below. A squadron of Mary Poppins flew into the Stadium and the Child Catcher from *Chitty Chitty Bang Bang* raced around the track with his wagon cage.

The great British Saturday night in – and out – was celebrated with a medley of pop hits from six decades, including the music of David Bowie, The Who, the Sex Pistols, The Clash and a live performance by Dizzee Rascal. Clips of popular TV shows, films, soap operas and adverts were projected on to a house in the centre of the arena. 'Frankie and June say … Thanks Tim' told the love story of a young couple who meet via social networking on the internet and then connect through social media. In a magnificent cameo the British inventor of the world wide web, Sir Tim Berners Lee (who gave his invention to the world without personal gain) appeared on stage, seated calmly at a desk, working on his computer.

The evening was full of unexpected gems. The Queen and her corgis delighted spectators by greeting James Bond actor Daniel Craig in Buckingham Palace with the line, 'Good evening, Mr Bond', before stuntmen dressed in their identical clothes made a spoof entrance into the arena by parachute. Rowan Atkinson's Mr Bean gave

a perfectly timed comic accompaniment to the 'Chariots of Fire' theme tune, performed by Sir Simon Rattle and the London Symphony Orchestra.

Danny Boyle said he took the job of masterminding the Opening Ceremony as a tribute to his late father, who had ignited his love of the Olympic Games. Many of those watching found the Ceremony a very emotional experience, not least Boris Johnson, Mayor of London, who described it as 'a brilliant show … inventive … intelligent … peculiar and particular to Britain'.

Lord Coe took to the podium to welcome the world to London. 'I have never been so proud to be British and to be a part of the Olympic Movement,' said the Chair of the London 2012 Organising Committee.

The lighting of the Olympic Cauldron provided a magnificent climax, surrounded as it had been by inevitable speculation about who would have that honour. A dramatic conclusion to the 8,000-mile Torch Relay saw David Beckham and a young footballer, Jade Bailey, powered up the Thames by speedboat to deliver the Olympic Flame to five-time gold medal winner Sir Steve Redgrave. The great rower entered the Stadium through a guard of honour, fittingly composed of the men and women who built the Olympic Park. The Cauldron, crafted in the shape of a flower of copper petals, each of which was brought in by a competing country, and which would bloom for the duration of the Games, was lit by seven young athletes nominated by seven past British Olympic heroes, literally enacting the passing of the Olympic Flame to a new generation. The petals were sent to the countries to keep at the end of the Games. The evening concluded with the parade of Olympic athletes from all 204 nations, the arrival of the Olympic Flag and a musical finale with performances by Sir Paul McCartney and the Arctic Monkeys.

Sir Chris Hoy, the winner of four Olympic Cycling titles before London 2012, proudly leads Team GB into the Olympic Stadium. Hoy noted before the Ceremony that bare-handed was the only way to carry the flag, and he paraded the Union flag around the Stadium without a holster.

The final Torchbearers

Seven young athletes were nominated by seven of Britain's greatest Olympians to light the Olympic Cauldron in the Opening Ceremony.

Callum Airlie, 17 (sailor; by Shirley Robertson)
Jordan Duckitt, 18 (Chairman of the London 2012 Young Ambassador Steering Group; by Duncan Goodhew)
Desiree Henry, 16 (sprinter; by Daley Thompson)
Katie Kirk, 18 (pentathlete and runner; by Dame Mary Peters)
Cameron MacRitchie, 19 (rower; by Sir Steve Redgrave)
Aidan Reynolds, 18 (javelin thrower; by Lynn Davies)
Adelle Tracey, 19 (middle distance runner; by Dame Kelly Holmes)

Journey's end. The Olympic Flame burns proudly in the centre of the Olympic Stadium. Copper petals placed by each competing team rose up to form the magnificent Cauldron in the climax to the Opening Ceremony.

Right: A 13-metre-tall remake of Marc Quinn's famous marble portrait of 'Alison Lapper Pregnant' is unveiled as a centrepiece to the Paralympic Opening Ceremony.

Opposite: East London is lit up as spectacular fireworks explode over the Olympic Stadium during the Paralympic Games Opening Ceremony.

The Paralympic Games Opening Ceremony

'Look up at the stars, and not down at your feet. Try to make sense of what you see, and wonder about what makes the universe exist. Be curious.'

The Opening Ceremony of the London 2012 Paralympic Games began with a rare public appearance from Professor Stephen Hawking, one of Britain's most brilliant scientists, who was diagnosed with Motor Neurone Disease at the age of 21. In an inspired and thought-provoking opening his distinctive electronic voice reverberated around the Olympic Stadium, urging the global audience to seek knowledge and understanding, and to challenge perceptions and stereotypes.

Hawking, a highly respected theoretical physicist, has spent a lifetime trying to unlock the secrets of who we are and where we came from. His words launched a spectacular sequence based on his own 'Big Bang' theory of the universe's origin. The audience of millions were whizzed through the cosmos in an explosion of light, dance and daring acrobatics. Performers included Australian artists 'Strange Fruit' on tall sway poles and 42 deaf and disabled acrobats, trained at the Circus Space in London, who twisted and twirled on wires suspended high above the Stadium.

Entitled 'Englightenment', the Opening Ceremony proved a powerful and multifaceted event. Themes of discovery and defying boundaries were interwoven with a celebration of the inspirational spirit of the Paralympic Games.

The spectacle embraced science, sport, learning and music through a volunteer cast of more than 3,000 adults, 100 professional artists and 100 children from three schools in the six east London Host Boroughs.

In an echo of the 'Isles of Wonder' theme that had introduced the Olympic Games, the Paralympic Opening Ceremony drew upon *The Tempest* as a source of inspiration. Ian McKellen gloriously assumed the role of Prospero and Nicola Miles-Wildin, a young disabled actress, played his daughter Miranda.

The unfolding drama, directed by Jenny Sealey and Bradley Hemmings, featured a historic voyage of exploration, observed from an upturned umbrella. Books, iconic symbols of knowledge and learning, flew round the ship, portraying the bold expansion of human horizons. A giant, floating golden apple paid homage to Sir Isaac Newton's discovery of gravity, with a mass apple crunch – created by 62,000 people in the audience simultaneously biting into apples they received on entering the Stadium – adding to the fun.

London 2012 was a proud homecoming for the Paralympic Games as Lord Coe, the Chair of LOCOG, explained in his welcome speech. His lectern, a stylised map of the British Isles forged from parts of sports wheelchairs and runners' blades, was created by artist Tony Heaton, a former England Wheelchair Basketball player. Lord Coe paid tribute to the pioneering work of Dr Ludwig Guttmann, whose first Stoke Mandeville Games for paralysed war veterans in 1948 was the inspiration for the modern Paralympic Games.

The Ceremony's spectacular climax was heralded by the Paralympic Flame. The Flame appeared at the top of the Orbit accompanied by Royal Marine Joe Townsend. Margaret Maughan, who won Great Britain's first Paralympic gold medal, for Archery, at Rome 1960, lit the first of 166 petals of Thomas Heatherwick's beautiful Cauldron, in a magnificent and moving finale.

'I declare open the London 2012 Paralympic Games.'

Her Majesty Queen Elizabeth II

Chapter Three
The London 2012
Olympic Games

Aquatics – Diving

Precision. Just 17 and 18 years old, China's Yuan Cao and Yanquan Zhang won gold in the Synchronised 10m Platform.

'If we are strong at diving it comes from good coaching, diving every day and hard work. Nothing more.'

Yuan Cao, gold medallist in the Men's Synchronised 10m Platform

Men's Olympic gold medallists

3m Springboard: **Ilya Zakharov (RUS)**

Synchronised 3m Springboard: **(CHN) Yulong Luo, Kai Qin**

10m Platform: **David Boudia (USA)**

Synchronised 10m Platform: **(CHN) Yuan Cao, Yanguan Zhang**

London 2012

Men's events

China scores high for Synchronised 10m Platform gold

China's Yuan Cao and Yanguan Zhang broke the Olympic record, scoring 486.78 to win the men's Synchronised 10m Platform gold medal.

There had been big hopes that the home fans would see a medal for British star Tom Daley and his diving partner Pete Waterfield. The pair led the competition at the halfway point, but a slight over-rotation on their fourth dive ended their challenge.

Chinese teenagers Cao, 17, and Zhang, 18, showed discipline and nerve under pressure, executing near-perfect final dives to win gold. The silver medal went to the Mexican pairing of German Sanchez Sanchez and Garcia Navarro (468.90). They delivered a spectacular inward four and half somersaults dive that had a 4.1 degree of difficulty and had never been seen at the Olympic Games.

The American duo of Nick McCrory and David Boudia won the bronze medal with a score of 463.47. It was the second Olympic Aquatics

bronze for McCrory's family; his uncle, Gordon Downie, won a bronze medal for Great Britain in the 4 x 200m Freestyle Relay at the 1976 Montreal Games.

Brilliant Boudia takes gold in 10m Platform

In an electric final USA's David Boudia was the surprise gold medallist in the 10m Platform Diving competition. He responded to the pressure from China's Bo Qiu and Britain's Tom Daley with a masterful performance at the Aquatics Centre.

The venue crackled with anticipation and Daley's status as the poster boy of diving attracted a stellar audience, including footballer David Beckham and British pop band One Direction. There was drama for Daley's first dive, when he claimed he was distracted and disorientated by the blinding flash lights from scores of cameras, resulting in a poor dive. He appealed to the referee and was allowed to dive again.

The final proved a nail-biting contest which climaxed in the sixth and final round. Daley had a 0.15 lead over Boudia, but the American saved the best until last, scoring a phenomenal 102.60 with a majestic back two and a half somersault, two and a half twist dive with a 3.6 degree of difficulty. His smooth entry into the pool with hardly a ripple secured gold with a score of 568.65.

China's Bo Qui also performed the same faultless final dive to win the silver medal with a score of 566.85. Daley, by contrast, had chosen his so-called easiest dive, a reverse three and a half tuck somersault, for his sixth and last dive. He could not hold on to his slender lead, but his score of 556.95 took the bronze medal.

The 18-year-old schoolboy from Plymouth, awaiting his A-level results, could finally release

months of tension by jumping into the pool with his teammates. Daley's achievement in winning a medal was an impressive testament to his mature and level-headed character. He performed in the face of immense pressure from the media microscope and the heartache of personal tragedy. Just over a year before London 2012 Daley's beloved father, who had followed him around the world, died of brain cancer at the age of just 40.

Women's events

Champions Chen and Wang win Synchronised 10m Platform

China set another Olympic Diving record when Ruolin Chen and Hao Wang won gold in the women's Synchronised 10m Platform with a huge score of 368.40 points.

The 2011 world champions were 25.08 points ahead of Mexico's 15-year-old Alejandra Orozco Loza, making her Olympic Games debut, and her teammate Paola Espinosa Sanchez. The pair won a second Diving silver medal for their country

after the men's success the day before. Canada's Roseline Filion and Meaghan Benfeito, a further 5.70 points behind, took bronze.

There was ecstatic cheering from the home crowd for Britain's 2012 European champions Sarah Barrow and Tonia Couch, who led after the first round and finished fifth.

Wu wows crowd in 3m Springboard

China's Minxia Wu won her sixth Olympic medal when she took gold in the women's 3m Springboard contest, triumphing over her teammate Zi He by a massive 34.80 points to finish on 414.00. Mexico continued its impressive run of performances at London 2012, with the bronze medal going to Laura Sanchez Soto who scored 362.40.

Wu, who trains for four hours each day, is jointly (with China's Guo Jingiing) the most decorated Olympic diver in history. The 26-year-old says her bravery comes from learning from failure. She calms her competition nerves by picturing each dive in her mind as she stands on the board. Earlier in the week Wu became the first woman to win three consecutive synchronised titles, after winning the 3m Synchronised Springboard competition with He.

Taking the plunge

Award-winning Baghdad-born architect Zaha Hadid, designer of London 2012's astonishing Aquatics Centre with its floating, wave-like roof, also redefined the design of its diving platforms. Normally a structure of two pieces, vertical and horizontal, the 10m board at London 2012 is a single, curving statue of concrete that curls around a twisting eight-tonne cage of steel. The dramatic result is the first entirely bespoke structure ever created for an Olympic Games.

Above left: When bronze felt like gold. Great Britain's Tom Daley came of age by battling through a difficult qualifying session on his way to the men's 10m Platform bronze medal.

Left: Into the record books. China's Ruolin Chen and Hao Wang dive to gold with an Olympic record in the Synchronised 10m Platform event in front of a packed Aquatics Centre.

Aquatics – Swimming

Sweet revenge. Clement Lefert (right) and Yannick Agnel of France celebrate beating the USA quartet in the men's 4 x 100m Freestyle Relay four years after losing out on the gold at Beijing 2008.

Open air Olympic Swimming

Today's swimmers have it easy compared with the competitors at the first three Olympic Games. They had to brave the Mediterranean Sea (1896), the River Seine (1900) and an artificial lake (1904). It was not until the first London Olympic Games in 1908 that a pool was built and even that was in the open air – in the middle of the White City Stadium, which also hosted the Athletics, Cycling, Fencing, Gymnastics and Wrestling.

Men's events

France on top in the 4 x 100m Freestyle Relay

Much was made of the rivalry between the USA and Australia before this encounter. Both teams started well, but the final result heralded the start of a great week for the French in the Aquatics Centre.

For France, the gold medal was also sweet revenge for their agonisingly narrow defeat at the hands of the all-conquering Americans at Beijing 2008. As it was, the Americans received the perfect start, with Nathan Adrian handing Michael Phelps a commanding lead over Australia. Phelps, who had

yet to show his true form in the competition after a disappointing swim in the 400m Individual Medley on day one, turned on the heat. He clocked an impressive 47.15 to keep the USA on track for gold.

When Australia faded on the second and third legs, it was France who offered the biggest challenge to the USA – though even then the favourites had the seemingly unstoppable 'successor' to Phelps, Ryan Lochte, to swim the glory final leg. In fact Lochte suffered for having already swum two 200m heats and was clearly not at his best, proving a suitable target for the fast-finishing Yannick Agnel (FRA). Agnel, second at the turn, swept past the faltering Lochte in the final 25m, leaving the American unable to respond. Agnel's touch stopped the clock at 3:09.93, with the USA coming home second (3:10.38). The Russian Federation pipped Australia to the bronze medal in 3:11.41. It was France's second gold medal of the night, the USA's 500th Olympic medal in the pool and Phelps' first-ever silver of an illustrious career.

Jamieson streaks to 200m Breaststroke joy

There were few highlights for the Host Nation in the pool but Celtic fan Michael Jamieson rose to the occasion with a sparkling silver medal and a Commonwealth record.

Four days short of his 24th birthday, the Scotsman swam in the wake of past Olympic Breaststroke champions – Frederick Holman, David Wilkie, Duncan Goodhew and Adrian Moorhouse – to clock a scintillating four lengths. He came mighty close to upstaging Daniel Gyurta, the Hungarian world champion who took the gold medal in a world record 2:07.28; Jamieson was just 0.15 seconds adrift. Both men had to work hard for their medals after Kosuke Kitajima

(JPN), the two-time 100m and 200m Olympic Breaststroke champion, set the early pace and was inside the world record at halfway.

At this stage Jamieson was fourth, behind his teammate and training partner at the University of Bath Andrew Willis, but on the third length the race changed. Gyurta, who as a 15-year-old claimed silver behind Kitajima at Athens 2004, took control, edging ahead of his old rival. Jamieson took up the challenge and, with the crowd on its feet and roaring him on, surged into second place and came within a stroke of snatching the gold medal. Ryo Tateishi of Japan swam his teammate Kitajima into fourth place in 2:08.29. Jamieson's race was shown to 50,000 fans on a big screen before Celtic's home match against HJK Helsinki. He said, 'It's been a pretty special week.'

Clary steals Lochte's 200m Backstroke limelight

Ryan Lochte was billed as the swimmer to succeed Michael Phelps as the greatest, but he did not have the best of weeks. As defending champion he was expected to triumph in the 200m Backstroke but was upstaged, both by USA teammate Tyler Clary and by Japan's Ryosuke Irie.

Lochte led from Irie at the first turn, but Clary came between the two and it was neck and neck along the final length. The last few metres saw Clary reach the wall first in an Olympic record 1:53.41, while Irie claimed the silver in 1:53.78 as Lochte was relegated to the bronze (1:53.94). Clary said, 'I'm using this as a stepping stone for Rio. I'm on cloud nine and I want more of this.'

Above left: On course for silver. Team GB's Michael Jamieson on his way to the silver medal in the 200m Breaststroke final. He finished agonisingly close to a gold medal and a world record.

Above: Flying the flag. Michael Jamieson and Andrew Willis both featured in the 200m Breaststroke final. Despite qualifying first and third respectively for the final, only Jamieson made the podium.

Historic 16th gold for Phelps in the 200m Individual Medley

Michael Phelps doing what he does best and winning gold – his 16th – to become the first man to win the same event at three Olympic Games. It made up for his disappointing showing at the longer event at the start of the week, and was all the sweeter for being revenge of sorts over his teammate Ryan Lochte. Phelps led from start to finish to clock 1:54.27, with Lochte taking the silver (1:54.90). Laszlo Cseh of Hungary claimed the bronze in 1:56.22.

Phelps claims 100m Butterfly triple

He might not have dominated the pool as he had at Beijing 2008, but the week in London was still very much about Michael Phelps. In the 'fly' he was to mark his last individual race by winning gold in 51.21. This was the third Olympic Games in a row in which Phelps won 100m Butterfly gold. The race was also notable for throwing up a unique dead heat for the silver medal, when Chad le Clos of South Africa (who beat Phelps to gold in the 200m Butterfly) and Evgeny Korotyshkin of the Russian Federation both touched in 51.44.

Golden farewell for Phelps with the 4 x 100m Medley

Michael Phelps dived into an Olympic Games pool for the final time, and it was only fitting that his extraordinary career should close with yet another gold medal, his fourth of these Games. It was his 18th gold medal in all, taking his overall tally to 22 in four Olympic Games. No other athlete from any sport has ever won more than nine.

The USA won in 3:29.35 from a strong Japanese quartet in 3:31.26, followed by the Australians (3:31.58). Afterwards Phelps was presented with a Lifetime Achievement Award trophy by FINA, the swimming world governing body.

Michael Phelps – Born to Swim

There will be many a pub argument over what constitutes the Greatest Athlete of All Time, but featuring heavily in any debate will be Michael Phelps. The American swimmer retired after the London 2012 Olympic Games, having won an extraordinary total of 22 medals, 18 of them gold. That tally, which includes his remarkable eight gold medals in eight events clean-sweep at Beijing 2008, means that Phelps overtakes Larisa Latynina, the Soviet gymnast who won 18 medals, nine of them gold, between 1956 and 1964, as the holder of the most Olympic medals.

Born in June 1985 in Maryland and coached by Bob Bowman, Phelps is built for swimming. At 195cm tall, he has a long torso and short legs, with an arm span of 6ft 7in and size 14 feet.

'I couldn't ask to finish on a better note. I've done everything I ever wanted to do.'

Michael Phelps

Golden finale. Michael Phelps bows out with a stunning Butterfly leg for the USA in their 4 x 100m Medley Relay final. The USA took the gold medal on the final day of Swimming.

The Aquatics Centre

The London 2012 Aquatics Centre is made from Welsh steel and concrete, and its 12,000-square-metre wave-shaped roof is one and a half times larger than Wembley's football pitch. The venue was built on the site of a former salvage yard, once Britain's biggest scrap fridge mountain. During construction workers removed and cleaned 160,000 tonnes of soil contaminated with petrol, tar, arsenic and lead. The Aquatics Centre now houses a 50m competition pool, 25m diving pool and 50m warm-up pool, lined with 866,000 ceramic tiles. Despite its voluptuous curves, all the ceiling joints of the Aquatics Centre were crafted in straight lines to help backstroke swimmers to swim straight.

Defending champion Rebecca Adlington reflects on losing her title but gaining the bronze medal in an impressive 400m Freestyle swim.

Women's events

A Chinese star rises in the 400m Individual Medley

To find a 16-year-old swimmer breaking the world record on the first night of Swimming finals at London 2012 was surprise enough. However, when it was noted that the closing 50m of China's Shiwen Ye was quicker than Ryan Lochte had managed in his final of the men's event earlier in the evening, it sent shockwaves through the sport. Ye, who took up swimming aged six when a teacher noticed her unusually large hands and directed her parents towards the sport, was timed at 28.93 for that last Freestyle 50m, compared with Lochte's 29.10. She overtook the pre-race favourite, Elizabeth Beisel of the USA, and touched with a world record of 4:28.43, slicing more than a second off the mark set by Stephanie Rice at Beijing 2008. It made Ye the youngest gold medallist in the 400m Individual Medley in Olympic history, and the youngest world record holder in the event for 34 years. China also took the bronze medal with the 17-year-old Xuanxu Li (4:32.91), while Beisel came home for silver in

4:31.27. Ye commented that, 'There is room for improvement.' The world waited to see if that would come in the 200m Individual Medley.

Shiwen Ye double in the 200m Individual Medley

Shiwen Ye completed the Individual Medley double, winning the women's 200m event and lowering the Olympic record she set in the semi-final with 2:07.57. However, it was noticeable that her victory was nowhere near as emphatic as it had been in the 400m Medley. The 16-year-old sensation was slowest off the blocks and turned only fourth after the Butterfly leg behind leader and defending champion Stephanie Rice of Australia. Ye made her Backstroke and Breaststroke count, however, and pulled away in the final, Freestyle leg. Alicia Coutts eventually took silver in 2:08.15. With American Caitlin Leverenz slipping into bronze (2:08.95), Rice left London without adding to the three gold medals she won at Beijing 2008.

Adlington claims another 400m Freestyle medal

The extent by which this sport moves on was never better illustrated than in this final, when Britain's Rebecca Adlington took the bronze medal despite swimming faster than she had to win gold at Beijing 2008.

Trailing in sixth place at the halfway point, as Camille Muffat of France (4:01.45) and Allison Schmitt of the USA (4:01.77) set the early pace to secure the gold and silver medals, the defending champion left her surge until the final 50m.

With the home crowd urging her on, she made enough headway to grab her spot on the podium in 4:03.01. But this was about differences of expectation, as Adlington explained afterwards. 'Gold wasn't my expectation, it was the people's expectation,' she said. 'Everyone has been saying to me "hey, are you going to get a gold?" like I'm just going to pick up a drink, like it's so easy.'

Lithuania shocks the world with 100m Breaststroke gold

Surprises continued at the Aquatics Centre when an unknown 15-year-old pupil at Plymouth College swept to victory in 1:05.47 ahead of a stellar field that included the gold and silver medallists from Beijing 2008. Sadly for the Host Nation, Ruta Meilutyte is not British but Lithuanian. When she was four years old, Ruta's mother Ingrida was killed by a car on a zebra crossing in Vilnius. Her father, Saulius, came to the UK in search of work and, having settled in Plymouth, brought Ruta to join him. She had already shown promise as a swimmer and was chosen for the Olympic squad in 2011. Coached by Jon Rudd, an overwhelmed Meilutyte could barely speak afterwards. 'I can't believe it,' she said. She was not alone.

Rebecca bows to talented teenager in the 800m Freestyle

Britain's Rebecca Adlington did her best to make the most of her bronze medal at the end of an exhausting week's work, but there was no denying that a 15-year-old American had proved this was very much a young person's game. Swimming in her first championship for her country, Katie Ledecky swept to victory in 8:14.63, a USA record as Adlington, aged 23, saw the second of her two Olympic titles taken away – though not her world 800m record.

It was one of the best performances seen at the Olympic Games and one that neither Adlington (8:20.32) nor the silver medallist, Mireia Belmonte Garcia (ESP), could live with. The Washington schoolgirl took an early lead and, with the first three swimming at sub-world record pace, Adlington expected the main challenge to come from Denmark's Lotte Friis, the bronze medallist behind her at Beijing 2008.

But Ledecky did not slow, and she simply pulled away. With 200m still to go, she had established an unassailable lead and joined the legend of USA

swimming, Janet Evans, in winning the longest of the events in the pool. She was also the latest teenager to cause a sensation at London 2012, following the gold medal exploits of China's Shiwen Ye and Lithuania's Ruta Meilutyte. With 100m to go, Mireia Belmonte Garcia moved ahead of Adlington to make the touch in 8:18.76 for her second silver medal of the Games after finishing second in the 200m Butterfly.

Through the tears, Adlington acknowledged the passing of the baton. 'That was painful,' she said. 'Katie is absolutely incredible.' There were also mutterings about retirement, but much about Adlington's future will only be decided once the dust has settled. As for Ledecky, she accepted that the new breed of swimmers had taken over. 'I think it is really neat. There must be a new generation coming up now that some of the older swimmers are retiring.'

'She is a talented and vigilant worker. When you've got talent and work ethic you've got a great kid.'

Jon Rudd, Ruta Meilutyte's coach, on her success

New kid on the block. Ruta Meilutyte won a surprise gold for Lithuania in the 100m Breaststroke then returned to school in Plymouth to complete her GCSE studies.

10km Marathon Swim

Mellouli moves from pool to men's Marathon Swim triumph

Two pool swimmers triumphed in the men's and women's races, held in the scenic surroundings of Hyde Park's Serpentine. The men's event saw Oussama Mellouli of Tunisia, a gold medallist at the 1500m Freestyle at Beijing 2008, race away to glory becoming the first swimmer to win a medal in the pool and in the 10km Marathon Swim event.

Mellouli came into the Games nursing a persistent shoulder injury, but was still able to produce a decisive move at 7km to head the field into the final circuit.

A quick last kilometre sealed victory, though it was a tired Mellouli who touched first in 1:49:55.10. Germany's Thomas Lurz, the bronze medallist at Beijing 2008, was second in 1:49:58.5 while Canada's Richard Weinberger took bronze in 1:50:00.30.

Afterwards Mellouli suggested that he had suffered enough. 'After winning this gold I will definitely think about retiring … I can't do any better than this.'

Winning return for Risztov in women's 10km Marathon Swim

Hungary's Eva Risztov, a veteran of the Sydney 2000 and Athens 2004 Olympic Games, also made the move from the Olympic pool to triumph in the open water. She had even swum the heats for her country the week before in the 400m and 800m Freestyle events, and in the 4 x 100m Relay. In the end she decided on the 10km Marathon Swim for London 2012, with her victory coming in only her seventh race at the distance.

Disqualified at the world championships when she was caught up in the pack, Risztov, 26, chose to swim this race from the front. She had a clear lead at halfway. For a time she had Britain's Keri-Anne Payne for company. Risztov switched over to backstroke at the one-hour mark to check on her rivals.

Resisting a late surge by the group of four who included Payne, Risztov touched to claim her first Olympic gold medal in 1:57:38.20. She was just 0.04 seconds ahead of Hayley Anderson of the USA and Martina Grimaldi of Italy, who stopped the clock at 1:57:41.80. Payne, the two-time world champion and silver medallist at Beijing 2008, came into the race as the favourite. But Payne lost valuable time in trying to get a drink at the third-lap feeding station, eventually missing out on the bronze medal by less than half a second.

Left: Last one in. The start of the women's 10km Marathon Swim in Hyde Park. Thousands lined the banks of the Serpentine to watch Hungary's Eva Risztov take gold.

Far left: Inside the Aquatics Centre, where capacity crowds filled the space with cheers.

Below left: Water off a duck's back. Tunisia's Oussama Mellouli on his way to an historic victory in the 10km Marathon Swim. In Hyde Park's the Serpentine, the ducks and swans had to make way for the world's best open-water swimmers.

Hyde Park – The Serpentine

There were no heats, only a final, in both men's and women's 10km Marathon Swimming events. The 25 athletes swam six laps of the Serpentine, a man-made lake in Hyde Park created in the 1730s at the behest of Queen Caroline, wife of George II. At that time, Hyde Park was very much countryside on the outskirts of the city. Today it is home to the Serpentine Swimming Club, which attracts attention every year for its Christmas Day race for the Peter Pan Cup, an event that was first held in 1864.

Aquatics –
Synchronised Swimming

Synchronicity. Natalia Ishchenko and Svetlana Romashina, the Russian Federation gold medallists, perform their Petrouchka routine in the Duets event. The Russian Federation are dominant in the sport, having won all the synchronised swimming gold medals at the 2011 world championships and at London 2012.

'We don't want to reveal our secrets, but to stay upside down on our head underwater is no joke. We prepare our new routine for about a year. We think of an image first and then we find the music.'

Natalia Ishchenko, gold medallist Synchronised Swimming Duets

Daring dolls win gold in Synchronised Swimming Duets

Russian Federation's Natalia Ishchenko and Svetlana Romashina were the gold medal winners in the Duets competition watched by 17,000 mesmerised fans at the Aquatics Centre. The Russian Federation's Petrouchka routine, which scored 197.030, featured sharp and dramatic shapes. It saw dolls come to life and included a daring and powerful double flip to start.

The silver medal went to Spain with a score of 192.900. Ona Carbonell Ballestero and Andrea Fuentes Fache swam a Tango with fast, mirrored movements. China's Xuechen Huang and Ou Liu won the bronze medal, scoring 192.870.

Russian Federation's 'Lost World' routine wins Teams event

The Russian Federation treated Synchronised Swimming fans to an intricate display of artistic and technical skill as their 'Lost World' routine won the gold medal in the Teams event. The defending champion swimmers, who scored 197.030, wove an embroidery of pinpoint precision across the pool. They sculled in unison with dramatic choreography to create breathtaking patterns and leaps through the water.

China's delicate butterflies fluttered and twirled across the Aquatics Centre in an absorbing routine which scored 194.010 to win silver. The bronze medal went to the Spanish 'Sea Monsters' routine, with the swimmers wearing silver fish-skin swimsuits, brought the creatures of the deep to life in an athletic display which scored a total of 193.120.

Great Britain finished sixth, scoring 175.440 after their enchanting Peter Pan routine saw Tinkerbell leaping from the pool and a vicious crocodile snapping through the water. Former Winter Olympic gold medal-winning ice skater Robin Cousins helped with the choreography and the voice of actor Michael Crawford was heard in the soundtrack.

Aquatics — Water Polo

Gold at last. The USA players showing gold medal form on their way to winning the Water Polo final. It was the country's first after winning silver and bronze in three previous Olympic Games.

'What an amazing feeling. I can't explain this. This is the top of the top.'

Samir Barac, USA Water Polo gold medallist and captain

Men's event

Croatia coast to victory in Water Polo

Croatia beat Italy 8–6 to become Olympic champions in the Olympic Park's magnificent Water Polo Arena. They are the first Balkan nation to win the title since the break-up of the former Yugoslavia.

In the final both Miho Boskovic and Maro Jokovic scored two goals in the second half, much to the delight of Croatian fans. Cheering spectators made the Water Polo Arena a sea of distinctive red, white and blue flags, emblazoned with a red and white checked shield.

This young team, mostly aged under 30, won the FINA World League Finals in the run-up to the Olympic Games, their tough and physical style reflecting that of Serbia and Montenegro. By taking London 2012 Olympic gold, they signalled that Croatia will be the nation to beat at Rio 2016.

In a dramatic bronze medal match Serbia beat Montenegro 12–11, recovering from a three-goal deficit and scoring in the final minute to finish third.

Women's event

First gold for USA in Water Polo final

The USA won their first gold medal in women's Water Polo, defeating Spain 8–5 in the final to take the gold medal.

Spain, competing for the first time in the Games after rising swiftly in the women's game, went ahead twice, but were eventually overpowered. The USA were determined to take home a gold medal from London 2012 after winning bronze at Athens 2004 and silver at Sydney 2000 and Beijing 2008.

In the bronze medal match, Australia beat Hungary 13–11 in extra time. The match was taken to extra time after Australian goalkeeper Alicia McCormack mistakenly thought she could hold on to the ball in the final seconds while her team was leading 11–10. The quick-thinking Dora Antal swam underwater, stole the ball and backhanded it into the goal to level the scores and give Hungary one last chance. However, Australia then scored twice in extra time to secure the bronze medal.

The Water Polo Arena

The Water Polo Arena, overlooking the Aquatics Centre and the Olympic Stadium, brought its own note of drama and innovation to the Olympic Park. Designed as a temporary venue, the exterior was wrapped in a silver-coloured, recyclable PVC membrane and topped with inflated, self-supporting cushions to make a wave-like roof. Inside the Arena, referees and public were placed on opposite sides of the pool to allow both good views of the action.

The Russian Federation team performs a spectacular move during their Teams technical routine in the Synchronised Swimming competition. Their 'Lost World' routine won the defending champions another gold medal, as their dominance of the sport continued.

Archery

The Italian men's team celebrate after a final arrow inner gold from Michele Frangilli wins gold in front of the historic Pavilion at Lord's Cricket Ground.

Lord's Cricket Ground

The world's most famous cricket ground is named after Thomas Lord, an entrepreneur and bowler who bought the then rural site for the Marylebone Cricket Club in 1814. In a bold move, the architects Populous set two temporary stands for 5,000 spectators on the cricket pitch, to create an axis linking the ground's two most iconic buildings – the red-brick main pavilion and the aluminium pod built for the media in 1999. The International Archery Federation agreed to move the north–south axis of shooting 39 degrees south, so that both buildings could be revealed.

'My first dream came true by being here and on top of that I have a gold medal, so I am a very happy man.'

Jin Hyek Oh

Men's events

Italy's golden arrow secures Team Competition victory

An inner gold finish from Michele Frangilli won the gold medal for Italy in the Team Competition at the magnificent Lord's Cricket Ground. The Italian kept his nerve to snatch victory over the USA with Archery's equivalent of one run in the last over. Italy, silver medallists at Beijing 2008, came into the London 2012 Games ranked 9th in the world, but beat the USA, ranked world number one, 219–218.

Frangilli, who has written a book about archery techniques and who once shot a strawberry off a cheesecake in a New York promotional event, confessed that he closed his mind to both the blustery weather conditions and the noise of the crowd. 'I have been chasing this medal for 16 years,' he declared, 'and the arrow at the 10, that was a dream.'

The young USA team had knocked out the favourites and defending champions Korea in the semi-final. This major shock saw the Koreans fail to make the Team Competition final for the first time since Barcelona 1992, despite breaking two world records in the ranking round and equalling their world record score of 227, set at Beijing 2008, in their quarter-final match against Ukraine. Korea eventually beat Mexico to win the bronze medal by 224–219.

New order flourishes in the Individual Competition

The final event of the Olympic Archery competition ended with a series of firsts and medals for Korea, Japan and China.

Top of the pile was Jin Hyek Oh (KOR), a 30-year-old lover of soft drinks and the elder statesman of the team. He became the first Korean to win the Individual Competition with a 7–1 victory over Takaharu Furukawa, who emulated the best-ever performance by a Japanese archer in this event. Oh, who adapted well to the variable winds that blew at the final, shot 28s and 29s and secured the gold medal with a 10.

The bronze medal match proved more competitive, with Xiaoxiang Dai scoring a shoot-off win with a dead-centre 10 against outsider Rick Van der Ven of the Netherlands to earn China its first individual medal in men's Archery.

Women's events

Team success for Asian superstars

Korea once again dominated the women's Team Competition, beating China 210–209 to win their seventh successive Olympic gold medal in fluctuating sunshine and torrential rain at Lord's Cricket Ground.

Hyeonju Choi, Sung Jin Lee and Bo Bae Ki, wearing designer sun hats and dripping with diamond earrings, are the superstars of the sport, radiating the glamour and energy of a chart-topping girl band. The character of the group, the joyful 24-year-old Bo Bae Ki, shot a final arrow scoring nine for victory. 'I was so lucky that I didn't have to score ten … talking to a sports psychologist gave me a big chance to maintain a stability of mind in that stressful moment,' said the athlete, whose training included handling snakes to enhance her bravery in competition.

She described winning gold as the greatest moment of her life and explained that being in London was the fulfilment of a childhood dream.

Japan beat the Russian Federation 209–207 to win bronze, the country's first medal in Archery. Ren Hayakawa hoped that in a nation where judo and swimming were more popular, the team's Olympic medal would inspire young people to take up the sport. 'Our bronze medal will make archery more popular with children in Japan,' she said.

The famous Long Room in the Lord's Pavilion was dressed up for London 2012 with plush sofas and bright purple cushions. Japan's Miki Kanie, speaking in the Marylebone Cricket Club's members' lounge, said, 'I feel very honoured to be in rooms that we are not usually allowed to enter.'

Korea keeps Individual Competition gold after Mexican shockwave

The Mexican archers caused all the drama with their emergence as a world power, but there was no surprise in Bo Bae Ki claiming her second gold medal of the London 2012 Olympic Games. Bo Bae Ki, who was introduced to the sport as part of her school curriculum, had to fight all the way, however, as Aida Roman (MEX), her opponent in the final, took her to the last arrow and a shoot-off. Both archers hit eight, but Ki's arrow was judged to be nearer the centre and won the gold 6–5. The closing stages of the competition were all about Mexico, with Mariana Avitia also taking the bronze medal 6–2 as she and Roman won their country's first medals in Olympic Archery.

Alison Williamson, the senior member of Great Britain's women's Archery team, was competing in her sixth Olympic Games. She lost to Mongolian Bishindee Urantungalag in the Individual Competition, following the women's team defeat by the Russians on the first day of the Games.

'Despite the result this is definitely the stand-out Games for me. The crowd was brilliant and the venue absolutely amazing.'

Alison Williamson

Shooting with style. Korea's spirited archer Bo Bae Ki scored nine with her final arrow to win Team gold. She sought the help of a sports psychologist to help her concentration at London 2012.

'I've been to five Olympic Games, but this is special to me because I'm a Londoner. As a cricket fan, working at Lord's is a bit like being set loose in the sweetshop.'

Robert Parsons, 79, Lord's Cricket Ground Games Maker

The use of the historic Lord's Cricket Ground as the site for the Archery competition was a huge success. The axis of the field of play was adjusted so that the two famous architectural elements, the pavilion and the Media Centre were linked.

Athletics

'It was wonderful … I knew it would be like this. I can feel that energy and I am extremely happy.'

Usain Bolt, 100m gold medallist, thanks the Olympic Stadium crowd

Men's track events

Lightning Bolt strikes again in 100m final

There were doubts before these Olympic Games about his form and fitness, but Usain Bolt of Jamaica proved yet again that he is the world's fastest man by retaining the title he had won so spectacularly at Beijing 2008.

In one of the most highly anticipated blue riband races for decades, the 25-year-old superstar of

the sport crossed the line in an Olympic record of 9.63, ahead of all those hoping to relieve him of his crown. In becoming the first man in history to win the 100m at successive Olympic Games, Bolt had also run the world's second fastest time – one that only he had bettered.

By his own admission, he was only '95 per cent fit' after niggling problems with his back and hamstrings, so there was no time to waste in those 41 strides for any theatrics. Bolt had to work hard for this victory, and it was all the more impressive for that.

After a relatively poor start, he was upright at 40m and ahead at 60m. From then on the 198cm-tall Bolt was all puffed cheeks and concentrated effort until he dipped with a glance at the trackside clock. There was also a raised index finger aimed at all those who had suggested that maybe he could not reproduce enough magic to secure this second 100m title.

Behind him was Yohan Blake, his 22-year-old training partner. Nicknamed 'the Beast', he was in reality the young pretender who had beaten Bolt at the Jamaican Olympic trials. Blake, who had won the 2011 World Championships 100m title when Bolt was disqualified for a false start, clocked 9.75 while the early leader Justin Gatlin, back at the top after a four-year doping ban, took bronze in 9.79.

Behind them were the two other Americans, Tyson Gay and Ryan Bailey. Both are great sprinters, but they were blown away in a final in which seven of the eight men broke 10 seconds, a first in Olympic history. After the excitement of the three British gold medals on 'Super Saturday', this was exactly what the Olympic Stadium needed. Chants of 'U-sain, U-sain' rang out from the 80,000 crowd, relishing a 100m final worthy of all the pre-Games hyperbole.

Bolt the showman re-emerged after the race to

strike his Lightning Bolt pose, perform a somersault and show that big booming smile as he paraded the Jamaican flag on a lap of honour. 'I slipped a little in the blocks,' he confessed. 'I don't have the best reactions, but I secured it and that's the key. My coach told me to stop worrying about the start and concentrate on the end because that's my best.'

Blake was more than happy with silver and his chance for revenge was not far away. Both men had to recover quickly for the heats of the 200m, hard on the heels of the 100m.

Bolt eyes legend status with 200m victory

As the irrepressible Usain Bolt led a Jamaican clean sweep of the medals in a thrilling 200m, it was the American Wallace Spearmon who summed up what had just been achieved. 'Those guys are on another planet right now,' Spearmon conceded. 'You just have to say "Congratulations".'

This, after all, was Bolt's favoured distance – the one in which he first came to prominence as a sprinter of rare quality when he became the youngest-ever world junior champion, aged 15, in 2002. Shrugging off the doubts over his stamina coming into these Olympic Games, the defending champion led around the bend and stretched out on the straight, always holding off the approaching Yohan Blake.

Bolt's time of 19.32 was outside his world record, but it equalled the previous best mark set by Michael Johnson at Atlanta 1996. All those years ago, people thought Johnson's record would last for decades, but Bolt made it look like jogging. He was that good.

Blake, who had beaten Bolt at the Jamaican trials, had to make do with a silver medal again, posting a season's best time of 19.44 while the little-known Jamaican Warren Weir, 22, was third with 19.84, a personal best. Spearmon's time of 19.90 put him in fourth place.

With two titles secured in front of another packed house at the Olympic Stadium, there was still the 4 x 100m Relay to go. For Bolt, looking forward to being hailed as 'a legend' as he paraded his way round yet another lap of honour, the Relay could not come soon enough.

Opposite: Lightning strikes twice. Usain Bolt makes history by winning his second successive Olympic 100m final in an Olympic record time.

Kemboi maintains Kenyan hold on Steeplechase

Exuberant Kenyan Ezekiel Kemboi danced for the 80,000 crowd on 5 August after adding the 2012 Olympic Steeplechase title to the one he claimed at Athens 2004. He celebrated by veering across the track to lane eight before stepping over the finish line in 8:18.56. 'It was to show that I am stepping aside from the Steeplechase to concentrate on the Marathon,' the 30-year-old revealed.

It was Kenya's eighth Olympic Steeplechase gold medal in a row. 'This is our event,' Kemboi explained, 'this is what we do best.' Long-time rival Mahiedine Mekhissi-Benabbad claimed France's first Athletics medal of the Games with silver in 8:19.08 while a second Kenyan, Abel Kiprop Mutai, took the bronze with 8:19.73.

Jamaican jubilation. Usain Bolt (left) celebrates with silver medallist Yohan Blake (centre) and bronze medallist Warren Weir (right) after the first-ever Jamaican clean sweep of the medals in the men's 200m final.

Right: New generation. Nineteen-year-old Kirani James of Grenada on his way to winning his country's first Olympic medal in the men's 400m. He was also the first athlete not from the USA to go under 44 seconds.

Below right: Simply the best. David Rudisha, whose father had won a 4 x 400m Relay silver medal at Mexico City 1968, chose the biggest stage of all to produce his finest performance. The Kenyan won a sensational 800m final with a new world record.

Resurgent Sanchez grabs 400m Hurdles gold

For six years Felix Sanchez (DOM) had been virtually written off as a force in one-lap hurdling, but at London 2012 the 2004 Olympic champion took everyone by surprise. He reproduced his best form to snatch back the title with 47.63 – exactly the same time as he clocked at Athens 2004.

The Dominican Republic athlete, who famously wore a red plastic souvenir bracelet with flashing lights during an unbeaten run of 35 finals between 2001 and 2004, sobbed uncontrollably as he stood on the podium. It emerged that he was remembering the grandmother who had brought him up and who had died in 2008.

Behind Sanchez the USA's Michael Tinsley was a surprise silver medallist in 47.91 while the world number one, Javier Culson of Puerto Rico, clocked 48.10 for the bronze. Most shocked of all was Team GB's world champion Dai Greene, whose lack of fitness after surgery at the turn of the year left him struggling in fourth place.

First gold for Grenada in 400m

On a night of surprises and upsets in the Olympic Stadium, Kirani James continued his sensational progress by adding Olympic gold to the world title he won in 2011. His victory came from a 400m final that contained no USA team athletes for the first time in modern Olympic history.

The 19-year-old took the first Olympic medal of any colour for Grenada (pop. 110,000) in 43.94. He finished ahead of Luguelin Santos, 18, of the Dominican Republic and Lalonde Gordon, 23, of Trinidad – a Caribbean clean sweep and from the part of the world now dominating world-class sprinting.

After the semi-final James, a world youth and world junior champion, swapped bib numbers with Oscar Pistorius, the South African who was the first double-amputee runner to compete at the Olympic Games.

Rudisha world record to win 800m

Lord Coe called it 'the performance of the Games, in any sport', and few would dispute that David Rudisha's (KEN) world record in the Olympic Stadium was among the greatest moments of London 2012. The 24-year-old world champion came to the Games intent on breaking Vebjorn Rodal's (NOR) Olympic record of 1:42.58, but from the start he was clearly on course for something faster. Leading

through 400m in 49.28, he opened up along the back straight and then launched his finishing effort around the final turn. The young Botswanan Nijel Amos gave chase, but there was no catching the imperious Rudisha.

His eyes lit up as he caught sight of the time as he crossed the line and the crowd responded with rapturous applause. He had broken the world record for the third time, and his 1:40.99 fulfilled the pledge that he made to himself 'to make Lord Coe proud'. Amos took the silver with a world junior and Botswana record of 1:41.73, a time that once stood as a world record to Seb Coe, and Timothy Kitum, another Kenyan, collected the bronze.

'Lord Coe is a good friend of mine,' Rudisha revealed afterwards. 'I came here in February and he took me around this Olympic Stadium. I wanted to come here and make him proud. I've waited for this moment for a very long time. I had no doubt about winning and I was praying for good weather. Today the weather was beautiful and I decided to go for the world record.'

Fabulous finale. The Jamaican 4 x 100m Relay team closed the Athletics programme in the Olympic Stadium by retaining the Olympic title, breaking the world record in the process. (Clockwise from bottom left) Yohan Blake, Usain Bolt, Nesta Carter and Michael Frater claimed they kept their baton-changing practice to a minimum.

In the greatest 800m ever seen, everyone behind Rudisha and Amos clocked either a season's best or a personal best. Among them was Britain's Andrew Osagie who was eighth in 1:43.77, a time that would have won the previous three Olympic finals.

Jamaican world record in 4 x 100m Relay

In the most fitting of finales to the Athletics programme in the Olympic Stadium Usain Bolt anchored the Jamaican quartet to a memorable world record of 36.84 – improving the mark they set at Beijing 2008.

It was the Games' fourth Athletics world record and the fourth of Bolt's stellar career, now including six Olympic gold medals. All the talk of Bolt's injury worries and waning powers were swept away in one glorious week; this was a final victory to savour.

The Jamaican changeovers, beginning with Nesta Carter and Michael Frater, were faultless. When Bolt took the baton from Yohan Blake, he was a stride behind the USA's Ryan Bailey, but the result was never in doubt. The USA team took silver, with Trinidad and Tobago being promoted to bronze medal position after the Canadians were disqualified.

Bolt almost blotted his copybook by pretending to hand the yellow baton to an official at the end of the race and then running away with it as a keepsake. The rules required that the baton be returned, but Bolt was given it later in any case – a memento of an astonishing week in which he had established himself as the greatest sprinter of all time. 'It's always a beautiful feeling to end like this,' said Bolt. 'I knew a world record was possible and the team gave it their all.'

> 'In my opinion we have seen the two best athletes in the sport tonight.'
>
> Michael Johnson, four-time Olympic gold medallist, pays tribute to Usain Bolt and David Rudisha

Bahamas triumph in 4 x 400m Relay

The USA used to be able to count the 4 x 400m Relay as its own after a winning record in the Olympic Games stretching back to 1952, but in London the Bahamas beat the top-quality quartet into second place.

Chris Brown, Demetrius Pinder, Michael Mathieu and Ramon Miller claimed Bahamas' first ever men's Olympic gold medal with a national record of 2:56.72. Their victory came after the most dramatic of final legs, when Miller overtook Angelo Taylor of the USA in the last 30m. Trinidad and Tobago took the bronze medal after holding off the fast-finishing Briton Martyn Rooney. His magnificent final leg of 44.1 seconds gave Team GB fourth place.

Missing from the USA team in the final was Manteo Mitchell, who had managed to complete his 400m lap in the heat despite sustaining a broken leg.

'I've been here since the beginning watching the Stadium grow and it's been a terrific experience. It's an amazing achievement and I've done my little bit to make it happen.'

Brian Thomas, Olympic Stadium worker

Magical moment. Mo Farah becomes the first Briton to win the men's Olympic 10,000m and the third of the three British athletes to win gold on 'Super Saturday'.

'I've never experienced anything like this ... this is the best moment of my life.'

Mo Farah, 10,000m gold medallist

Anything goes. The London 2012 Olympic mascot Wenlock hugs Mo Farah as he celebrates winning gold in the men's 10,000m.

Pure Mo magic in the 10,000m

This was British athletics at its very best. Mo Farah's 10,000m triumph capped a fantasy night for a sport that normally struggles for a British gold medal. This was a night when three came within the space of 45 minutes, and the most dramatic of those belonged to Farah. This was the night that Farah took on the Africans over 25 laps and beat them, sprinting from the front around the final circuit and crossing the line in 27:30.42. A euphoric crowd of 80,000, already hoarse from cheering the gold medals won by Jessica Ennis and Greg Rutherford, found a second wind to acclaim Farah's historic achievement, in an event in which it was once thought impossible to overcome the Kenyan and Ethiopian dominance.

Farah ran a careful, strategic race, remaining with the defending champion Kenenisa Bekele (ETH) until only five laps remained, when he moved to third. He followed Tariku Bekele, the younger of the Ethiopian brothers, to the front and was in second place at 800m, racing away at the bell to take a metre lead. Another move with 90m to go and the 29-year-old had crossed the line, ending the sequence of four consecutive Ethiopian golds.

It was fitting that the silver medal was won for the USA by Galen Rupp, Farah's training partner, with 27:30.90. Both men belonged to the group of athletes coached by former marathon runner Alberto Salazar in Oregon, to where Farah and his family had decamped in 2010.

Bronze went to Tariku Bekele on 27:31.43, the younger brother of Kenenisa Bekele who had tried in vain to track Farah throughout the race.

'I can't believe it,' said Farah. 'It's something I have worked so hard for with 120 miles in training, week in, week out.'

Mo achieves distance double in 5,000m

It seemed inconceivable that having won the 10,000m the week before, Britain's Mo Farah could pull off this double. Only six men in history had achieved such a feat, including the great Emil Zatopek of Czech Republic and Lasse Viren from Finland – but this was a historic Olympic Games in which British athletes were achieving extraordinary things. When Farah was handily placed throughout the slow-run race, and then moved into the lead with less than two laps to go, the impossible became suddenly possible. Given that Farah had already admitted to being tired after the greatest week in his life, the Kenyans and Ethiopians had played into his hands by allowing the race to drift along. They gave Farah the perfect platform from which to launch his winning effort, with his famous burst of speed.

The strike came even before the bell and Farah was off. He was chased hard by the pack, led by Ethiopia's Hagos Gebrhiwet, Morocco's Abdalaati

Iguider and Kenya's Thomas Pkemei Longosiwa. There was a time when Farah would have been swallowed up by men such as these, but not now. The Briton pressed harder on the accelerator and found more speed, his face showing his effort and sheer desperation to get to the finish line first. The nearer it came, the less serious their gold medal challenge appeared.

Even before he crossed the line, to a standing ovation from the Stadium crowd, Farah's unforgettable celebrations had begun. His hands first crossed and then stretched wide as his mouth opened and the reality hit home. He had run the last mile in four minutes and the last lap in 52.94 seconds, contributing to an overall time of 13:41.66. Ethiopian Dejen Gebremeskel took silver with 13:41.98 and Longosiwa of Kenya bronze with 13:42.36.

Left: Determination. Mo Farah runs through the pain on his way to winning his second gold medal of the London 2012 Olympic Games in the 5,000m final.

110m Hurdles gold falls to USA

Top-ranked American Aries Merritt won the 110m Hurdles in what was a competition littered with injuries and falls. Among the casualties were the Chinese superstar and Athens 2004 champion Xiang Lui, who succumbed to an Achilles tendon injury just as he had done at Beijing 2008. The final also saw world record holder Dayron Robles pull up injured.

'The greatest feat in the history of British athletics.'

Brendan Foster, 10,000m Olympic bronze medallist at Montreal 1976, acknowledges the scale of Mo Farah's achievement

One day like this. Mo Farah's face says it all as he completes an historic double to win the men's Olympic 5,000m ahead of Dejen Gebremeskel of Ethiopia and Thomas Longosiwa of Kenya on the final night of track action in the Olympic Stadium.

Ugandan surprise. Draped in his national flag, Stephen Kiprotich heads for the finish line of the men's Marathon in The Mall. He was only the second Ugandan ever to win Olympic gold after 400m hurdler John Akii-Bua.

'I didn't believe it could be me … I've joined the champions and I'm very happy.'

Stephen Kiprotich,
Marathon gold medallist

Men's walks draw record crowds

The vast crowds which lined the route of the men's 20km Race Walk on 4 August 2012 were rewarded with an Olympic record and a major breakthrough, as Ding Chen, 19, became the first Chinese walker to win Olympic gold. He crossed the line in The Mall in 1:18:46, with compatriot Zhen Wang taking the bronze medal behind Erick Barrondo of Guatemala.

Big crowds were also in central London for the 50km Walk on the 11 August, which saw a victory for Sergey Kirdyapkin of the Russian Federation in a new Olympic record of 3:35:59. Australia's Jared Tallent won silver, as at Beijing 2008, while Tianfeng Si of China took bronze.

Britain's Dominic King was cheered home to finish last of the 51 walkers, crossing the line more than 39 minutes behind Kirdyapkin.

Uganda powers to Marathon gold

There were surprises on both sides of the barriers lining the men's Marathon route on the final day of the Olympic Games. Stephen Kiprotich ran the race of his life to take the first gold medal for Uganda since the legendary John Akii-Bua won the 400m Hurdles at Munich 1972, and unprecedented crowds watched the field wind its way through the centre of London from its start in The Mall.

Unlike the women's race a week earlier, the men's event was blessed with glorious sunshine. Even the London Marathon has not drawn such crowds, often 20-deep and hanging from every vantage point as the race unfolded.

In a field containing champions and a world record holder, Kiprotich's victory was a major shock. The sixth of seven children, he moved to Kenya to train in Eldoret in the Rift Valley, home to the world's elite marathon runners; and it was the Kenyans who had to watch from the chasing pack as the 23-year-old made his move, powering away from the rest with three miles to go.

Away and clear, Kiprotich waved to the crowd on The Embankment and winked at the television camera. As he made his way to the finish, in front of Buckingham Palace, he grabbed a Ugandan flag from the crowd, draped it around his shoulders and jogged through the finish line in 02:08:01. It was to be Uganda's second-ever Olympic medal.

Abel Kirui (KEN), the two-time world champion, had to be content with the silver medal in 02:08:27 and Wilson Kipsang Kiprotich (KEN) the reigning London Marathon champion, was third in 02:09:37. These were the last medals awarded at the London 2012 Olympic Games and they were presented to the athletes, as is traditional, later that day, during the Closing Ceremony in the Olympic Stadium.

Men's field events

Rutherford emulates 'Lynn the Leap' in the Long Jump

On the night that will go down in history as 'Super Saturday' three Britons won gold in the Olympic Stadium. The most unlikely of them, Greg Rutherford, gloriously succeeded the likes of Lynn Davies, Bob Beamon, Carl Lewis and Dwight Phillips as the Long Jump champion with a remarkable jump of 8.31m.

The 25-year-old from Milton Keynes, whose great-grandfather Jock won three league championship titles with Newcastle United, has struggled with injury throughout his career; before Beijing 2008 he also had to contend with the death of his grandfather. He did not come into the London 2012 Olympic Games as a favourite, but he was fit and healthy. Rutherford had remodelled his jumping technique in recent years to emulate the take-off favoured by Lewis, who took Olympic gold four times between 1984 and 1996.

His fourth-round jump was enough to beat the rest, allowing Rutherford, who might have become a footballer after training with the Aston Villa academy as a 14-year-old, to fulfil a lifelong dream. On such a night, when his every effort was propelled along the runway by the jet-engine noise of an 80,000-strong crowd still revelling in Jessica Ennis' Heptathlon triumph, Rutherford did enough to beat Mitchell Watt of Australia, on 8.16m, and the American Will Claye on 8.12m.

'Looking at the others, I knew that no one had the spark that's been there in this event in recent years,' he admitted. 'No one dominated the event. I wanted to get a good jump in early and make them chase. I was aware of the crowd and they gave me the lift I needed.'

In an Olympic Games bearing the slogan 'Inspire a generation', Rutherford hoped that he could play his part. 'I'm hoping there are a couple of kids out there who are thinking, "I'll do long jump now; that ginger guy was pretty good".'

History maker
Majewski wins Shot Put

Tomasz Majewski of Poland became only the third man in history to win two Olympic Shot Put titles, and the first to retain his title since 1956. His best effort of 21.89m came in the final round of an intriguing contest, with the 30-year-old taking the title by just three centimetres from David Storl of Germany. Reese Hoffa of the USA claimed the bronze medal with 21.23m while his teammate Christian Cantwell was fourth.

After the contest on 3 August Majewski praised the performance of the young German, youngest of the 12 finalists. 'David Storl is young, he is explosive,' he said. 'The next Olympic Games will be his, but this one is mine.'

'This is what I have dreamed of my whole life and to do it in London is just incredible. I might wake up in a minute.'

Greg Rutherford, Long Jump gold medallist

Leaping for gold. Greg Rutherford becomes the first Briton to win the Olympic Long Jump since Lynn Davies at Tokyo 1964 with this leap of 8.31m.

Right: Breakthrough. Great Britain's Robbie Grabarz cleared two heights, 2.25m and 2.29m, to win a bronze medal in the men's High Jump a year after almost giving up the sport.

Far right: Staying ahead of the game. Ashton Eaton (centre) of the USA produced a season's best in the 110m hurdles to retain the lead he held throughout the competition as he won the men's Decathlon gold medal.

Pars hits par to win Hammer

Krisztian Pars became the fifth Hungarian to take the Hammer gold medal, on 5 August 2012. The Hungarian run of success began with the legendary Imre Nemeth at the London 1948 Olympic Games.

Pars, 30, came into the Olympic Games in the form of his life and was simply too good for the rest, his being the only throw beyond the 80m mark. His winning score, coming in the third round, was a relatively modest 80.59m, with the closest throws of defending champion Primoz Kozmus of Slovenia and Koji Murofushi of Japan, the 2011 world champion, falling more than a metre shy. Kozmus took silver with 79.36m and Murofushi bronze with 78.71m, both season's bests. 'There will be quite a festival now in my hometown,' said Pars, who comes from Szombathely, near the Austrian border.

Up and Ukhov in the High Jump

Ivan Ukhov, one of the great characters of the High Jump event, found a new celebrity status in London by taking Olympic gold. Competing in rainy conditions that do not usually suit him, as he could not wear the normal high jump shoes with spikes in the heel, there was an ad hoc element to Ukhov's performance; at one stage the tousle-haired Russian lost his competition vest and hastily had to pin a spare number on a T–shirt. The 26-year-old, overlooked for Beijing 2008, sailed over 2.33m, 2.36m and 2.38m to secure the gold, while Erik Kynard of the USA, who tried to stay with Ukhov, landed the silver as the only other man to clear 2.33m.

It was a dramatic night as both the world champion Jesse Williams of the USA and Olympic champion Andrey Silnov (RUS) failed to live up to their best. Britain's Robbie Grabarz cleared only two heights, but his 2.29m meant he took bronze, sharing equal third place with Mutaz Essa Barshim of Qatar and Derek Drouin of Canada. It made for a crowded podium.

'I should have jumped higher than that and should have got one better medal, but I got a bronze medal and it's incredible … it's fantastic.'

Robbie Grabanz, High Jump bronze medallist

Exhausted Eaton wins Decathlon

The USA's world record holder Ashton Eaton enjoyed a fabulous two days to win the Decathlon title in front of crowds that multi-event athletes only dream about. The striking aspect of this 10-element event is that, normally, most of it is played out in front of near-empty stadia. At London 2012, the Olympic Stadium was full for the first element, the 100m, and the last, the 1500m. In between, three quarters of the 80,000 crowd stayed behind at lunchtime on the first day to watch the Decathlon high jump.

The 24-year-old racked up points with his 100m time of 10.35, the fastest-ever in an Olympic Decathlon, followed by a long jump of 8.03m and a throw of 61.96m in the javelin. By the time the athletes lined up for their 1500m race, the outcome was no longer in dispute. Eaton won gold with 8,869 points from his teammate, Trey Hardee, for the first American one–two since 1956. For Hardee, second to Eaton in the 100m and close behind him throughout the ten events, the silver medal was particularly welcome following a foul in the pole vault at Beijing 2008 and an elbow injury in the 2011 world championships. Cuban Leonel Suarez took the bronze medal with 8,523, a season's best score.

Hurdling Harting takes Discus gold

Robert Harting celebrated his Olympic gold medal by ripping off his vest and leaping over the barriers set out for the women's 100m Hurdles final. The 204cm-tall German's eccentric display was understandable. He had just won the Discus competition with his fifth-round effort of 68.27m to become the fourth German to hold the title and the first for 12 years to win an Athletics Olympic gold.

Ehsan Hadadi's first-round distance of 68.18m survived to land him silver – Iran's first-ever Athletics medal at the Olympic Games. The bronze went to the defending champion, Gerd Kanter of Estonia, who threw 68.03m.

Walcott shocks with golden Javelin strike

Less than a month after winning the world junior title in Barcelona, Keshorn Walcott (TRI) shocked the senior athletes by collecting the Olympic gold medal as well. Walcott became the first non-European to win the Javelin Throw since 1952.

The 19-year-old's first surprise was to take the first-ever lead in the competition with 83.51m, and then improve to 84.58m, a Trinidad and Tobago national record, in the second round. It was a mark that the very best throwers from Europe, struggling with the wind, were unable to match, with Norwegian Andreas Thorkildsen, the defending champion, finishing a surprising sixth. Oleksandr Pyatnytsya of Ukraine took the silver medal with 84.51m while the bronze went to Antti Ruuskanen of Finland who managed 84.12m.

This was Trinidad and Tobago's first Olympic gold medal in Athletics since Hasley Crawford's 100m triumph at Montreal 1976, and its first ever in a field event. On his return home, Walcott received a £100,000 reward and 20,000 acres of land. A lighthouse was named in his honour, and the day of his arrival was also declared a national holiday by Trinidad and Tobago's Prime Minister.

Indoor Pole Vault champion soars to Olympic gold

Renaud Lavillenie, the most confident of all the pole vaulters in the Olympic Stadium, boldly moved straight to a 5.97m vault in the final on 10 August, going clear on his second attempt. He became the fourth Frenchman to win the gold medal and the first since Atlanta 1996.

Already European outdoor and world indoor champion, Lavillenie had not enjoyed the best of build-ups, but took the title with an Olympic record of 5.97m, ahead of Germans Bjorn Otto and Raphael Holzdeppe. Both cleared 5.91m on their first attempt, but failed to go any better. Their medals were decided based on their record at the previous height of 5.85m. Otto cleared this height on the second attempt, while Holzdeppe took three attempts.

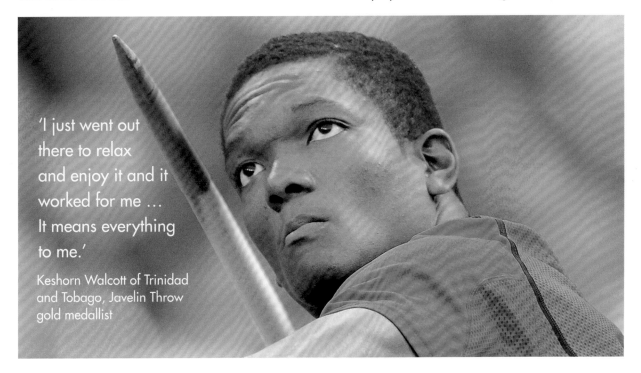

'I just went out there to relax and enjoy it and it worked for me … It means everything to me.'

Keshorn Walcott of Trinidad and Tobago, Javelin Throw gold medallist

Above left: Party on. Germany's Robert Harting celebrates winning the Olympic Discus gold medal by ripping off his vest. Harting's win saw him extend his unbeaten record, which stretches back to August 2010.

The big shock. Trinidad and Tobago's Keshorn Walcott won the men's Javelin Throw with the shortest winning distance since Seoul 1988, but it was a personal best, a national record and too good for the rest.

'I used to compete in triathlon so this is very exciting. The enthusiasm of the British people has been amazing ... I'm really impressed by people's love of sport.'

Fernanda Strasser - German and Spanish interpreter

Eager spectators, photographers and journalists fill the streets of London to catch a glimpse of the competitors in the men's Marathon, the final Athletics event of the London 2012 Olympic Games.

Above: Close run thing. Jamaica's Shelly-Ann Fraser-Pryce (centre) retains her Olympic 100m title ahead of the favourite, Carmelita Jeter (second right) of the USA.

Women's track events

Fraser-Pryce back on top in the 100m

Jamaica's Shelly-Ann Fraser-Pryce caused something of an upset by upstaging the pre-race favourite, Carmelita Jeter of the USA, to win the 100m in 10.75 – an astonishing time considering the breezy, cool conditions in the Olympic Stadium.

The 25-year-old, who took the lead at half way became the first woman to retain the title since the USA's Gail Devers won at Barcelona 1992 and Atlanta 1996. It was not quite the clean sweep the Jamaicans managed at Beijing 2008, however. Fraser-Pryce crossed the line just 0.03 seconds ahead of Jeter, who challenged hard all the way in what she described as a 'power-filled final', with fellow Jamaican Veronica Campbell-Brown taking the bronze medal in 10.81. Jeter, who ran a season's best time, had narrowly beaten Campbell-Brown in one semi-final, while in the other Fraser-Pryce finished ahead of Allyson Felix, also of the USA.

10,000m win puts Dibaba into history books

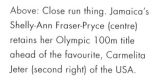

Ethiopia's Tirunesh Dibaba became the first woman to win successive Olympic titles at 10,000m on 3 August. Her victory followed another consummate performance over 25 laps on the opening evening of Athletics in the Olympic Stadium.

The only other woman to win two 10,000m titles since the race entered the Olympic programme was her cousin, Derartu Tulu, who won at Barcelona 1992 and Sydney 2000. Dibaba, 26, unleashed her trademark sprint over the final 600m to win in 30:20.75, ahead of Kenyans Sally Kipyego (30:26.37) and Vivian Cheruiyot (30:30.44). 'I have worked very hard for this,' said the delighted champion.

Richards-Ross takes 400m in near carbon copy final

It was so close to being a rerun of their race at the Beijing 2008 Olympic Games – but both Sanya Richards-Ross and Britain's Christine Ohuruogu, the bronze and gold medallists there, had been through enough in the intervening four years to ensure that this final would have a different result. Richards-Ross, the 2009 world champion from the USA, led as usual into the final 50m. This left Ohuruogu, after three years of injury and indifferent form, to make her customary late charge from sixth place coming off the final turn. The Briton almost made it, but her best time since her Beijing 2008 triumph still left her 0.15 seconds adrift at the line as Richards-Ross claimed the title she craved in 49.55.

DeeDee Trotter (USA) who admitted having spent 25 minutes on her extravagant eye makeup, was third in 49.72.

'I worked so hard for that and I prepared for this moment over and over for the last four years,' admitted Richards-Ross. This was the USA's first gold medal on the track at London 2012, with Richards-Ross becoming only the second American to hold the title after Valerie Brisco-Hooks in 1984.

Ohuruogu, who was brought up within a 10-minute walk of the Olympic Stadium, was initially distraught at losing her title, but admitted later, 'I should be really proud of myself … To have done what I did, having had three years which were not that great means I should be quite happy.'

Gelana defies the rain in Marathon

Inspired by Fatuma Roba, the Atlanta 1996 champion, Ethiopia's Tiki Gelana survived a fall at a drinks station to win the women's Marathon in a rain-soaked central London, setting a new Olympic record of 2:23:07.

The 24 year old from Bekoji, 100 miles south of Addis Ababa, improved the record set by Japan's Naoko Takahashi at Sydney 2000. It proved a fascinating race on the Olympic course of one 2.2-mile loop followed by three of eight miles that took in some of the capital's most iconic sights.

In the early stages the 118 competitors had to splash through vast puddles as the rain lashed down, but the carnival atmosphere persisted. Runners could not resist waving to the crowds who lined every section of the route. As the sun dried the streets, so the leaders pushed on in their quest for Olympic glory and, predictably, it was

the Ethiopians and Kenyans who forged ahead. With eight miles to go, Gelana was one of five leaders with a 17-second lead on the rest. Up with her were Kenyans Mary Keitany, the two-time London Marathon champion, the world champion Edna Kiplagat, Priscah Jeptoo, and Mare Dibaba of Ethiopia in what was looking like a battle between Ethiopia and Kenya.

The surprise package turned out to be the Russian Tatyana Arkhipova. She surged from the pack to catch the leaders and, as Keitany tried to inject some pace, so Arkhipova matched her efforts.

Gelana rounded the Queen Victoria Memorial alone to cross the line and kiss the red tarmac in The Mall – the finish of the London Marathon since 1994. Jeptoo was just five seconds adrift in second for the closest finish in the women's Olympic Marathon's short history. Arkhipova was rewarded for her tenacity with the bronze medal in a personal best of 2:23:29.

'It was a great race,' said Gelana. 'The rain made it very interesting. I love running in the rain. I have been doing that since I was a small child. Roba [Olympic gold medallist Fatuma Roba, also from Bekoji, the 'town of runners'] is my hero. I am extremely happy to share history with her.'

The women's Olympic Marathon

As recently as 1980, the furthest women were permitted to run on the track was 1500m. Resistance to the women's Marathon lay in the long-held belief that it was simply too far for them to run. Pressure to include the classic distance in the women's programme came largely from female runners who were competing in big city races around the world. Only in September 1981 was the women's Marathon finally added to the Olympic programme for Los Angeles 1984.

Opposite: Silver lining. Great Britain's Christine Ohuruogu's silver medal in the women's 400m represented an astonishing comeback after three years of injury problems following on from Beijing 2008.

Below: The women's Marathon sets off in front of huge crowds on a rainy Sunday morning in The Mall. The location provided a stunning backdrop for the start and finish of the race.

'This is no time to freeze because it's the Olympic Games. This is what you do every single day. You aren't going to forget how to hurdle or run. So you just have to do it.'

Advice given to Sally Pearson before her 100m Hurdles final

Third time lucky for Felix in 200m

After taking the silver medal at Athens 2004, the USA's Allyson Felix was expected to win gold at Beijing 2008, only to be denied by Jamaica's Veronica Campbell-Brown. At London 2012 the graceful 26-year-old always looked like a champion-in-waiting in the heats, and in the final she had enough in reserve to hold off another Jamaican, the 100m champion Shelly-Ann Fraser-Pryce. Felix clocked 21.88 to claim Olympic gold, with Fraser-Pryce equally delighted to win the silver medal with 22.09, a personal best. Carmelita Jeter (USA), the 100m silver medallist, took the bronze in 22.14. 'I've waited so long for this moment,' said Felix. 'It's been a long road. You can't lose sight of your dream.'

Right: Breaking down barriers. The USA team of (left to right) Allyson Felix, Carmelita Jeter, Bianca Knight and Tianna Madison broke an East German world record to win the 4 x 100m Relay.

Inspired Pearson gives a 100m Hurdles masterclass

Sally Pearson is not British, but there was no more popular winner that night in the Olympic Stadium, when she took gold in a dramatic 100m Hurdles.

Inspired by Cathy Freeman's 400m victory on the 'Magic Monday' of the Sydney Olympic Games, the Queenslander gave a masterclass in hurdling to win Australia's first Athletics gold medal at London 2012. Her British relatives in the crowd saw the 25-year-old clock an Olympic record of 12.35, finishing a hair's breadth ahead of the USA's Dawn Harper, whose dip for the line almost brought her gold. Only 0.02 of a second separated the two, with Kellie Wells (USA) taking bronze on 12.48. Both Harper and Wells ran personal best times.

Pearson, who admitted to being very nervous before the first heat, had won 32 races in a row before losing to Wells at Crystal Palace three weeks before the Games. She finished her London 2012 heat in 12.57, the fastest heat time ever run at an Olympic Games.

USA scorch to world record in 4 x 100m Relay

One of the longest-surviving world records was obliterated when the USA team of Tianna Madison, Allyson Felix, Bianca Knight and Carmelita Jeter clocked 40.82 to win the Olympic women's 4 x 100m Relay title.

Significantly the previous record of 41.37 belonged to East Germany and had been set back in 1985. Knight, who ran the third leg, said, 'I knew we could get the Olympic record but the world record? I didn't see that.' Jamaica, a long way back in second place on 41.41, set a national record, while Ukraine took the bronze medal on 42.04.

The USA team, which had failed to qualify for the final at Beijing 2008, made a powerful start and held on to their fierce pace. Jeter, silver medallist in the 100m, stormed down the final leg to take the gold medal.

Felix was also part of the USA team – along with DeeDee Trotter, Francena McCorory and Sanya Richards-Ross – who won gold in the 4 x 400m Relay, finishing more than three seconds ahead of the Russian Federation and Jamaica.

'The atmosphere is electric because the crowd bring you alive ... I fed off them.'

Jennifer Suhr, Pole Vault gold medallist

Left: Jennifer Suhr of the USA coped best with the conditions to win the women's Pole Vault in a competition where even the two-time champion Yelena Isinbayeva (RUS) faltered.

Far left: Unchallenged. Sandra Perkovic won the first Athletics gold medal for Croatia in the women's Discus Throw with a national record and the longest winning throw since Atlanta 1996.

Women's field events

Croatia takes first gold medal with Discus Throw triumph

Sandra Perkovic won Croatia's first-ever Olympic gold medal in Athletics when she landed a national record of 69.11m in the third round of the competition. No Croatian had ever qualified for an Olympic Discus Throw final before, and the only other medallist from that country previously was the high jumper Blanka Vlasic, forced to miss London 2012 through injury.

Perkovic was not seriously challenged, with the silver medal going to Russian Darya Pishchalnikova (67.56m) and bronze to China's Yanfeng Li (67.22m).

Breeze blows Suhr to Pole Vault triumph

On a breezy evening in east London when the heights were more modest than would normally be expected, it was the Team USA pole vaulter Jennifer Suhr who kept her cool to improve on the silver medal she won at Beijing 2008. The winning height in only the fourth women's Olympic Pole Vault competition was 4.75m and, while Suhr and Yarisley Silva went over on their second attempt, the American took the gold medal because of the Cuban's initial failure at 4.45m.

Yelena Isinbayeva, the Russian world record holder who won gold at Athens 2004 and Beijing 2008, had competed only sparingly in the intervening years and could manage just 4.70m to take the bronze medal.

There were mixed fortunes for Holly Bleasdale, Team GB's new Pole Vault star. She had raised hopes by qualifying for the final in fourth place, clearing 4.55m at her second attempt. She failed to make an impression in the final, going out of the competition at 4.45, but shortly after revealed that she had just accepted her boyfriend Paul Bradshaw's proposal of marriage. '6th in the Olympics and @bradshaw proposes to me,' she tweeted excitedly. 'Epic day!!!'

Rypakova reaps Triple Jump reward

For the first time since the event was added to the Olympic programme in 1996, there were no 15m jumps in the Triple Jump final on 5 August. Former heptathlete Olga Rypakova emerged as the best on the night to win gold for Kazakhstan. Her leap of 14.98m in the fourth round saw off the challenge of Caterine Ibarguen of Columbia and Olha Saladuha of Ukraine, who took silver and bronze. The competition marked the end of the line for the 36-year-old Russian Tatyana Lebedeva, a two-time world champion and medallist at the previous three Olympic Games.

Soaring high. Great Britain's Jessica Ennis cleared 1.86m in a rain-affected high jump to maintain her lead in the early stages of the Heptathlon.

Elements of the Heptathlon

100m hurdles
High jump
Shot put
200m
Long jump
Javelin
800m

Jess perfect to win Heptathlon

Most Olympic champions will admit that relief is the overwhelming emotion in that moment of victory, and Jessica Ennis' expression as she crossed the line at the end of the 800m said it all. The 26-year-old closed her eyes and smiled as the Olympic Stadium erupted in a crescendo of noise. In those few seconds, Ennis felt the weight of expectation fly from her shoulders.

Among the images that flashed through her mind were the endless hours spent training at the English Institute of Sport in her hometown of Sheffield, where she and her coach Tony Minichiello have nurtured and honed her outstanding talent. Four years before, she had been ruled out of competing at Beijing 2008 after fracturing her ankle in an early-season heptathlon and in this, her first Olympic Games, she was among the favourites to win gold in the most complex of events. The Heptathlon comprises seven elements over two days, when anything could go wrong at any time.

But Ennis, who won the world title in 2009 only to lose it in 2011, did not put a foot wrong in the two days in the Olympic Stadium. More than that, she excelled in the first event, the 100m hurdles, setting a British record of 12.54 – and never looked back. Only once did she briefly lose the lead after the shot put.

The fierce competition from world champion Tatyana Chernova of Russian Federation and defending champion Nataliya Dobrynska of Ukraine never materialised. After another personal best of 22.83 in the 200m at the end of day one, Ennis had a healthy lead going into her traditionally more difficult second day.

Her long jump had been a concern, especially since she had been forced to change take-off legs after her ankle injury. However here, after an average opener, she sailed out to 6.40m and then 6.48m on her final two attempts. The javelin throw, so often a painful experience for British heptathletes, was a breeze, with 47.49m providing yet another lifetime best.

It all meant that the 800m was little more than a formality for the psychology graduate – from Sheffield University, naturally. Even then she made the race into a fabulous finale, sprinting away from the field to cross the line in 2:08.65. 'I am just so happy. I want to thank everyone who has supported me … I just had to give it everything at the end,' she said.

Ennis's total of 6,955 points, a new British record, included three personal bests in the first six elements. She finished a huge 306 points ahead of Lilli Schwarzkopf, who took silver for Germany, and 327 ahead of the Russian Tatyana Chernova who took bronze.

There were more smiles and plenty of emotion for this most popular of home-grown Olympic champions – never more so than when she stood on top of the podium, the Stadium reverberating to the sound of the national anthem. That, as Minichiello revealed afterwards, was when the enormity of what had been achieved brought tears even to his eyes.

'I am honoured to have witnessed this.'

Denise Lewis (GBR), Olympic Heptathlon champion, Sydney 2000

Left: Like a bullet. Jessica Ennis had the best possible start to the Heptathlon competition when she clocked a British record of 12.54 for the 100m hurdles in front of a packed house. It was the fastest time ever recorded during a Heptathlon.

'I told myself at the start that I'm only going to have one moment to do this in front of a crowd in London and I just wanted to give them a good show.'

Jessica Ennis, Heptathlon gold medallist

Left: Curtain call. The star of the show Jessica Ennis joins hands with the rest of the heptathletes to take a bow on 'Super Saturday'. The intense two-day competition leads to an atmosphere of mutual respect and admiration.

Badminton

Déjà vu. China's Dan Lin once again overcame his long-time rival Lee Chong Wei of Malaysia in a re-run of their final at Beijing 2008.

Superstar Lin retains men's Singles title

Dan Lin, the sport's biggest superstar with a rock-star profile in China, retained his Olympic title and celebrated in style. He overcame his fiercest rival Chong Wei Lee (MAS) at Wembley Arena, in what was a repeat of their Beijing 2008 final.

This was another epic encounter between the two, whose rivalry matches that of any in sport. Played at lightning speed, it was won by the charismatic Lin through the narrowest of margins: 15–21, 21–10, 21–19. While he sprinted around the court in joy, Lee was devastated at failing again to land the most important title of them all.

After playing 13 major finals during the four years they have dominated the sport, this could be the men's last encounter, as both have previously talked about retirement.

Hopes for a Chinese clean sweep of the gold medals were kept alive when four-time world champions Yun Cai and Haifeng Fu overcame number three seeds, Mathias Boe and Carsten Mogensen of Denmark, 21–16, 21–15 in the men's Doubles. It was the first victory in men's Doubles for China since the sport, invented when a string was run across the great hall of Badminton House in Gloucestershire, was added to the Olympic programme in 1992.

London 2012 women's Singles

Xuerui Li, a late choice by the Chinese, won the Singles gold medal, beating top seed Yihan Wang 21–15, 21–23, 21–17. Saina Nehwal took India's first Badminton medal with bronze after her opponent, Xin Wang of China, had to withdraw injured.

Finishing strong. Olympic Singles champion Xuerui Li was a late addition to China's team at London 2012. She admitted to having problems with her stamina, but her winning streak continued.

China triumph in troubled women's Doubles

Yunlei Zhao (CHN) made Olympic Badminton history when she became the first player to win two gold medals at the same Olympic Games. She followed her Mixed Doubles success by partnering Qing Tian (CHN) to a 21–10, 25–23 victory in the women's Doubles over the number four seeds, Mizuki Fujii and Reika Kakiiwa of Japan. The Russian Federation won its first medal in the event by taking the bronze.

The event was earlier mired in controversy, when four pairs, including world champions Xiaoli Wang (CHN) and Yang Yu (CHN), were involved in matches in which neither team appeared to want to win – because of the chances of being drawn next against the top Chinese team. They were disqualified by the Badminton World Federation (BWF) for 'not using one's best efforts to win a match'.

China dominates Mixed Doubles

In an all-China final, victory went to Nan Zhang and Yunlei Zhao. They beat Chen Xu and Jin Ma 21–11, 21–17 as the nation underlined its domination of the Badminton tournament.

It was the first time that a single nation had won both gold and silver medals in this event since Korea had achieved the feat in 1996. With eight medals at London 2012, China overtook Korea as the most successful Badminton nation. Only two European countries have ever made an impact on the medal tables in the mixed discipline, one of them being Britain in 2000 and 2004. The other, Denmark, took the bronze medal at London 2012, courtesy of Joachim Fischer and Christinna Pedersen.

Basketball

Men's events

Spain give the USA a scare in Basketball final

In a repeat of the final at Beijing 2008, Spain came closer still to toppling the USA, winners of the gold medal in five of the previous six Olympic Games.

In the end, there were only seven points in it as the USA, coached for the last time by Mike Krzyzewski, eventually claimed the title again 107–100. The match on the final day of the Games was watched by Arnold Schwarzenegger, London Mayor Boris Johnson, David Beckham and his sons and even Henry Kissinger, as well as members of the Spanish royal family.

It was Spain, the European champions, who started more strongly at the North Greenwich Arena, with Juan Carlos Navarro scoring freely to help them to a 12–7 lead. The USA team, including the 33-year-old Kobe Bryant, came back and attempted to reassert their authority, but they had managed only a single point lead at half-time.

Shortly into the second period Spain took the lead; every time the USA's Kevin Durant scored a three-pointer, Navarro responded in kind. The USA had come to these Games never doubting they would win. They even counted the President and First Lady among their fans for their early games at London 2012. Yet the Spanish proved more than a match for them – and in their NBA stars, including the 213cm-tall brothers Marc and Pau Gasol (the latter arguably the best player on the pitch), they had the players to make the so-called 'Dream Team' work very hard for their victory.

Alongside Bryant, the USA's Kevin Durant, Carmelo Anthony and LeBron James starred as the pre-tournament favourites finally overcame the toughest of opponents. It was a tense but exciting finale for Krzyzewski, who had won 61 games with only one loss, to Greece in 2006. Stars and Stripes ponchos fluttered and wild celebrations erupted as Bruce Springsteen's hit 'Born in the USA' blasted from the giant speakers in the arena.

The bronze medal match saw a compelling contest, with the Russian Federation beating Argentina 81–77. In the last minute Alexei Shved managed both a crucial steal and a three-pointer for the Russians to seal the match. The Great Britain squad, playing in their first Olympic Games, finished ninth of the 12 teams with performances that included a win against China 39–24, their first Olympic victory in the event since London 1948, and a narrow loss to Spain.

Left: Looking up. LeBron James (back) and Kevin Love challenge Spanish guard Rudy Fernandez during the USA push for points in their close encounter for the Basketball gold medal at the North Greenwich Arena.

'This here tonight is right up there at the top of anything I have ever achieved in basketball.'

Kobe Bryant, Basketball gold medallist

USA's golden line-up

Tyson Chandler
Kevin Durant
LeBron James
Russell Westbrook
Deron Williams
Andre Iguodala
Kobe Bryant
Kevin Love
James Harden
Chris Paul
Anthony Davis
Carmelo Anthony

USA's golden line-up

Lindsay Whalen
Seimone Augustus
Sue Bird
Maya Moore
Angel McCoughtry
Asjha Jones
Tamika Catchings
Swin Cash
Diana Taurasi
Sylvia Fowles
Tina Charles
Candace Parker

Airborne threat. France's Edwige Lawson-Wade takes aim, but there was no way past Sue Bird and the all-conquering USA, who went on to win their fifth consecutive Olympic Basketball title.

The Basketball Arena

The bold Basketball Arena, another of London 2012's temporary venues, was among the most striking structures on the Olympic Park. Sheathed in white recyclable PVC stretched over a modular steel skeleton, the dynamic facade combined curves and hollows to echo the sporting movement inside.

The facade was lit at night during Games-time to create a dramatic lighting show of ever-changing colours. The interior of the vast arena, also used for Handball and Wheelchair Rugby, features a vivid black and orange colour scheme depicting the 'energy burst' hallmarks of LOCOG's design scheme. The later stages of the Basketball tournament were held in the larger North Greenwich Arena venue.

Women's events

Fifth straight Olympic Basketball gold for USA

The first half of the USA double came when the women's team enjoyed a 86–50 win over France. In chalking up the country's fifth consecutive Olympic gold medal, they also extended the squad's unbeaten run to 41 games, stretching back to Barcelona 1992.

Candace Parker's 21 points and 11 rebounds made her the stand-out player on this occasion. On the way to collecting their third Olympic gold medal Tamika Catchings, Diana Taurasi and Sue Bird were also all given standing ovations when coach Geno Auriemma took them out of the game with two minutes remaining. All 12 USA players made the scoresheet as the team established its superiority in the second quarter and put the game

beyond doubt in the third, with Parker's run of 19 unanswered points securing the match.

France played their part as well. The team established its own impressive seven-match winning run during the tournament, with silver becoming the first Olympic medal for France in a women's team sport.

Previously Celine Dumerc had led the French brilliantly, but, confronting the best team in the tournament, the point guard found herself too often shackled by the attention of Taurasi. The French also let too many rebound opportunities slip away and, with every mistake, the USA pounced to pile on the agony.

Australia beat The Russian Federation 83–74 to claim the bronze medal, and their fifth consecutive Olympic medal in women's Basketball.

Team GB's campaign did not go as well as they would have liked, losing all five of their matches to finish bottom of Group B in the qualifying stages.

Boxing

Left: Flat out. Cuban teenager Robeisy Carrazana Ramirez hits the canvas after exuberantly celebrating his Fly Weight (52kg) gold medal. Ramirez defeated Tugstsogt Nyambayar of Mongolia to take the title.

Far left: Tense and technical. Ireland's John Joe Nevin (left) was an aggressive opponent but Team GB's Luke Campbell (right) showed wit and maturity to win the men's Bantam Weight (56kg) division gold medal.

Men's events

Luke Campbell battles to Bantam Weight (56kg) gold

Luke Campbell of Team GB showed wit and maturity to beat Ireland's John Joe Nevin to win the gold medal in the Bantam Weight (56kg) final. He became the first British Bantam Weight Olympic champion since the 1908 Games in London – over a century ago.

It proved a tense and technical bout. The start was wary on both sides, with Campbell going on to take the first round 5–3 and Nevin, a strong and smart boxer, fighting back to win the second 5–4. Campbell's swift countering saw his old friend and rival on the canvas in the final round, spurring the Briton to a confident finish in which he landed a hard left punch and put up a wily defence against an aggressive Nevin.

Campbell, 24, described by Lennox Lewis as a impressive 'classical fighter', was proclaimed Olympic champion 14 –11. He raised his arms aloft and the tears of joy and relief flowed from the man who wanted to bring back a gold medal for his young son. 'I'm very emotional and this is something I've worked for all my life. It was a difficult … technical fight … I was on my game tonight,' he observed. Declaring Muhammad Ali his inspiration, he admitted that he could not believe that he had emulated his hero to become Olympic champion. He also acknowledged the support from his home city and the St Paul's Amateur Boxing Club. 'I am very proud to be from Hull … I love you all,' he smiled.

Cuban teenager takes Fly Weight (52kg) gold

Cuban teenager Robeisy Carrazana Ramirez gave a fast and powerful display to win the gold medal in the Fly Weight (52kg) final, defeating Mongolia's Tugstsogt Nyambayar.

Both fighters showed class and style in a tough match, but it was Ramirez, leading by one point going in to the third and final round, who eventually prevailed 17–14. The 18-year-old's performance was notable for a strong left hook and variety of hard punches.

In victory Ramirez twirled delightedly around the ring and executed a series of push-ups on the canvas.

Ireland's Michael Conlan, from Belfast, and the Russian Misha Aloian took the bronze medals following their respective semi-final defeats.

'It's a day I've dreamed of for a long, long time … I'm lost for words. It means everything.'

Luke Campbell, Bantam Weight gold medallist

Great Briton. Team GB's latest boxing hero, 22-year-old Anthony Joshua, who won the Super Heavy Weight (+91kg) title after defeating Italy's defending Olympic champion Roberto Cammarelle. Joshua spoke eloquently after the fight and has the charisma to become a global boxing star.

'Today is a Sunday … a holy day … today I was blessed.'

Anthony Joshua, Super Heavy Weight gold medallist

The big champions

As Cassius Clay, Muhammad Ali won gold as a Light Heavy Weight (81kg) boxer at Rome 1960. Many of his rivals and successors as world champion came through the Olympic division of men's Heavy Weight (91kg), which changed to Super Heavy Weight (+91kg) after 1980.

Tokyo 1964: **Joe Frazier (USA)**
Mexico City 1968: **George Foreman (USA)**
Los Angeles 1984: **Tyrell Biggs (USA)**
Seoul 1988: **Lennox Lewis (CAN)**
Atlanta 1996: **Wladimir Klitschko (UKR)**

Dramatic gold for Joshua in Super Heavy Weight +91kg

Team GB's Anthony Joshua won a dramatic countback against the defending gold medallist, Italy's Roberto Cammarelle, to take the men's +91kg division title in a courageous and painful fight.

Joshua, 201cm tall and 114kg in weight, is still a novice in international boxing, with only 43 amateur bouts to his name. He faced the 32-year-old reigning Super Heavy Weight +91kg gold medallist and was trailing by three points heading into the third and final round, but he moved well and unleashed a final storm of punches, including a hard, crunching right-hand shot which rocked the Italian policeman and left him flailing until the bell. Joshua remained calm to deliver a barrage of blows in the last few minutes, finding himself level at 18–18 with the Italian at the conclusion of the bout. Under Olympic Boxing rules, the decision then goes to countback, which the 22-year-old north Londoner was judged to have won by three points. The Italians appealed, but it was turned down and Joshua was declared champion. The result was greeted by a deafening roar from the ExCeL crowd, among them former Olympic Super Heavy Weight +91kg champions Wladimir Klitschko, Audley

Harrison and Lennox Lewis, who compared himself to Joshua. 'He has a lot of talent, great power and a lot of potential', he wrote on the BBC website.

Joshua emerged into the media spotlight as a mature young man, and an eloquent and intelligent gold medallist. Questions on whether he would move into professional boxing met with a thoughtful response, as Joshua explained that he would like a shot at the world amateur title.

'It's never been about money … to leave the Great Britain set-up just for money would be a big mistake … I didn't grow up with loads of money. I learned to cope. I'm happy with life. My mum's a really grounded person, so's my dad … It keeps my feet on the ground. These memories are priceless,' declared the new Olympic champion, who now has the opportunity to develop into an inspiring global Boxing star.

Second gold for Lomachenko in Light Weight (60kg)

Ukraine's Vasyl Lomachenko beat Korea's Soonchul Han 19–9 to win the Light Weight (60kg) title, becoming the 12th man in 108 years of Olympic Boxing to win two gold medals.

The 24-year-old world champion, held by some to be the world's best amateur, is coached by his father, Anatoly Lomachenko – one of Ukraine's most revered boxing trainers. The number one seed in his division, he dominated with skilful footwork and hand speed, winning the first round 7–2. Han raised his game in the second, which he took 4–3, but Lomachenko asserted himself again in the final round, winning 8–4. The Ukranian's victory established him as one of the greats of Olympic amateur Boxing, following his earlier gold medal at Beijing 2008 in the now discontinued Feather Weight category. 'Ukraine are strong in every division, and Lomachenko is the jewel in the crown,' observed Richie Woodall, Boxing bronze medallist at Seoul 1988.

The bronze medals were won by Yasniel Toledo Lopez of Cuba, and Evaldas Petrauskas of Lithuania.

the third. Sapiyev dominated the match with a highly skilled performance that Evans could not disrupt, to be awarded the gold with a final score of 17–9. Kazakhstan have now triumphed in this division for the third Olympic Games in a row.

There was consolation for Evans, however, described by Athens 2004 silver medallist Amir Khan as someone 'with a very bright future in front of him'. His silver medal made him Wales's most successful boxer, overtaking Ralph Evans who won bronze at Munich 1972. The bronze medals at London 2012 went to Taras Shelestyuk of Ukraine and Andrey Zamkovoy of the Russian Federation.

Under the spotlight. Team GB's Freddie Evans heads into the ring to face Serik Sapiyev of Kazakhstan who won Welter Weight (69kg) gold. Evans emerged to the sound of The Clash's classic song, London Calling.

'I am still young at 21, so I have done well and am over the moon.'

Fred Evans, men's 75kg division silver medallist

Sapiyev outpoints tired Evans for Welter Weight (69kg) gold

Welshman Fred Evans enjoyed a sensational run to the final, winning four bouts and beating the world number one, Taras Shelestyuk of Ukraine, in the semi-final. His encounter with the accomplished Serik Sapiyev from Kazakhstan, however, proved a fight too far.

Sapiyev is the 28-year-old two-time world champion at Light Welter Weight. In the match he was too quick and too accurate with his jabs for the Team GB's unseeded 21-year-old, who was hoping to be the first Welshman to win an Olympic Boxing gold medal. Against the background of the ExCeL crowd's enthusiastic support for Evans, the Kazakh won the first round 4–2 and the second 6–3 before confirming his superiority with a flurry of jabs in

More gold for Zou as he retains Light Fly Weight (49kg) title

Shiming Zou of China retained his Light Fly Weight (49kg) title and took a third Olympic Boxing medal after a tough and controversial final bout against Thailand's Kaeo Pongprayoon.

Zou, China's first Boxing gold medallist when he won at Beijing 2008 and the first Light Fly Weight successfully to defend his title, was awarded the fight 13–10. The decision did not go down well with Pongprayoon, who fell to his knees and pounded the canvas in protest. The Thai's cause had not been helped by a two-point penalty awarded against him with only nine seconds left on the clock.

Losing semi-finalists Paddy Barnes of Ireland and Russian David Ayrapetyan took the bronze medals.

Boxing gold medallists

Light Fly Weight (49kg): **Shiming Zou (CHN)**
Fly Weight (52kg): **Robeisy Ramirez Carrazana (CUB)**
Bantam Weight (56kg): **Luke Campbell (GBR)**
Light Weight (60kg): **Vasyl Lomachenko (UKR)**
Light Welter Weight (64kg): **Roniel Iglesias Sotolongo (CUB)**
Welter Weight (69kg): **Serik Sapiyev (KAZ)**
Middle Weight (75kg): **Ryota Murata (JPN)**
Light Heavy Weight (81kg): **Egor Mekhontcev (RUS)**
Heavy Weight (91kg): **Oleksandr Usyk (UKR)**
Super Heavy Weight (+91kg): **Anthony Joshua (GBR)**

Usyk too strong in Heavy Weight (91kg)

In a tense match Oleksandr Usyk of Ukraine turned the tables on Clemente Russo to win the Olympic Heavy Weight (91kg) title – four years after the Italian had put him out of the tournament in the quarter-finals at Beijing 2008.

Russo had the consolation of the silver medal in 2008. He was forced to accept it again at ExCeL where Usyk, the reigning world champion, came from behind to triumph. In the second round it looked as if Usyk had scored a knockdown and, while the referee ruled that Russo had stumbled, the Ukrainian still came out on top 7–5. The 25-year-old, who enjoys writing poetry, was finally awarded the bout 14–11; he promptly broke into a celebratory dance. Tervel Pulev of Bulgaria and Teymur Mammadov of Azerbaijan took the bronze medals.

The medal brought Ukraine's London 2012 Boxing tally to a highly respectable four, the others being a silver in Light Welter Weight (64kg) and two bronzes in Welter Weight (69kg) and Light Heavy Weight (81kg).

Women in the ring

Although women's Boxing was added to the Olympic programme for the first time at London 2012, the sport had appeared once before at the Games. The IOC Museum in Lausanne contains a picture of a women's bout at the 1904 St Louis Games, when even men's Boxing enjoyed only exhibition status. Reports of rudimentary fights featuring women emerge from 18th-century London, but women's boxing only became established in the 1970s. The sport was approved by the IOC for inclusion in the Olympic Games in 2001.

History in the making. Team GB's Nicola Adams wins the Fly Weight (51kg) gold medal bout against China's Cancan Ren. Adams became the first women's Olympic Boxing gold medallist.

Women's events

Adams' shuffle wins historic Fly Weight (51kg) gold

Team GB's Nicola Adams emulated her boxing heroes Muhammad Ali and Sugar Ray Leonard to win the first Olympic Boxing medal for women in the women's Fly Weight (51kg) category.

Adams, 29, cruised to a 16–7 victory over three-time world champion Cancan Ren of China. She gave a masterful display of lightning-quick boxing with sublime footwork and powerful left-right combinations. In the second round Ren was on the canvas, but fought back with impressive hand speed. Adams, though, was hungry for gold. She retained her composure and discipline, leading 14–5 into the final round. She dominated the rest of the match to become the first women's Olympic champion, with the bronze medals going to India's Chungneijang Mery Kom Hmangte and Marien Esparza of the USA.

The beaming boxer with a megawatt smile began training in a Leeds boxing gym while waiting for her mother to finish aerobics classes. After her Olympic victory she was congratulated ringside by Amir Khan, silver medallist at Athens 2004. An ExCeL crowd of over 10,000 went into overdrive when Adams finished the closing seconds of the fight with an Ali-like Adams shuffle, going on to bow and punch the air on each side of the ring. 'I have wanted this all my life and I have done it,' she said. 'To be taking the gold medal back to Leeds will be special.' British boxing has seen memorable nights before, but this one was truly historic.

Watching the fight was Barbara Buttrick, the Yorkshirewoman who founded the Women's International Boxing Federation. She also fought in the 1950s when she was known as The Mighty Atom. She commented: 'I would never have dreamed women boxers would ever get into the Olympic Games, now they've got that credibility.'

'Rocky, the female version, would be quite cool.'

Nicola Adams, women's Fly Weight gold medallist

Irish eyes smile as Taylor boxes to Light Weight (60kg) gold

A sea of green, white and gold and boisterous cheering welcomed Ireland's Katie Taylor into the ring at ExCeL as she faced the Russian Federation's Sofya Ochigava in the fight for the Light Weight (60kg) gold medal.

It was a tough and scrappy contest, with Taylor appearing too eager in the opening flurries of the fight. Ochigava toyed with her opponent and Taylor was a point behind at halfway. In the final round, the Irishwoman slipped and was down on the canvas, but she kept her cool, landing some powerful punches to become Olympic champion 10–8 at the bell.

Taylor, 26, fell to her knees and pointed skywards as Irish fans sang a rousing chorus of patriotic songs to celebrate their country's first women's Boxing medal – and its first gold of London 2012. Mavzuna Chorieva of Tajikistan and Adriana Araujo of Brazil took bronze.

Earlier in the competition Taylor defeated Team GB's Natasha Jonas, who had made history as the first woman to win an Olympic Boxing match with a victory over the USA's Quanitta Underwood 21–13. The 28-year-old from Liverpool had won bronze at the World Championships in China in May 2011, where she became the first woman to qualify for the Boxing team at London 2012. Taylor, who holds four world championship and five European titles, admitted she had to work 'so hard' to take the match 26–15.

Shields blocks Torlopova for Middle Weight (75kg) crown

The USA's Claressa Shields became the first women's Olympic Middle Weight (75kg) champion after beating the Russian Nadezda Torlopova. It was an impressive 19–12 victory for the teenager who, at 17, became the second-youngest boxer ever to take Olympic gold.

Torlopova, 16 years older than her opponent, began well and the first round was drawn 3–3. She faded over later rounds, however, allowing Shields to double the USA's women's Boxing tally, their first medal being a Light Weight (60kg) bronze. Shields' story of Olympic success is one of triumph over adversity. She comes from a tough neighbourhood in Flint, Michigan, and spent her childhood moving from home to home. Yet she is a dedicated student in college and has taken an Olympic gold medal. As the USA national anthem played, Shields stood on the podium smiling with her hand on her heart – a fitting finale to her Olympic journey, or a Hollywood movie.

Bronze medals were awarded to Jinzi Li, of China and Marina Volnova from Kazakhstan.

Green, white and gold. Ireland's Katie Taylor (right) celebrates winning the Olympic title in the Light Weight (60kg) gold medal bout against Russian Sofya Ochigava. Taylor's win was Ireland's first gold medal of London 2012.

'I wanted the good life ... I didn't want my sister or my little brother to go without a meal again ... I am the second oldest so I had to step up.'

Claressa Shields, women's Middle Weight gold medallist

'In the Olympics people have just a split second to deliver and that makes it all so exciting. I've seen so many families and little kids watching sport … boys and girls with their mums and dads … all coming to live sport for the first time … this will be inspirational for the next generation of sports people.'

Michael Vaughan, Former England Cricket Captain

Anthony Joshua greets fans after winning Great Britain's third gold medal in Olympic Boxing at London 2012. Joshua won gold in the Super Heavy Weight +91kg division.

Canoe Slalom

Splashing time. Tim Baillie (left) and Etienne Stott on their way to a surprise Canoe Slalom gold medal for Great Britain at the Lee Valley White Water Centre.

The Course

The Lee Valley White Water Centre, 30 km north of the Olympic Park and part of the Lee Valley Regional Park, was the first of the brand new venues to be completed. It has a 300m Olympic-standard competition course with a 5.5m descent, plus a 160m intermediate/training course with a 1.6m descent for use in the venue's legacy mode. A system of pumps creates the white water, generating 13,000 litres of water per second to power down the course, fed from a specially created 10,000-square-metre lake.

Olympic gold medallists

Men's Kayak (K1):
Daniele Molmenti (ITA)

Men's Canoe Single (C1):
Tony Estanguet (FRA)

Men's Canoe Double (C2):
GBR **(Tim Baillie, Etienne Stott)**

Women's Kayak (K1):
Emilie Fer (FRA)

Men's events

Canoe Double produces gold and silver for Team GB

The British pair of Tim Baillie and Etienne Stott, ranked six in the world, staged an upset in the Canoe Double. Even they did not expect to win this most challenging of events in the swirling currents of the Lee Valley White Water Centre. Stott even admitted leaving his Team GB medal-winner's tracksuit in its packaging at the bottom of his kitbag at the start as they set out for the event.

The slowest of the six crews to qualify from the semi-final, Baillie and Stott were the first to paddle. They produced the performance of their lives in front of the noisy 12,000-strong crowd, with a time through the 23 gates of 106.41 seconds proving unbeatable. They were joined on the podium by the British number one pair of David Florence and Richard Hounslow who, as the last to go down the 300m course, made the trip just 0.36 seconds slower (106.77) to take silver. 'We attacked it hard all the way and it was probably just about the sprint to the finish,' admitted Hounslow, heralding the British gold and silver as 'fantastic'.

Even more surprisingly, the Slovakian twins Peter and Pavol Hochschorner – the dominant force in the sport, who had been looking for their fourth consecutive Olympic title at London, took bronze. They hit a pole at gate 17, incurring a two-second penalty which gave them the third-placed time of 108.28 seconds.

It was an extraordinary day for Canoe Slalom in Britain, which had never won this event before. The moment was celebrated by raucous spectators, placed as close to the action as possible by the Centre's design, with Team GB's double triumph leading to a water-born celebration as both crews jumped in. 'To win is just mad,' said a delighted Stott, who had recently had shoulder surgery. 'The run we had, I was hoping it might be good enough for a medal … It is brilliant.'

Women's events

Second French gold in Kayak Single

Following Tony Estanguet's historic third win in the men's Canoe Single event, it was the turn of Emilie Fer to claim France's second gold medal at the Lee Valley White Water Centre. She won gold in the women's Kayak Single with a faultless run.

Fer, a gold medal winner in the K-1 team event at the 2006 ICF Canoe Slalom World Championship in Prague, had only finished seventh at Beijing 2008. She clocked 105.90 to take gold ahead of Jessica Fox (106.51), world junior champion from Australia and the daughter of Richard Fox, Britain's former world champion, and Myriam Fox-Jerusalmi, who also won bronze at Atlanta 1996.

The world number two, Maialen Chourraut, took the bronze medal (106.87), Spain's first Olympic medal in Canoe Slalom.

Canoe Sprint

won the bronze medal in 36.657.

McKeever set an Olympic record in the heats, which saw the surprise departure of favourite Piotr Siemionowski of Poland, but came behind Craviotto and de Jong in the semi-finals, where only 0.024 seconds separated the men.

A tough final was in prospect, but in the event the Briton's strength dominated, enabling him to strike a relentlessly smooth and fast rhythm and to draw on the support of a 30,000 capacity crowd who roared him home. 'I was really buzzing and I wanted to do well,' said McKeever.

Your number's up. Ed McKeever swaps accountancy for kayak racing to win gold for Great Britain in the Canoe Sprint at Eton Dorney.

Olympic gold medallists

Men's Kayak Single (K1) 200m: **Ed McKeever (GBR)**

Men's Kayak Single (K1) 1000m: **Eirik Veras Larsen (NOR)**

Men's Kayak Double (K2) 1000m: **HUN (Rudolf Dombi, Roland Kokeny)**

Men's Kayak Four (K4) 1000m: **AUS (Jacob Clear, Dave Smith, Tate Smith, Murray Stewart)**

Men's Canoe Single (C1) 1000m: **Sebastian Brendel (GER)**

Men's Canoe Single (C1) 200m: **Yuri Cheban (UKR)**

Men's Canoe Double (C2) 1000m: **GER (Peter Kretschmer, Kurt Kuschela)**

Women's Kayak Single (K1) 200m: **Lisa Carrington (NZL)**

Women's Kayak Single (K1) 500m: **Danuta Kozak (HUN)**

Women's Kayak Double (K2) 500m: **GER (Franziska Weber, Tina Dietze)**

Women's Kayak Four (K4) 500m: **HUN (Krisztina Fazekas, Katalin Kovacs, Danuta Kozak, Gabriella Szabo)**

Men's events

Cleaver McKeever strikes gold in Kayak Single (K1) 200m

Ed 'The Cleaver' McKeever (GBR) became the Usain Bolt of the Canoe Sprint when he blasted to the men's Kayak Single 200m gold medal at Eton Dorney, near Windsor.

The sprint champion of the water rocketed off the start with his famously powerful first stroke. He led throughout the race, setting a ferocious pace to become the first Olympic medallist at this distance, with a time of 36.246. Spain's Saul Craviotto took the silver (36.540) and Mark de Jong of Canada

Women's events

Kiwi first in Kayak Single (K1) 200m

New Zealand's world champion Lisa Carrington battled against a strong headwind to win the women's Kayak Single 200m. The 23-year-old politics student took her country's first women's Canoeing medal in a time of 44.638. Carrington said it had always been her dream to win Olympic gold.

Ukraine's Inna Osypenko-Radomska won the silver medal (45.053) to add to the silver she picked up in the 500m event. Hungary's Natasa Douchev-Janics took the bronze medal (45.128).

Cycling — BMX

Left to right: Lativia's Maris Strombergs, France's Joris Daudet, Colombia's Carlos Mario Oquendo Zabala, Australia's Sam Willoughby and Switzerland's Roger Rinderknecht take a jump during the BMX Cycling men's semi-finals.

'My whole life I am trying to win this. I want to win it again. I want go out the gate and win it again. It's unbelievable.'

Mariana Pajon, women's BMX gold medallist

The course

The men's track was 450m long and the women's 440m while the entire venue covered a total area of 160m by 90m, slightly larger than the size of a football pitch. The 14,000 cubic metres of soil used to build the track were excavated during the building of the Olympic Park, part of a massive recycling operation that followed the clearance of the site. Comments from riders and the sport's governing body following the test event in 2011 led to several modifications to the first straight and some of the jumps.

Men's event

Strombergs takes all the honours in BMX defence

Maris Strombergs is 25 years old and considers himself a veteran after taking up BMX riding when he was five. He was still quick on the track, though, keeping his Beijing 2008 title with 37.576.

In doing so, he became the first Latvian to take two gold medals at the Olympic Games, the winner of his country's first gold medal at London 2012, and the first man to win an event in both of its appearances at the Games.

'It gets tougher against these young kids. I can see myself in them. When you get older, you start thinking more. During the races, the nerves got the best of me but deep down I was still confident and I'm happy that I was able to put together one good race.'

The BMX Track played its part in making this one of the most exciting sports on offer and the 6,000 sun-scorched fans squealed their approval as riders soared through the air or clattered to the ground in the competitive heats and semi-finals. Britain's great hope Liam Phillips was among those who came a cropper on the tight bends and he

was a disappointed eighth in the final after his foot became unclipped from the pedal and he crashed on the last bend.

His long-time rival Sam Willoughby took silver for Australia. The bronze medal went to Carlos Mario Oquendo Zabala of Colombia.

Women's event

Pajon gold for Colombia in BMX thriller

Colombia does not win many Olympic medals, but on the final day of BMX racing in London there were two for the country to celebrate. Before the bronze in the men's race, Mariana Pajon won Colombia's second-ever gold medal at the Olympic Games after the 2011 world champion, who carried the flag at the Opening Ceremony, had enjoyed a near-flawless competition.

She and silver medallist Sarah Walker of New Zealand led from the dramatic start, hurtling out of the gates at the top of an 8m ramp and were never headed. Laura Smulders, the 18-year-old from the Netherlands, tracked the pair of them to take the bronze medal.

Pajon, who was badly injured in a car crash earlier this year, said, 'Off the track I'm all woman but on the track I change completely and I become aggressive and I race like a man. Then at the end of the race I become a girl again and of course I cried. I cried a lot of tears. This is a dream come true.'

The capacity crowd, which included Prime Minister David Cameron, was mainly there to cheer on Britain's Shanaze Reade, who was hoping to win the gold medal she had missed so spectacularly at Beijing 2008. Reade, a three-time world champion, missed again, this time failing to get a good enough start, and trailed in sixth.

Cycling – Mountain Bike

Men's event

Close finish to Mountain Bike ride

The most gruelling of the Olympic Cycling events took place on the Mountain Bike track, perched on a grassy hill in the Thames Estuary at Hadleigh Farm in Essex.

After 90 minutes of dramatic and exciting racing, the Olympic men's Mountain Bike title was won by Jaroslav Kulhavy of the Czech Republic. He won after a huge last-gasp effort, beating Switzerland's Nino Schurter by just one second.

The two racers were at the front from the start at Hadleigh Farm, packed for the second day running with 20,000 mountain bike fans who were to witness an epic contest. With the finish just over the brow of the final hill Schurter was in front, still battling to keep ahead. As the riders sped into the last hairpin bend, Kulhavy stood up on his pedals for one last push. He grabbed the vital inside line and charged to victory by less than a bike length.

The bronze medal went to Italy's Marco Fontana, who lost his saddle on the final descent of the Rock Garden.

Not everyone completed the challenging ride. French double Olympic champion Julien Absalon limped out of the race with a puncture on the first lap while Great Britain's Liam Killeen, 30, crashed out of the race on the boulders at Deane's Drop during the second lap. Killeen injured his left ankle in the fall, undergoing surgery to pin his tibia and fibula.

Women's event

Brilliant Bresset wins Mountain Bike gold

For the women's event, 30 riders tackled the rocky tracks and steep climbs in a race that was run over six laps of the five-kilometre course, constructed from 500 tonnes of unforgiving rock and 3,500 tonnes of crushed stone.

Frenchwoman Julie Bresset, 23, dominated the race, freewheeling over the finish line in a time of 1:30:52 to win the Olympic title. The 40-year-old defending champion, Germany's Sabine Spitz, raced to the silver medal with 1:31:54, while Georgia Gould of the USA pedalled to bronze with 1:32:00. Great Britain's Annie Last, 21, who trained for London 2012 in the tough terrain of the Alps, finished in eighth place.

On a scorching summer's day that was cooled by a stiff Thames breeze, Bresset brilliantly mastered the tricky and technical course. She showed superhuman skill on her Olympic debut, using power, speed, endurance and determination to survive the stony tracks and the bone-shaking vibration of her 10kg carbon-fibre bike. The punishing track included the rocky staircase known as Triple Trouble, the death-defying Leap of Faith sheer drop and the grinding Breathtaker and Snake Hill climbs.

The sunshine and natural amphitheatre provided a stunning venue that gave the enthusiastic crowd a perfect view of the Olympic action.

Julie Bresset of France on her way to the gold medal in the women's Mountain Bike race. The course included gruelling obstacles such as Triple Trouble and the Leap of Faith.

'I put everything into this race, all my energy. I am amazed. This race was really important.'

Jaroslav Kulhavy (CZE), Mountain Bike gold medallist

Above left: The Czech Republic's Jaroslav Kulhavy who took gold in the men's Mountain Bike competition. He pulled away in the final climb, and won the gold with a sprint finish.

Cycling – Road

Right: Great Britain's Tour de France winner, Bradley Wiggins, blasts to gold in the Time Trial. He was watched by 250,000 cycling fans on the roads around Hampton Court Palace and Bushey Park.

Far right: King of the Time Trial. Bradley Wiggins takes to his throne as Olympic Champion and the most decorated British Olympian of all time with seven medals, four of them gold.

Men's events

'King' Wiggins storms to gold in Time Trial

'I don't think my sporting career will ever top this now. That's it. It will never, ever get better than that. Incredible.'

Bradley Wiggins,
Time Trial gold medallist

'Wiggomania' erupted at Hampton Court Palace when Britain's Tour de France winner Bradley Wiggins rocketed home to win gold in the Time Trial and become the country's most decorated Olympian with seven medals.

A roaring and adoring crowd lined the 49km route, thunderously banging on the hoardings and willing Wiggins to victory. The quarter of a million screaming and cheering fans, many sporting the trademark 'Wiggo' sideburns, witnessed a spectacular time of 50:39.54. Germany's Tony Martin won the silver medal with 51:21.54 and, in a suitably fairytale finish for a royal Palace, Britain's Chris Froome, the runner-up on the Tour, took bronze (51:47.87). Wiggins and Froome

had been the Hillary and Tenzing of the mountains and roads of France; but in London they were the Lion and the Unicorn of Hampton Court Palace, proclaiming Britain's dominance in world cycling. Froome paid tribute to his teammate's enormous achievement, commenting, 'Brad has a huge engine for time trials ... he can keep up the speed and power.'

Whippet-thin Wiggins, a London-raised boy, was characteristically down to earth in victory. He hugged his wife and two young children and then stopped to salute the thousands of fans outside the Palace gates before freewheeling to the purple winner's throne and his place on the podium.

Afterwards Wiggins laughed off talk of a knighthood, preferring to speculate that his new status as the king of cycling could encourage more people to get on their bikes. 'I guess someone will be inspired by this ... this is a facility that costs nothing ... people can get out on the same roads as the Olympic Time Trial and pretend they're us. That is the thing about cycling. It is accessible to anybody.'

The only hint of Wiggins' ruthless competitive streak came when he said, 'There was only one colour for me today – gold.'

Vinokurov steals Road Race thunder

Alexandr Vinokurov from Kazakhstan won gold in a surprise victory, with Colombia's Rigoberto Urán Urán taking silver and Norway's Alexander Kristoff bronze.

Great Britain's world champion Mark Cavendish had been the pre-race favourite, but for the British team it proved an unhappy outing on Box Hill; he finished 29th. A staggering 1.5 million spectators lined the 250km route that began in The Mall and headed for the Surrey Hills, where riders completed nine gruelling 15.9km loops.

In the final kilometres through Fulham and Chelsea Vinokurov made his decisive move. Urán Urán responded, but made the fatal error of glancing over his left shoulder in The Mall, only to see Vinokurov accelerate from his right and cross the line, in a time of 5:45:57.

Women's events

Gang of three in compelling climax to Road Race battle

This was the event in which the Host Nation opened its medal account with a magnificent silver for Yorkshire's Lizzie Armitstead – although even she could not stop the Dutch Marianne Vos, the outstanding pre-race favourite.

The critical break for the eventual medallists came as the race left the Box Hill circuit for the

'I'm just so happy that I committed to the breakaway … I'm proud of Team GB. We stuck together, raced the race and ultimately it worked out.'

Lizzie Armitstead,
Road Race silver medallist

Gold at last. Marianne Vos of the Netherlands (left) crosses the line ahead of Britain's Lizzie Armitstead to win the Road Race on The Mall. Vos broke her run of five consecutive second places at the world championships and her sixth place finish at Beijing 2008 with the win.

The Olympic Road Race Course

Starting and finishing in The Mall, riders travelled southwest through the suburbs to Surrey, with the men cycling 250km and the women 140km. The men's route included nine laps of a 15.9km circuit of Box Hill on Surrey's North Downs, and the women's two. Box Hill, a magnet for hundreds of cyclists every weekend, features Zig Zag road, the Butterfly Bend and Dormouse Drive. It is also an area of outstanding natural beauty, supporting bats, moths, butterflies, orchids and the hill's namesake, the Box Tree.

Top of the world. Silver medallist Elizabeth Armitstead of Great Britain, gold medallist Marianne Vos of the Netherlands, and bronze medallist Olga Zabelinskaya of the Russian Federation beat the elements and the opposition to fill the podium places in the women's Road Race.

last time, with over 45km still to ride and the peloton hard on their wheels. The leading group of four riders was reduced to three 33km from the finish line with the loss of Shelly Olds, but, riding hell for leather, they continued to elude the chasing pack. As at Beijing 2008, the climax to the Road Race was a thrilling affair, fought out in torrential lashing rain, as Vos, Armitstead and Russian Olga Zabelinskaya – their medals secured – prepared to launch their sprint to the line after having established a 40-plus-second lead over the peloton.

Vos, who had claimed the Points Race title in the Velodrome at Beijing 2008 and holds world titles in road cycling, track and cyclo-cross, struck first with just 175m to go. Despite the roars of the thousands of British fans along The Mall, Armitstead's final effort left her half a length short at the line, for a well-deserved silver medal. She and Vos achieved the same time of 3:35:29, with Zabelinskaya posting 3:35:31.

Two months before the Games Vos had suffered a broken collarbone in a race in the Netherlands, and still rode on for 63km to finish second – and

she was not going to be denied in London. She explained, 'It was a hard race with the weather conditions, but I felt good. We made it a hard race with the Dutch squad making early attacks. That was the plan … during the race I thought that this might be the day that it is all coming together.'

Age does not weary Armstrong in Time Trial win

Kristin Armstrong of the United States successfully defended her Olympic women's Time Trial title at the majestic Hampton Court Palace. The 38-year-old's time of 37:34.82 was the more impressive after she broke her collarbone in a racing accident in May. World Champion Judith Arndt from Germany took the silver medal with 37:50.29, and Russian Olga Zabelinskaya, who was third in the women's Road Race, gained another bronze with 37:57.35. Zabelinskaya, whose father won Cycling gold at Moscow 1980, occupied the purple throne hot seat for most of the race before Armstrong and Arndt set a blistering pace to reel in her lead. Britain's Emma Pooley, who had won silver at Beijing 2008, came in sixth, on a course that did not play to her hill-climbing strengths. 'I'm pretty disappointed,' said Pooley, 'but if someone else is better than you then they deserve to win.' Lizzie Armitstead, who admitted to finding the Time Trial very hard going, finished in 10th place.

Armstrong, who came out of retirement to compete in London and crashed out of the Road Race, became the oldest gold medallist in Olympic Road Cycling history. The former triathlete stood on the podium wearing a huge smile and carrying her 23-month-old son Lucas in her arms. 'I am now officially retired,' she declared.

Cycling — Track

Men's events

Rock star welcome for Team GB's Sprint men

The Olympic Track Cycling events enjoyed an explosive start in the electric atmosphere of a rock concert. A capacity crowd of 6,000 took their seats in the sleek, sexy and tightly engineered Velodrome, one of the showpiece venues of the Olympic Park.

Thin Lizzy's hit 'The Boys Are Back In Town' pumped out of the speakers at maximum volume as Great Britain's defending Olympic champions lined up for the Team Sprint final, led by the veteran knight of the track, Sir Chris Hoy. Hoy, 19-year-old new boy Philip Hindes and Jason Kenny smashed the world record in a stunning time of 42.747 on the way to the gold medal race against five-time world champions France, but there were more heroics to follow.

On the big screen Dame Kelly Holmes, finger on lips, 'shushed' the crowd for the starting hooter. Then a deafening wave of roaring followed the cyclists around the track as Hindes set a blistering pace on the first lap. Jason Kenny powered around the Siberian pine to hand over to Hoy, who produced an unprecedented ride of strength and aggression to claim gold and another world record (42.600).

The cheering and flag-waving home crowd went wild in the pressure cooker of the Velodrome, where temperature and air speed are perfectly controlled for fast, world record-breaking performances. France, who trailed Team GB by 0.413 seconds, took the silver, as they did at Beijing 2008. In the bronze medal heat Germany (43.209) triumphed over Australia by 0.146.

The tears flowed as the Velodrome rocked to David Bowie's 'Heroes' and Team GB waved to ecstatic fans on their victory lap. Hoy, 36, admitted that he had struggled to control his emotion as he received his fifth Olympic gold medal, equalling the record held by rower Sir Steve Redgrave.

The Sport

Changes to the Olympic Games Cycling programme after Beijing 2008 meant that men and women were treated equally in terms of number of events. The seven men's events and three women's events were amended by the Union Cycliste Internationale (UCI) to become five events for each.

As a result the men's and women's Individual Pursuit and Points Races and the men's Madison were dropped from the programme. The women's Team Pursuit, Team Sprint and Keirin were introduced as well as the Omnium (cycling's version of the Decathlon). The UCI also decreed that each nation could enter only one athlete or team in each event.

Above: Heads down, this could be fast. Team GB's Edward Clancy, Geraint Thomas, Steven Burke and Peter Kennaugh retain the title they won at Beijing 2008 and set a new world record in men's Team Pursuit.

Above right: Jason Kenny (left), boldly selected over Chris Hoy, wins the second heat against Gregory Bauge of France on his way to taking gold in the men's Sprint.

'It was amazing how fast we were going. I needed a bigger gear, my legs were almost going too fast for me.'

Ed Clancy, Team Pursuit gold medallist

Incredible Team GB smash Pursuit world record

Team GB set a new world record (3:51.659) to take gold in the men's Team Pursuit, beating Australia by almost three seconds – an enormous gap in pursuit cycling.

The huge crowd, which included Tour de France winner and Time Trial gold medallist Bradley Wiggins, knew they were watching something special when the British team flew round the early stages at speeds of around 40 miles per hour. Such momentum signalled that they were on schedule to break their own world record.

Ed Clancy and Geraint Thomas, Team Pursuit gold medallists at Beijing 2008, joined forces with Steven Burke and Peter Kennaugh to dominate the race. They executed a series of changes with power and precision, encouraged by an exuberant crowd. 'It felt like everyone here was cheering for us,' Clancy said later. 'It was just incredible'. The Australians pushed hard, but the big boys of British cycling cranked up the pressure to beat their own world record, set at Beijing 2008, for the third time.

After the race Kennaugh, 23, said the British

quartet enjoyed a unique camaraderie. 'We bounce off each other. It's much easier when you're not stressing about the race, you're just laughing and joking,' he laughed.

In the race for the bronze medal, the Russians paid the price for trying to contain New Zealand, who won in an impressive 3:55.952.

Outstanding Kenny wins Sprint

Britain's Jason Kenny became a double gold medal-winning Olympian on Day 11, stepping out of the immense shadow of Sir Chris Hoy to win the men's Sprint in scintillating style.

The quiet and modest 24-year-old from Bolton was picked for the Sprint ahead of Britain's cycling hero. He justified his selection with vicious velocity to beat Frenchman Gregory Bauge 2–0 in a best of three contest, with times of 10.232 and 10.308. Shane Perkins of Australia won the bronze medal in two races against Nijsane Nicholas Phillip of Trinidad and Tobago, the only cyclist representing his country at the Velodrome.

Bauge was always the big threat and there was history between the two riders. Kenny had become world sprint champion in 2011, handed the title after Bauge forfeited his crown for missing a doping control test. At the world championships in April 2012 Bauge beat Kenny, but that second place galvanised the British rider into action. His Olympic gold was a glorious victory, the perfect reward for refocusing and training harder. He had also made a personal sacrifice, moving from his beloved Bolton to be closer to the Team GB training base at the Manchester Velodrome – first visited by Kenny on a school trip aged 11.

In the Olympic final Kenny treated the excited crowd to one of the best exhibitions of Track Cycling of the 2012 Games. He broke the world record in qualifying and said that although he had felt lonely competing individually rather than as a team, he had not been intimidated by the imposing figure of Bauge. Nor had he thought about Hoy until the start of his winning second race.

'I didn't think of it until the last ride. I knew Chris would never lose the final killer ride,' laughed Kenny, adding that the tremendous noise of the cheering fans in the final half lap had given him the fractional advantage to win gold.

Danish delight in Omnium

It was a Cycling gold for Denmark as Lasse Norman Hansen won the first medal in the men's Omnium, the multi-discipline event which is Track Cycling's equivalent of the Heptathlon or Decathlon in Athletics.

Over two days of intense competition in six events, Hansen battled and prevailed. His 27 points gave him the edge over Frenchman Bryan Coquard, who took silver with 29, and Britain's Ed Clancy, who won the bronze medal with 30.

'I know I said I was off Twitter until after tomorrow, but that was PHENOMENAL by Jason Kenny. So happy and proud of him, well deserved, mate.'

Cycling icon Chris Hoy joins in praise of Jason Kenny after his Sprint victory

Great Dane. Lasse Norman Hansen celebrates winning the gold for Denmark after the 1km time trial, the final element of the men's Omnium.

Clancy's scores in four out of the six elements would have been enough for gold, but finishes of 11th and 10th in the 30km points race and 15km scratch race respectively brought him to bronze medal position. Hansen had his own troubles. He survived a crash in the scratch race, but, battered and bruised, caught the pack and then lapped the other riders to put himself in the perfect position for gold in the final 1km time trial.

Cheers and tears as Keirin brings Hoy sixth gold

Sir Chris Hoy ignited the rocket burners and propelled himself into Olympic legend, winning an astonishing sixth gold medal in the men's Keirin. In so doing he overtook rower Sir Steve Redgrave's record of five golds to join fellow cyclist Bradley Wiggins as Britain's most decorated Olympians with a total of seven medals.

Hoy was like a shark waiting to attack in the early circuits of the track, before striking with killer instinct and injecting a burst of speed. With two laps to go, there was a scare and the crowd

Team GB Cycling medals at recent Olympic Games

Beijing 2008
8 gold
4 silver
2 bronze
Total: 14 medals (ranked 1st)

Athens 2004
2 gold
1 silver
1 bronze
Total: 4 medals (ranked 3rd)

Sydney 2000
1 gold
1 silver
2 bronze
Total: 4 medals (ranked 6th)

missed a collective heartbeat as Hoy seemed momentarily to be under pressure. He never lost control, however, skilfully judging power and pace to edge away and take the Olympic title with a remarkable time of 10.306. Maximilian Levy of Germany won silver, and bronze medals were awarded to both Dutch veteran Teun Mulder and Simon Van Velthooven of New Zealand, who finished equal third.

Then came the celebrations for the nice guy of British sport, a consistently modest and admirable ambassador for cycling. He rode off the Olympic track for the final time through a guard of honour of his coaching staff as the world's elite cyclists applauded and cheered. The moment was shared by Hoy's mother, who had hidden her face in her hands for most of the race, and father, who unfurled the familiar family flag proclaiming 'Chris Hoy – The Real McHoy'. Thousands of fans in the Velodrome, as well as those watching on the big screen in the Olympic Park and on television at

home, shared the emotion as Hoy shed tears during the National Anthem.

Yet it was not the final farewell to Hoy. The 36-year-old Scot thanked his wife and family, backroom coaching staff and fans, confirming that this was the finale to his Olympic career. He would, however, aim to retire from competition at the Commonwealth Games in Glasgow in two years time.

'I'm in shock. This is surreal. It is what I always wanted – to win gold in front of my home crowd. This is the perfect end to my Olympic career.'

Sir Chris Hoy, gold medallist in the Keirin and Team Sprint

Below: Applying the burners. Cycling icon Chris Hoy crosses the line first in the Keirin on the final day of Track Cycling in the Velodrome.

Below right: Welcome to the Pleasuredome. Chris Hoy celebrates an emotional victory in the Keirin and his sixth gold medal at the Olympic Games, a record for a British athlete.

disqualified for an illegal changeover – the equivalent of dropping the baton in Athletics.

China qualified for the women's Team Sprint by setting a new Olympic and world record, then apparently going on to beat world champions Germany in the gold medal race. Yet moments after cycling a lap of honour carrying the Chinese flag, Jinjie Gong and Shuang Guo were relegated to the silver medal position for an illegal takeover. The German duo Miriam Welte and Kristina Vogel, who finished in 32.798, were crowned Olympic champions, and the bronze medal went to Australia, who beat Ukraine in 32.727.

Left: In a busy and controversial session Germany's Kristina Vogel (right) and Miriam Welte were crowned champions in the women's Team Sprint. China was relegated to silver medal position and Team GB's Pendleton and Varnish were disqualified earlier in the event.

Below: On the rebound. Victoria Pendleton, seen ahead of China's Shuang Guo, bounces back from her disqualification in the Team Sprint to take Keirin gold.

Women's events

Drama in the Team Sprint

The women's Team Sprint competition was full of drama during a tense session in the Velodrome. China won the gold, then lost it, while Britons Victoria Pendleton and Jessica Varnish, who set the first world record of the afternoon, were

Keirin gold crowns Team GB's Queen of the Track

The Queen of British cycling Victoria Pendleton delighted home fans in the Velodrome with victory in the Keirin, banishing the misery of her Team Sprint disqualification the day before.

So, as Pendleton lined up for the Keirin – an event once described by BBC radio presenter Terry

'I can barely believe it right now … Thank you so much to everyone who's helped me get here. The crowd have been fantastic and it really helped me today.'

Victoria Pendleton, women's Keirin gold medallist

Wogan as like watching six crazy cyclists chasing a pizza delivery boy – fans were willing a gold medal for their heroine in her swansong Olympic Games. And this time it was to be tears of joy for the 31-year-old poster girl of British cycling.

Australia's Anna Meares, so often Pendleton's nemesis, was to make the first move in the Keirin, as the motorised durny bike peeled away. Pendleton responded and jumped ahead, raising a fleeting concern she had moved too soon. However, her lightning speed held off all challengers in a masterclass of sprinting for gold, which she took with a time of 10.965. Meares, the pre-race favourite, finished fifth.

Half a wheel behind Pendleton in the silver medal position was China's Shuang Guo, who lost the gold medal in the Team Sprint after being relegated. A surprise bronze went to Wai Sze Lee, in a historic first Cycling medal for Hong Kong, China.

Britain tops Track Cycling medals table			
	G	S	B
GBR	7	1	1	9
AUS	1	1	3	5
GER	1	1	1	3
DEN	1	0	0	1
FRA	0	3	0	3
CHN	0	2	1	3
USA	0	2	0	2
NZL	0	0	2	2
CAN	0	0	1	1
HKG	0	0	1	1
NED	0	0	1	1

'Fab Three' conquer the world in Team Pursuit

Pop music pounded out across the Velodrome and Sir Paul McCartney waved his arms in the air as Britain's supreme Team Pursuit champions Laura Trott, Joanna Rowsell and Dani King broke another world record to take gold in the Team Pursuit. Their time of 3:14.051 was a staggering sixth world record in six competitive races.

The magnificent British trio produced a ride in the final, against the USA, that was nothing short of phenomenal. They were flying so fast that they were catching their quarry and could see the USA team, who finished with 3:19.727, in front of them on the final lap. The contest for the bronze medal was also close – a Commonwealth clash in which Canada beat the world silver medallists Australia with a time of 3:17.915 (two seconds faster than

'Words can't describe how I feel … When London won the Olympic Games I was not even riding a bike – this journey has been crazy for me.'

Dani King, women's Team Pursuit gold medallist

A magnificent ride from Team GB's King, Rowsell and Trott brings gold medals and a new world record on the fast and fercious track of Siberian pine.

the USA in the gold medal race).

There were emotional scenes as the British team hobbled up the steep bank of the track in cycling shoes to greet friends and family. 'It's mad. This has been my dream since I was eight,' laughed Trott, 20, who beamed with joy on the podium wearing her first Olympic medal. Rowsell praised the football match atmosphere inside the Velodrome, 'I could tell we were winning by the sound of the crowd,' she laughed.

After the Victory Ceremony McCartney led the British celebrations – a Fab Four survivor leading a chorus of *Hey Jude* in tribute to a 'Fab Three'.

Aussie rules in Individual Sprint

Australia's Anna Meares conquered her arch-rival Victoria Pendleton of Team GB in the women's Individual Sprint, denying the Briton a fairytale end to her cycling career.

An air of drama settled over the track for another chapter in the decade-long rivalry between the two women. Tension mounted as Pendleton, the defending champion, won the first race of three by 1000th of a second: 11.218 to Meares' 11.348. Moments later she suffered her second infringement of the Olympic Games when she was relegated to second place for straying out of the sprinter's lane after a clash with Meares.

In race two Meares toyed with Pendleton,

creeping up to the top of the bank and cycling at snail's pace before blasting away to win the gold medal 2–0. The old adversaries cycled around the track holding hands before Meares punched the air and threw her helmet into the air. The British crowd cried, 'Vicky, Vicky, Vicky', and Pendleton, in floods of tears, declared that she was relieved that it was all over and could now move on.

The bronze medal was a fight between China's Shuang Guo and Kristina Vogel from Germany, with Guo winning the medal 2–0.

New star rises in the Omnium

As Victoria Pendleton bade farewell to cycling, a new British superstar emerged from the Velodrome. Twenty-year-old Laura Trott produced a gutsy performance to take the gold medal in the multi-event Omnium.

Two points behind the USA's Sarah Hammer after the scratch race, she snatched victory with an Olympic record in the 500m time trial in the final element of the competition. The dramatic close (Trott won 19–18) delighted the cheering crowd and brought the British rider, from Hertfordshire, her second gold medal following her Team Pursuit success. Hammer won the silver, with Annette Edmondson of Australia taking bronze with 24.

Trott, born with a collapsed lung, first took up cycling to help control her asthma, and a high acid lining to her stomach often makes her sick after racing. Yet she has proved herself to be an inspirational cyclist at her first Olympic Games. On her celebratory lap of honour she beamed and waved to the crowd carrying a Union flag emblazoned with 'Go Trotty'. With her blonde plaits flying in the breeze, the fresh-faced, double gold medallist looked like a 1950s sixth-former cycling home from school.

She said her dad had given up cricket to ferry her to cycling events and thanked her parents for the sacrifices they had made to help her become an Olympic champion. 'I can't believe this has happened to me,' she said.

The Velodrome

From the outside the Velodrome is a stunning piece of architecture with its iconic curved roof, red cedar wood cladding, glass wall and natural ventilation. Economic with materials and able to harvest rainwater from its roof, as well as ventilate without air conditioning, it is one of the most environmentally friendly of the London 2012 venues. Form and function are interlinked; among those who played a part in its design was Sir Chris Hoy, while veteran track designer and cyclist Ron Webb came out of retirement to conceive the track. Completed 18 months ahead of the Games, the Velodrome will in future form the centrepiece of a VeloPark for use by the local community, clubs and elite athletes

'I thought I was going to be sick on the start line, which didn't help matters. But I just got going and the crowd just drove me home. I was so happy.'

Laura Trott, women's Omnium gold medallist

After her final race before retirement, silver medallist Victoria Pendleton (left) congratulates the new Olympic Sprint champion, Anna Meares of Australia.

'It was inspiring to be at the Olympic Games and to have a million people lining the route of the Road Race ... that's a record crowd for an Olympic event. People were talking about cycling being cool ... they wanted to get their bikes out of the shed. I'm confident there will be a huge legacy from these Olympics.'

Stewart Kellett, Director of Recreation, British Cycling

The Cycling Road Race route took cyclists past an estimated one million spectators in central London, and out into the beautiful countryside of Surrey before finishing back at The Mall, close to Buckingham Palace.

Equestrian – Dressage

Great Britain's Carl Hester performs an immaculate routine on his majestic horse Uthopia in the Dressage Team Competition. Team GB's gold medal ended the seven-year German domination of the sport.

The Sport

Dressage is a French term, most commonly translated to mean 'training'. It tests the communication between riders and their horses, effectively testing the horse's ability to perform a series of pre-defined moves by responding to its rider, who in turn must appear calm and in control. The horses are always beautifully turned out and their riders adhere to a strict dress code. Sometimes referred to as 'horse ballet', horse and rider demonstrate their skill in front of judges who score from zero to 10.

Bechtolsheimer, Dujardin and Hester take Team Competition gold for Team GB

They looked beautiful and performed brilliantly. In one of the great spectacles of London 2012, Team GB's stylish horses and riders ended the seven-year German domination of the sport by winning the gold medal in the Dressage Team Competition at Greenwich Park.

Charlotte Dujardin and her horse Valegro (stable name Blueberry), who are said to have a telepathic bond, broke the Olympic Dressage record in qualifying, scoring 83.286 per cent. They then produced an ice-cool performance in the finale to help Great Britain to a final score of 79.979 per cent. The Germans were runners-up with 78.216 per cent to win the silver medal, and the Netherlands won bronze with 77.124.

Dujardin's mentor Carl Hester and his horse

Uthopia (nickname Uti) delighted the crowd with an immaculate routine that scored 80.571 per cent. 'It is a dream come true,' he said. The third member of the team, Laura Bechtolsheimer and Mistral Hojris (Alf), posted 77.794 per cent.

It was a thrilling moment for the British equestrian fans. They had provided a memorable atmosphere at the magnificent Greenwich Park venue, with its glorious views over London. Many young riders went home dreaming of future Olympic Games, noting that Dujardin had only begun competing internationally 18 months before.

'It is an incredible feeling for all three of us and I think we'll all really proud of each other and of our horses.'

Laura Bechtolsheimer, Team Competition gold medallist

'I can't believe it. It was only last January that we did our first Grand Prix and now we have two Olympic gold medals.'

Charlotte Dujardin, two-time Dressage gold medallist

Dujardin and Valegro triumph with Individual Dressage gold

Great Britain's new Dressage darlings, Charlotte Dujardin and her glossy-coated, chocolate brown champion Valegro, produced an amazing routine to win the gold medal in the Individual Dressage Competition.

Dujardin's delightful dance across the arena offered a masterclass in the art of Dressage. Valegro skimmed over the sand in extended trot to the sound of 007's 'Live and Let Die', followed moments later by half passes to 'The Great Escape'. Horse and rider then struck a patriotic note, cantering to 'Land of Hope and Glory' before slowing to a walk as music from the hymn 'I Vow To Thee My Country' drifted over the arena. The inspired and artistic display was rounded off with double pirouettes to the chimes of Big Ben.

There was not a dry eye in Greenwich Park as the crowd burst into rapturous applause and loud cheering. The pair scored an incredible 90.089 per cent, an Olympic freestyle record.

Dujardin, from Enfield, grew up showing ponies. The 27-year-old was given the chance to work with her mentor, fellow Team GB competitor Carl Hester, after meeting him at a talent-spotting day. Dujardin's mother asked if he would give her daughter a lesson; Hester saw she was a special horsewoman and invited her to work at his yard in Gloucestershire where the heavenly partnership with Blueberry was perfected. She becomes the fourth British woman to win double gold at an Olympic Games, and also emulates rider Richard Mead who took two gold medals at Munich 1972.

The silver medal was won by Adelinde Cornelissen from the Netherlands (88.196 per cent), whose routine included music from 'The Nutcracker Suite'. Bronze went to Britain's Laura Bechtolsheimer (84.339 per cent), who rode Mistral Hojris to music from the popular 'Lion King'.

Greenwich Park

Greenwich Park, London's oldest Royal Park, dates back to 1433. It is home to the National Maritime Museum and the Prime Meridian Line, from where Greenwich Mean Time is established. The main arena featured an innovative purpose-made platform made of plywood, aluminium and steel, and held above ground by more than 2,000 pillars. Placed on the axis with the Queen's House, it was designed in the shape of a horseshoe to allow glorious views of the Old Royal Naval College and the city skyline behind.

Equestrian – Eventing

Great Britian's Zara Phillips (centre) carries on the family tradition, flanked by members of the Eventing team.

Team GB's Eventing Team

Nicola Wilson and Opposition Buzz
Mary King and Imperial Cavalier
Zara Phillips and High Kingdom
Tina Cook and Miners Frolic
William Fox-Pitt and Lionheart

The Sport

The competition for the Olympic Individual and Team Eventing gold medal took place over four days and included Dressage, Cross-Country and Jumping. The highlight was the cross-country test over a specially designed 5.7km course, including 42 jumps, that wound its way through the beautiful Greenwich Park. Scores are cumulative in this ultimate test of horse and rider, and while teams consist of up to five riders, only three results count towards the final score.

German gold in dominant Team Eventing display

Germany retained their Team Eventing title at the spectacular Greenwich Park with a powerful display of horsemanship. They finished ahead of Team GB, who won silver, and New Zealand, who took the bronze.

London 2012 saw Equestrian events placed at the heart of the Olympic Games for the first time. Riders competed in the World Heritage-listed Greenwich Park, once a hunting and jousting ground for King Henry VIII. Royal connections were maintained by the Queen's granddaughter Zara Phillips, in her first Olympic Games; her mother the Princess Royal is also an Olympian and her father,

Captain Mark Phillips, won Team gold at Munich 1972. In an emotional ceremony before a cheering British crowd, Phillips received her silver medal from her mother.

Germany, who scored 133.70 to win gold, demonstrated a consistent mastery of the three disciplines of dressage, cross country and jumping. Their dominance had secured the gold medal even before their last rider, Ingrid Klimhe, completed her round, but the battle for silver and bronze was close and tense. Both Great Britain and New Zealand, fielding two riders in their fifties, proved that in equestrian sport experience counts. New Zealander Mark Todd, riding in his eighth Olympic Games, first won gold at Los Angeles, while Team GB's Mary King, who suffered a broken neck in a fall in 2001, was competing in her sixth Games. She produced a vital and impressive clear round on Imperial Cavalier, matching that of Andrew Nicholson for New Zealand. Finally Tina Cook, daughter of the late Grand National-winning trainer Josh Gifford, completed a cool, clear show jumping round with just one time penalty to clinch the silver for Team GB on 138.20; New Zealand took bronze with 144.40. 'It was very much mind over matter,' she explained later. Her horse Miner's Frolic had survived a life-threatening disease only 12 months earlier.

Phillips said her parents were immensely proud. 'It's an awesome experience. We've had a great time ... it's been a great team effort,' she smiled.

Individual Eventing sees Jung's dream come true

Germany's Michael Jung became the first rider to hold the World, European and Olympic titles when he won gold in the Individual Eventing Competition, riding his horse Sam. The triple crown came on Jung's 30th birthday. His Olympic Individual title made this a double gold birthday present, as earlier in the day he had helped Germany to take gold in the Team Competition.

The finale to the competition took place in the unique show jumping arena in front of the Queen's House, designed by Inigo Jones. The jump designs reflected a magnificent range of British history and landmarks, including Stonehenge, Nelson's Column and Trafalgar Square, red postboxes and Abbey Road, The Beatles' famous recording studio.

Only four penalty points separated the first four riders and the gold medal was not decided until the final moment of the competition. Jung had jumped clear to put pressure on Sweden's Sara Algotsson Ostholt, riding Wega. Poised to take gold, she clipped a pole on the last fence in a heartbreaking moment, missing out on the Olympic title to take silver.

The bronze medal was another triumph for Germany as Sandra Auffarth and Opgun Louvo

completed the jumping phase without penalties. British hopes had been with Zara Phillips, who ended in eighth place, Tina Cook and Mary King who, in an unhappy coincidence, both brought down the first and third fences. They finished sixth and fifth respectively.

After receiving his medal, Jung paid tribute to his mount, Sam. 'Every competition with Sam is very easy,' he said. 'He makes everything easy for me.'

Germany's Michael Jung, and his horse Sam, make a splash winning Team and Individual Gold in Eventing. Jung became the first rider to hold the European, World and Olympic Eventing titles.

Equestrian – Jumping

Jumping for joy as Team GB win gold

After a wait of 60 years, Team GB's gold medal in the Jumping Team Competition was a tribute to mature horsemanship and the skill of orthopaedic surgeons. A litany of injuries, including broken vertebrae, knee and hip operations and a ruptured spleen, failed to hinder Britain's veterans. They showed exquisite horsemanship to win the Olympic Team title in a thrilling jump-off against the Netherlands.

Sporting survivors Nick Skelton, riding Big Star, and Peter Charles on Vindicat, both in their 50s, rode with Ben Maher (Tripple X) and Scott Brash (Hello Sanctos) to give Britain their first Olympic Jumping title since Helsinki 1952. It was also the

first Jumping medal of any colour for Great Britain since Los Angeles 1984.

After the final phase of action, both Team GB and the Netherlands, including Gerco Schroder riding a horse called London, had four faults.

The Sport

Known in the UK as Show Jumping, the Olympic Individual and Team competition took place over five rounds in the main arena. Riders were timed as they tackled jumps that included parallel rails, triple bars, water jumps and simulated stone walls. A jump not cleared correctly means penalty points, with the individual gold medallist being the rider who completes the course in the fastest time and with the fewest penalties.

'It's been a long time coming. I've been to a lot of Games and made a lot of mistakes, but I've finally got there … The crowd was behind each one of us. Without them, this would not have been possible.'

Nick Skelton, Jumping gold medallist in his fifth Olympic Games

The gold medal thus had to be decided in a jump-off – a nerve-wracking equivalent of football's penalty shoot-out. Skelton and Maher jumped like lightning and were faster than the first Dutch riders, while Brash's one mistake was cancelled out by errors from the next two Dutchmen. One clear round would bring gold – but Vindicat had picked up penalties from three of the previous rounds. In the temporary Greenwich Park arena the 23,000-strong crowd held its breath, and then roared with joy as Charles jumped clear to win gold. 'I just had to focus on the arena,' he said later. 'I was very keen to get the job done and not let the lads down.'

Saudia Arabia, who had been the shock leaders overnight, claimed bronze, the country's first Olympic Team medal.

Sun shines on Swiss in Individual Jumping Competition

In the sunshine, Switzerland's Steve Guerdat a and his horse Nino des Buissonnets gave the cheering crowd a fabulously faultless riding lesson in Greenwich Park's magnificent arena. They displayed great equestrian skill and equine athleticism to take the gold medal.

The Olympic Jumping course, with its red London bus, was quirky and tough for Equestrian competitors. Team GB's veteran horseman Nick Skelton described it as 'not crazily big, but with tricky lines.' Among the fences was a difficult triple combination, including a water jump that sorted the medallists from the also-rans.

Guerdat, whose hero is fellow countryman Roger Federer, was the only rider to jump without faults. Holland's Gerco Schroder won silver after a jump-off against Ireland's Cian O'Connor, who was awarded bronze.

British hopes rested on Skelton and Big Star, but he knocked a rail down at Cutty Sark to finish equal fifth. It was the only mistake made by the horse, whom Skelton had called 'perfect', in the five rounds of a tiring competition. Saudia Arabia emerged as contenders for Olympic Equestrian honours in the future, when Kamal Bahamdan, who won a Team bronze, finished fourth.

Jumping fences in Greenwich Park

A range of beautifully designed fences in Greenwich Park Arena included the following themes:
Old Royal Naval College and
    the Queen's House
Naval Ship of the Line
Magna Carta and the Birth
    of Justice
English Country Garden
Gazebo and Bridge
Lighthouse and Thames Barge
Greenwich Mean Time Clocks
1908 and 1948 Olympic
    Fences
Royal Observatory of
    Greenwich
Nelson's Column from Trafalgar
    Square
Stonehenge
Tower Bridge
Royal Mail
Abbey Road

'I am proud, but I am more happy for the people behind me. They have helped me so much as a team and this gold medal is theirs, not mine.'

Steve Guerdat, Individual Jumping Competition gold medallist

Tripple X and rider Ben Maher of Great Britain fly over Stonehenge. The Olympic Equestrian events included imaginative obstacles which featured famous London landmarks like Abbey Road, Nelson's Column and Tower Bridge.

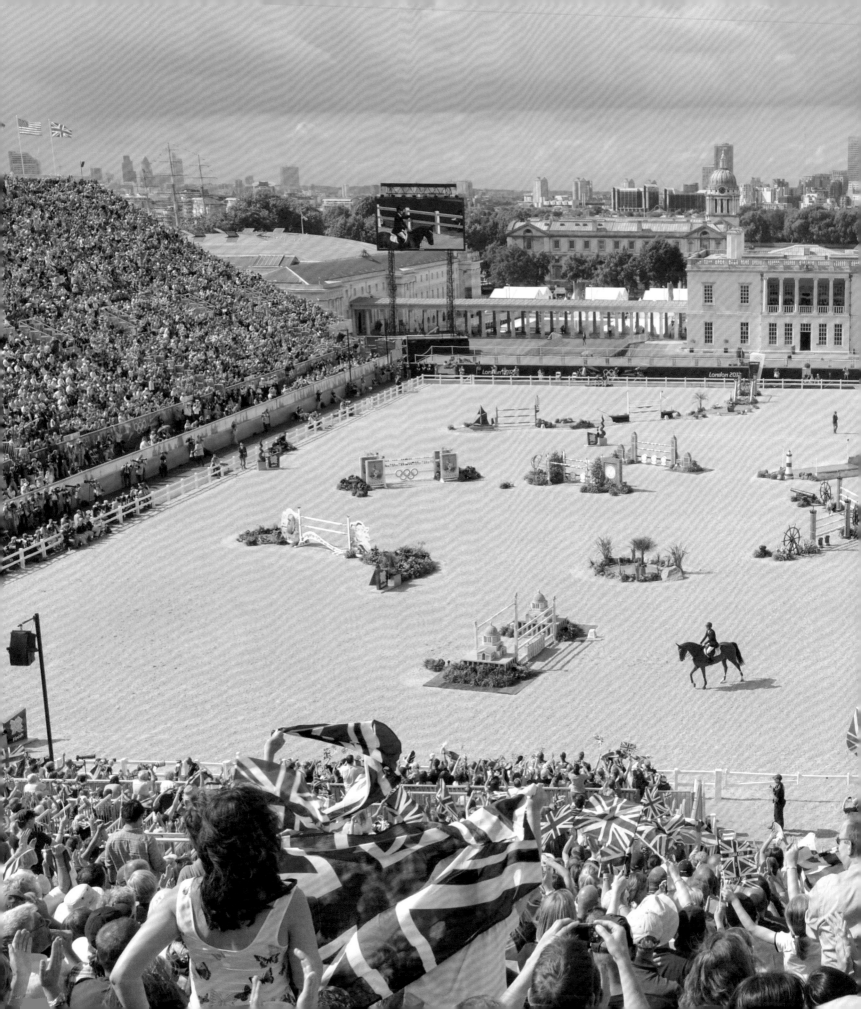

'The crowd just carried you round in a wave of screams and roars ... it was special ... I'm sad it's over.'

William Fox-Pitt, Team GB Equestrian Eventing Team Competition Silver medallist

Greenwich Park, the London 2012 venue for Equestrian events and elements of the Modern Pentathlon. It afforded spectators a dazzling view of London landmarks and perfect sightlines of horses and riders.

Fencing

No way through. Suguru Awaji (left) was among the Japanese fencers who pushed Andrea Cassara (right) and the all-conquering Italians hard in the Fencing men's Team Foil final. However, the Italian's Fencing prowess eventually won out.

'I'm the first African fencer who has won an Olympic medal and that makes me proud, especially because this was also my father's dream.'

Silver medallist Alaaeldin Abdulelkassem pays tribute to his father, who died earlier in the year.

Men's events

New star from Egypt in Individual Foil

A piece of history was made at a packed ExCeL with a first-ever medal for an African fencer. It followed an epic, 37-minute contest that brought the crowd to its feet at the level of skill on show.

Alaaeldin Abdulelkassem of Egypt took the silver medal, with Sheng Lei of China seizing his country's first Individual Foil title 15–13. In also winning Egypt's first medal in London, the 21-year-old African champion had enjoyed a sensational passage to the final, overcoming Italy's Andrea Cassara who had come into the competition as the world champion and hot favourite for the gold medal. 'I really can't believe what I've done,' he said. The bronze medal went to Byungchul Choi of Korea who defeated Andrea Baldini of Italy 15–14 in the bronze medal contest.

Italian fencers win Team Foil gold

Italy's prowess as a Fencing nation at these Games was never better illustrated than in the Team Foil event, in which Andrea Cassara, Andrea Baldini and Giorgio Avola overcame a persistent Japan to win gold 45–39.

In a battle of attrition that took the Italians by surprise, Japan pushed the top-seeded nation to the limit, producing a dazzling display. It was not until the last two bouts that the Italians managed to gain ground on their plucky opponents. 'We didn't expect such a tough final,' Avola admitted. 'They fenced really well.'

The bronze medal match saw Germany decisively overpower the USA by 45–27.

The result meant that Italy matched France's record of seven gold medals in this event overall.

Korea sweep to first Team Sabre gold

Korea secured its first Olympic Fencing Team gold in the men's Team Sabre event at ExCeL after a one-sided match against Romania which ended 45–26.

Koreans Junghwan Kim, Young Woo Won and Bongil Gu dominated the Romanian trio of Rares Dumitrescu, Tiberiu Dolniceanu and Florin Zalomir and both teams brought on substitutes to make sure they also received a medal. Italy maintained its medal count in London, and in the wider competition, by taking the bronze 45–40 against the Russians. Italy substituted the competition's oldest man, Luigi Tarantino, 39, with Luigi Samele. He proved a sparkling replacement, winning 19 hits to give Aldo Montano (ITA) a cushion of nine hits for the final bout.

Women's events

Triple delight for Italy in Individual Foil

Italian domination of the event continued with a clean sweep of the medals. It was not three-time Olympic champion Valentina Vezzali who took the gold, however, but her teammate, Elisa Di Francisca. Separating the two in the medals was Arianna Errigo, who beat Vezzali in their semi-final.

The final itself was fought to extra time after Di Francesca had come from 11–8 down, with 45 seconds of normal time remaining, to snatch the 12–11 victory by a single point. This was the first time that Italy had won all the medals in a women's event in any sport at the Olympic Games. After claiming her eighth Olympic medal, Vezzali signalled her intention to carry on to Rio 2016. 'Now I have a big motivation to continue because when there is a problem like losing, I want to resolve it,' she said.

Sit-in overshadows Ukrainian Individual Epée win

The gold medal was won by Ukraine's Yana Shemyakina, but her dramatic 9–8 win in extra time over 2008 Olympic champion Britta Heidemann (GER) was overshadowed by a controversial sit-in. The protest, staged by beaten Korean semi-finalist A Lam Shin, held the competition up for more than an hour.

Pandemonium erupted at the end of Shin's match against Heidemann, whose winning hit came as the clock showed just a second left. Shin, who had priority, believed that the time was up and the hit should be disallowed. Korean officials called for the Directoire Technique (the International Fencing Federation's ruling body) to question the length of that final, crucial second. When the ruling went against Shin, she sat on the piste and refused to leave, evoking memories of Korean boxers' sit-in protests at the 1964 and 1988 Olympic Games.

The International Fencing Federation later went some way to acknowledge that a mistake may have been made, deciding to make a special award to Shin for her 'aspiration to win and respect for the rules'.

Kim ends Zagunis' reign in the Individual Sabre

The surprise winner of the women's Individual Sabre was Korea's Jiyeon Kim, who beat Russian Federation's Sofya Velikaya in the final 15–9. Yet it was her victory against all the odds over Mariel Zagunis, USA Flagbearer at the Opening Ceremony, that caused the biggest shock of the competition.

Zagunis had held the title from its introduction to the Games at Athens 2004. She was on her way to a comfortable win over Kim in their semi-final when the Korean launched an astonishing comeback from 12–5 down. Kim scored the next 11 hits and ended the match by winning 15–13 against the sport's poster girl. Zagunis had little left for her bronze medal bout, with the medal going 15–10 to Olga Kharlan of Ukraine.

Broken teeth battle for Greece's lone fencer

Vassiliki Vougiouka, Greece's only fencer, battled hard in her Individual Sabre quarter-final against the eventual gold medallist Jiyeon Kim, despite struggling with the pain of two broken teeth after an accidental clash of masks in an earlier match. Tired and in pain, wearing a temporary guard on her teeth, she finally succumbed 15–12. Vougiouka came to London as a medal prospect despite having to balance her Individual Sabre training programme with final-year university studies – in dentistry.

Clean sweep. Elisa Di Francisca and Arianna Errigo contest the final of the women's Individual Foil event as Italy takes the top three spots for the first time.

Football

Right: Golden generation. Korea's gifted young players celebrate with their coach Hong Myung Bo (top) after beating Japan to the bronze medal at the Millennium Stadium in Cardiff.

Opposite: Too good. Brazil's goalkeeper Gabriel (right) dives in vain as Oribe Peralta scores Mexico's second goal in the men's Football final at Wembley Stadium.

Men's events

Korea beat Japan to Football bronze

Korea claimed their first-ever medal in the Olympic Football tournament by defeating Japan 2–0 in the bronze medal match at Cardiff's Millennium Stadium.

The goals came either side of half-time from Arsenal's Chuyoung Park and Korea's captain Jacheol Koo, but this was to prove a close-fought contest as Japan pushed Korea hard. They thought they had reduced the deficit with three minutes to go when Japanese captain Maya Yoshida headed in from a corner. His effort was disallowed by the referee, however, in response to the player's

earlier foul on Sungryong Jung in the Korean goal, enabling the bronze medallists to secure only their second victory of the competition.

Hong Myung Bo, the Korean coach, hailed this generation of players as a 'dream team' – following in the footsteps of the squad that reached the semi-finals of the World Cup in 2002, when Bo was captain.

Among the teams beaten by Korea on the way to their bronze medal was Team GB, making their first appearance in the tournament since 1960. Their quarter-final encounter finished 1–1 after normal and extra time, and it was the Koreans who won the ensuing penalty shoot-out 5–4.

The losers of the bronze medal match, Japan, had previously claimed the mighty Spain among their conquests. At the group stage, Japan defeated the World Cup winners 1– 0 in a shock result to record their first victory over Spain at any level.

Marvellous Mexico deny Brazil in Football final

This was supposed to have been the match that saw Brazil finally add the Olympic title to its five World Cups. Yet in the event it was Mexico who scored early, stole the show and took the Football gold.

Some of the 86,162 spectators at Wembley Stadium were still finding their seats when Mexico pounced on some nervous defending by the Brazil and Manchester United defender Rafael da Silva. Their boldness enabled the unmarked Oribe Peralta to fire home the opener from the edge of the penalty area after just 28 seconds.

Brazil were immediately forced to chase the game. Coach Mano Menezes attempted to inject some enterprise into his attacking options by sending on Hulk for Alex Sandro in the 32nd minute. Soon after the Porto striker's long range

'Winning this gold medal on the sacred pitch of Wembley makes it even more special.'

Luis Fernando Tena, the Mexican coach

shot did force a save from Jose Corona in the Mexican goal. Despite their pressure, however, the previously free-scoring Brazil, overwhelming favourites for the competition, failed to make an impact on the Mexico defence. The first half ended with no further goals.

Brazil began the second half brightly but Mexico held firm, with Diego Reyes playing well and Corona proving unbeatable. The goal that sealed the gold medal came in the 75th minute. Peralta's clever run evaded the Brazilian defence and he headed home from a Marco Fabian free kick to score his fourth goal of the Olympic competition.

Brazil had to press hard. Their frustration boiled over when Juan Jesus argued with Rafael before being substituted with five minutes still left on the clock. Brazil's reward came when Hulk broke away to score in the 91st minute. Moments later Oscar might even have levelled the match, but his close-range header missed the target.

So a delighted Mexican team claimed its first gold medal at London 2012, and its first medal

Mexico's golden line-up

Israel Jimenez
Carlos Salcido
Hiram Mier
Darvin Chavez
Hector Herrera
Javier Cortes
Marco Fabian
Oribe Peralta
Giovani dos Santos
Javier Aquino
Raul Jimenez
Diego Reyes
Jorge Enriquez
Nestor Vidrio
Miguel Ponce
Nestor Araujo
Jose Rodriguez

Celebrating a shock victory. The Mexico players celebrate after pulling off a victory over the competition favourites Brazil to win gold in the men's Football final.

of any colour in the Football tournament. Brazil once again missed out on the only title to elude the country, despite acquiring three silver and two bronze medals over the years.

Luis Fernando Tena, the Mexico coach, described his squad as '18 warriors' and added a special dedication for his gold medal. 'I dedicate this to my late father,' he said. 'He is still kicking a ball up in heaven.'

His star striker, Peralta, the first man to score two goals in an Olympic final for 20 years, said, 'I dreamed about this moment. It is one of those things you don't get to live every day. Brazil were the favourites, but we knew that would put some extra pressure on them.'

That pressure will only intensify on the Brazilian team that lines up at Rio 2016.

> 'There were some really fantastic matches and it has been a great advert for the women's game.'
>
> Megan Rapinoe, women's Football gold medallist

Running into trouble. Mana Iwabuchi of Japan comes up against Christie Rampone of the USA in their women's Football final at Wembley Stadium.

USA's golden line-up

Hope Solo
Heather Mitts
Christie Rampone
Becky Sauerbrunn
Kelley O'Hara
Amy le Peilbet
Shannon Boxx
Amy Rodriguez
Heather O'Reilly
Carli Lloyd
Sydney Leroux
Lauren Cheney
Alex Morgan
Abby Wambach
Megan Rapinoe
Rachel Buehler
Tobin Heah
Nicole Barnhart

Women's events

Three strikes and you're in ...
USA take Football gold

The USA maintained their dominance with a 2–1 victory over Japan to take their third consecutive gold medal in women's Football. It was also their fourth in the five Olympic Games since the sport was added to the programme in 1996.

Significantly, the crowd for the final at Wembley was 80,203. The figure comfortably beat the previous record for a women's Olympic Games Football match of 76,481, dating from the last match at Atlanta 1996 between the USA and China.

A brace of goals for Carli Lloyd – the first coming as early as the eighth minute – saw off an impressive Japan. The action-packed match, a brilliant advertisement for the women's game, was played out in front of Sepp Blatter, President of the world governing body FIFA.

Japan pulled a goal back through Yuki Ogimi after 63 minutes, but could not find an equaliser.

The thrilling game meant revenge of sorts for the USA, who had lost to Japan on a penalty shoot-out in the 2011 World Cup Final.

In the bronze medal match, held at the City of Coventry Stadium, Canada beat France 1–0. Midfielder Diana Matheson headed home the only goal just as the match seemed to be heading for extra time.

The experienced Canadian team had also ended Team GB's hopes in the quarter-final after the Host Nation had seemed in medal-winning form during the group stage. Most notable was a magnificent 1–0 victory over Brazil following a strike by Steph Houghton in the second minute. Over 70,000 excited supporters created an electric atmosphere at Wembley Stadium as Team GB held off the challenge from Brazil, ranked fourth in the world.

Record crowd. All talk of ticket sales was forgotten as a record crowd for women's Football of 80,203 filled Wembley Stadium to see the USA beat Japan to win the women's Football gold medal.

Gymnastics – Artistic

Team GB bronze medallists (left to right) Daniel Purvis, Max Whitlock, Louis Smith, Kristian Thomas and Sam Oldham, who won Great Britain's first Gymnastics Team medal for 100 years.

Men's events

Tense Team finale delights North Greenwich Arena crowds

London-born pop star Pixie Lott rocked the arena ahead of the men's Team Competition, singing 'Someone Like You' – but nobody guessed that by the end of the evening that 'someone' would be Team GB. A dramatic turn of events at the North Greenwich Arena saw the British team win bronze, with China taking gold and Japan silver.

In an electric session Team GB originally finished in second place, but the Japanese appealed their star gymnast Kohei Uchimura's dismount score on the pommel. For a nail-biting five minutes the judges reviewed video evidence and did their maths, eventually awarding silver to Japan. Ukraine, who had been in the bronze medal position, left London empty-handed.

China produced a series of near-perfect routines

'It's a beautiful day for the sport and British Gymnastics.'

Team GB captain Louis Smith celebrates the country's first Team medal since Stockholm 1912.

and led throughout the competition. Feng Zhe, who had the highest parallel bar score, explained how they maintained such dominance. 'We didn't have any faults. That's our secret. We conquered ourselves,' he laughed.

British fans, including the Duke of Cambridge and Prince Harry, went wild when Kristian Thomas executed a magnificent, straight-legged, backward double somersault that scored 16.550 – the highest mark in the competition. 'It's the first time I've pulled it off in competition. The blood, sweat and tears paid off,' said Thomas, who at 180cm is unusually tall for a gymnast.

Team GB, who failed to qualify from the world championships for London 2012, only winning their place at the Visa International Gymnastics test event 199 days before the Games, were ecstatic with the country's first team medal for 100 years. Sam Oldham described the result as, 'Madness … outrageous'. Team captain Louis Smith, who had won the Pommel Horse bronze at Beijing 2008, said the team had responded to the support of the home crowd. 'We set out to enjoy ourselves. It was beautiful,' he smiled.

Kohei Uchimura said he was sorry for challenging his score but added, 'It is strange to say that I feel sorry, but that is the scoring system.' Andre Gueisbuhler, Secretary General of the International Gymnastics Federation, said the judges reviewed Uchimura's dismount 10 times before correcting his score. 'Britain is a country of fair play,' observed Gueisbuhler. 'I'm sure nobody would have wanted a medal given because of a wrong score.'

The USA, who started as favourites for the gold medal, never recovered from a disastrous start when John Orozco unceremoniously sat down on the pommel horse. 'I blame myself and take responsibility,' said the young star from the Bronx.

Superstar Uchimura wins Individual All-Around Competition

Japan's 23-year-old Kohei Uchimura, known as 'Super-Mura', combines the looks of a pop star with the poise of a ballet dancer. In taking the Individual All-Around title he confirmed his status as the world's greatest gymnast, ending Japan's 28-year wait for the most highly regarded medal of Olympic Artistic Gymnastics.

The impish three-time world champion and silver medallist at Beijing 2008 finally tamed the pommel horse, the apparatus that cost him gold in 2008 and the Team title in London 2012, to post an unbeatable score of 92.690.

German soldier Marcel Nguyen won the silver medal with 91.031 points and 20-year-old Cuban-born American Danell Leyva took the bronze on 90.698. 'If I spoke Japanese, I would tell him [Uchimura], he is the best gymnast that has lived so far,' Leyva said.

Berki wins by a nose on Pommel Horse

There was more excitement in the North Greenwich Arena as Hungary's Kristian Berki and Great Britain's Louis Smith completed the competition with exactly the same score of 16.066 for their routines.

The judges awarded the gold medal to double world champion Berki, whose stunningly smooth execution gained fractionally higher marks than that of Smith, bronze medallist at Beijing 2008. The 23-year-old reggae-loving Briton, once a contestant on television talent show 'The X Factor', won worldwide admiration for his mature and gracious acceptance of his heartbreaking defeat in front of the home crowd. The bronze medal was won by

'You have to look at the positives. I can't sit here with my face screwed up just because I got a silver at the Olympic Games. Great Britain are making history – it's a fantastic day for the sport.'

Louis Smith, Pommel Horse silver medallist

Support for Team GB

Ahead of London 2012 Britain's gymnasts were part of UK Sport's 'no compromise' investment strategy, receiving more than £10 million of National Lottery funding. Teenager Sam Oldham acknowledged that this had propelled them on to the podium. 'I want to thank the National Lottery players,' he said. 'They fund our training costs, this is their medal.' The team's success was orchestrated by Yorkshireman Eddie Van Hoof, the technical director of British Gymnastics, who put their stunning victory down to plain hard work.

Star quality. Great Britain's Louis Smith performing on his way to the silver medal on Pommel Horse. Smith, 23, went one better than his historic bronze medal at Beijing 2008.

Britain's 19-year-old Max Whitlock with a score of 15.600. He took home two medals from his first Olympic Games after winning the bronze in the Team event.

Sitting in a TV studio with the British gymnasts, the legendary Olympic gold medal-winning Russian gymnast Olga Korbut congratulated them on their achievement. 'This is just the beginning,' she promised. 'This will see more boys in the gym.'

Carnival for Brazil in the Rings Competition

There was a shock in the competition for the gold medal on the Rings, the event for the strongmen of the Olympic Games, when the title was awarded to Brazil's Arthur Nabarrete Zanetti.

The 22-year-old, participating in his first Olympic Games, was the last competitor to perform, scoring 15.900 with an impressive display of strength and concentration. He beat the four-time world champion, China's Chen Yibing, who finished the competition with a total of 15.800. Matteo Morandi, who serves in the Italian Air Force, took the bronze medal with 15.733 points.

Zanetti, whose father makes his training equipment to help save money, will be competing on home soil at the next Olympic Games at Rio 2016. He explained that he had worked on his mental strength and stayed calm to win Brazil's first Olympic Gymnastics medal.

Olympic strongman. Brazil's Arthur Nabarrete Zanetti who came first in the Rings final. He qualified fourth, but pulled off an impressive routine to take home gold.

Women's events

Glittering USA take first Team Competition gold since Atlanta 1996

The Team USA gymnasts came to London 2012 and sparkled, winning their first Team gold since hosting the Olympic Games at Atlanta 1996. The USA team of Gabby Douglas, Alexandra Raisman, McKayla Maroney, Kyla Ross and Jordyn Wieber posted a final score of 183.596 after dazzling the crowd at the North Greenwich Arena.

The Russian challenge for the Olympic title wobbled and died on the beam where Aliya Mustafina and Victoria Komova made costly errors. The young Americans, by contrast, executed their routines with near-perfect precision, balancing smiling Stateside showmanship with a gritty determination. The Russians finished with a final score of 178.530 to take the silver medal, while Romania edged ahead of defending Olympic champions China to win the bronze with 176.414 points.

Smooth win for Russian on Uneven Bars

Aliya Mustafina of the Russian Federation returned to stunning form with a challenging and smooth routine to win gold in the Uneven Bars.

The gymnast spent a year out of competition after tearing her anterior cruciate ligament in an awkward landing on the vault in the 2011 European Championships. Her remarkable score of 16.133 added the Olympic title to the Team silver and Individual All-Around bronze medals. China's Kexin He, the reigning Olympic champion, pirouetted to the silver medal with a fabulous twisting double back somersault dismount which earned her a score of 15.933.

To the delight of the cheering British fans, 27-year-old Beth Tweddle, competing in her last Olympic Games, performed a spectacular routine to take the bronze medal with a score of 15.916.

Britain's most successful female gymnast, who missed out on a medal at Beijing 2008 by just 0.025, underwent keyhole knee surgery only weeks before the 2012 Games, sleeping hooked up to an ice machine every night to ensure that she could compete. Her Bars routine was the best in qualifying, but she was still delighted to win an Olympic medal at last. 'I know I've done the years of hard work, my coach has too, and she'd have been as gutted as me if we'd come away with nothing,' she admitted. Tweddle, who won Commonwealth, European and World titles in her long career, is credited with spearheading the resurgence of British gymnastics on the world stage.

'Flying Squirrel' captures Individual All-Around Competition gold

Gabrielle Douglas, the USA's 'Flying Squirrel', took the third consecutive Olympic gold for her country in the Individual All-Around competition. Featured on the front cover of *Time Magazine*'s Summer Olympic Special ahead of London 2012 – an honour once bestowed on Nadia Comaneci, the Romanian gymnast who scored a perfect 10 at Montreal 1976 – the 16-year-old captivated the crowd at the North Greenwich Arena. A bright and bubbly star, she is likely to inspire a new generation of gymnasts.

As with most sports champions, there is a tale of sacrifice behind the Douglas dazzle.

She is coached by Liang Chow, the man who guided USA gymnast Shawn Johnson to gold on the beam at Beijing 2008, and who Douglas first saw on television. The determined young gymnast, deciding he was the coach for her, went on to move 1200 miles from Virginia to live with a host family in Iowa, where Liang has his gym.

Douglas, the first African American to win Gymnastics gold, excelled with breathtaking performances full of poise, grace and character on the uneven bars, beam, vault and floor. She displayed the perfect combination of athleticism and artistry, mixed with a touch of charm and cheek, to win the gold medal with a final score of 62.232. Her most spectacular move was a death-defying arched leap on the beam when, remarkably, Douglas touched the back of her head with her pointed toes. The Russian Victoria Komova ended a whisker behind Douglas in the silver medal position, on 61.973 points, while her compatriot Aliya Mustafina took bronze with 59.566.

Above: The Flying Squirrel. USA's Gabrielle Douglas, one of the star gymnasts of London 2012. She took home the first Gymnastics gold medal for an African American in the Team Competition final, before following it up with Individual All-Around gold.

Left: One of the great pioneers of British gymnastics. Beth Tweddle performing to win the bronze medal on the Uneven Bars. Tweddle's success in the past decade has helped inspire a new generation of British gymnasts to international success.

'I'm a very happy and grateful man. London promised an athletes' Games and that's exactly what we got.'

Jacques Rogge, IOC President

Handball

'We were superb. The players were outstanding, the fans incredible. What a magnificent game, atmosphere and occasion.'

Claude Onesta, French Handball coach

Hotshot Luc Abalo scores for France, despite the best efforts of Sweden's goalkeeper Johan Sjostrand. France won the men's Handball gold medal in the Basketball Arena on the Olympic Park.

Men's events

Croats cruise to Handball bronze

Croatia beat a tired Hungarian team 33–26 to become the bronze medallists in men's Handball. The gold medal winners at Atlanta 1996 and Athens 2004 swiftly charged to a half-time five-goal lead over the exhausted Hungarians, who had failed to recover from a draining quarter final 34–33 win over medal favourites Iceland in extra time.

Croatia's fast winger, Ivan Cupic, swarmed around the turquoise court and himself struck five times in the first half. The Croats cruised to victory in the second half with strong defending from goalkeeper Mirko Alilovic and seven goals from

Blazenko Lackovic, six from Domagoj Duvnjak and five scored by Manual Strlek.

The Croatian team, who had been aiming for a record third Handball gold medal at London 2012, still joyfully celebrated their bronze.

'Allez Les Bleus' – France snatches Handball gold

There was an incredible atmosphere for the men's Handball gold medal match on the final day of the Olympic Games, with France beating Sweden 22–21 to become the first team to retain the title.

Noisy, passionate French and Swedish fans were joined at the Basketball Arena by hordes of new home crowd Handball fans. Their enthusiasm created a degree of sporting fervour normally seen on the football terraces at the FA Cup final at Wembley. They stamped their feet, loudly roaring on the teams, with the French in fine Gallic voice singing 'Allez Les Bleus'.

The exciting and dramatic final culminated in a flurry of goals during the dying seconds of the game. Extra time loomed, as Sweden won a penalty and moved to just one goal behind at 21–20, with 70 seconds remaining. The powerful French hit back in the last minute with a Luc Abalo goal, bringing the final score to 22–20. The sound of the crowd was deafening as the determined Swedes surged on, scoring again (22–21) and leaving France to endure an agonising 18-second countdown before securing their historic Olympic title.

It was the fourth time that Sweden had finished in the silver medal position in Olympic Handball. Niklas Ekberg was nonetheless proud to be the tournament's 'golden arm', top scoring with 50 goals (one more than Ivan Cupic of Croatia).

Women's events

Viva Espana as youthful Spain takes Handball bronze

Spain battled through two periods of extra time to defeat Korea 31–29 and win the bronze medal in women's Handball.

It was a gutsy victory for the less experienced Spanish team, with the Koreans, Olympic champions at Seoul 1988 and Barcelona 1992, missing six penalty shots. Spanish goalkeeper Mihaela Ciobanu proved the heroine of the hour, saving four out of five of the penalties she faced.

In a roller-coaster match where nothing separated the two teams, the scoreline went from 13–13 at half-time to 24–24 at full-time. It was the first time at London 2012 that a Handball game would be decided in extra time and even the additional 10 minutes failed to produce a result, all square at 28–28.

Jessica Alonso scored the game's final goal late in the second spell of extra time to win the bronze medal for Spain, making only their third appearance at the Olympic Games.

Second gold for Norway Handball drama

Olympic Handball champions Norway kept their title with a victory in the women's Handball. They defeated the surprise finalists Montenegro, making their Olympic debut, 26–23. The silver was Montenegro's first Olympic medal since the country separated from Serbia-Montenegro in 2006.

The final proved a thrilling encounter, roared on by an enthusiastic crowd in the Basketball Arena, where Norway's Linn Jorum Sulland and Katarina Bulatovic of Montenegro each scored 10 goals. Bulatovic was the 'golden arm' top scorer of the women's London 2012 Handball tournament, with a tally of 53 goals. The goal-scoring heroines dominated the fast and furious first half of the final, with Norway ahead 13–10 at half-time.

The gold is still ours. Norway's Camilla Herrem and Heidi Loke show what it means to retain the women's Olympic Handball title after their defeat of Montenegro.

Montenegro kept pace in the second half, blocking the Norwegian attack. In the final minutes there was a flurry of goals, as both teams battled to get their hands on the gold medal. With two minutes to go Sulland scored her ninth goal to take the score to 24–22, and then her tenth to take it to 25–23.

The Norwegians celebrated with a lap of honour carrying their national flag while the Montenegro team, delighted with their silver medal, danced on court.

Handball, although not a mainstream sport in the UK, proved a big hit with the British spectators who embraced the exciting atmosphere and fast-paced play.

'This gold feels very heavy and I love it hanging around my neck. It is the biggest achievement you can have in Handball.'

Linn Jorum Sulland (NOR), Handball gold medallist

Hockey

Chasing the bronze. Australia's Fergus Kavanagh chases Barry Middleton of Great Britain as the two sides battle for the bronze medal. It would be Team GB's men who would go home empty-handed.

Hanging onto the title. Maximilian Mueller vies for the ball during Germany's match with the Netherlands for the Hockey gold medal at the Riverside Arena.

Men's events

Aussies rule in Hockey bronze medal match

Australia won the bronze medal match in the men's Olympic Hockey tournament, beating Great Britain 3–1.

Both teams came into the game smarting. Australia had suffered a surprise semi-final defeat to Germany, while in the other semi-final Team GB endured a 9–2 thrashing by the Netherlands, the country's worst-ever defeat.

Australia's Simon Orchard struck first in the 17th minute. Britain grabbed an equaliser in the 29th from an impressive set-piece penalty corner, forced by teenager Harry Martin, in which Ian Lewers deflected an Ashley Jackson pass.

Australia edged ahead in the second half when Jamie Dwyer scored from a loose ball in the 48th minute. The bronze medal was secured by Kieran Gover's goal from a rebound in the 57th minute.

Dramatic German triumph in tense Hockey final

In a thrilling climax to the men's Hockey tournament Germany scored a late winning goal to beat the Netherlands 2–1 and retain their Olympic title.

Both teams had played exciting Hockey throughout the Games, but the final began with 10 minutes of skilful defensive play. In the 16th minute Dutchman Billy Bakker created the first goal-scoring opportunity, with his reverse-stick shot being kicked away by German goalkeeper Max Weinhold.

Weinhold proved to be a tough obstacle in the German goal. Moments later his nimble foot action again denied Bakker; Germany's Benjamin Wess defended the rebound. Jan Philipp Rabente made a strong charge from the right, acrobatically scoring as he skidded along the ground.

Relishing their 1–0 lead, the Germans made a confident start to the second half. Christopher Zeller whacked a shot against the post in the 46th minute before the Dutch turned up the heat to equalise from a penalty corner. Mink Van Der Weerden, the tournament's leading goal scorer, powerfully flicked the ball home to score his eighth goal of London 2012.

The winning goal was scored with less than five minutes on the clock. The trigger was again Rabente, who panicked the Dutch defence with an attacking run. He scored after scurrying around the back of the goalpost to tap in a deflection from Florian Fuchs.

Women's events

Broken jaw bronze for Team GB

Team GB's women's Hockey captain Kate Walsh showed true Olympic courage in one of the bravest battles of the Games. She led her team to a 3–1 bronze medal victory against New Zealand, despite playing with a broken jaw.

Walsh, 32, fractured her jaw in three places when she was hit in the face with a stick during her side's 4–0 defeat of Japan. She returned to compete in the remaining Pool A games and played the medal match wearing a plastic chin brace following surgery to insert a metal plate in to her jaw bone. 'Once I'd got out of surgery, and the surgeon was so confident, there was no stopping me,' she explained. 'I was going to get back out on the pitch and in the team.'

Great Britain, supported by an enthusiastic crowd, played with focus and patience after their semi-final defeat by Argentina. All three goals, scored from penalty corners by Alex Danson, Cristo Cullen and Sarah Thomas, came in the second half, with New Zealand's Stacey Michelson grabbing a late goal in the 68th minute.

Celebrations in the stands and on the pitch greeted Great Britain's victory. The team had secured their first women's Olympic Hockey medal since Barcelona 1992, and only their second Olympic bronze ever.

Dutch orange quashes Argentina to take Hockey final

There was a euphoric sea of orange at the Riverbank Arena when the Netherlands took their third Olympic gold medal in women's Hockey, beating world champions Argentina 2–0.

The Dutch, who won gold at Beijing 2008 and Los Angeles 1984, dominated the first half with superior possession and fast, stylish play. They failed to score from two penalty corners, however, while Noel Barrionuevo flicked wide for Argentina in the 10th minute.

After the break, the defending champions stepped up the pressure. They went ahead in the 45th minute, when captain Maartje Paumen's shot was parried by the goalkeeper and the attacking Carlien Dirkse van den Heuvel pounced, sending the ball rocketing into the net. The Netherlands fans, including a noisy brass band, broke into exuberant celebrations. Captain Paumen then took the score to 2–0 with a superb penalty corner drag flick which flew into the net just below the crossbar. It made her the leading goal scorer in women's Olympic Hockey history, boasting a total of 14 goals.

It proved a heartbreaking final for Argentina captain Luciana Aymar. The seven-time world player of the year, marking her 35th birthday, failed to win Olympic gold for the fourth time.

Rallying call. Disappointed at missing out on the gold medal, Great Britain's women were determined to get something out of the Hockey tournament. Alex Danson (right) celebrates with teammates after scoring during their bronze medal match against New Zealand.

'We vowed that we weren't going home empty-handed … we just had to put it all together.'

Kate Walsh, women's Hockey bronze medallist

Judo

Olympic gold medallists

Extra Lightweight (-60kg):
Arsen Galstyan (RUS)

Half-Lightweight (60–66kg):
Lasha Shavdatuashvili (GEO)

Lightweight (66–73kg):
Mansur Isaev (RUS)

Half-Middleweight (73–81kg): **Jae-Bum Kim (KOR)**

Middleweight (81–90kg):
Dae-Nam Song (KOR)

Half-Heavyweight (90–100kg): **Tagir Khaibulaev (RUS)**

Heavyweight (+100kg):
Teddy Riner (FRA)

Superstar of the mat. France's Teddy Riner (right) was always the favourite to land the Heavyweight Judo title in London. His legions of fans were not disappointed.

Men's events

France powers to Heavyweight gold and landmark 200th medal

ExCeL took on a distinctly Gallic feel on the final day of competition as a predominantly French crowd gathered for the crowning of the charismatic Teddy Riner (FRA) as Olympic champion. They were not to be disappointed. The five-time world champion came through the day undefeated and beat a frustrated Alexander Mikhaylin (RUS) in the final of the +100kg category to claim France's 200th gold medal at a summer Olympic Games.

Like so many of the other matches, Riner's victory was sealed with a decisive penalty yuko as his opponent Mikhaylin was penalised with shido, or warnings, for defensive postures.

At 207cm tall and 128kg, Riner's natural attributes are obvious. Born on the Caribbean island of Guadeloupe during a family holiday, he was raised in Paris and is easily the biggest name in judo. His aim now is to defend the title at Rio 2016.

Mikhaylin's silver was the fifth medal for the Russian Federation at these Games. For Japan, however, the Games proved a disaster, with no gold medals for the men's team – unprecedented at the Olympic Games.

Earlier the competition had witnessed the extraordinary appearance of Ricardo Blas Jr, who at 219kg was more than 63.5kg heavier than any other athlete at the Olympic Games. He made it through to the last 16 before being defeated by Oscar Brayson of Cuba.

Swift Russian success in the Extra Lightweight brings first ExCeL gold

The gold medal on the first day of competition at ExCeL went to Russian Federation's Arsen Galstyan in double-quick time. In the division of up to 60kg he threw Japan's Hiroaki Hiraoka to the mat for an ippon within 41 seconds.

Later in the week the fate of the bronze medal hung around the neck of Brazil's Felipe Kitadai puzzled observers. Having joked that he would take his bronze medal everywhere, Kitadai had to confess that he had damaged it while having a shower. A small dent was detected on the medal, and there was also damage to the small ring holding the ribbon. Kitadai told Globoesporte. com, 'I even took it into the shower, but I was afraid to get it wet so put it in my mouth while I soaped myself. But it ended up slipping.' The IOC was forced to consider a request for a new medal from the Brazilian Olympic Committee.

Women's events

Local heroine takes Half-Heavyweight silver

Gemma Gibbons (GBR), the new Olympic Games Judo silver medallist in the 70–78kg category, became Britain's first judoka to make the podium since 2000. The 25-year-old grew up and trained in Greenwich, just across the river and two train stops away from ExCeL, where she enjoyed a sensational tournament. Coming in ranked 42nd, Gibbons went on to defeat world champion Audrey Tcheumeo (FRA) with a last-gasp ippon in her semi-final.

As the 10,000-strong crowd roared its approval, the Briton looked to the heavens and mouthed, 'I love you, Mum', in tribute to the woman who had scrimped and saved so that, from the age of six, she could practise her judo at the local Metro Club in Blackheath. Gibbons' mother, Jeanette, died from leukaemia in 2004. 'She was everything to me,' said Gibbons. 'We did not have a lot of money and what she had went into my judo career.'

Left: Throwing in an upset. Arsen Galstyan of Russia (left) caused an upset with his ippon after only 41 seconds of his Extra Lightweight final against Japan's Hiroaki Hiraoka on the first day of competition at ExCeL.

Below: Against the odds. Britain's Karina Bryant (right) overcame Iryna Kindzerska (UKR) to claim bronze in the +78kg division to win her first medal in four Olympic Games appearances despite the Ukrainian's 25kg weight advantage.

Her talent and tenacity could not take her all the way to the gold, though. Lying in wait for the Briton was the formidable Kayla Harrison (USA), who had her own point to prove.

With Prime Minister David Cameron and President Putin in the crowd, it was Harrison who held the upper hand throughout the final. Yet with seconds left on the clock only two yukos separated the competitors. From the sidelines Jimmy Pedro, Harrison's coach and the man to whom she attributes her success, screamed, 'You're the Olympic champion if you fight smart'. She did, and she was.

Heavyweight medal doubles Britain's Judo success

Team GB waited 12 years for a Judo medal at the Olympic Games, only to have two arrive at London 2012 within the space of 24 hours. Inspired in part by Gemma Gibbons' heroics in battling to her silver medal in the Half-Heavyweight on the Thursday, Karina Bryant clinched bronze in her fourth Olympic Games in the +78kg division.

At 33, the 183cm-tall Bryant had enjoyed much success in the sport without achieving her ultimate goal of a podium place at the Olympic Games. The chants of a 10,000 capacity crowd at ExCeL provided her with overwhelming support. 'I've dreamt of getting a medal since I was a kid,' said Bryant. 'I couldn't have asked for a better stage than this. The crowd was amazing, and Gemma did so well in her first Olympic Games. She was a complete underdog. It made me so emotional. I was definitely inspired.'

The gold medal – and Cuba's first in Judo – went to Idalys Ortiz. She was awarded a judge's decision over Mika Sugimoto of Japan, having already handed a first defeat in five years to the 2008 Olympic Games champion, Wen Tong of China, in the semi-final.

Left: The Half-Heavyweight Olympic medallists share their success. (Left to right) Silver medallist Gemma Gibbons, gold medallist Kayla Harrison, and bronze medallists Mayra Aguiar and Audrey Tcheumeo.

Opposite and below:
Points to prove. Kayla Harrison of the USA (white) overcame Britain's Gemma Gibbons to win the Half-Heavyweight event when both women had very personal reasons for wanting that precious gold medal.

Modern Pentathlon

Riding high. David Svoboda of the Czech Republic on Fellow Van T in the riding element of the men's Modern Pentathlon. He finished this section in first place, before eventually taking the gold medal.

Elements of the Modern Pentathlon

Fencing
Swimming (200m Freestyle)
Riding (12 fences)
Combined event (running and shooting)

Men's event

Czech gold for Svoboda in Modern Pentathlon

David Svoboda, a military officer from the Czech Republic, won the men's Modern Pentathlon gold medal with a fine all-round performance.

Modern Pentathlon is the sport introduced to the Olympic Games by Baron Pierre de Coubertin in 1912. It is inspired by a 19th-century legend in which a young French cavalry officer was sent on horseback to deliver a message. To complete his mission he has to swim, fence, shoot and run – the five challenges that face competitors today.

The 27-year-old began the day well. Svoboda won 26 of his fencing bouts to equal the Olympic record of 1024 points. This feat meant that, despite a disappointing swim, he was never out of the top two. A good performance in the riding at Greenwich Park – the point at which Svoboda's Beijing 2008 campaign had come unstuck after his horse fell on him – set him firmly on course for the gold medal.

The challenge for Modern Pentathletes is that their rides are chosen at random, with horse and rider having only 20 minutes to become acquainted before the competition begins. Similar problems to Svoboda's at Beijing 2008 befell China's Wang Guan, forced to withdraw after falling from his horse, and Korea's Hwang Woojin, who was thrown from the same horse and was lucky to avoid a nasty injury.

The final element, the new combined event of shooting and running, saw Svoboda and China's Zhongrong Cao vying for the gold medal. The 3,000m run is now interrupted at 1,000m intervals by three sessions at the shooting range, from where

'It sounds like a cliché, but that is what it was, a dream come true.'

David Svoboda (CZE), Modern Pentathlon gold medallist

Opposite: Fans from all over the world cheer madly for their countrymen at the Modern Pentathlon

Pentathletes have to fire a laser pistol at five targets within 70 seconds. Svoboda finished home and dry and, after waving to the crowd, he was able to stroll across the finish line. His 5928pts were an Olympic record as Cao took silver with 5904 and Hungary's Adam Marosi picked up the bronze with 5836.

Britain's Nick Woodbridge and Sam Weale finished in 10th and 13th place respectively. Woodbridge showed real promise in the swimming to come second in that element, while Weale scored well to take seventh place in the riding.

Women's event

Asadauskaite triumphs in Modern Pentathlon

The Modern Pentathlon, which featured the last medals to be won at the London 2012 Olympic Games, saw gold awarded to Lithuania's Laura Asadauskaite, the world number one, with 5408 points. It was, she explained, the one Olympic medal missing from the household since her husband Andrejus Zadneprovskis, also a Modern Pentathlete, had already won a bronze medal at Beijing 2008 and a silver at Athens 2004. 'This is the first Olympic gold medal in our family,' said a delighted Asadauskaite. 'I am immensely excited. I had a great deal of support from the people of Lithuania. It is only a small country. So this means the world to them.'

Nor was the Host Nation to be denied on this final day. Since the women's Modern Pentathlon was added to the Olympic programme at Sydney 2000, Great Britain has always been successful. It won two medals on the sport's first appearance, with Stephanie Cook taking gold and Kate Allenby bronze at Sydney 2000. This was followed by bronze for Georgina Harland at Athens 2004 and silver for Heather Fell at Beijing 2008.

Right: In the centenary year of the Modern Pentathlon at the Olympic Games, David Svoboda comes home to take the gold medal in the men's event. He had a one-second advantage going into the combined event, but held on to take gold.

'Holding a pistol when you've just run 2km, coordinating your breathing, you've got sweaty palms, your heart's racing – it's tough, it's a challenge. But I've pictured and trained my mind for that moment.'

Samantha Murray (GBR), Modern Pentathlon silver medallist

Bottom right: Take three. Great Britain's Samantha Murray (left), Brazil's Yane Marques (centre) and Laura Asadauskaite of Lithuania (right) shoot it out for the final medals of the Olympic Games as the women's Modern Pentathlon nears its climax.

At London 2012 the honours belonged to Samantha Murray from Preston, a French and Politics student who trains with the British Modern Pentathlon squad at the University of Bath. Murray had not shone in the initial fencing round, losing seven bouts in succession before she began to improve, but an excellent 2,000m swim and a good riding element on Glen Gold brought her into medal contention. She entered the combined event (a 3,000m cross country run interwoven with three rounds of shooting from a 10m range) in fourth place and at first struggled with her shooting, but remained calm. Finally the 22-year-old came through in the final 1,000m of the run/shoot phase to snatch the silver medal with 5356 points. She finished just ahead of Yane Marques of Brazil, who had matched Asadauskaite throughout the competition and finally took bronze on 5340.

Large cheering crowds were there to greet

Murray as she ran the final stage through Greenwich Park and entered the arena for the last time. 'It was a complete dream to have a home crowd screaming for me, and I could have carried on running for another 10 minutes because I was just loving it so much,' said Murray.

Above: Early start. Great Britain's Samantha Murray celebrates a victory in the women's Modern Pentathlon fencing phase, which began at 8am in the Copper Box on the final day of competition at the Olympic Games.

Far left: One for the family collection. Laura Asadauskaite of Lithuania wins the last gold medal of the Olympic Games as she crosses the finish line in Greenwich Park to become the women's Modern Pentathlon Olympic champion.

Left: Rising to the challenge. Samantha Murray of Team GB started 2012 ranked 78th in the world and began the Olympic Modern Pentathlon at number seven. Her silver medal meant she ended the year ranked world number three.

Overleaf: Competitors in the fencing element of the Modern Pentathlon.

Rowing

The German crew celebrates Olympic gold in the men's Eight at Eton Dorney.

Team members of winning Eight

Filip Adamski
Andreas Kuffner
Eric Johannesen
Maximilian Reinelt
Richard Schmidt
Lukas Mueller
Florian Mennigen
Kristof Wilke
Martin Sauer (Cox)

Men's events

Undefeated German Eight continue their reign

This was a thriller, and one that left the vast partisan crowd at Eton Dorney almost as exhausted as the eight men representing Team GB after their tussle with a German crew undefeated in four years. In the end the world champions Germany prevailed, reaching 40 strokes a minute as they powered over the final 800m to see off a determined British effort in 5:48.75. The Brits, who had come to the final through victory in the repechage, edged ahead approaching the 1500m mark, but, spent by their surge, faded to third (5:51.18), with Canada, the champions at Beijing 2008, coming through for the silver medal in 5:49.98. For the 40-year-old Greg Searle in the British boat, it was the end of a remarkable comeback, 20 years after he rowed to gold in the Coxed Pair with his brother Jonny at Barcelona 1992. 'I think my wife would say that I am retired now,' he observed.

South African strength for the Lightweight Four

As the Host Nation claimed its third Rowing medal in the Olympic regatta, for the Northern Irish brothers Peter and Richard Chambers, Rob Williams and Chris Bartley, it was South Africa who made history. They took the country's first-ever gold in an Olympic Rowing event, crossing the line in 6:02.84, while Sizwe Ndlovu at stroke became the first black African medal winner in the sport.

Defending champions Denmark opened the race up by surging into what appeared to be a commanding lead and hanging on to it until 1500m, when the real battle looked to be between slow-starting Britain and Australia for the minor medals. The old rivals battled it out, but, as Australia faded, it was not Britain or Denmark who thrived but the South Africans. Their boat managed to cover the final 500m faster than the first, with a surge that took them across the line just 0.25 ahead of Britain who took silver (6:03.09).

'That was brutal, really, really brutal,' Chambers said. 'We were just fighting and fighting even to get ourselves back in contention, and we did a cracking job. To even get the silver was impressive from where we came from.' Bartley added, 'I don't remember that much of the last 250m, to be honest. The pain is so extreme and it took me a little while to compose myself.'

German triumph over Croatia for the Quadruple Sculls crown

Germany continued their very good form in the regatta with a dominating performance in the Quadruple Sculls. They combatted breezy conditions at Eton Dorney to finish with clear water ahead of the much fancied Croatia crew in 5:42.48.

Even when the Croatians (5:44.78) and then the Australians (5:45.22) looked like challenging, the Germans found another gear in the final 500m.

Phillipp Wende (GER) said, 'We are very proud to be the first German Olympic champions in this event since 1996 but we don't think too much about whether we can dominate the next five or 10 years. We are just proud to be Olympic champions and that's all.'

'I don't think we could have given more. We said we wanted to look in the mirror and say we've given it all, and we did that.'

Greg Searle, bronze medallist in the men's Eight

Inspiring a generation. The hope is that a first Rowing gold for South Africa can bring more people to the sport at home. The crew (left to right) James Thompson, Matthew Brittain, John Smith and Sizwe Ndlovu, came from behind to snatch a sensational victory.

New Zealand success in the Double Sculls

When the experienced pair in the Slovenian boat raced into an early lead, it looked as if Iztok Cop and Luka Spik were going to pull off a remarkable repeat of their victory at Sydney 2000. They extended their lead to a length at 500m, but world champions New Zealand and Italy chased hard. It all came down to the final 500m, when Cop and Spik ran out of steam. New Zealand captured the gold in 6:31.67, and Italy the silver (6:32.80), but Cop and Spik emerged from their boat with smiles on their faces after claiming bronze in 6:34.35. 'The plan was to win a medal,' Cop explained. 'We knew there were fine crews that could beat us, and we did all we could.'

New Zealand's Double Sculls gold medal team of Nathan Cohen and Joseph Sullivan in perfect synch at Eton Dorney.

Dominant New Zealanders win the Pairs

Eric Murray and Hamish Bond finished seventh in the Four at Beijing 2008, but came to London 2012 as the outstanding crew in the entire regatta. Their gold medal performance (6:16.65) in the Pairs was a magnificent demonstration of power into a stiff headwind that no other crew could match.

Having clawed back France's early lead, the New Zealanders were ahead at halfway before taking four lengths from the opposition in the next 500m. From then, the only contest left was for the silver medal, with British pair George Nash and William Satch finding themselves in a three-way battle with France and Italy. France eventually took the honours in 6:21.11, but the British bronze in 6:21.77 was a hint of future greatness from Nash and Satch.

Single Sculls luck for Drysdale

Mahe Drysdale (NZL) is no stranger to bad luck before a major race. Four years ago he was expected to win the Single Sculls at Beijing 2008, but an untimely bout of food poisoning meant that he struggled to finish third. Then before coming to Eton Dorney, he was knocked off his bike while training. There was no stopping him on the lake, however. The 201cm-tall Drysdale won New Zealand's third gold of the Games in 6:57.82 ahead of Ondrej Synek (6:59.37), the Czech rower who was also second at Beijing 2008. Behind them Alan Campbell, from Coleraine in Northern Ireland, like the Chambers brothers who won a medal in the Lightweight Four, took Britain's first medal in the event since 1928 – and then crawled out of his boat with exhaustion after a 7:03.28 row.

Notable among the single scullers who did not win a medal was one Hamadou Djibo Issaka of landlocked Nigeria. Despite being more than a minute slower than the rest of the men's Single Sculls field, he was roared home by the crowd every time he raced.

'I think we turned it on in the second half, kept it simple, raw, basic. It feels like a dream has come true today.'

William Satch, bronze medallist in the Pairs

Eton Dorney

Not many schools can boast their own Olympic-standard rowing course, but Eton College has provided many of Britain's Olympic rowers. The Eton Dorney Rowing Centre, with its 2000m, eight-lane course and separate return lane sits in a 400-acre park near Windsor, some 25 miles west of London. The course, which also staged the Canoe Sprint events, boasts Windsor Castle as one of its more illustrious neighbours.

Four consecutive golds for Team GB Four

Billed as the showdown between Great Britain and Australia, this final did not disappoint as a relentless battle between the two old rivals ensued over the full 2000m course.

Within 500m they were both clear of the field, with the Team GB crew of Alex Gregory, Pete Reed, Tom James and Andrew Triggs Hodge hanging on to the slightest of leads. At halfway, the advantage was just 0.6 seconds. As Australia pushed, so Britain responded with the telling point coming in the final quarter as the crews came within earshot of what became known over the week as the 'Wall of Noise' or even the 'Dorney Roar' as 35,000 fans screamed their support. Britain held on to win by a quarter of a length in 6:03.97 and retain the title won at Sydney 2000, Athens 2004 and Beijing 2008, a record of four consecutive gold medals only matched by East Germany from 1968 to 1980. The USA came through to take the bronze (6:07.20). 'It was impeccable rowing,' said Triggs Hodge. 'It took four years to make that. It was a masterpiece.'

At the finish, Gregory described his emotion as 'relief, just massive relief.' He added, 'I was so confident we could hold on. Everything's been worthwhile. My little boy will take the medal to school with him in a few years and tell about his dad being an Olympic champion.' Reed went straight to the point, 'I was praying that the line came before the Australians. The hours, the hours we do, the pain – it's all worth it.'

'We had the very best race we could.'

Mark Hunter and Zac Purchase, silver medallists in the Lightweight Double Sculls

Thrilling finale for Lightweight Double Sculls

The Olympic regatta could not have chosen a more epic and dramatic finale than that provided by the British and Danish crews in the Lightweight Double Sculls, when both crews rowed themselves to exhaustion and a thrilling finish.

In a race that had to be restarted after Britain's Zac Purchase's seat suffered a malfunction, he and partner Mark Hunter established a one-second lead from the Danes at 500m, effectively laying down a marker as the defending champions. The lead was maintained but without ever being convincing and it was the Danes, who as favourites had lost out to the Britons in the Beijing 2008 final, who had most left in the tank in the last quarter.

With the line rapidly approaching, the two Britons could not hold on as the two-time former world champions Mads Rasmussen and Rasmus Quist surged across the line to win by 0.61 seconds (6:37.17). New Zealand completed their impressive medal tally with another bronze in 6:40.86. The silver (6:37.78) meant that Great Britain had finished the Rowing competition on top of the medal table, with their four golds equalling a British record set fittingly at London 1908.

Left: Oarsome foursome. Great Britain's (top to bottom) Alex Gregory, Pete Reed, Tom James and Andrew Triggs Hodge maintained the country's winning streak in the Four, established by Cracknell, Foster, Redgrave and Pinsent at Sydney 2000.

Below: Near miss. Mark Hunter (left) and Zac Purchase were devastated to lose their Olympic title at Eton Dorney. They were pipped on the line by Denmark in the Lightweight Double Sculls.

The famous 'Dorney Roar' goes up as 30,000 spectators at Eton Dorney cheer in loud support of the athletes. Team GB's rowers formed Great Britain's most successful Rowing team to date, netting an impressive nine medals overall.

Women's events

Magnificent Pair bring Team GB's first gold

A remarkable performance by Heather Stanning (GBR) and Helen Glover (GBR) in the Pair thrilled 35,000 ecstatic fans at Eton Dorney and brought Team GB its first gold medal of London 2012.

Both women, products of the World Class Start programme which found and developed athletes with minimal rowing experience, appeared calm and focused in their first Olympic final. Glover, a 25-year-old PE teacher from Penzance, has only five years' experience in the sport, yet she and 27-year-old Stanning, a Royal Artillery Captain, had been unbeaten all year and qualified for the final with a British record.

'I'm absolutely shattered and absolutely ecstatic, all at the same time … I want to collapse, but I'm just so overjoyed, I just want to jump around at the same time.'

Heather Stanning, Double Sculls gold medallist

First Ladies. Helen Glover and Heather Stanning break new ground as the first women to win an Olympic Rowing gold for Great Britain. Little did they know that others would very quickly follow.

Hopes, and tension, were riding high as a magnificent start carried Glover and Stanning quickly ahead of the German boat, a lead they retained over the 2000m course. Three and a half seconds clear at the halfway point, the British Pair dominated from the front, relishing the 'Wall of Noise' from jubilant home supporters, including Princes William and Harry, in the last 500m. They crossed the line in 7:27.13, but their gold medal had never been in doubt. Australia took silver with 7:29.86 and New Zealand bronze with 7:30.19, but the race, and the day, belonged to Glover and Stanning.

This was a particularly historic medal for British rowing. Not only was this Team GB's first gold medal of the London 2012 Games – it was also the first won by the country's women rowers. On top of that, it was Britain's 25th gold medal in Rowing at the Olympic Games, and marked the first time that the Host Nation had won this event. The result sparked celebrations across the UK providing an inspiration to the sporting world and beyond.

Ukraine strikes first gold in Quadruple Sculls

Ukraine won their first Rowing Olympic gold medal with an impressive display, leading from start to finish to cross the line in 6:35.93 ahead of world champions Germany (6:38.09) and the USA (6:40.63). This was Ukraine's 100th medal at the Summer Olympic Games, but only the country's second in women's Rowing, following a silver in the Quadruple Sculls at Atlanta 1996. For Team GB it proved a disappointing follow-up to Glover and Stanning's Pair victory, as the British quartet were never in the hunt and trailed in sixth.

Left: Unbeatable. USA's women's Eight celebrate a four-year unbeaten run and retaining their Olympic title.

Team members of winning Eight

Erin Cafaro
Zsuzsanna Francia
Esther Lofgren
Taylor Ritzel
Meghan Musnicki
Eleanor Logan
Caroline Lind
Caryn Davies
Mary Whipple (Cox)

USA unrivalled in dominant Eight

Defending champions the USA continued their extraordinary domination of this event with another resounding victory and another gold medal, winning in 6:10.59. Unbeaten since 2006, they led from the start and only Canada (6:12.06) offered a serious challenge in the closing 500m – though even they had to fend off the Dutch crew (6:13.12) for the silver medal. The strongest British crew seen in the event for years were fifth.

Mary Whipple, the USA cox with a voice that encouraged them to victory, summed up what it takes to be this good. 'I think it takes selflessness and the ability to come together as a group,' she said.

Grainger finally the bride in golden Double Sculls

Katherine Grainger's (GBR) elusive gold medal came at Eton Dorney in the most one-sided race of the entire regatta. The 36-year-old and her partner Anna Watkins, 29, led from the start, pulling away

to a commanding lead that was never threatened. They crossed the line in 6:55.82, well ahead of the Australian silver medallists (6:58.55).

The real deal. Katherine Grainger (right) kisses the gold medal she craved as she and Anna Watkins celebrate their emphatic win in the Double Sculls final at Eton Dorney.

'The best Olympic regatta ever'

The Rowing regatta at the London 2012 Games was praised by Denis Oswald, president of the sport's world governing body FISA, as 'the best Olympic regatta ever'.

Crosswinds during the event had required some difficult decisions on lane allocation, but FISA Secretary General Matt Smith acknowledged that, 'we have to accept the outdoor aspect of it. We cannot expect perfect conditions'. The lake at Eton Dorney won praise as the best Olympic venue, with 97% satisfaction among visitors.

Over 400,000 spectators witnessed record-breaking performances from Great Britain, whose tally of nine medals, including four golds, was their most successful ever. New Zealand came second with three golds, and South Africa took their first ever gold medal. Nigeria were memorably represented at the Games by Hamadou Djibo Issaka, who was warmly cheered home as he finished his Single Sculls race in last place.

'We only wanted one medal. We had a great race. There is so much trust and confidence in each other … We knew we would win from halfway.'

Anna Watkins, Double Sculls gold medallist

Watkins and Grainger came into the race as double world champions, unbeaten in 22 races since coming together in 2010. Having had gold snatched from her before, however, Grainger was not going to let anything slip. Experience counted as the three-time silver medallist Grainger, and Watkins, bronze medallist at Beijing 2008, quickly forged a lead of almost a second over the rest in the first 500m. Rowing with grace and remarkable composure, they increased the gap after 1000m, resisting repeated pushes from the tenacious Australian boat.

The delighted crowd roared and chanted 'GB, GB' as Watkins and Grainger became only the second female crew after Helen Glover and Heather Stanning to win an Olympic Rowing title.

Afterwards, Grainger confessed that the joy of victory was everything she had imagined it to be. 'Blood, sweat and tears are behind it, but it's all been worth it,' she said. 'I did seriously consider my future after Beijing. If I was going to continue it had to be for the right reasons. Once I'd made the decision though, there was never any doubt.'

Britain's Katherine Copeland (left) can barely contain herself after she and Sophie Hosking take the gold medal in the Lightweight Double Sculls. After only rowing together in three previous regattas, their victory was unexpected.

Gold medals and stamps for GB's Lightweight Double Sculls

Katherine Copeland's (GBR) wide-eyed, open-mouthed expression at the end of the race spoke volumes for the shock she was feeling at being an Olympic champion, but even lip-readers could not make out her comment to the stroke, Sophie Hosking. Only later did she reveal that what she actually said was, 'We're going to be a stamp.' And she was.

Such an accolade was thoroughly deserved for this win, the least expected of the week's Rowing golds. The performance of Copeland and Hosking, a team who had only rowed in three previous regattas, was nothing less than sensational. In a remarkable week for the sport in Great Britain, she and Hosking had crewed the third women's gold-medal winning boat as the Host Nation dominated the medals table at Eton Dorney.

Achieving the fastest qualifying time in the heats gave the British crew the slightly more sheltered lane six in the final when crosswinds forced a redraw. At halfway they shared the lead with the early pace-setters Greece (7:12.09) and China (7:11.93), before making their decisive move in the middle 1000m. Then the Britons simply pulled away from the rest, to finish in 7:09.30.

After the race Hosking revealed that she had been inspired by her dad, a British rowing world champion in the 1980s. 'My dad is an inspiration in that he never gives less than 100 per cent,' she said.

'I can't believe this is real, that we just won … we just won the Olympic Games.'

Katherine Copeland, Lightweight Double Sculls gold medallist

First Czech success in Single Sculls

Miroslava Knapkova secured an easy win and a first Olympic gold medal for the Czech Republic, racing away from the rest of the field to open up an unassailable lead. The world champion was never threatened and crossed the line in 7:54.37. At one stage she held a seven-second advantage as Fie Udby Erichsen of Denmark and Kim Crow of the USA vied for the silver medal. Erichsen eventually won Denmark's third Olympic medal in the sport with the silver (7:57.72) while Crow took bronze, Australia's first medal in women's single sculls, with 7:58.04.

Too easy. The Czech Republic's Miroslava Knapkova acknowledges the Eton Dorney crowd after her runaway win in the Single Sculls.

Sailing

Rule Britannia. Great Britain's Ben Ainslie on top of the podium for the fourth Olympic Games in a row. He came through a tough series of races to win the Finn gold medal in his boat, *Rita*.

'I'm not going to do a Steve Redgrave, but I can't see myself in one of these again. It's killing my back. There's no better way to bow out.'

Ben Ainslie, gold medallist in the Finn class

Sailing at London 2012

Ten events were contested at Weymouth and Portland: six for men, four for women. There were three disciplines – match racing, fleet racing and windsurfing.

The events featured were: the men's and women's Two Person Dinghy (470); the men's and women's Windsurfer (RS:X); the men's Keelboat (Star); the men's Skiff (49er); the men's Heavyweight Dinghy (Finn); the men's One Person Dinghy (Laser); the women's One Person Dinghy (Laser Radial) and women's Match Racing in the Elliott 6m.

Men's events

Ainslie wins the Finn class for a record fourth gold

The home waters off Weymouth and Portland and the huge crowds packing the shoreline did not make it any easier for Ben Ainslie, but he came through a difficult week magnificently to win a record fourth consecutive Olympic Sailing gold medal. The 35-year-old was proclaimed the greatest Sailing Olympian of all time for his tally of five medals at five Olympic Games.

Success in Weymouth meant Ainslie overtook the great Dane, Paul Elvström – who won four gold medals up to 1960 – as the most decorated sailor in Olympic history. His haul began at Atlanta 1996, aged 19, when he took the silver medal in the Laser class. Three golds followed, at Sydney 2000 (Laser), Athens 2004 (Finn) and Beijing 2008 (Finn).

For Ainslie, who learned to sail in Restronguet Creek on the River Fal in Cornwall 'as an 8-year-old in a duffle coat and wellies', the six days battling the elements and opposition for this historic gold medal probably rated as the toughest of his life.

Nothing about it was plain sailing. For a start, he had to fight for his place as the Finn representative and had undergone surgery on his back at the beginning of the year. In Weymouth he faced the best sailors in the world, including Denmark's Jonas Høgh-Christensen, who won their first six races. It was then that Ainslie, the oldest man in the field, clicked into gold medal-winning gear.

'After those six races, I was very concerned and had to make something happen,' he explained.

'The others teamed up on me and I was seriously unhappy. But they also made a big mistake because they made me angry, and you don't want to do that.' The fightback was launched, with Ainslie defeating Høgh-Christensen in the seventh race. On the last day of fleet racing he had impressively slowed up whilst leading, to cast his wind shadow over Høgh-Christensen, slowing him down just enough to let Pieter-Jan Postma (NED) through to second in order to reduce the gap in points to just two. To win gold Ainslie had to finish ahead of Høgh-Christensen in the final race, and be in the top six should Postma win the race.

In the event Ainslie, while covering Høgh-Christensen further back in the field, came close to missing out on his historic gold. Postma, set in a comfortable third, was threatening to move to second and possibly go on to take the race. Then he struck Dan Slater's boat, incurring a penalty turn and dropping to fifth and out of serious contention. Ainslie ended the race ninth, ahead of Høgh-Christensen who was tenth, while Frenchman Jonathan Lobert won the race. The final scores, with Ainslie and Høgh-Christensen both on 46 points and Lobert on 49 to take bronze, with Postma edged out of the medals in fourth place, show how tight the event had been. Celebrating with orange flares in his boat *Rita* for the cheering hordes around the Nothe Fort, the champion acknowledged that the Weymouth course had been the hardest he had ever raced on. 'It's at times like this you are supposed to come out with something clever but I am speechless,' he admitted. 'It's been an amazing experience. This was the place to do it, in front of a home crowd.'

Swedish first with Star gold

In a dramatic final defending champions Iain Percy and Andrew Simpson had to settle for silver in the Star class. Sweden's Fredrik Loof and Max Salminen sprung a surprise by winning their country's first gold medal in Sailing for 36 years. Percy and Simpson, both 36, were in the lead going into the final, and appeared to be on course to retain the title they won at Beijing 2008. They held an eight-point lead over Brazil and a 12-point lead over Sweden, needing only to finish higher than sixth in the final, double points-scoring medal race. Conditions were against them, however. Light winds favoured the Swedish crew who took an early lead as the Britons tried desperately to keep pace, cheered on by crowds gathered around Weymouth's Nothe Fort. A gust of wind at the end sealed their fate. 'We tried our hardest, but it wasn't to be,' said Simpson after finishing the race in eighth position. The Britons ended with 34 points, with Sweden on 32.

The final race also saw Brazil's Robert Scheidt and Bruno Prada finish seventh with 40 points, slipping from silver to bronze. The consolation for Scheidt was that he had secured his fifth Sailing medal, a successor to two previous golds and two silvers. The 39-year-old, who has been known to suffer from seasickness, has won a medal at the last five Olympic Games.

'It feels cruel sometimes,' admitted Percy, who described the supporters watching on shore as a 'highlight' of his Games. 'It was ridiculous conditions at the end,' he added. 'We feel a little robbed, but that is the way it goes.'

'I learned to sail for fun so it's been a long road, but I have had a lot of support over the years and I am just so glad to have done it.'

Ben Ainslie, gold medallist in the Finn class

Blown away. Defending champions Iain Percy (pictured) and Andrew Simpson of Great Britain had to settle for silver as the Swedish crew of Fredrik Loof and Max Salminen came through in the medal race to snatch gold.

Right: Tactical sailing. Australia's Tom Slingsby (left) secured the Laser gold medal by keeping his closest rival, Pavlos Kontides of Cyprus (right), at bay in the final medal race.

Far right: Medallist on board. Great Britain's Nick Dempsey gets a little help from his friends to celebrate his silver medal in the RS:X competition. It was the discipline's final appearance at the Olympic Games.

'I still don't understand how huge an achievement this is for my country, the first-ever Olympic medal. I guess when I have it around my neck and I get back home with my compatriots I will understand.'

Pavlos Kontides (CYP), Laser silver medallist

Slingsby caps return with Laser gold

The Australian five-time world champion, who quit the sport after a disappointing regatta at Beijing 2008, returned to the top of the podium.

Tom Slingsby, 27, had gone to Beijing 2008 as the favourite, but finished in only 22nd position. His return to the Laser class could not have been more triumphant, as he mounted a strong challenge in the opening 10 races. By the final medal race only Cypriot Pavlos Kontides could deny the Australian the gold medal. The race saw Slingsby stick close to his rival, depriving him of wind. He finished ninth, Kontides tenth, and the medals were settled. Briton Paul Goodison finished seventh after an injury to his back on the first day put him out of medal contention, but hinted at a possible return to competing at Rio 2016. 'The Olympic Games is so special ... I'd love to do it again,' he said.

For Kontides, the satisfaction lay in winning his country's first Olympic medal in any sport. The bronze medal went to Rasmus Myrgren of Sweden.

Flying Dutchman wins RS:X

Dutchman Dorian Van Rijsselberge dominated the men's RS:X event at Weymouth and Portland. It was Windsurfing's final appearance in the Olympic Games, with the event due to be replaced by Kiteboarding at Rio 2016.

Van Rijsselberge took a commanding 22-point lead into the medal race with Britain's Nick Dempsey needing only to finish sixth for the silver. Poland's Przemyslaw Miarczynski won bronze.

Dempsey, bronze medallist at Athens 2004, had finished a frustrating fourth at the Beijing 2008 Games, but this time he was determined to win a medal. The Briton, who lives in Weymouth, had promised his son a medal at London 2012 – and after the Victory Ceremony he placed it around the little boy's neck. The silver medallist, who said the huge crowd on the shoreline had lifted him on to the podium, also paid tribute to his wife Sarah Ayton, winner of Yingling gold with Sarah Webb (now Gosling) and Pippa Wilson at Beijing 2008. 'I couldn't have done it without her,' he said.

Australia take control to win 49er

With Australia replacing Great Britain as the top Sailing nation at the London 2012 Olympic Games, Nathan Outteridge and Iain Jensen raced to a comfortable victory in the 49er class.

The Australian pair could only finish fourth in the medal race, but had already secured their gold medal. New Zealand took the silver medal and the only real race was for the bronze, with Team GB's Stevie Morrison and Ben Rhodes battling it out against Allan Norregaard and Peter Lang of Denmark.

The British pair from Exmouth had been world champions and favourites at Beijing 2008, where they finished ninth. At London 2012 they could only finish fifth in a tense medal race with light wind, while Denmark mounted the podium as bronze medallists. 'In China we weren't good enough, whereas here I think we were,' said a disappointed Rhodes. 'It's done, it's gutting, but we've got an awful lot to be proud of.'

Australian gold rush in 470 class

The offshore winds fell away for the 470 medal race, forcing a day's delay. Again the Australians proved themselves masters of the conditions as the crews took to the waters in the much lighter six-knot breezes for the windward–leeward course.

The highly respected Mathew Belcher and Malcolm Page were too strong for the rest. They finished ahead of Team GB's Luke Patience

and Stuart Bithell, sailing in their first Olympic Games, who pressed them hard through the event. The British pair were assured of silver as they entered the medal race, but needed to finish with at least one boat between them and the Australians to snatch gold. A compelling tactical contest in the light wind ensued, eagerly followed by the crowd in a packed spectator area. In the event Sime Fantela and Igor Marenic of Croatia won the medal race, but a second place for the Australians landed the gold medal – the country's third of the Olympic regatta. Patience and Bithnell, who had started more strongly, finished two places behind them in the race to secure silver, while Argentina took the bronze.

The result saw Great Britain lose to Australia its place at the top of the Sailing medals table, achieved at Beijing 2008. They had, however, returned medals in more than half of the ten classes, exceeding the pre-Games target of four, and both Patience and Bithnell, 26 and 25 respectively, were confident of future success. 'I'm sure that we'll get a chance one day, and I'm sure we've got the faith and belief that on that day we'll be good enough and prepared enough,' Patience declared. An exuberant celebration followed the final race, with both Australian and British crews intentionally capsizing for victory swims.

Left: Ruling the waves. Nathan Outteridge and Iain Jensen (left) made it gold for Australia in the 49er class ahead of the New Zealanders Peter Burling and Blair Tuke (centre). Britain's Stevie Morrison and Ben Rhodes (right) were pushed into fifth place.

Below: Mathew Belcher (right) and Malcolm Page (left) of Australia celebrate in the Olympic Rings after winning gold in the men's 470 Sailing at the Weymouth & Portland Venue.

'It's amazing, we've sailed brilliantly for four years and this week was one of our best weeks so far.'

Nathan Outteridge. Gold medallist in the 49er class

Women's events

Xu takes gold in Laser Radial

The final race in the Laser Radial class was intriguingly open, with four competitors having a chance of taking the gold medal. China's Lijia Xu, the Netherlands' Marit Bouwmeester, Ireland's Annalise Murphy and Belgium's Evi Van Acker were separated by only one point.

It was to be Xu, 27, bronze medallist at Beijing 2008, who took her Laser Radial over the line in first place in the double-points medal race, despite incurring a penalty point. In so doing she claimed only China's second Olympic Sailing title. 'I just give it all for joy and I gave it my best for Weymouth and the world and my country, China,' said the delighted Xu.

Second over the line in the medal race was Bouwmeester, who took silver for the Netherlands, with Van Acker securing bronze. A disappointed Murphy finished fifth in the medal race, placing her fourth overall and out of the medals. Team GB's Alison Young, competing in her first Olympic Games, finished fourth in the medal race, just ahead of Murphy, to take fifth place overall.

Spanish gold for Alabau Neira in RS:X

Marina Alabau Neira made winning her Windsurfing gold look easy. She led the rankings throughout the first 10 races with four wins and four other top-three finishes. Then she crossed the line first in the medal race, 27 seconds ahead of the rest. Finland's Tuuli Petaja took silver and Poland's Zofia Noceti-Llepacka the bronze.

Team GB's Briony Shaw, who finished fourth in the final, ended in seventh place overall, 12 points behind the bronze medal position.

The 26-year-old Alabau Neira, who described herself as 'super-happy … super-excited' after her victory, became the last gold medallist in Windsurfing. The sport is scheduled to be replaced by Kiteboarding at Rio 2016.

Gold for New Zealand crew in 470

Some skilful sailing by the New Zealand pair of Jo Aleh and Olivia Powrie put them on top of the podium in the women's 470 class, after a wind shift in the medal race put paid to the hopes of the British crew, Hannah Mills and Saskia Clark.

The two crews went into the final race neck and neck on 33 points. Each was guaranteed at least

'I am proud of the gold, especially as I'm in Britain, because British and European countries are good. I want to take this experience back to China so more can experience the beauty of sailing.'

Lijia Xu, Laser Radial gold medallist

One in four. China's Lijia Xu won the final to secure the Laser Radial gold medal in a competition in which four women could have triumphed. Xu established a decisive lead from the start of the medal race to secure only the second Olympic Sailing title for China.

'I've got a silver, which is good, but it's an upgrade in Rio that I want.'

Saskia Clark, women's 470 class silver medallist

a silver – finishing first of the two would determine who took gold. The British boat started well, but was caught by a sudden wind shift on the first leg and lost momentum. New Zealand tacked sharply right and caught the new wind, giving Aleh and Powrie an unbeatable lead. They eventually won the race by 41 seconds from Italy. The British pair, who had only sailed together since February 2011, finished almost two and a half minutes behind.

The Netherlands' Lisa Weterhof and Lobke Berkhout finished sixth in the medal race to claim the bronze medal.

Spain surprise to win Match Racing title

There was an upset for Australia at Weymouth and Portland, and it came in the Match Racing, when Spain's Tamara Echegoyen Dominguez, Sofia Toro Prieto Puga and Angela Pumariega Menendez took the gold medal, the last of the Olympic regatta.

The first signs of problems for the Australian crew came in the third match, with the score tied at 1–1. Skipper Olivia Price was swept overboard when the boat rolled on its side in Weymouth Bay,

making fellow crew members Lucinda Whitty and Nina Curtis swing back to collect her. Spain won that race by 1 min 1 sec, but the Australians came back to level the series 2–2. They were penalised in race five, however, and finally succumbed to the strong Spanish challenge to take silver. The bronze medal was won by Finland.

'We of course surprised ourselves,' admitted Puga after the race. 'We said before the Olympic Games that we would try to pass the quarter-finals and as each race went very well we said "why not go become Olympic champion?" It is a dream.'

Above: Viva Espana. Tamara Echegoyen Dominguez, Sofia Toro Prieto Puga and Angela Pumariega Menendez of Spain sprung a surprise by winning gold in the women's Match Racing. It was the final race of the Olympic Sailing programme in Weymouth and Portland.

Above left: Outmanoeuvred. Hannah Mills (left) and Saskia Clark (right) lost out to Australia for the gold medal in the women's 470 class but the Britons have vowed to come back for Rio 2016.

Overleaf: Olympic Sailing in the men's Laser class in the waters of Weymouth Bay.

'There have been so many people involved in making these Games so special ... thanks so much to everyone involved ... the volunteers and the whole nation for getting behind the team.'

Ben Ainslie, Team GB
gold medallist

Shooting

Peter Wilson, Team GB's Double Trap gold medallist. The early bad weather of the British summer had hampered Wilson's training on the range, but he hit his last two clays to become Olympic Champion.

Olympic gold medallists

10m Air Rifle: **Alin George Moldoveanu (ROM)**

50m Rifle Prone: **Sergei Martynov (BLR)**

50m Rifle 3 Positions: **Niccolo Campriani (ITA)**

50m Pistol: **Jongoh Jin (KOR)**

25m Rapid Fire Pistol: **Leuris Pupo (CUB)**

10m Air Pistol: **Jongoh Jin (KOR)**

Double Trap: **Peter Wilson (GBR)**

Skeet: **Vince Hancock (USA)**

Trap: **Giovanni Cernogoraz (CRO)**

Men's events

Royal coaching for Double Trap champion

Team GB's Peter Wilson was coached to the gold medal by former Olympic champion Sheikh Ahmad Al Maktoum, a member of the Dubai Royal family who won gold in the Double Trap at Athens 2004.

Wilson, 201cm tall and a former pupil of Britain's leading sports school Millfield, lost his funding for a year after failure at Beijing 2008 and worked as a waiter in a pub. However, the Sheikh who had retired from competing, recognised Wilson's talent and offered to train him for free. Wilson revealed that the two marksmen had become friends whilst competing at Athens 2004 after sharing tips about playing squash. 'I have the greatest admiration for him. He's one of the world's greatest shooters. He invited me to Dubai and we had a handshake over coffee. He saw something in me,' he explained.

Thirty-six-year-old Wilson, a farmer's son from Sherborne in Dorset, was on target throughout, but it was a close finish, with Wilson hitting the last pair of clays to win gold. 'I just really focused on my technique. I looked at the scoreboard and knew I needed one to win, but I hadn't banked on it being that close and wanted to hit both. It was exciting and a dream come true,' laughed Wilson, who explained that Britain's bad weather ahead of the Games had kept him off the range and hampered his training. Sweden's Hakan Dahlby won the silver medal and the bronze went to the Russian Vasily Mosin.

Double Trap is more widely known in Britain as clay pigeon shooting, and Wilson encouraged people to visit their nearest range and try the sport. 'I hope I've spurred on a resurgence in competitive shooting and I challenge anyone of any age to give it a go,' he urged.

'Immaculate' for Skeet champion

The USA's Vince Hancock retained his Olympic Skeet title and became the first shooter to win back-to-back gold medals in the event. Denmark's Anders Golding won silver and Nasser Al Attiya, from Qatar, a former winner of the Dakar Rally, took the bronze.

Hancock, 23, who serves in the US Marksmanship Unit, hit all of his 25 targets in the six-man final and only missed two in the entire session. He finished with a score of 148/150, which he said reflected his competitive spirit. 'Even playing tic tac toe with my wife I'm competitive,' he admitted. Hancock described the range at the Royal Artillery Barracks as perfect. 'We had the best targets and the best machines. Everything was immaculate.'

Women's events

First gold of the Games in 10m Air Rifle

China's Siling Yi, the world number one, took the first gold medal of London 2012 in front of IOC President Jacques Rogge, with a victory in the 10m Air Rifle at The Royal Artillery Barracks. Polish soldier Sylwia Bogacka took silver and Dan Yu, also of China, won bronze.

Yi was the first athlete to qualify for the London 2012 Games. She shed tears of relief after her victory and declared that all the attention from the media made her feel like a movie star.

Malaysia's Nur Suryani Mohd Taibi, who competed while eight months pregnant, finished 34th in the competition.

Jam, cars and Skeet gold for Rhode

The Skeet gold medallist, the USA's Kim Rhode almost failed to make it to London; her flight was cancelled twice and her dog ate her air ticket. The gold in London was her fifth successive Olympic medal, and she became the most successful woman shooter in Games history.

Rhode, 32, from Tucson, Arizona, who makes jam and restores vintage cars in her spare time, claimed victory ahead of China's Ning Wei who won the silver medal and Danka Bartekova (SVK) who took bronze. Despite it being a warm day, all the competitors struggled in the breeze. 'The targets were moving around with the wind,' explained Rhode. 'It's all about overcoming the bumps, the stars aligning and walking away with the medal.'

The Royal Artillery Barracks

Like the Equestrian athletes at Greenwich Park, the shooters were put at the heart of the action with an impressive, historic backdrop, with the event being staged at The Royal Artillery Barracks in Woolwich, south-east London. The heritage of the site dates from 1716, and for 200 years it was the centre of the UK arms industry. Spectators entered the site from Ha-Ha Road, and the three rifle ranges were made from a simple steel frame, covered by a stretched fabric, with ventilation holes looking like blocks of Swiss cheese. All were designed as temporary structures, to be removed after the Games.

Olympic gold medallists

10m Air Rifle:
Siling Yi (CHN)

50m Rifle 3 Positions:
Jamie Lynn Gray (USA)

25m Pistol: **Jangmi Kim (KOR)**

Skeet: **Kim Rhode (USA)**

Trap: **Jessica Rossi (ITA)**

Poland's Sylwia Bogacka, eventual silver medallist in the 10m Air Rifle, keeps a close eye on China's Siling Yi. She went on to win the first gold medal of London 2012.

Table Tennis

Right: Grand Slam. China's Jike Zhang on his way to becoming the youngest ever winner of the sport's grand slam. His gold medal at London 2012 added to his World Cup and World Championship titles.

Far right: Clean Sweep. Hao Wang (right) and Jike Zhang combine forces to ensure China's victory in the men's Team final. This victory meant another clean sweep of the gold medals for the world's powerhouse of table tennis.

Men's events

China gathers gold and silver in Table Tennis

China's Jike Zhang hurdled the barriers guarding the court and kissed the gold medal step on the podium after winning the men's Table Tennis title against his countryman Hao Wang at ExCeL.

The unstoppable Zhang, 24, won 4–1 (18–16, 11–5, 11–6, 10–12, 13–11) to complete the Table Tennis grand slam. His Olympic success followed victories in the World Cup in Paris in 2011 and the Rotterdam 2011 world championship.

Zhang dominated the first three games before a fight back from Hao, the Olympic champion at Athens 2004 and Beijing 2008, gave him the fourth game. But Zhang, who first started playing table tennis at the age of five, prevailed in the final close game to win gold. In the bronze medal match Dimitrij Ovtcharov of Germany beat Chuang Chih-Yuan of Chinese Taipei 4–2 (12–10, 9–11, 8–11, 13–11, 11–5, 14–12).

As his players took gold and silver medals the Chinese coach, Guollang Liu, was moved to kiss

a plastic cup printed with pictures of his daughters to show his appreciation of his family.

'I didn't have them at the last Olympic Games,' he declared. 'I wanted to express that they are the most important thing to me. I wanted to make them proud, to give them something precious to remember.'

Clean sweep for China in Team event

China underlined their supremacy in this sport, jokingly termed 'Chinaball', by taking home all the available medals once the men had defended their Olympic Team title, defeating Korea by an impressive 3-0.

The most exciting tie saw China's world number one player, Jike Zhang, take on Korea's Saehyuk Joo. The Korean put up a brilliant defence to take the second game and level the contest at 1–1 before Zhang's bullet-like forehand blasted him to a 3–1 victory.

China's Long Ma also beat Korea's Seungmin Ryu, while in the doubles Hao Wang and Zhang were 3–0 winners against Sangeun Oh and Ryu. Germany won 3–1 against Hong Kong, China in the bronze medal match.

24 years of Olympic success

Known as *ping pang qiu* in China, table tennis was famously the country's national sport under Chairman Mao. Chinese players have dominated the medal table since it was introduced to the Olympic programme for the 1988 Games in Seoul, taking 24 of 28 gold medals. This was never better illustrated than at Beijing 2008, where China won gold, silver and bronze medals in both men's and women's Singles competitions and gold in both Team events, the first time a country had won every available medal.

Women's events

First medal to China in women's Table Tennis

China's Xiaoxia Li won the women's Table Tennis gold medal, beating a furious Ning Ding, also of China, who berated the umpire for penalising her serve during the match. Chinese players have now won all seven of the women's Olympic Singles titles since the sport was introduced to the Games at Seoul 1988.

Although Li dominated the match winning 4–1 (11–8, 14–12, 8–11, 11–6, 11–4), it was a controversial contest. Ding was red-carded for an illegal serve and for dawdling back to the table following a break, with each card earning Li an extra point. Ding's serve was judged to be failing to reach the required 16cm in height and possibly moving backwards. After the match Ding, who had been favourite to win the gold medal, said she thought the umpire was being too strict.

Li, so often the number two to Ding, played with power and inspiration to win the Olympic title. She controlled the enthralling match from the start to join a long, proud line of Chinese Olympic Table Tennis champions.

In the bronze medal match, Singapore's Tianwei Feng beat Kasumi Ishikawa, of Japan, 4–0 (11–9, 11–6, 11–6, 11–5)

Chinese women power to Team success

China's women reiterated their dominance in the Team competition, with Japan also taking their first medal in the women's Table Tennis Team final. The defending Olympic champions only lost four games before triumphing with the gold medal. China's Xiaoxia Li set the tone by beating Japan's Ai Fukuhara in the first Singles match. Japan's new star Kasumi Ishikawa was then despatched 3–0 by China's Ning Ding, with her distinctive tomahawk serve. Yue Guo and Li beat Sayaka Hirano and Ishikawa 3–1 in the Doubles match. However, Japan's silver medal was an historic first, achieved after beating Singapore in the semi-final.

In the third place playoff for the bronze medal, the silver medallists from Beijing 2008, Singapore, defeated Korea 3–0.

Above left: Unstoppable. Xiaoxia Li went into her women's Singles final against compatriot Ning Ding ranked number two in the world. However, she prevailed to make her childhood dream come true.

Above: Winning combination. Finalists in the Singles, Xiaoxia Li (left) and Ning Ding combined forces as China beat Japan in the women's Team final.

'This has been my dream since being a little girl. I dreamed of being an Olympic champion. I want to thank my parents; they have sacrificed a lot to make my dreams come true.'

Xiaoxia Li, Table Tennis gold medallist

Taekwondo

Turkish delight. Servet Tazegul (blue) served up Turkey's first gold medal of the London Olympic Games. He justified his tag as 'the favourite' by beating Iran's Mohammad Bagheri Motamed in the final of the –68kg category.

The Sport

Taekwondo, which translates into English as 'the way of foot and fist', is based on an ancient Korean martial art. The aim is to land kicks and punches to four scoring zones on an opponent's body, with each contest consisting of three sets of two-minute rounds. Its white uniforms are known as doboks and competitors wear coloured protective equipment; the one in blue is referred to as chung, while the competitor in red is hong. Taekwondo was introduced to the Olympic Games as a demonstration event in 1988 and as a full medal event in 2000.

Olympic –58kg category

Joel Gonzalez Bonilla of Spain won the gold medal match in the –58kg category. The world champion overcame Daehoon Lee of the Republic of Korea 17–8 to take the gold medal. 'I have been through so much hard work to reach this gold, so much support, but also so much pain, but in the end it all paid off,' a delighted Bonilla said.

Men's events

First gold for Turkey in –68kg

Before Cakir Alptekin's 1500m victory on the track, Turkey's first gold of London 2012 came at ExCeL, where the favourite Servet Tazegul triumphed in the –68kg division.

Since winning the bronze medal at Beijing 2008, the 23-year-old world champion has dominated the division. He duly became only the second taekwondoka to win two medals in this event at the Olympic Games after Hadi Saei of Iran.

Another Iranian, Mohammad Bagheri Motamed, faced Tazegul in the final. It began slowly as each competitor scored one point in the first round. Tazegul took a 5–3 lead in round two before Bagheri Motamed, who had shown the best of form going into the contest, scored and both men received penalties.

Tazegul eventually justified his top ranking by winning 6–5, with the bronze medals going to Terrence Jennings of the USA and Rohullah Nikpah of Afghanistan. The result meant that, combined with his bronze medal at Beijing 2008, Nikpah has won both his country's two medals at the Olympic Games.

Lutalo justifies selection with –80kg medal

At ExCeL, 21-year-old Lutalo Mohammad more than justified the faith shown in him by the selectors. His relief at winning a bronze medal was evident in his joyous dancing with the Union flag after defeating Armenia's Arman Yeremyan. 'It's not the colour of medal I wanted, but it's hard earned,' said Mohammad as he celebrated becoming the first Briton ever to win a Taekwondo medal. The other bronze went to Mauro Sarmiento of Italy.

The competition provided a number of surprises, most notably in its two finalists. In the event it was Sebastian Eduardo Crismanich of Argentina who beat Spain's Nicolas Garcia Hemme 1–0 in a close-fought contest to win the gold medal, a first in Taekwondo for Argentina. Other men expected to feature, such as top seed Ramin Azizov of Azerbaijan, the two-time Olympic champion Steven Lopez and world –87kg champion Yousef Karami of Iran, all lost early in the contest.

The significance of his medal was not lost on Crismanich. 'I would like to give all the people of Argentina a piece of this medal,' he said.

Obame makes history with silver in +80kg

A first-ever Olympic medal in any sport for Gabon meant that the Taekwondo programme closed on a historic note at ExCeL.

The silver medal was awarded to Anthony Obame on a judges' decision following a dramatic and nail-biting final won by Italian police officer Carlo Molfetta. It was Italy's first gold medal in the sport, serving to underline Europe's emergence as a new Taekwondo powerhouse at the Olympic Games, thereby ending Korea's dominance.

Molfetta levelled the contest at 9–9 with a headshot just 15 seconds before the end, bringing about extra time. No further points were scored although Molfetta was the more active. The judges' decision went to Molfetta, who had overcome far bigger opponents on his way to the final, and he duly acknowledged the part Obame had played in a terrific finale to the Olympic competition.

For Obame, a 23-year-old student living in Paris, London 2012 is only the start. 'We have to try to get more medals in the future,' he said. 'For now it's just me, but I hope that other people from Gabon will win medals at other Olympic Games and have the same success as me.'

The bronze medals went to Xiabo Liu of China and Robelis Despaigne of Cuba.

The Olympic Games saw five gold medals go to European taekwondoka, who also collected 16 of the 32 medals on offer. Since the sport was added to the programme at Sydney 2000, only one previous title had been won by a European.

Women's events

Jones the 'head hunter' wins –57kg

Aged just 19 and participating in her first Olympic Games, Britain's Jade Jones provided the Host Nation with a fairytale gold medal – one very much hewn by the inhabitants of Flint in north Wales (population 12,000).

Locals there have funded Jones' progress from a talented youngster to Olympic champion by dipping into their own pockets, and she repaid their generosity with a sensational series of performances at ExCeL. Many of her supporters were there to witness Britain's first gold medal in this sport, including her grandfather Martin Foulkes who introduced Jones to taekwondo. As she rose through the ranks to represent her country, he drove her to and from GB Taekwondo's Performance Academy in Manchester four times a week.

Those who could not make it to London were gathered round televisions in pubs and clubs in the small town that once raised more than £1,000 to help Jones travel to the Youth Olympic Games in Singapore, where she also won gold.

Jones's progress to the final was decisive. Once there the one-time tomboy, nicknamed the 'head hunter' because of her penchant for head shots, set about her task against the former double world champion, Yuzhuo Hou of China.

Jones won 6–4 and celebrated in the packed arena, launching her headgear into the air and parading with the Union flag and the Red Dragon flag.

The bronze medals went to Marlene Harnois of France and Li-Cheng Tseng of Chinese Taipei.

Flint edged. Jade Jones (blue), from Flint in north Wales, produced a sensational series of performances including the final against the more experienced Yuzhuo Hou of China. She won Britain's first Olympic Taekwondo gold medal.

'I'm from a little town. I don't have super amounts of money and I couldn't afford to go to qualification tournaments, but everyone in Flint has helped raise funds for me to go events like the Youth Olympic Games.'

Jade Jones, –57kg gold medallist

Olympic gold medallists

–49kg: **Jingyu Wu (CHN)**

–57kg: **Jade Jones (GBR)**

–67kg: **Kyung Seon Hwang (KOR)**

+67kg: **Milica Mandic (SRB)**

Tennis

Turning the tables. Britain's Andy Murray races in to the net on his way to overturning his Wimbledon defeat to Switzerland's Roger Federer. Murray took the gold medal in their Olympic final clash.

'The atmosphere was unbelievable. I felt much more comfortable on the court … the crowd helped me get a few extra miles an hour in the last couple of serves.'

Andy Murray, Team GB gold medallist

Men's events

Magnificent Murray wins Singles

Exactly four weeks previously, Britain's Andy Murray had been inconsolable after losing to Roger Federer in the Wimbledon final. Yet in the Olympic Games Murray was to come out on top, winning in straight sets 6–2, 6–1, 6–4.

In the sunshine of Wimbeldon, with Massive Attack blasting out of the sound system and the All England Club dressed in Olympic purple violet, it was a fun-filled people's final – noisy, raucous and joyful. 'Andy … Andy … Andy,' cried the passionate and patriotic fans as a Mexican wave rippled around Centre Court. Murray, embracing the Olympic atmosphere, appeared determined but relaxed as he managed to save two break points in the opening game of the match. The 25-year-old Scot broke Federer's serve in the sixth game and took the set 6–2, assisted by a series of scorching backhands that ruffled and frustrated the Wimbledon champion.

A long cat and mouse game at 2–0 in the second set offered Federer six break points, but Murray held on. He played with grit and determination, using his racket like a cricket bat to gain the advantage and making his own luck as the ball stayed in or trickled over the net to take yet another point. Federer, wearied by a marathon four-and-a-half-hour semi-final with Juan Martin Del Potro (ARG) that ended 19–17 in the third set (the longest Tennis match in Olympic history), tried to turn on the heat, but every time Murray kept control. He ended the match with an ace to notch his first victory over the Swiss in a five-set match – and to take Olympic gold. Federer swiftly marched off court, leaving Murray to soak up the adoration of fans who had witnessed the first British win in the Olympic men's Singles final since the London 1908 Olympic Games.

With the gold medal around his neck, Murray had come of age – a champion at last. He said that he had been inspired to win the gold medal by watching Britain's Mo Farah triumph in the 10,000m the previous evening. Jubilant and smiling, he described winning the Olympic competition as the greatest achievement of his career. 'This is number one for me ... the biggest win of my life. It's been a lot of fun, unbelievable. I felt fresh and not nervous. It was the best way to come back from Wimbledon. I will never forget it.'

In the match for the bronze medal, Argentina's Del Potro beat Serbia's Novak Djokovic 7–5, 6–4. Del Potro described the medal, the first for Argentina at London 2012, as a gift for his nation.

Twin Slam for USA in men's Doubles

It was a Tennis golden slam for the USA's twin brothers Mike and Bob Bryan, who defeated second seeds Michael Llodra and Jo-Wilfried Tsonga of France 6–4, 7–6. The brothers, bronze medallists at Beijing 2008, said playing for their country brought a fresh intensity to their game. 'We play with a little extra fire, magic, passion

when we're playing for our country,' explained Bob Bryan. Julien Benneteau and Richard Gasquet of France won the match for the bronze medal, beating Spain's David Ferrer and Feliciano Lopez 7–6, 6–2.

Veteran Mirnyi goes for gold in Mixed Doubles

Andy Murray returned to Centre Court with Laura Robson and went down 6–2, 3–6, 8–10 to the top seeds Max Mirnyi and Victoria Azarenka of Belarus, who took the Mixed Doubles gold medal.

Veteran Mirnyi, 35, became the oldest player to win a medal since Tennis returned to the Olympic Games in 1988. Murray and Robson were the surprise duo in the Mixed Doubles, having only got through to the competition on a wildcard entry. Robson later revealed that because of their other matches the couple had not had any time to practise together as a duo ahead of the final.

The bronze medal match was won by the USA's Lisa Raymond and Mike Bryan. They defeated the German pair Sabine Lisicki and Christopher Kas 6–3, 4–6, 10–4.

'It has been a dream come true for me to achieve gold because I think every athlete in the world is dreaming about this prize. You don't get so many chances.'

Victoria Azarenka, Mixed Doubles gold medallist

Below left: Brothers Mike (left) and Bob Bryan enjoy a team hug after beating France's Michael Llodra and Jo-Wilfried Tsonga in the men's Doubles gold medal match.

Below: Great Britain's Laura Robson (near right) and Andy Murray, a new wildcard pairing for the Olympic Mixed Doubles, win a valuable point against Belarus' Victoria Azarenka (far right) and Max Mirnyi. Murray and Robson took the silver medal after losing 8–10 in the final set.

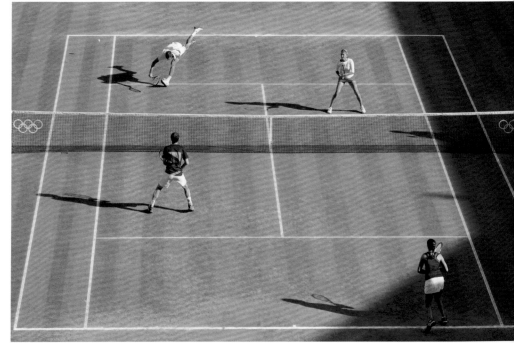

Golden moment. In this rare image of a British Tennis player winning at Wimbledon, Andy Murray jumps for joy at beating Roger Federer, possibly the greatest player the world has ever seen.

Power play. Serena Williams demolished the Russian Federation's Maria Sharapova to emulate her sister Venus in taking the Olympic women's Tennis Singles gold medal.

'The crowd at Wimbledon is so quiet, you don't hear much talking – but here you do. It's exciting, you really get to see the fans … it's awesome.'

Serena Williams, gold medallist in women's Singles and Doubles

Women's events

Serena powers to Singles golden slam

The USA's Serena Williams, 30, became only the second woman in history to grab Tennis's golden slam when she outplayed the Russian Federation's Maria Sharapova to win the gold medal 6–0, 6–1. It was an emphatic victory for Williams, who added the Olympic title to her wins in the four majors – Wimbledon, the Australian, French and US Opens. Williams, who played with deadly accuracy on court, celebrated her win by leaping into the air and dancing a jig she later described as 'West Coast' on Centre Court.

Victoria Azarenka from Belarus beat Russian Maria Kirilenko 6–3, 6–4 to win bronze, the first Olympic Games Tennis medal for her country.

Treble for Williams sisters in Doubles

Serena and Venus Williams cemented their dominance of the Olympic Tennis Doubles court by winning their third gold medal. The sisters defeated Andrea Hlavackova and Lucie Hradecka from Czech Republic 6–4, 6–4.

The USA pair, who also took gold medals at Sydney 2000 and Beijing 2008, have won every set they have played in Olympic Doubles. At London 2012, when torrential summer rain forced the closure of the Centre Court roof, they became the first 'indoor' Olympic champions since 1912. 'Olympic gold, golden slam, Singles and Doubles. That's awesome,' mused a delighted Serena.

The bronze medal was won by Russians Maria Kirilenko and Nadia Petrova who defeated Liezel Huber and Lisa Raymond of the USA 4–6, 6–4, 6–1.

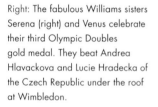

Right: The fabulous Williams sisters Serena (right) and Venus celebrate their third Olympic Doubles gold medal. They beat Andrea Hlavackova and Lucie Hradecka of the Czech Republic under the roof at Wimbledon.

Triathlon

In at the deep end. Athletes dive into the start of the men's Triathlon, a 1500m swim in the Serpentine in London. The Triathlon route took in the surroundings of Hyde Park, a royal park which has been open to the public since 1637.

The Triathlon takes centre stage

There is some evidence of a triathlon-type event featuring three sports staged in France during the 1920s, but the first swim-bike-run version of the modern event took place in San Diego, California in 1974. The triathlon's rapid growth in popularity and television appeal saw it added to the Olympic Games programme at Sydney 2000, which adopted the internationally accepted distances of a 1500m swim, a 40km bike ride and a 10km run. The London 2012 event was the most compact and spectator-friendly so far, with all three elements taking place in and around Hyde Park.

Men's event

Brilliant Brownlee brothers in the Triathlon

Britain's Alistair Brownlee, who won the gold medal in the men's Triathlon, prepared for London 2012 by digging a big hole in his front garden. He filled it with a training pool complete with an underwater treadmill, which he used to cure a torn Achilles tendon. It gave a whole new meaning to the British wartime phrase 'Dig for Victory', and the Olympic title confirmed Brownlee's status as the world's toughest triathlete.

After a 1.5km swim, a 43km cycle race and a 10km run, Brownlee coolly jogged down the blue carpet and strolled across the finish line carrying

'I woke up this morning and I was really nervous. I was like a kid at Christmas, looking forward to the race.'

Alistair Brownlee, Triathlon gold medallist

a Union flag draped around his shoulders, in a time of 1:46:25. Eleven seconds behind him was Spain's Javier Gomez who won the silver. There was more metalwork for the Brownlee household when the Olympic champion's younger brother Jonathan finished with a bronze, collapsing on the line only 30 seconds behind his sibling. This was despite serving a 15-second time penalty for jumping on his bike too early in the transition phase from swimming to cycling.

Right: The Triathlon course itself proved to be one of the stars of the Games, as fans packed the dramatic route through central London. Here Alistair Brownlee, the first Briton to win the Triathlon since the sport entered the Olympic programme in 2000, powers past the Serpentine.

Below right: Brothers in arms. Britain's Alistair (right) and Jonathan Brownlee celebrate winning gold and bronze medals in the Olympic Triathlon after training for the race together around their home in Yorkshire.

'I saw the board and I saw the number 31. I thought it was Alistair and I thought "Alistair, you idiot, you've got a penalty." I looked down at my arm and I thought "Oh no, it's me".'

Jonathan Brownlee, Triathlon bronze medallist on his time penalty

Hundreds of thousands of people lined the Triathlon route which began in the Serpentine in Hyde Park and snaked around Park Lane, Rotten Row and Knightsbridge. Vincent Luis of France tried to stay with the leaders, but only the Yorkshire-born Brownlee brothers and Gomez, a legendary double world champion, had the power and pace to get on the podium. It was the first time in Olympic Triathlon history that Britain had won medals.

Triathlon cyclists pass under Wellington Arch, originally created to commemorate the Duke of Wellington's victory at Waterloo. Appropriately Britons took gold and bronze in the event, with Javier Gomez taking silver and two Frenchmen, David Hauss and Laurent Vidal, coming fourth and fifth.

Women's event

Triathlon dramatic dead heat finish

Londoners and tourists headed into Hyde Park in their thousands to watch the women's Triathlon. Like the men's, the central London route took in famous landmarks such as Buckingham Palace, Hyde Park Corner and Constitution Hill. Spectators witnessed a sensational conclusion when, after 1500m of swimming in the Serpentine, 43km on the bike and 10km running on roads of the Royal park, two athletes finished with exactly the same time. In a dramatic photo finish, Switzerland's Nicola Spirig was awarded the gold medal and Lisa Norden of Sweden the consolation prize of silver. Two seconds behind them came Australia's Erin Densham, who once underwent surgery to correct an irregular heartbeat, to take bronze.

The day began overcast and drizzly, forcing the athletes to wear wetsuits for the swim because the water temperature had dipped below 20 degrees. A wet and greasy road claimed its first casualty when Beijing 2008 bronze medallist and early favourite, Emma Moffat from Australia, crashed out in the cycle phase. On the final lap of the run five athletes were in with a chance of medals, but it was Spirig and Norden who lunged for the line. The women simultaneously posted times of 1:59:48, but the Olympic Triathlon's first photo finish captured Spirig as just 15 centimetres in front.

Britain's hopes for the Olympic Triathlon were not fulfilled with Helen Jenkins, former world champion and winner of the London 2012 test event, finishing fifth. She apologised for her failure to take a much-desired medal in front of the passionate home crowd, explaining that she had struggled with a knee injury ahead of the Games. 'I've been training through a lot of pain. We've had a lot of tears, and unfortunately I wasn't 100 per cent on the run today.'

Above: Making a splash. The lower water temperature meant that wetsuits were obligatory for the first leg of the women's Triathlon in Hyde Park's Serpentine.

Left: Photo finish. The dramatic conclusion to the women's Triathlon shows Nicola Spirig (right) and Lisa Norden finish with exactly the same time. Spirig was eventually awarded the gold medal, with Australia's Erin Densham, shown behind, coming in to take bronze.

Volleyball

Dramatic victory at Earl's Court. The Russian Federation team celebrate after stunning Brazil to win the gold medal in men's Volleyball. They completed a staggering comeback to take the gold medal after being two sets down.

The Russian Federation's golden line-up

Nikolay Apalikov
Taras Khtey
Sergey Grankin
Sergey Tetyukhin
Alexander Sokolov
Yury Berezhko
Alexander Butko
Dmitriy Muserskiy
Dmitriy Ilinykh
Maxim Mikhaylov
Alexander Volkov
Alexey Obmochaev

Brazil's golden line-up

Fabiana Claudino
Danielle Lins
Paula Pequeno
Adenizia Silva
Thaisa Menezes
Jacqueline Carvalho
Fernanda Ferreira
Tandara Caixeta
Natalia Pereira
Sheilla Castro
Fabiana Oliveira
Fernanda Rodrigues

Men's event

Russian Federation fight back to seize Volleyball gold

The Russian team staged a dramatic turnaround from two sets down to snatch the men's Volleyball title 3–2 against Brazil.

The South Americans dominated for most of the match at Earl's Court and appeared to be coasting to victory. Determined to follow the women's team to a gold medal, they were ruthless, taking the first two sets 25–19 and 25–20. At 22–19 in the third set they even brought on Giba, their injured and retiring captain, to savour the medal-winning moment. This move seemed to anger and fire up the Russian Federation team, and they stunned the Brazilians by saving several match points to take the third set 29–27. Rejuvenated, the Russian Federation dominated the fourth set, which they took 25–22, as the pre-match favourites became less agile and confident around the court. They went on to win the last set 15–9 and to take gold in an astonishing turnaround, with Dmitry Muserskiy at the net scoring an impressive 31 points. The Russian Federation had become the first team in Olympic history to secure the Volleyball title from two sets down.

It was their fourth Olympic Volleyball title and the first gold since 1980. The bronze medal went to Italy, who beat Bulgaria 3–1 to extend their unbroken run of taking Olympic medals in the sport to five Games.

Women's event

Brazil takes Volleyball gold

The USA gave defending champions Brazil a scare when they won the opening set of the final 25–11 within the first 20 minutes, but the Brazilians fought back to take the gold medal in the fourth set 3–1.

The USA, unbeaten in 21 matches running up to the Olympic final, were ranked number one in the world and pre-event favourites at London 2012. Their coach Hugh McCutcheon had been hoping to enjoy the distinction of having coached both men's and women's Volleyball teams to gold. He began coaching the women after leading the USA men to the Olympic title at Beijing 2008.

At Earl's Court Brazil quickly regrouped, led by their captain Fabiana Claudino. They began to dominate at the net, taking the second and third sets 25–17 and 25–20. Jacqueline Carvalho, top scorer with 18 points, helped drive her side to the gold medal as Brazil took the fourth set 25–17. The USA had to accept silver, as at Beijing 2008.

Earlier in the day Japan beat Korea 3–0 to win bronze (25–22, 26–24 and 25–21).

'Soccer in Brazil is not a sport, it is a religion, so volleyball is the first sport in Brazil.'

José Guimarães, Brazilian women's Volleyball coach

Volleyball – Beach

Far left: On the beach. With its temporary venue in Horse Guard's Parade, Beach Volleyball had a stunning backdrop illuminated by floodlights. Players had the unique opportunity to serve from 'the Downing Street end'.

Left: Triple crown. Kerri Walsh Jennings (right) and Misty May-Treanor celebrate winning their third consecutive Olympic title in the all-USA Women's Beach Volleyball final.

Women's event

May-Treanor and Walsh Jennings enjoy Beach Volleyball hat trick

The Germans may have won the men's title but there was no such upset on offer in the women's tournament, where the spirit of the Copacabana came to London's heart of government. The USA dominated and provided both teams for the final.

Misty May-Treanor and Kerri Walsh Jennings confirmed their status as the most successful pairing in the sport. They took their third consecutive Olympic title 21–16, 21–16 against compatriots Jennifer Kessy and April Ross, with the match held under floodlights on a glorious evening at Horse Guards Parade. The bronze medal went to the Brazilians, who came from behind to beat China 11–21, 21–19, 15–12.

There was only one blip on the champions' progress, which came in a pool match. Austria's Doris and Stefanie Schwaiger became the first and only team to win a set against the USA in 12 years of Olympic competition.

For May-Treanor, 35, the gold medal brought her glittering career to a close. 'It's hard to stay on top … It's time for me to be a wife and mom. It's time for me now to help the next generation.'

Men's event

Breakthrough for Germany in Beach Volleyball thriller

It was fitting that the best in men's Beach Volleyball was saved until the final; the 15,000 enthusiastic fans packed into the temporary venue in the unlikely setting of Horse Guards Parade deserved nothing less. On a sultry summer night, with the match played under floodlights, Germany became the first nation other than the USA or Brazil to win gold since the sport was added to the Olympic programme for the Atlanta 1996 Games.

The German pair of Julius Brink and Jonas Reckermann beat the Brazilians, Emanuel Rego and Alison Cerutti, by 23–21, 16–21, 16–14. The match proved a thriller worthy of its setting, with Brazil saving three match points to draw level in the deciding set, only to fall to an initially controversial line call. European teams also featured in the bronze medal match as Latvia overcame the Netherlands by 19–21, 21–19, 15–11.

Horse Guards Parade

Among the most inspired of the London 2012 venues, this is the parade ground where Trooping the Colour takes place and which dates back to 1745. It was transformed for the Games, with a lower seating bowl running around four sides while an upper tier in horseshoe shape showed surrounding architecture, including the London Eye, to spectators. Over 4115 tonnes of sand from Surrey created the beach for the 16m x 8m court, while the temporary arena boasted a capacity similar to that of Centre Court at Wimbledon.

Weightlifting

Surprise package. Only 19 years old and 152cm tall, Yun Chol Om of DPR Korea broke the Olympic record. He took the gold medal from Group B of the 56kg category.

'Here, at the age of 24, I gave everything tonight, everything for this triumph. It's not just a gold medal for me, it's a triumph.'

Ilya Ilyin after retaining his 94kg title

Men's events

Om sensation in 56kg

History was made at ExCeL when the tiny Yun Chol Om from DPR Korea became the first weightlifter to win the Olympic gold medal from the B Group of lifters. More than that, he became only the fifth lifter to clean & jerk three times his own bodyweight as he set an Olympic record of 168kg, also equalling the world record held by the triple Olympic gold medallist, Turkey's Halil Mutlu.

It was an extraordinary performance and one the 19-year-old attributed to the leaders in his country, past and present.

It was DPR Korea's first Olympic gold medal in men's Weightlifting and the first Olympic gold medal in any sport since Kim Il won the 50kg Wrestling title at Atlanta 1996. In a competition that saw an unusually high number of failed attempts in the clean & jerk, the silver medal went to Jingbiao Wu. He continued China's run of winning at least one medal in the event at every

Games the country has entered since making its Olympic debut in 1984.

The bronze medal, the first ever in Weightlifting for Azerbaijan, went to Valentin Hristov, who was watched by the country's president Ilhan Aliyev.

Lu dominates the 77kg

Unusually exuberant celebrations on the stage followed Xiaojun Lu's gold medal and world record-breaking final lift as the Chinese lifter underlined his grip on the 77kg category.

After success with a 175kg snatch at his second attempt, Lu rushed to his coach Jie Yu. He lifted him off the ground too, before waving to the crowd and acknowledging the cheers inside ExCeL. It was Lu's second world record. Earlier, in the clean & jerk, he took 204kg to set the new world record mark for the total with 379kg.

His younger teammate Haojie Lu claimed the silver medal. He had appeared threatening and in contention for gold until he had to call a halt to his competition after injuring his left arm in his attempt at the 175kg snatch.

Ilyin retains title in 94kg

Kazakhstan's Ilya Ilyin became the third man to win the 94kg category twice, following in the iconic footsteps of Arkady Vorobiev of the Soviet Union (1956 and 1960) and Akakios Kakhiashvili of Greece (1992 and 2000).

Contesting what was dubbed 'the group of death' because it was so competitive, Ilyin completed six successful attempts. He twice broke the world record total with 413kg and 418kg, and also set a new clean & jerk world record of 233kg.

Russian Alexandr Ivanov secured the silver medal, with the bronze going to Anatoli Ciricu of

Olympic gold medallists

56kg: **Yun Chol Om (PRK)**

62kg: **Un Guk Kim (PRK)**

69kg: **Qingfeng Lin (CHN)**

77kg: **Xiaojun Lu (CHN)**

85kg: **Adrian Edward Zielinksi (POL)**

94kg: **Ilya Ilyin (KAZ)**

105kg: **Oleksiy Torokhtiy (UKR)**

+105kg: **Behdad Salimikordasiabi (IRI)**

Moldova. Ilyin, three-time world champion at the age of 24, claimed his perfect diet consisted of chicken and horsemeat. He added, 'The Olympic Games are just so great. You have to take care of yourself, and find your inner balance. If you choose a sport that is perfect for you early on, you will be successful.'

Barbell drama

Behdad Salimikordasiabi and Sajjad Anoushiravani caught the spectators' imagination in taking gold and silver for Iran in the +105kg division, but neither became the Games' most photographed lifter. That accolade went to defending Olympic champion Matthias Steiner, a competitor in the same category. Steiner was sent to hospital for X-Rays after buckling under the 196kg bar during his snatch. The weight crashed on to his head and neck, pinning the German under the barbell. Remarkably, he managed to walk away unhurt.

Women's events

Rim wins 69kg for DPR Korea's third gold

A fabulous Weightlifting competition for DPR Korea saw Jong Sim Rim win the country's third gold medal in the women's 69kg category at just 19 years old. She took the lead with her first attempt of 142kg after most of the competitors had completed the clean & jerk. The gold medal came with her clean & jerk of 146kg and 115kg in the snatch, giving her a combined total of 261kg.

Roxana Daniela Cocos of Romania offered a challenge, but it was short-lived as she dropped the barbell at 146kg. She did win the silver medal, however, as Maryna Shkermankova of Bulgaria took the bronze.

Zhou wins +75kg as China retains top ranking

Lulu Zhou won her country's third gold medal in the women's Weightlifting at ExCeL. She set a world record total of 333kg as China maintained its authority over the sport at the Olympic Games.

This was a competition of multiple world records. Zhou tried to bring the curtain down with an attempt to take the clean & jerk record to 190kg, but she failed. The silver medal went to Tatiana Kashirina of the Russian Federation, while Armenia's Hripsime Khurshudyan took the bronze.

Like most of the lifters Zhou has her own mantra, shouted out before she makes her effort. The enthusiastic crowd enjoyed returning the cry of 'Fung Song' without understanding what it meant. 'It means relax,' explained a bespectacled Zhou after her victory. 'I tell myself to relax so that I can lift weights relaxing.'

Above: Sim Jong Rim celebrates her gold medal in the 69kg category on the podium. She noted that, 'Even when the training was tough, I did my best and trained harder.'

Left: Lulu Zhou lifts for gold in the +75kg category at ExCeL. She was selected back in primary school to start weightlifting because of her 'strong physical condition'.

Olympic gold medallists

48kg: **Mingjuan Wang (CHN)**

53kg: **Zulfiya Chinshanlo (KAZ)**

58kg: **Xueying Li (CHN)**

63kg: **Maiya Maneza (KAZ)**

69kg: **Sim Jong Rim (PRK)**

75kg: **Svetlana Podobedova (KAZ)**

+75kg: **Lulu Zhou (CHN)**

Wrestling – Freestyle

Wrestling legend. Uzbekistan's Artur Taymazov (right) wrestles Georgia's Davit Modzmanashvili (left) in the men's Freestyle Wrestling 120kg gold medal bout.

The Sport

Often called 'catch as catch can', Freestyle Wrestling entered the Olympic Games in 1904. Competitors wear soft leather boots and red or blue wrestling leotards. There are seven weight categories for men and four for women, who first took part at Athens 2004. The rules are similar for both sexes, but double-headlocks are banned in women's Wrestling. Bouts are fought on a 12m x 12m octagonal mat with a combat circle 9m in diameter.

Olympic gold medallists

Men's 55kg: **Dzhamal Otarsultanov (RUS)**
Men's 60kg: **Toghrul Asgarov (AZE)**
Men's 66kg: **Tatsuhiro Yonemitsu (JPN)**
Men's 74kg: **Jordan Ernest Burroughs (USA)**
Men's 84kg: **Sharif Shaifov (AZE)**
Men's 96kg: **Jacob Stephen Varner (USA)**
Men's 120kg: **Artur Taymazov (UZB)**
Women's 48kg: **Hitomi Obara (JPN)**
Women's 55kg: **Saori Yoshida (JPN)**
Women's 63kg: **Kaori Icho (JPN)**
Women's 72kg: **Natalia Vorobieva (RUS)**

Men's event

Taymazov takes triple gold in 120kg Freestyle Wrestling

Artur Taymazov, Uzbekistan's most decorated Olympian, won his third successive gold medal in the men's 120kg Freestyle Wrestling final, beating Georgia's Davit Modzmanashvili in straight periods.

Russian-born Taymazov, 33, equalled the achievement of his boyhood heroes, the Russian Federation's legendary Greco-Roman wrestler Alexander Karelin, and Aleksandr Medved, the great Soviet wrestler. Medved had been the first to achieve the Olympic triple in Freestyle Wrestling.

Taymazov, who won silver at Sydney 2000 and gold at Athens 2004 and Beijing 2008, did not drop a point in the competition. In the final, the athletic super heavy weight prevailed 1–0 in a tight first round. In the second, even more closely fought, Taymazov bulldozed his huge opponent off the mat to retain the Olympic title.

The bronze medals were won by Bilyal Makhov of the Russian Federation and Komeil Ghasemi of Iran – a country that made a real impact in Olympic Wrestling at London 2012 by winning a total of six medals, three of them gold. Both were close matches, Makhov's taking three sets and Ghasemi scoring a winning point nine seconds from the end of the second set to secure victory.

Women's event

Yoshida dominates to grasp 55kg Freestyle Wrestling gold

With ferocious strength and lightning footwork, Japan's Saori Yoshida won the gold medal in the women's 55kg Wrestling competition. She defeated Canada's Tonya Lynn Verbeek at ExCeL in a rerun of the Athens 2004 final.

The victory confirmed Yoshida's status as the greatest female wrestler in the world. The 29-year-old, who began wrestling at the age of three, has now won three consecutive Olympic gold medals and nine world titles.

Before the Games, Yoshida had identified Verbeek as her biggest rival, but in the event the Canadian was overwhelmed by her opponent's speed and skill. The Japanese wrestler, who once held a winning streak of 119 consecutive victories, fought like the tiger printed on her bright blue leotard. She finally secured the Olympic title when she grabbed the Canadian's leg and drove her off the mat. Verbeek challenged the point, but she was overruled, allowing Yoshida, who trains against men, to retain her Olympic crown. In a remarkable performance, Japan won three of the four women's Wrestling gold medals at London 2012.

The bronze medallists were Colombia's Jackeline Renteria Castillo and Yuliya Ratkevich of Azerbaijan, the latter coming through the repechage to secure her medal.

Wrestling – Greco-Roman

Left: Cuba's Mijain 'The Kid' Lopez Nunez (right) defeats Heiki Nabi of Estonia (left) to win the gold medal and the Olympic 120kg Greco-Roman Wrestling title. Nunez noted he was tempted to continue to Rio 2016 if 'all goes well'.

Far left: Iran's Gholamreza Rezaei savours his gold medal in the 96kg Greco-Roman Wrestling. Iran took three out of seven Olympic titles in Greco-Roman Wrestling.

The Sport

Greco-Roman Wrestling formed part of the first ancient Olympic Games in 708 BC and appeared in the programme of the Athens 1896 Games. Competitors in Greco-Roman Wrestling are only allowed to use their upper bodies and arms to attack, with the aim to force the back of the opponent's shoulders on to the ground. The suplex is the most dramatic throw and bouts include arm locks and bear hugs. Contests are fought over three periods of two minutes in duration. Ways to win include showing technical superiority or holding both the opponent's shoulders to the ground (a pin).

Three for Iran as Rezaei claims 96kg Greco-Roman Wrestling gold

Iran took their third gold medal in Greco-Roman Wrestling at London 2012 when Ghasem Gholamreza Rezaei won the men's 96kg final against the Russian Rustam Totrov.

It was a stunning victory for the strong and athletic Rezaei, who had finished only 16th at Beijing 2008 and taken bronze in the 2007 world championships. The 26-year-old resisted Totrov's lift and takedown attempts to lift the Russian clear of the mat in the first period and successfully defend a par terre in the second. He won the match 2–0, 1–0, whereupon his coach celebrated by running on to the mat, picking up his athlete and slamming him down on his back.

London 2012 proved to be Iran's most successful Olympic Games for Greco-Roman Wrestling, in which it had never before won gold. Hamid Mohammad Soryan Reihanpour took the 55kg title and Omid Haji Noroozi won the 60kg event.

The bronze medals were won by Armenia's Artur Aleksanyan and Jimmy Lidberg of Sweden.

Cuba's 'Terrible Kid' takes 120kg Greco-Roman Wrestling gold

Cuba's Mijain 'The Kid' Lopez Nunez retained his 120kg Greco-Roman Wrestling Olympic title by defeating Heiki Nabi of Estonia at ExCeL.

The 29-year-old teacher, who had already beaten reigning world champion Riza Kayaalp on his way to the final, cruised to victory over Nabi, lifting him off the mat in the first round. His greater size and strength allowed him to take control, finishing the first period with a dramatic gut wrench and defending tactically on the floor to take the second. Lopez Nunez, also known as 'The Terrible' because of his fierce fighting skill, is only the third super heavy weight to win successive Olympic gold medals. His medal gave Cuba its first Wrestling gold at London 2012.

Lopez Nunez, the Cuban Flagbearer at the London 2012 Opening Ceremony, said that after winning gold and retaining the Olympic crown he was considering defending his title at Rio 2016.

The bronze medals were won by Turkey's Riza Kayaalp and Johan Euren of Sweden.

Olympic gold medallists

55kg: **Hamid Mohammad Soryan Reihanpour (IRI)**
60kg: **Omid Haji Noroozi (IRI)**
66kg: **Hyeon-Woo Kim (KOR)**
74kg: **Roman Vlasov (RUS)**
84kg: **Alan Khugaev (RUS)**
96kg: **Ghasem Gholamreza Rezaei (IRI)**
120kg: **Mijain Lopez Nunez (CUB)**

Olympic Games Closing Ceremony

The curtain came down on the 'greatest show on earth' with a Closing Ceremony that was loud, funny, clever, sentimental, occasionally daft and very British. It was entirely fitting that the country which has given so much music, culture and modern art to the world should close with a fantastic, brilliantly choreographed end-of-show party.

The aim, according to director Kim Gavin, was to 'celebrate the athletes, the volunteers, London itself, the country and the world at these extraordinary Games' with 'a mashed-up symphony' of all that is good about Britain spanning the last 50 years. And the result was just that – an extraordinary 'last night' party with a musical sweep that acknowledged classic hits

such as The Beatles' *Here Comes The Sun* and embraced the ephemeral pop of The Spice Girls. The fabulous Olympic Stadium was filled at one time or another, and sometimes all at once, with 108 vehicles, a volunteer cast of 3,500, including 380 children from 10 schools in the six east London Host Boroughs, singers, dancers and acrobats. All this was illuminated by the audience pixels, those 70,799 small panels of nine LED pixels mounted between the seats.

Gavin's party threw caution to the wind on a set of London landmarks featured against the backdrop of a Damien Hirst painting that evoked an ever-changing Union flag. The unforgettable show had Ray Davies stepping from a black cab to sing *Waterloo Sunset*, Madness performing *Our House* on the back of one of the 10 trucks and Ed Sheeran, Nick Mason, Richard Jones and Mike Rutherford playing Pink Floyd's *Wish*

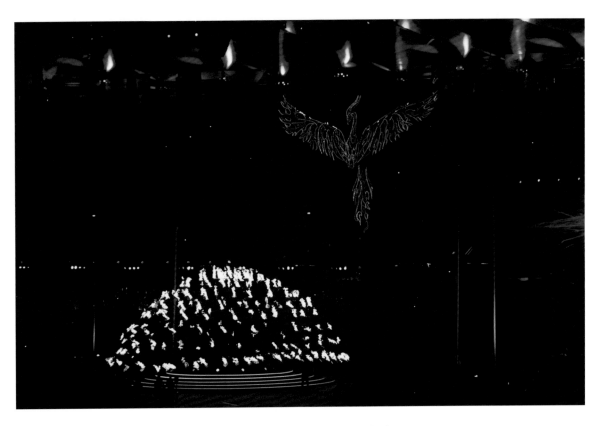

You Were Here. High above the Olympic Stadium there was even a tightrope-walking businessman spontaneously bursting into flames in a recreation of Pink Floyd's celebrated album cover.

Such ingenuity also signalled the 'anything goes' atmosphere that pervaded the show. Eric Idle sang *Always Look on the Bright Side of Life*; there was a real-life human cannonball.

Into the mix went the Mod era of the early 1960s, flower-power, dancers and supermodels celebrating British fashion, George Michael, given centre stage for two songs, and, via the big screens, John Lennon singing his immortal *Imagine*, over 30 years after his death, accompanied in the Olympic Stadium by the Liverpool Philharmonic Youth Choir and Liverpool Signing Choir. Throw in images of the late Freddie Mercury, a flavour of Queen, Tinie Tempah, Jessie J and Taio Cruz, a 50m-diameter inflatable octopus and the London Symphony Orchestra and the inspirational 'mashed-up symphony' was almost complete. Pele, the world's greatest footballer, played his part as Rio 2016 gave a taste of what lay ahead, but this in essence was London's show.

The rousing finale was provided by The Who and their seminal track *My Generation*. The Closing Ceremony was over, but the celebration was set to continue all the way to the Paralympic Games and beyond.

This was underlined by the formalities which preceded The Who, when first Lord Coe, Chair of LOCOG, and then Jacques Rogge, the President of the IOC, congratulated all those who had contributed to London 2012. The biggest cheer came for the 70,000 volunteers and Games Makers, who, said Coe, had given 'their time, their boundless enthusiasm and their goodwill and who have the right to say "I made London 2012".' He added, 'This may be the end of these two glorious weeks in London. But what we have begun will not stop now. The spirit of these Olympic Games will inspire a generation … On the first day of these Games I said we were determined to do it right. I said that these Games would see the best of us. On this last day I can finish with the words: When our time came – Britain, we did it right.'

President Rogge, whose 'verdict' on an Olympic Games is always keenly anticipated, said that the London Olympic Games had been 'happy and glorious', and so they were. The measure of London 2012, as of any major tournament, was how organisers dealt with any potential issues, and these were all settled quickly and as fairly as possible. This was a Games of outstanding achievements in every part of every venue. If it was possible to raise the bar from the friendliness of the Sydney 2000 Games and the sheer splendour of Beijing 2008, London had done it. London had done it right.

Above: The Cauldron opens outwards to mark the end of the Olympic Games, watched over by a phoenix, symbol of rebirth through fire. The Cauldron will stay dark for two weeks until it is relit with the Paralympic Flame.

Top left: Sir Winston Churchill as portrayed by actor Timothy Spall.

Left: London calling. Models of the Royal Albert Hall, Big Ben, the London Eye, 30 St Mary Axe ('The Gherkin') are wrapped in newspaper as the set is revealed at the start of the Closing Ceremony.

'It's not every day you are asked to get into Big Ben and come out of the top of it as Churchill reciting Shakespeare.'

Timothy Spall, Closing Ceremony performer

'It continued where the Opening Ceremony left off. It was kind of surreal and bizarre and crazy. It's got humour – all the things the British are good at.'

Julian Lloyd Webber, Closing Ceremony performer

'That mixture of street culture, music, fashion and sport – these are the ways working-class kids have come through and become something in the world.'

Annie Lennox, Closing Ceremony performer

Chapter Four
The London 2012
Paralympic Games

Paralympic Archery

Matt Stutzman of the USA competes in the Individual Compound – Open at The Royal Artillery Barracks where he won the silver medal. Stutzman was born without arms, learning to use his feet for everything instead.

Classification

Standing
Athletes compete standing

Wheelchair 1 (W1)
Impairment of arms, legs and trunk

Wheelchair 2 (W2)
Impairment of legs and trunk

Men's events

Russian 1–2–3 in Individual Recurve – Standing

Three Russian Federation archers were on target in the men's Individual Recurve – Standing, dominating the event and taking all three medals at The Royal Artillery Barracks.

The gold medallist was Timur Tuchinov, who beat fellow countryman Oleg Shestakov 7–3 in the final. Russian Mikhail Oyun, 22, crushed USA archer Eric Bennett 6–0 to take the bronze medal.

The Russian triple medal haul represented an impressive recovery from Beijing 2008, when the nation failed to win any Paralympic Archery medals. Tuchinov, 25, who holds the title of Honoured Master of Sport in Russia, said it felt wonderful to be the Paralympic champion, insisting that facing a teammate in the gold medal match had calmed his nerves. 'It's not the first time that we have competed against each other. Playing with a teammate is actually more calming,' he explained.

The 22-year-old Shestakov, who said the silver medal was the best performance of his life, agreed. 'We have faced each other in Russian championships, but the responsibility is higher in the Paralympic Games,' he observed. 'I feel a sense of duty in front of my fellow countrymen.'

Finnish teenager wins gold in Individual Compound – Open

Jere Forsberg of Finland won the gold medal in the men's Individual Compound – Open when he defeated Matt Stutzman of the USA. Both men were competing at their first Paralympic Games.

Forsberg, 18, was cheered on by the President of Finland, Sauli Niinisto, as he took to the field for the final against the phenomenal Stutzman, 29. The American's technique of controlling his bow with his feet attracted a lot of media attention. Sitting on a low stool, Stutzman holds the bow up by extending his right foot. He then loads the arrows with his left foot and pulls back the bow string with his teeth before releasing it.

Forsberg's accurate shooting saw him race into a 4–0 lead before Stutzman composed himself and focused on the 10, bringing the score to 5–3. Both archers scored perfect 30s in the final set to take the score to 6–4. The new champion, who said winning was an incredible experience, described his opponent as an amazing guy.

In the match for the bronze medal Dogan Hanci of Turkey triumphed over Spain's Guilermo Rodriguez Gonzalez 6–2.

Women's events

Gold and silver for Britain in Individual Compound – Open

ParalympicsGB's Danielle Brown retained her women's Individual Compound – Open title in a thrilling all-British final, defeating teammate Mel Clarke at The Royal Artillery Barracks.

Brown, a law graduate, was just 18 years old when she won gold at Beijing 2008. She became one of the star faces of London 2012, appearing on billboards and in television advertisements.

The British athletes drew the first two sets, with Brown taking the third. Clarke, 30, responded to the challenge, shooting two 10s and a nine to win the fourth set. The teammates then entered a nail-biting final shoot-out, supported by a rapt home crowd.

First Clarke went ahead, hitting the inner gold for 10 to Brown's nine. Then the defending champion shot another nine, while Clarke wobbled with an eight. Tension mounted, with the gold medal resting on the final arrows. Brown composed herself and shot a ruthless nine, to which Clarke replied with a seven, her lowest score of the day. A relieved Brown, who trains at the National Sports Centre in Shropshire, thus secured gold again with a final score of 6–4. She later admitted that her home Paralympic Games had put her under extra strain. 'The whole crowd was behind us and lifted us tremendously, but I think we were both nervous at times and fired a few loose arrows,' she revealed.

In the all-Russian battle for bronze, Stepanida Artakhinova beat Marina Lyzhnikova 7–3.

Korea claim first gold in Team Recurve – Open

Korea secured a historic victory in the women's Team Recurve – Open, beating China, the defending Paralympic champions, 199–193. Hee Sook Ko, 45, Hwa Sook Lee, 46, and Ran Sook Kim, 45, took the gold medal and secured their nation's first team title in women's Paralympic Archery.

The Koreans flirted with danger by starting slowly and using up precious minutes before firing their arrows, but gradually their patience paid off. Needing only to score four with their final shot, they finished with a flourish by scoring 10 to take the gold medal. Afterwards Ran Sook Kim thanked her enthusiastic supporters. Her teammate Hee Sook Ko, who won bronze at Sydney 2000, shared her delight in the nation's first gold medal in Team Archery. 'In 2000, I was the only female archer … a senior member of the Korean Archery Federation promised me that they would organise a female Archery team for future competitions,' Ko explained. 'This win reminds me of that moment.'

The battle for the bronze medal saw Iran beat Italy 188–184, in a team which included women's Individual Recurve – W1/W2 gold medallist Zahra Nemati. Great Britain went out of the competition when they met Korea for a place in the semi-finals and were defeated 183–175.

> 'Before we came to London we promised ourselves to make history and we did it.'
>
> Ran Sook Kim, Korean Team Recurve – Open gold medallist

Fangxia Gao (left) and Huilian Yan (right) of China compete in the final of the women's Team Recurve – Open. They took the silver medal after the defending Paralympic champions were beaten by Korea in the final.

Paralympic Athletics

Classification

Athletes are allocated a two-digit number. The first digit indicates the nature of their impairment, the second its impact on their event-specific performance. The lower the number, the greater the impact of their impairment on the field of play. For example, a runner in class 11 will have little or no sight and will use a guide runner, while a runner in class 13 will have limited sight and cannot use a guide runner.

T before a number is for Track,
F is for Field.
11-13 Visual impairment
20 Intellectual impairment
31-38 Cerebral palsy athletes; 31-34 race in a wheelchair, or field athletes who throw while seated
40-46 Athletes with an impairment that affects their arms or legs, including amputees
51-58 Wheelchair racers or field athletes who throw while seated

Athletes generally compete against athletes with the same sport class. But similar classes are combined to make certain classes more competitive.
At London 2012, classes F37 and F38 compete together in the Long Jump. T11-13 relay squads must have at least one T11 athlete, one T12 and a maximum of one T13; T35-38 squads must have a maximum of two T38 athletes and T42-46 squads a maximum of two T46s; T53-54 squads must have at least one T53 athlete.

Men's track events

Peacock struts his stuff to win 100m – T44 gold

As the athletes lined up, the shouts of 'Pea-cock, Pea-cock' by the 80,000-strong crowd reverberated inside the Olympic Stadium and Peacock had to ask for quiet, silencing the crowd in an instant. After a faulty start when Brazil's Alan Oliveira stumbled on his carbon-fibre blades, hush descended until the race exploded into life with Jonnie Peacock, the 19-year-old world record holder from Great Britain, who lost his right leg to meningococcal septicaemia when he was five, establishing an early lead.

This was supposed to have been a showdown between Peacock, the young pretender, and Oscar Pistorius, the 'Blade Runner' and defending champion from South Africa, but the duel never took off. Instead, Peacock was out in front and heading for gold before Pistorius could get into his running.

Peacock crossed the line in a crescendo of noise, glancing at the trackside clock which had stopped at 10.90, a Paralympic record. Richard Browne (USA), the 21-year-old from Flowood, Mississippi was the only one to get close to Peacock and he was second in 11.03 while Arnu Fourie proved himself South Africa's top sprinter by taking the bronze ahead of Pistorius in 11.08.

On a night when David Weir and Hannah Cockcroft had also won gold for the Host Nation, Peacock celebrated wildly on a lap of honour that included a hug for his mother and an embrace from Pistorius.

Peacock said: 'It was fantastic to go into that stadium with 80,000 people cheering and it was hard to keep relaxed. What happened though was surreal. I'm not sure I will ever get over it.'

Shvetcov heads off Blake to win 400m – T36

Evgenii Shvetcov of the Russian Federation enjoyed a fabulous Paralympic Games, winning over 100m, 400m and 800m. The 400m – T36 saw the 24-year-old run a world record of 53.31 to beat Great Britain's Paul Blake, despite slowing in the final 10 metres. Roman Pavlyk, the former world record holder from Ukraine was third in 55.18. Blake, who clocked 54.22, also picked up a bronze medal in the 800m – T36, where he and Shvetcov were separated by the winner's teammate, Artem Arefyev.

Richard the Lionheart roars to gold in 200m – T42

World champion 200m – T42 sprinter, Great Britain's Richard Whitehead broke his own world record with a time of 24.38 to win gold at

Left: Richard Whitehead crosses the finish line first after catching the field from behind to win gold in the 200m – T42.

Opposite: Jonnie Peacock struts his stuff across the line for gold in the 100m – T44.

London 2012. He treated the cheering crowd to a spectacular surge of speed in the final 25 metres to come from last place and beat the USA's Shaquille Vance (25.55), who won silver, and bronze medallist Heinrich Popow, of Germany (25.90).

Whitehead said that his race strategy was inspired by Dame Kelly Holmes, who won double gold at Athens 2004 by saving her best for the end of her races.

The 32-year-old from Nottingham is a versatile sportsman; he is the double leg amputee world record holder in both the half marathon (1:14:59) and marathon (2:42:52); and also represented Great Britain in sledge hockey at the Turin 2006 Paralympic Games. The senior member of the ParalympicsGB track squad, and the new Paralympic champion, smiled and flexed his biceps as he crossed the line, saying that he hoped his medal would produce a lasting legacy.

Pistorius wins his individual gold in the 400m – T44

In a fitting conclusion to the Athletics programme at the Paralympic Games, Oscar Pistorius successfully defended his title in the men's 400m – T44.

The most famous Paralympian of them all had already won gold in the 4 x 100m Relay – T42-46 but, by his own standards, Pistorius had not enjoyed the best of Games going into the final event after defeats in the 100m – T44 and 200m – T44.

With Alan Oliveira (BRA), who had beaten Pistorius in the 200m – T44, not fit enough to challenge, Pistorius was given the freedom to turn on the style and win comfortably in a Paralympic record 46.68. Oliveira's challenge lasted only until 200m when injury reduced him to little more than a jog. Blake Leeper of the USA took the silver medal in 50.14 and his teammate, David Prince the bronze in 50.61.

Somebody special? Oscar Pistorius throws a bouquet of flowers on the podium during the medal ceremony for the 400m – T44.

'It was very, very special for me. I was very nervous and quite tired but the crowd kept me going and, for once, I was thinking about something other than the race coming round the final straight.'

Oscar Pistorius, 400 – T44 gold medallist

Weir rocks the Stadium in the 5000m – T54

Home-loving, patriotic Londoner David Weir won a stunning gold medal in the men's 5000m – T54 in his own backyard, where his speed and experience proved unbeatable against a top-class field.

In the final 800m of the race, there were four contenders for the gold medal as Weir, Kurt Fearnley of Australia, Switzerland's Marcel Hug and Julien Casoli of France stalked each other, waiting to make the decisive charge for the line.

As the home crowd roared on their hero, Weir burst to the front with a phenomenal thrust of wheelpower, coming off the final bend with his powerful arms propelling him to victory in a time of 11:07.65.

As he crossed the line, the 33-year-old father of two raised his arms and blew kisses to the crowd, savouring the Paralympic track title that had eluded him for so long. 'This was the one I wanted to win and it was special doing it in my home town. The crowd gave me such a massive lift. It's indescribable what it does for you,' explained Weir, who has 'to win' in Japanese symbols tattooed on his chest.

Fearnley took the silver medal, clocking 11:07.90, with Casoli winning the bronze medal in a time of 11:08.07.

Double gold for Weir after winning 1500m – T54

Great Britain's David Weir added the 1500m – T54 gold medal to the 5000m – T54 title in another thrilling track final at the Olympic Stadium.

Roared on once again by the home crowd, Weir punched the air as he crossed the line in 3:12.09, with Prawat Wahoram of Thailand clocking 3:12.32 to win the silver medal and Gyu Dae Kim of Korea, the bronze in 3:12.57.

Taking the inside line, Weir powered ahead at the bell. His distinctive high-elbow action and hands slamming into the wheel rims with relentless pace saw him sprint clear to the line.

Fabulous fourth gold for Weir in Marathon – T54

If there was a single, outstanding athlete on show at the Paralympic Games, it had to be David Weir, who crowned 10 days of astonishing performances on the track by outsprinting a world-class field in The Mall to win the Marathon – T54. After a campaign that began with the 5000m – T54, took in the 800m – T54 and 1500m – T54, the 33-year-old summoned up enough energy, guile and determination to win a fourth gold medal in a race

'It was a dream come true tonight. It's taken hard work and dedication to get here. I was in great form coming into this and everything I have done in the last year has been for this.'

David Weir,
ParalympicsGB four-time
gold medallist at London
2012

Wheelpower. In the 1500m – T54 final, David Weir thrills the crowd with his second gold-medal performance.

Left: The 'Weirwolf' howls in victory after crushing the competition in the 1500m – T54 final.

'David Weir is the greatest wheelchair racer of all time.'

Jeff Adams, Paralympic gold medallist at Atlanta 1996 and Sydney 2000

Thousands of fans turn out to cheer David Weir through the streets of London to his fourth gold medal, in the Marathon – T54.

he described as 'the toughest of my life'.

To spectators, Weir appeared always in control, cruising around the city-centre course as part of a leading group of six, but only he knew the real story as the race developed in temperatures that hit 30 degrees Celsius. 'In the first five miles I was absolutely dying,' he admitted. 'I didn't think I was going to manage to cope. I felt like I had no energy and thought, "If they keep this speed up, I won't last another mile."'

After 26 miles, the gruelling race came down to a sprint and, inevitably, it was Weir who led the charge from the Queen Victoria Memorial in front of Buckingham Palace. Just as he had on the track, the Briton proved too good for the rest, crossing the line in front of thousands of cheering fans in 1:30:20, just a second ahead of Marcel Hug of Switzerland and Kurt Fearnley of Australia, rivals of old who had done all they could during the race to undermine Weir's explosive finish.

'Blade Runner,' Oscar Pistorius strides to a magnificent victory in the 400m – T44, leaving the field trailing behind him as the world watches, riveted.

Special delivery from the heart. Aled Davies (GBR) hurls the discus to win one of his two medals at the Paralympic Games, his other being in the Shot Put.

'I hope my medal will inspire more young people to try the shot. People think it's a sport for old, hairy men but it's a cool sport.'

Aled Davies, ParalympicsGB bronze medallist in Shot Put – F42/44

Aled Davies, ParalympicsGB gold medallist in the Discus Throw – F42, waves from the Victory Podium.

Men's field events

Davies puts more 'hustle in the muscle' in Discus Throw – F42

Welshman Aled Davies continued his dream of putting 'the hustle into the muscle' by winning the Discus Throw – F42 with a huge final throw of 46.14m that broke the European record and inspired wild jubilation in the Olympic Stadium.

Paralympic debutant Davies had at least one hand on the gold medal from early on after a first throw of 45.31m. Davies lapped up the adoration from the crowd and kissed members of his family. 'It's nice to give something back to everyone. I'm just so happy I performed. I've worked so hard to deliver and to give something back on the biggest stage,' he smiled.

The silver medal went to Iran's Mehrdad Karam Zadeh (44.62m) and China's Lezheng Wang was the bronze medallist with a throw of 42.81m.

First for Fiji in High Jump – F42

The High Jump – F42 caused a sensation on Twitter as Athletics fans were captivated at home and in the Stadium watching three men hop, leap and flop to the same stunning height of 1.74m.

The gold medal was awarded to Iliesa Delana, 27, of Fiji after a countback of successful jumps earlier in the competition. Fiji had previously never won a Paralympic or Olympic medal and a delighted Delana said he was looking forward to taking his medal home. 'I just made history. This is the first one and it was a gold,' he smiled.

Girisha Hosanagara Nagarajegowda of India

won his country's first medal of the Paralympic Games when he took the silver medal and the bronze medal went to Lukasz Mamczarz of Poland.

Crowd roars Christiansen to gold in Shot Put – F42/44

The first Athletics gold medal of the London 2012 Paralympic Games was won by Denmark's Jackie Christiansen in the Shot Put – F42/44 with a Paralympic record throw of 18.16m scoring

1012 points for the world record holder. With the sun shining and the Olympic Stadium full, the atmosphere was unprecedented for a Paralympic field event with the crowd roaring every throw. The 35-year-old Christiansen thanked the Athletics fans for their enthusiasm: 'It was really exciting out there. It was surely the biggest crowd I've seen in my lifetime. The crowd were great. They were with us all the way.'

Croatia's Flagbearer, Darko Kralj won the silver medal with a distance of 14.21m (987

Above: Jackie Christiansen of Denmark dominates the Shot Put – F42/44 to win the first Athletics gold of the Paralympic Games.

Above left: Giant leap for Poland. Lukasz Mamczarz of Poland jumps to the bronze medal in the men's High Jump – F42.

Club Throw

Unique to the Paralympic Games, this is for the most severely impaired athletes and takes place in the Shot Put circle. Athletes throw a wooden club, weighing 400 grams and similar in shape to a rounders bat or bowling pin. Throwing technique varies with some athletes launching the club backwards, over their head.

'Above all it was fun. The heartfelt welcome from the crowd made all the nerves disappear very quickly. It felt like the crowd was empathising with us.'

Markus Rehm, gold medallist Long Jump – F42/44

Leap of faith. Germany's Markus Rehm competes during the men's Long Jump – F42/44. He broke the world record twice during the competition to win the gold medal.

points), but the biggest cheer of the morning came for ParalympicsGB's 21-year-old Aled Davies who won the bronze medal with a throw of 13.78m (961 points), securing Great Britain's first Athletics medal of the London 2012 Paralympic Games.

World record for Dimitrijevic in Club Throw – F31/32/51

Serbia's Zeljko Dimitrijevic produced a stunning throw of 26.88m, setting a new world record and scoring 1010 points to win gold in the Club Throw – F31/32/51. The 42-year-old set the record with his first throw of the day in a final which saw several athletes setting personal bests as they were roared on by the cheering crowd.

There was just one point separating second and third places, with the silver medal going to Radim Beles from the Czech Republic at 26.67m (1004 points) and Algeria's Lahouari Bahlaz at 36.31m (1003 points) winning bronze.

Magic Markus world record in Long Jump – F42/44

Germany's Markus Rehm broke the Long Jump – F42/44 world record twice to win the gold medal in an exciting competition which saw the athletes buoyed up by a loud and enthusiastic Friday night capacity crowd in the Olympic Stadium.

The fun-loving Rehm responded to the support of the crowd and set an F44 world record of 7.14m in the first round, beating his own world record of 7.09m set at the Paralympic World Championships in 2011. After the first two jumps, all three German athletes in the competition occupied the top three slots and this, along with the incredible atmosphere, spurred Rehm to a huge gold medal winning leap of 7.35m (1093 points) in the third round.

His teammate Wojtek Czyz won the silver medal with a jump of 6.33m (983 points), while Denmark's Daniel Jorgensen overtook Germany's Heinrich Popow to clinch the bronze medal with a jump of 6.11m (959 points).

Sprint double. Hannah Cockroft of Great Britain crosses the line to complete a sprint double with her gold medal in the 200m – T34 event. She had won the 100m – T34 final earlier in the week.

Women's track events

Hurricane Hannah wins gold in 100m – T34

In an electrifying evening, Great Britain's 'Hurricane' Hannah Cockcroft won the gold medal in the women's 100m – T34 with a new Paralympic record of 18.06.

The execution of her race was Bolt-esque in its domination of the rest of the field. Cockcroft pushed away to a superb start, powering ahead to win by 10 metres and beating Dutch silver medallist, Amy Siemons (19.49) by almost a second and a half. Australia's Rosemary Little won bronze with a time of 19.95.

Cockcroft was always the favourite for gold having broken the Paralympic record in qualifying (18.24) earlier in the day but her victory in the final was stunning, propelling Cockcroft to star status.

Her sporting journey began with swimming and discus throw but she turned to the track after having a taste of track sprinting in Paralympic legend Tanni Grey-Thompson's racing chair in 2007.

Her original target was Rio 2016 but Cockcroft swiftly showed she had the speed and strength to be ready to race at London 2012 by breaking national records in 2010, becoming double sprint World Champion in 2011 and setting the first world record in the Olympic Stadium in May 2012 when she set a time of 18.56. Days later, she smashed that time, posting 17.60 at the Swiss Championships.

Like fellow Yorkshirewoman and Olympic Heptathlon champion, Jessica Ennis, Cockcroft has the charisma to reach out to people beyond the sports stadium and inspire the next generation.

Cockcroft completes the sprint double in 200m – T34

Just as she had done in the 100m – T34, Great Britain's Hannah Cockcroft dominated the longer sprint, powering away from the start and opening an unassailable gap before the athletes had completed the turn.

With her head down and arms pumping, Cockcroft had only the clock to beat as she hoped to improve her own world record on the way to winning her second gold medal of these Paralympic Games. She missed one of her targets by more than half a second but 31.90 was still a Paralympic record for her.

'I didn't know whether to cry or laugh or what to do. It's a little bit surreal when you're dreaming about it for so long and then it just happens in, what, 18 seconds.'

Hannah Cockcroft, 100m – T34 gold medallist

The rest of the field were a long way behind, with Amy Siemons of the Netherlands picking up the silver medal in 34.16 and her teammate Desiree Vranken the bronze in 34.85.

That's how it's done. Hannah Cockroft acknowledges the support of the crowd after a dominant performance in the 100m – T34 final. It was the first of her two gold medals at the Games.

'I may look calm but I am always extremely nervous before a race – any race – and I worried that the other girls had saved something up and they were going to going to get me in the 200m.'

Hannah Cockcroft, 200m – T34 gold medallist

Wolf leads the pack in 5000m – T54

The women's 5000m – T54 was a thrilling battle between the world's top two long-distance wheelchair racers, with Edith Wolf, of Switzerland, winning the gold medal in 12:27.87.

The race was decided in an exciting sprint to the line as Wolf, 40, the Beijing 2008 Marathon champion, perfectly timed her powerful thrust for victory to win her first-ever track medal.

The Beijing 2008 bronze medallist, Great Britain's Shelly Woods, made a speedy start as the 10-woman field raced a zippy first kilometre in 2:26.72. As Woods moved aside, the pace slowed and with all the athletes reluctant to dictate the pace, the lead changed several times in the next two kilometres.

Three laps from home, Wolf steered clear of the traffic and edged to the front, calculating her moment to make the decisive move. With 500m to go, she powered ahead, with Shirley Reilly of the USA, chasing from the final bend to set up a dramatic race down the home straight. Reilly was only half a wheel behind at the line, taking the silver in 12:27.91. The bronze medallist was Christie Dawes of Australia, who clocked 12:28.24.

Leader of the pack. Switzerland's Edith Wolf (right) leads the 5000m – T54 athletes on her way to winning the gold medal. She had Britain's Shelly Woods (left) for company for much of the race, but Woods finished out of the medals.

McFadden makes it a double in the 800m – T54

On a chilly and breezy evening, Tatyana McFadden (USA) made it double gold after an emphatic victory in the 800m – T54.

McFadden, 23, who had already won 400m – T54 gold, stormed to the line, her familiar white sleeves flashing as she powered to the gold medal in a time of 1:47.01, almost three seconds ahead of veteran Edith Wolf of Switzerland, who clocked 1:49.87. The bronze medal was won by Lihong Zou of China in 1:50.31.

McFadden said she was thrilled to have emulated the former Paralympic champion and world record holder, Chantal Petitclerc, of Canada, commenting: 'She's been my role model since I started racing aged 15. The first time I saw her I was like "Wow, who's that?" She led Paralympic sport and she is one of the people who made it great.'

Reilly takes gold in the Marathon – T54

On the sun-soaked streets of central London, the USA's Shirley Reilly won her third medal of her third Paralympic Games with gold in the Women's Marathon – T54. Her perfectly timed sprint saw her cross the line in a thrilling finish in 1:46:33 ahead of the fast-finishing Shelly Woods of Great Britain in 1:46:34. Sandra Graf of Switzerland was only another second behind as she and fourth-placed Amanda McGrory of the USA were given the same time.

Reilly, from Anchorage in Alaska, had already won silver in the 5000m – T54 and bronze in the 1500m – T54.

The 27-year-old Reilly, who had won the Boston Marathon in April, admitted it had been a tough race. 'I kept motivating myself to keep going because I was hanging on in there for a very long time,' she said. 'It was a very tactical race, with a lot of twists and turns. It was tough. I thought that with half a mile to go I could make a scrap of it and I was lucky that it was me who finished first.'

The silver medal was just as important to Woods, who had come into the Paralympic Games with high expectations. 'I'm so proud of myself,' she admitted. 'I've had such a tough week on the track but these Games have built my character. It was such a tough race with the toughest field I've ever faced. It was one of the hardest marathons I've ever done.'

Left: The USA's Tatyana McFadden savours the moment after winning her second gold medal of the Games. McFadden won the 800m – T54 final to add to her success in the 400m – T54.

Below: Sprint finish. The USA's Shirley Reilly (right) sprints to win the gold medal in the women's Marathon – T54. At the race's conclusion, she had (left to right) Sandra Graf of Switzerland, Amanda McGrory of the USA and Great Britain's Shelly Woods for company.

Airtime. Kelly Cartwright of Australia jumps to the gold medal in the women's Long Jump – F42/44. She set a new world record to beat Great Britain's Stef Reid into the silver medal position.

'I have worked hard. I had to have faith in myself and keep cool. I managed to do it with my last throw.'

Beverley Jones, ParalympicsGB bronze medallist in Discus Throw – F37

Women's field events

Cartwright leaps to gold in Long Jump – F42/44

Australia's Kelly Cartwright (F42) set a new world record of 4.38m (1030 points) to win the gold medal in the Long Jump – F42/44.

ParalympicsGB's Stef Reid (F44) won the silver medal in the F42/44 event and at the same time set a new Paralympic record of 5.28m (1023 points) in the F44 classification. The bronze medallist was Marie-Amelie le Fur, of France, the F44 world record holder, who was unable to close the gap with her final jump of 5.14m (1010 points).

Reid said she was pleased with the silver medal, commenting: 'If someone had told me four years ago, after I'd endured the hardest four years of my life, that I'd get a silver it would have been worth it. I have no regrets.'

Marvellous Maroua wins Club Throw – F31/32/51

Tunisia's Maroua Ibrahmi set a new world record to win the gold medal in the women's Club Throw – F31/32/51 with a magnificent 23.43m throw which scored 1064 points.

Silver medallist Mounia Gasmi from Algeria hit 22.51m, scoring 1052 points and Great Britain's Gemma Prescott won the bronze medal with a third round throw of 20.50m (1015).

Prescott said of her bronze medal: 'When I started (athletics), somebody invited me to have a go. I will pretty much give anything a go – bungee jumping off a bridge or jumping out of a plane. I am absolutely delighted with the bronze medal. It's amazing.'

Crowd help javelin to fly in Javelin Throw – F52/53/33/34

Germany's Birgit Kober broke her own world record with her final throw to win the gold medal in the Javelin Throw – F52/53/33/34.

Kober said the crowd had lifted her to a throw of 27.03m (1230 points). 'The Stadium gets so loud. When all the people clapped on my last attempt, it was really great. They helped the javelin to fly,' she laughed.

Kober's teammate, Marie Braemer-Skowronek won the silver medal with a throw of 20.43m (1018 points) and the bronze medal winner was Finland's Marjaana Huovinen whose first throw measured 19.47m (971 points).

World record for Pearson in Discus Throw – F51/52/53

Great Britain's Josie Pearson (F51) broke the world record three times on her way to winning the gold medal in the Discus Throw – F51/52/53. Her winning throw of 6.58m (1122 points) was

a huge 45cm longer than the existing world and Paralympic record set by Catherine O'Neill of Ireland at Beijing 2008.

This time round, O'Neill took the silver medal, throwing 5.66m (880 points), with Zena Cole (F51) of the USA winning bronze with a distance of 5.25m (771 points).

Pearson, 26, who played Wheelchair Rugby for Great Britain at Beijing 2008, turned to Athletics to give herself a new challenge. She said that the atmosphere in the Olympic Stadium on a hot and sunny Friday morning had inspired her to the Paralympic gold. She commented: 'It was amazing to perform in front of such a crowd, truly amazing. The roar of the crowd is something else.'

'I have always been very determined and I knew I wanted to be Paralympic champion. When you hear that the Games are going to be in your home country that's such an incentive to be the best at what you do.'

Josie Pearson, ParalympicsGB Discus Throw – F51/52/53 gold medallist

A capacity crowd at the Olympic Stadium cheers the men's 200m – T13 finalists to the finish line. Ireland's Jason Smyth (front) added the title to his 100m – T13 gold medal.

'I can't put into words what the crowd was like. They have made these Games. They have set them alight. If you want to know who was the star of these Paralympic Games, take a picture of the crowd. There's your star.'

Jonnie Peacock, Paralympic gold medallist in the 100m – T44

Boccia

The Sport

Pronounced 'Bot-cha', the sport designed for wheelchair athletes was introduced to the Paralympic programme at the New York/ Stoke Mandeville 1984 Games and is most often likened to bowls or petanque. The aim is to get a leather ball close to the white jack and competitors can throw, kick or use a ramp to get their ball onto the court. Points are awarded for every ball that is closer to the jack than their opponents'.

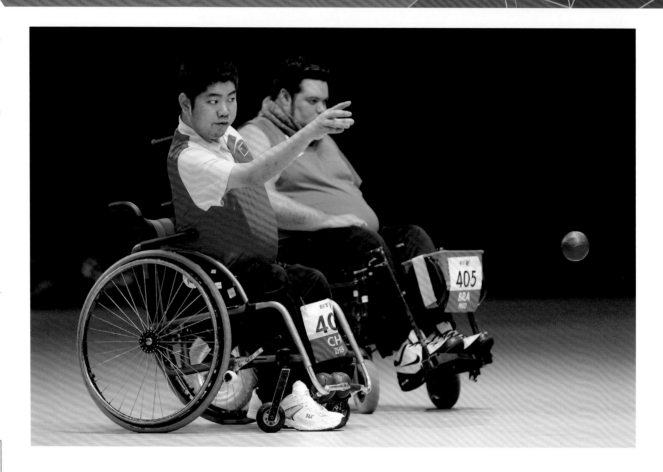

Risky manoeuvre. Yuansen Zheng of China makes a high-risk shot as he tries to overcome Dirceu Pinto of Brazil in the Individual – BC4 final.

Classification

Athletes have a severe impairment in all four limbs and use a wheelchair.
BC1 Athletes with cerebral palsy who use their hands or feet to propel a ball. May have a Sport Assistant.
BC2 Athletes with cerebral palsy who use their hands to propel a ball and have greater functional ability than BC1.
BC3 Athletes with any impairment who cannot independently kick or throw the ball three metres, and who therefore use a ramp.
BC4 Athletes with an impairment other than cerebral palsy who have a similar functional ability to BC1 and BC2 athletes.

Individual events

Brilliant Brazilian wins Individual – BC4

The exciting Individual – BC4 final went down to a tie-break after a gripping contest between the accuracy of Dirceu Pinto, from Brazil and the power of Yuansen Zheng, of China.

Zheng went 3–2 down in the third set when he tried to dislodge the jack with a risky, bullet-like shot but he clawed his way back in the fourth set to force the tiebreak.

Zheng, 23, who trains five hours a day, attacked by dislodging the jack with his third ball but Pinto, 31, fought back with a glancing blow off Zheng's ball to rest flush with the jack. Zheng's double lob on the jack failed to move it and Pinto, who leads projects to help disability athletes in his home town of Mogi das Cruzes, was the Paralympic champion.

In the bronze medal match, Great Britain's Stephen McGuire was beaten 5–3 by Brazil's Eliseu dos Santos.

Terrific Tadtong wins Individual – BC1

Thailand's Pattaya Tadtong added the Individual – BC1 gold medal to his Team gold when he beat Great Britain's David Smith 7–0 in the gold medal match at ExCeL.

The 4,000 spectators created an electric atmosphere and gave both players a lengthy standing ovation at the close of play. Tadtong threw

himself from his wheelchair, rolling on the court in celebration before his coach lifted him onto his shoulders so that he could salute the crowd. A smiling and laughing Smith acknowledged the fans with a high-speed lap of honour.

The two players could not have had more contrasting styles of play in the final, Smith playing aggressively at lightning speed and Tadtong, 33, eking out every second on the clock.

Smith, 23, smiled in admiration as Tadtong went 6–0 up in the third end after craftily clustering around the jack and playing brilliantly accurate shots each time the Great Britain player put him under pressure.

Smith praised Tadtong, commenting: 'I gave it my best shot but he was too classy for me on the day. No regrets, I'm happy. He was on fire.'

The bronze medal was won by Norway's Roger Aandalen, who was the 6–4 winner against Jose Carlos Chagas de Oliveira of Brazil.

Pairs event

Greece get gold in Pairs – BC3

Greece were the gold medal winners in the Pairs – BC3, beating Portugal 4–1 in the final at ExCeL.

The Greek team of Maria-Eleni Kordali, Nikolaos Pananos and Grigorious Polychronidis played with accuracy and nerve and made a flying start, winning the first three ends before Portugal took consolation from their win in the fourth and final end.

Georgian-born Polychronidis, 31, who began playing Boccia at university, said he was thrilled to win. He smiled: 'It's one of the best moments in my life and I was really proud to hear the national anthem. I've really tried for this medal and I couldn't be happier with this achievement.'

Above: Nikolaos Pananos plays a shot during the Pairs – BC3 gold medal match as his teammate Grigorious Polychronidis looks on. The Greek team beat Portugal in the final to win the gold medal.

Above left: Thailand's Pattaya Tadtong is held aloft by his coach as he celebrates winning the Individual – BC1 final. Tadtong's tactics and accuracy proved too much for Great Britain's David Smith who won the silver medal.

A need for speed. Cyclist and former racing car driver Alessandro Zanardi of Italy after winning the men's Road Race – H4.

The Course

In a change from the Olympic Games, the start and finish of the Paralympic Road Cycling was at Brands Hatch. The racing circuit near Sevenoaks in Kent, more famous for four wheels than two, is the site of Nigel Mansell's victory in the last F1 Grand Prix held there in 1986. Famous racing drivers to have competed there include Stirling Moss, Jim Clark, Barry Sheene, Jack Brabham, Ayrton Senna and Jenson Button.

Classification

B Visually impaired athletes who compete on a tandem with a sighted pilot on the front
C1-5 Athletes with an impairment that affects their legs, arms and/or trunk, who compete on a bicycle
H1-4 Athletes with an impairment that affects their legs, who compete on a handcycle
T1-2 Athletes with an impairment that affects their balance, who compete on a tricycle
In C, H and T classes, the lower the athlete's class number, the greater the impact of their impairment on their ability to cycle.

Men's events

Terrific Teuber takes gold in Time Trial – C1

Michael Teuber of Germany became a triple Paralympic champion when he raced to victory in the men's Time Trial – C1 in 25:16.43, adding a London 2012 gold medal to those of Athens 2004 and Beijing 2008. 'I focused on this race rather than the track. I trained for it for a whole year. I'm very happy,' declared Teuber, 44, adding that he was looking forward to racing at Rio 2016.

Great Britain's Mark Colbourne, more than 12 seconds behind Teuber, took the silver medal in a time of 25:29.37. The bronze medal went to Zhang Yu Li, of China, who completed the course in 26:23.11.

Colbourne, who won silver and gold on the track, was competing in his first Paralympic Road Race and said that he found it tough to race in the blustery breeze. 'It was windy out there, really windy,' he said. 'The temperature's good, but so, so windy.'

Former F1 driver claims Time Trial – H4 gold

Alessandro Zanardi of Italy, a former Formula 1 driver, returned to Brands Hatch to win a poignant gold medal in the men's Time Trial – H4. Zanardi, 45, riding a hand cycle at speeds averaging 38.6kph, clocked a time of 24:50.22 around the 16km course that included the famous Druids and Paddock corners. He was nearly half a minute quicker than Norbert Mosandl of Germany, who took silver with 25:17.40, and more than 45 seconds ahead of Oscar Sanchez of the USA, who won bronze with a time of 25:35.26.

Zanardi, who survived a horrific F1 crash during practice for the 1993 Belgian Grand Prix, had to have his legs amputated above the knee after a Championship Auto Racing Teams racing accident in Germany in 2001. In 2004, he returned to motor racing, competing in a specially adapted Touring car, and began hand cycling in 2007. The smiling Italian celebrated one of the most emotional gold medal victories of the Games by sitting on the track and holding his trike above his head. 'I am very happy,' said Zanardi, describing himself as 'thrilled' to be on top of the podium. 'I worked really hard for the last two years.'

Road Race – H4 thriller brings Zanardi second gold

An emotional day at Brands Hatch saw Italy's Alex Zanardi of Italy win the Road Race – H4 to become a double gold medal-winning Paralympian.

An exciting, classic Road Race saw the cyclists

riding in close formation in the peloton. Zanardi stayed calm and got the tactics right by resting on the uphill sections of the 64km course, catching up on the downhill slopes and conserving his power for the sprint finish. 'I managed my energies well,' he remarked. He crossed the line in 2:00:32, just 0.001 ahead of the South African rider, Ernst van Dyk, who won the silver medal. Wim Deleir of Belgium clocked 2:00:35 to take bronze.

Italian gold in the Road Race – C1/2/3

Italy clinched another Paralympic Cycling gold medal when Roberto Bargna won the Road Race – C1/2/3 title. He powered ahead to beat the rest of the peloton in an exciting sprint to the finish.

Bargna, 40, a keen amateur cyclist before he lost the use of his left arm in a motorbike accident, clocked 1:42:51. Both silver medallist Steffen Warias of Germany and the winner of the bronze medal, Australia's David Nicholas, posted the same time as Bargna, but the Italian just edged ahead. He had previously enjoyed second and third places in the world championships and was delighted with the result. 'It's been a crescendo,' he explained. 'I started in 2007 and then I entered the national team. After that, it's been one event after the other, one emotion after the other.'

Women's events

Triple gold for Storey after winning Time Trial – C5

Great Britain's super cyclist Sarah Storey won her third gold medal of the Paralympic Games at the historic Brands Hatch motor racing circuit. Her scorching victory in the women's Time Trial – C5 took her Paralympic gold medal tally to 10, five in Cycling and five in Swimming.

More than 7,500 spectators gathered around the fast, wide and smooth track on a glorious day for road racing. Storey, 34, immediately looked

as dangerous on the road as she had on the track, and by the halfway point in the 16km race she was already 50 seconds ahead of the rest of the field. Powering up Gorse Hill and over Scratchers Lane, she treated the crowd to a grandstand finish, beating Anna Harkowska (24:14.94) of Poland by more than a minute and a half, clocking a time of 22:40.66 and reaching average speeds of 42.3kph. Kelley Crowley of the USA won the bronze medal in a time of 24:14.51.

Storey, inspired by Team GB in the Olympic Games, said that she was determined to take gold in the Time Trial. 'Having watched the success of the Olympic team on the road, Bradley winning the Time Trial and Chris Froome getting the bronze medal, I just wanted to make sure I added my name to that list of success,' she revealed.

The home crowd was delighted when Storey's husband Barney joined her on the podium to celebrate. 'He's worked so hard with me all summer to make my power better. The power was there today,' she explained.

The cameras love her. Great Britain's great favourite Sarah Storey after her win in the Time Trial - C5.

'I have enjoyed every morning of training as much as this moment ... I really wish for everyone in this world to find their horizon to aim for because when it's your passion you're playing with every day, results are going to come.'

Alex Zanardi, Time Trial – H4 gold medallist

'It's just amazing with the crowds around the course and on the finish straight every single lap. I wanted to say thank you, but I had to keep my head down and make sure I made no mistakes.'

Sarah Storey, Road Race – C4/5 gold medallist

Storey gold in Road Race – C4/5

Great Britain's Sarah Storey became her country's most decorated female Paralympian when she won her fourth gold of the Paralympic Games in the women's Road Race – C4/5. It brought the super-cyclist her 11th Paralympic gold medal, in addition to her eight silver and three bronze medals, and beat the record set by wheelchair racer Baroness Tanni Grey-Thompson of 11 golds, four silvers and one bronze. 'To be even on the same page as Tanni, to have won 11 and make it a clean sweep for this week, is just a dream come true. I don't know if it'll ever sink in,' Storey observed.

The top three slots went to the same athletes who took the medals in the Time Trial. Storey finished the 64km race clocking 1:40:36 while Poland's Anna Harkowska finished over seven minutes behind to win the silver medal in 1:27:58 and Kelly Crowley of the USA won bronze in a time of 1:48:34.

Victorious and glorious. Sarah Storey celebrates gold in the women's Road Race – C4/5.

Golden girl Davis wins Time Trial – H1/2

The USA's Marianna Davis stormed to the gold medal in the Time Trial – H1/2 at Brands Hatch, speeding to victory in 31:06.39 over the undulating 8km course.

Davis, 39, a Paralympic Skiing medallist who has climbed two mountains over 4,000m, finished over two minutes ahead of Great Britain's Karen Darke (33:19.09), who took silver. Ursula Schwaller of Switzerland won bronze with a time of 34:56.55.

Davis, who also won gold in the Road Race – H1/2, explained that she had started cycling to get fit after giving birth to her daughter. 'It's a dream come true,' she remarked. 'You work hard and make a lot of sacrifices, so to be able to get my second Paralympic gold – it's awesome.'

Mixed events

Rolling Stone takes Road Race – T1/2 gold

Great Britain's David Stone defended his mixed Road Race – T1/2 title by winning gold on the final day of the Paralympic Road Cycling event at Brands Hatch. Stone, 31, who covered the 24km in 45:17, described it as the race of his life. He broke away from the pack close to the finish to take gold by an impressive seven seconds.

The silver medal was won in 45:24 by Giorgio Farroni of Italy and the bronze by David Vondracek from the Czech Republic, who posted 45:34.

London 2012 was Stone's third Games and he said would now target Rio 2016. 'It was the best race of my life. It makes the win better as it wasn't easy,' he said. 'It shows how much stronger the competition is compared to Beijing 2008. The field is so much harder now. It's good, it pushes me, it makes it a much better sport.' Stone's medal meant that ParalympicsGB finished at the top of the Cycling medal table.

Paralympic Cycling – Track

Great Britain's Mark Colbourne celebrates winning the men's Pursuit – C1. In his favoured event, he broke the world record twice in one day to add a gold medal to his silver won in the 1km Time Trial – C1/2/3.

'Three years ago I thought my life was over. If you face adversities in a positive way you never know what you can achieve.'

Mark Colbourne, Pursuit – C1 gold medallist

Men's events

Cool Colbourne wins gold in Pursuit – C1

Great Britain's Mark Colbourne set his second world record of the day to take the gold medal in the men's Pursuit – C1.

The Welshman first set a new world record in qualifying (3:53.970) before winning the gold medal race with 3:53.881. He beat China's Zhang Yu Li (4:01.826) by almost eight seconds, with Argentina's Rodrigo Fernando Lopez taking bronze in 4:04.559.

Colbourne, 42, described himself as 'completely euphoric'. He declared that winning the Paralympic title was a dream come true, and that he had modelled his racing tactics on those of Bradley Wiggins, the Olympic Time Trial Champion. 'I follow the Bradley Wiggins philosophy of going from A to B as consistently as possible and obviously it works. I try to maintain a Bradley Wiggins pace start to finish. I carried it through right to the end and didn't panic,' he explained.

On the opening day of the Paralympic Track Cycling events, Colbourne had claimed a silver medal in the 1km Time Trial – C1/2/3, this time losing to Zhang Yu Li. The pair of medals was a remarkable achievement for the extreme sports enthusiast, who only took up Paralympic cycling 18 months ago following a paragliding accident.

Fiesta and fireworks at 1km Time Trial – C4/5

Spanish teenager Alfonso Cabello won the men's 1km Time Trial – C4/5, clocking a time of 1:05.947 to set a new C5 world record in what proved a dramatic event.

Cabello's record-breaking run put pressure on the last competitor to ride in the competition, Great Britain's Jody Cundy. The defending Paralympic champion stuttered out of the gate, however,

Classification

B Visually impaired athletes who compete on a tandem with a sighted pilot on the front.
C1-5 Athletes with an impairment that affects their legs, arms and/or trunk who compete on a bicycle. The lower the number, the greater the impact on the ability to cycle.

'Hopefully tonight the audience got a glimpse of what was in there in my legs and enjoyed that.'

Jody Cundy, Pursuit – C4 bronze medallist

Flying the flag. The world champion Carol-Eduard Novak of Romania set a new world record to win the men's Pursuit – C4 gold medal. It was the first-ever gold medal for Romania at a Paralympic Games.

and had his appeal for a re-start refused. Cundy later spoke to the crowd and received a standing ovation after apologising for his angry reaction to the situation.

Cabello, 18, had to wait patiently while the matter was resolved. 'It was very difficult,' he observed. 'But I understood. If it had happened to me, I would have reacted the same way.'

The holder of the former world record (1:07.212), Great Britain's Jon-Allan Butterworth, won the silver medal. The ex-RAF serviceman, who lost his arm in a rocket attack on the Basra Air Station in Iraq, broke his own record with a time of 1:05.985, but finished 0.038 behind Cabello.

The bronze medal was won by Xinyang Liu of China, with a time of 1:07.638.

World champion Novak wins Pursuit – C4

World champion Carol-Eduard Novak of Romania set a new world record of 4:40.315 on his way to winning the gold medal in the men's Pursuit – C4. In the final Novak, a former champion speed skater, won in 4:42.000, brilliantly holding off Jiri Jezek of the Czech Republic, who took silver with 4:45.232.

Novak celebrated with his family and, in a warm display of sportsmanship, Jezek dropped to his knees to hail the new Paralympic champion. Both men hugged on the track.

The bronze medal was won by Great Britain's Jody Cundy, 33, who took just 1500m to catch Colombian Duenas Gomez.

Women's events

Paralympic record for Johnson in 1km Time Trial – B

Australia's Felicity Johnson set a new Paralympic record to claim the gold medal in the women's 1km Time Trial – B, contested by eight tandem riders. The world champion and world record holder,

piloted by Stephanie Morton, posted a time of 1:08.919. Great Britain's Aileen McGlynn, the defending champion, and her pilot Helen Scott secured the silver medal in 1:09.469. The 39-year-old mathematics graduate and her pilot also raced in an all-British bronze medal match in the women's Pursuit – B, narrowly beating Lora Turnham and Fiona Duncan.

After the race Johnson admitted that she could sense the British team trying to catch her. 'I could feel them nipping at our heels,' said the sports coach who works with young people with sensory disabilities. 'It was great motivation for us to try our best, considering it's their home turf and the track is really fast,' she added.

The bronze medal was won by New Zealand's Phillipa Gray and pilot Laura Thompson in a time of 1:11.245.

Storey strikes gold in Pursuit – C5

Great Britain's Sarah Storey powered to the gold medal in the women's Pursuit – C5 to claim an astonishing eighth (at the time) Paralympic title. It was ParalympicsGB's first gold of London 2012.

Storey signalled she meant business when she broke her world record in qualifying. Her time of 3:32.170 was quicker than Joanna Rowsell's 3:32.364 UCI Track Cycling World Cup win on the Olympic Park track in February. In the gold medal race she overwhelmed the silver medallist, Poland's Anna Harkowska (3:48.885), ruthlessly reeling in the half-lap gap to catch her with half the race still to run. The judges fired the pistol to signal the end of the race and the Velodrome erupted in thunderous applause. New Zealand's Fiona Southorn beat Crystal Lane of Great Britain to to take bronze with 3:52.695.

Storey, 34, is a Paralympian who has already won gold, silver and bronze medals in Swimming at Barcelona 1992, Atlanta 1996, Sydney 2000 and Athens 2004. An ear infection prompted her to switch to Cycling at Beijing 2008, where she took two gold medals. She then represented England at

the 2010 Commonwealth Games, almost making the Team GB squad for the London 2012 Olympic Games.

As she cycled round the track, celebrating her victory, Storey conducted the crowd in choruses of cheering. 'It was like having an extra family. 6,000 people and they've all come to sing with you when you win,' she laughed.

Second gold for Storey in 500m Time Trial – C4/5

Great Britain's Sarah Storey won her second gold medal of London 2012 in the women's 500m Time Trial – C4/5, smashing her personal best with a time of 36.997.

Storey defeated USA's Jennifer Schuble, the 500m specialist, who took the silver medal with 37.941. China's Jianping Ruan set a new C4 world record in the event posting a time of 38.425, factored at 38.194 to give her the bronze medal.

The factoring process is used in Paralympic events to take account of athletes with different classifications competing in the same event.

Earlier in the day Storey's husband Barney took gold in the men's 1km Time Trial – B, piloting Britain's Neil Fachie to a new world record of 1:01.351. This is the fastest time ever on a tandem, Paralympic or non-disabled.

Mixed event

China race to world record in Team Sprint – C1-5

The finale to the brilliant summer of Track Cycling at London 2012 saw intense competition in the Paralympic Team Sprint – C1-5, an event which includes men and women and a combination of classifications. The gold medal race proved a classic encounter between defending champions Great Britain and China, the previous Paralympic Games hosts.

China set a new world record time of 49.804 in qualifying, overtaking that set by Great Britain, also in qualifying, of 49.808. A tense final was in prospect, with China's world champion trio signalling that the four years since Beijing 2008 had made them hungry for gold. Crowd noise reached a crescendo as Xiaofei Ji (C4), Time Trial bronze medallist Xinyang Lui (C5) and Hao Xie (C2) faced the ParalympicsGB squad of Jon-Allan Butterworth (C5), Richard Waddon (C3) and 42-year-old Paralympic veteran Darren Kenny (C3), who had also taken bronze in the men's Pursuit – C3. The close race saw China's sprinters clock another dazzling world record time of 49.454, with Great Britain finishing in 49.519 – a heart-stopping 0.065 behind.

In the bronze medal race the USA team of Jennifer Schuble (C5), Sam Kavanagh (C4) and Joseph Berenyi (C3) beat the Czech Republic squad in a time of 52.749.

Left: Gold medal two of four. ParalympicsGB's Sarah Storey poses on the podium with her 500m Time Trial – C4/5 gold medal. It was her second gold medal in the London 2012 Velodrome before she turned her attention to the Road Cycling events.

'I think it's fantastic that the Velodrome is a sell-out ... Paralympic sport has certainly evolved. It's come a long way.'

Felicity Johnson,
1km Time Trial – B
gold medallist

(Front to back) China's Xiaofei Ji, Xinyang Liu and Hao Xie on their way to the gold medal and a world record time in the Team Sprint – C1-5. China beat the ParalympicsGB team in the gold medal race

Paralympic Equestrian – Dressage

Equestrian veteran. Great Britain's Lee Pearson on his horse Gentleman during the Championship Test: Individual – Grade 1b final. He has won 12 Paralympic medals since his debut at Sydney 2000, including 10 gold, but took the silver on this occasion.

The Sport

The Equestrian competition was a welcome addition to the Paralympic Games at Atlanta 1996 and has won acclaim with its innovative approach to horsemanship. Open to male and female athletes with any type of physical or visual impairment, the Dressage events test the riders' extraordinary horsemanship skills with a Freestyle section set to music.

Classification

Grades **Ia**, **Ib**, **II**, **III** and **IV**. The lower the impairment number the greater the impact on the ability to ride, the higher the less. For example, a Grade Ia rider will have an impairment that has more of an impact on his/her ability to ride than a Grade IV rider.

Individual Championships

Gold medal for debutant Baker in the Championship Test: Individual – Grade II

Taking part in her first Paralympic Games, 22-year-old Natasha Baker fulfilled a childhood dream to win Great Britain's first gold medal in the Greenwich Park arena. Riding Cabral, the European champion scored a Paralympic record for her Grade II class of 76.857 per cent, ahead of German riders Britta Napel (on Aquilina 3) and Angelika Trabert (on Ariva-Avanti), who took silver and bronze.

Baker, from Uxbridge in Middlesex, was inspired to ride at the Paralympic Games aged 10 after watching her current teammate Lee Pearson win gold at Sydney 2000.

'It means absolutely everything,' said the delighted champion. 'To come to my first Games and win a gold medal … I just never expected that in a million years. It is the most amazing feeling ever. My heart was going at a thousand beats a minute.'

Upset for Pearson as Formosa wins Championship Test: Individual – Grade 1b

In an historic upset Australian Joann Formosa, a 51-year-old artist from Victoria, rode her 19-year-old stallion, Worldwide PB, to victory with a score of 75.826 per cent. She was one of the oldest athletes in the Dressage competition, riding one of the oldest and smallest horses.

The result saw Lee Pearson of Great Britain, 38, suffer his first defeat in a Paralympic Games since his debut at Sydney 2000. The defending champion, who had taken three gold medals at each of the Sydney 2000, Athens 2004 and Beijing 2008 Paralympic Games, admitted that he had suffered an uncharacteristic bout of nerves before his round with Gentleman, a horse with whom he enjoys something of a love-hate relationship. On this occasion Pearson said he probably lost the title when Gentleman broke into an unscripted jog. After going in third, however, he led the competition with 75.391 per cent until Formosa posted her score. 'It's been a tough competition, a tough year and Gentleman is a tough horse to keep on top of his game. I'm genuinely delighted with silver,' said Pearson.

Austria's top-rated rider Pepo Puch won the bronze medal on Feeling Fine with a score of 75.043 per cent.

George wins Championship Test: Individual – Grade IV

Michele George of Belgium set the bar high on her own horse, Rainman, producing a brilliant ride to score 77.065 points. The figure proved out of reach for Great Britain's Sophie Wells, who had come into the competition as favourite at her first Paralympic Games.

Riding Pinocchio, Wells, 22, had won her grade in the Team test, two days before, raising hopes that she could win gold for the Host Nation, but she acknowledged that following George into the ring was a daunting prospect. 'I don't usually hear the commentary as I'm going into the ring, but today I heard it and understood what a good score Michele had got,' explained Wells. 'I knew then that I'd have to be at my best and do the best test I'd ever done to beat her.' She went on to score 76.323 points to claim silver, with New Zealand's Frank Hosmar, riding Alphaville, taking bronze on 73.097 points.

Individual Freestyle

Second gold for Baker in Freestyle Test: Individual – Grade II

Natasha Baker's Paralympic Games could not have gone any better after the 22-year-old Great British debutante secured her second gold medal with a Paralympic record in the Freestyle Test: Individual – Grade II competition.

Riding Cabral, an 11-year-old Polish-bred gelding nicknamed JP after the late Pope John Paul II, Baker dexterously managed a spot of improvisation in her routine, set to music composed specially for her by Ken Barnsley, the composer and keen dressage rider who died last year. 'At certain points I had to improvise,' she revealed. 'Everything was good until I got to the point where I am supposed to canter and I forgot what to do

Gold medal smile. Natasha Baker of Great Britain poses with her horse Cabral after winning gold in the Freestyle Test: Individual – Grade II. She said that Cabral was a 'star', adding that she 'couldn't have asked for any more from him.'

'I love my horse … when I'm riding, I'm free. Put me on a horse and I'm a different person.'

Joann Formosa, Championship Test: Individual – Grade 1b gold medallist

Above: Pepo Puch of Austria shows his delight after he and his horse Fine Feeling competed in the Freestyle Test: Individual – Grade 1b to take the gold medal.

Opposite: The stunning Greenwich Park arena, with Queen's House and the London skyline as a backdrop, provided the perfect setting for the Paralympic Equestrian events.

Puch has the crowd chanting in Freestyle Test: Individual – Grade 1b

The crowd in Greenwich Park chanted 'Pepo-Pepo' as Austria's Pepo Puch emerged triumphant in the Freestyle Test: Individual – Grade 1b test. The 46-year-old, who competed at the Athens 2004 Olympic Games before breaking his neck in a fall from his horse, responded in kind. 'The people are so sporting, so it's very special,' he said.

Riding his mare Fine Feeling to the stirring accompaniment of Strauss's Radetzky March, Puch scored 79.150 per cent to take the gold ahead of Katja Karjalainen of Finland on Rosie with 74.250 per cent. 'My horse was like a ballerina. As soon as she heard the music, she started to swing,' said Puch.

There was further disappointment for Great Britain's Lee Pearson, however. After his silver medal in the Individual Championships, Pearson could place only third in the Freestyle test with 74.2 per cent, a score that surprised many within the sport. The legendary rider thus completed his fourth Paralympic Games with a full set of gold, silver and bronze medals.

Puch told how his wife and trainer Michele was his biggest support through the difficult years after his accident. 'My five-year-old daughter Lou-Charlotte was one-and-a-half when I had my accident,' he explained. 'For the first few months, all I could do was move my neck from side to side, but I knew I wanted to play with her, so never wanted to give up.'

next, so I did a loop into a trot.' Her performance so impressed the judges that they awarded Baker 82.8 per cent, a score that wiped out the record mark set at the Athens 2004 Paralympic Games by Irene Slaettengren of Sweden.

In a result that reflected the order of the earlier Individual Championship, the silver and bronze medals went to Germany's Britta Napel on Aquilina 3 and Angelika Trabert on Ariva-Avanti.

Christiansen completes Home Nation success in Freestyle Test: Individual – Grade 1a

Sophie Christiansen completed Great Britain's astonishing run of success in the Equestrian competition by winning gold in the Freestyle Test: Individual – Grade 1a. Riding Janeiro 6, known as Rio, she performed a near faultless routine to music by Pink Floyd and Muse, as well as the chimes of Big Ben and the iconic Land of Hope and Glory.

Christiansen scored 84.75 per cent to become the first British athlete at the London 2012 Paralympic Games to win three gold medals. Her closest rival was Laurentia Tan of Singapore on Ruben James 2 who, despite being profoundly deaf and unable to hear the music, won the silver medal with 79 per cent. Helen Kearney on Mister Cool took the bronze with 78.45 per cent as Ireland celebrated a very successful first appearance in the Paralympic Equestrian event.

The enthusiastic crowd in Greenwich Park cheered wildly for Christiansen at the finale of Great Britain's most successful Paralympic campaign. No previous team had won medals in all five grades in the Individual and Freestyle competitions – a magnificent result. Will Connell, the Great Britain Performance Director, said: 'At Beijing 2008, we won 10 medals with seven riders. Here we've won 11 medals with five riders and exceeded our target. This is the first time anyone has won medals in all five grades in the Individual and Freestyle.'

Great Britain's Sophie Christiansen and her horse Janeiro 6 maintain absolute focus during the Freestyle Test: Individual – Grade 1a. Her gold in this event took her London 2012 tally to three gold medals, on each occasion scoring over 80.

A delighted ParalympicsGB quartet of (left to right) Sophie Wells, Lee Pearson, Deborah Criddle and Sophie Christiansen celebrate winning the Team – Open gold medal. Their strong individual performances secured them first place and ensured that the team exceeded their medal target.

'I think this has been our strongest team, but it has been the toughest gold to gain.'

Lee Pearson, member of Great Britain team who won Team – Open gold

Team – Open event

Great Britain maintains 100 per cent record with Team – Open gold

Strong individual performances and medals ensured that the Great Britain riders kept their record of winning every Paralympic, world and European team title since the sport joined the Paralympic Games programme at Atlanta 1996. Lee Pearson, the most decorated British rider, did not take gold, but his second place in the Championship Test: Individual – Grade 1b event secured him a 10th Paralympic gold medal.

Performing in front of sell-out crowds in Greenwich Park, the Paralympic riders' combined score of 468.817 points after the Team and Individual Tests came courtesy of a gold medal for Sophie Christiansen on Janeiro 6, known as Rio, in the Freestyle Test: Individual – Grade 1a. Silver medals for the 46-year-old Deborah Criddle, a triple gold medallist at Athens 2004, on LJT Akilles in the Freestyle Test: Individual – Grade III and Sophie Wells on Pinocchio in the Freestyle Test: Individual – Grade IV contributed to the impressive total. The Team silver medal went to Germany with 440.970 points while Ireland, in their first Paralympic Equestrian competition, claimed the bronze with 428.313 points.

'The gold is in memory of Jane Goldsmith, who pioneered para-dressage in Britain,' observed Christiansen's trainer Clive Milkins. 'She found Rio for us … without her influence, we wouldn't be where we are today.'

Paralympic Equestrian medals table

	G	S	B	
GBR	5	5	2	11
GER	2	3	2	7
BEL	2	0	0	2
AUT	1	0	1	2
AUS	1	0	0	1
IRL	0	1	2	3
SIN	0	1	1	2
FIN	0	1	0	1
DEN	0	0	2	2
NED	0	0	2	2

'It was incredibly uplifting and I felt proud to be British. I have never seen the Paralympic Games before and I didn't see disability, I just saw sport.'

Ellise Cooley, Spectator

Football 7-a-side was one of the biggest hits of the Games, attracting huge, very vocal crowds.

Football 5-a-side

Above: Brazil's Jeferson da Conceicao Goncalves (left) vies for the ball with France's Frederic Villeroux (centre) in the final.

Classification

Exclusively for athletes with a visual impairment. All four outfield players must wear eyeshades to ensure fairness.

Right: Serverino Gabriel da Silva of Brazil celebrates by showing some gymnastic skill after defeating France. The Brazilian team return to Rio 2016 in fine form, as Paralympic gold medallists.

Brazil go to Rio 2016 as two-time champions after Football 5-a-side triumph

All the magic of Brazil was on show at the Riverbank Arena in the team's 5-a-side Football triumph over France. The victory enabled the team, also champions at Beijing 2008, to go to their home Paralympic Games in Rio de Janeiro as two-time defending champions. Brazil, undefeated since the sport was added to the Paralympic Games programme at Athens 2004, secured the London 2012 gold medal without conceding a goal.

After qualifying for London 2012 by winning the world title in Hereford in 2010, the defending champions played France earlier in the competition without a goal being scored. All caution disappeared with medals at stake, however, on

one of the warmest days of the summer. Strikers Ricardo Alves and Jeferson Goncalves were in superb form in front of a full house, leaving France, the European champions, with no answer to their exquisite dribbling skills. Some brilliant close control by Alves earned Brazil a first-half penalty, scored by Gabriel Da Silva. In the second period the 22-year-old Goncalves twisted and turned in and out of the French defence until the ball rebounded off Martin Baron for an own goal.

At the other end of the pitch Fabio De Vasconcelos, Brazil's sighted goalkeeper, was equal to any of France's attempts, including eight-metre penalties from David Labarre and Frederic Villeroux. It was fitting, therefore, that the goalkeepers were awarded medals for the first time at the Paralympic Games.

The bronze medal went to Spain, but only after a dreaded penalty shoot-out decided their match against Argentina. Following a goalless draw in normal time, Antonio Martin Gaitan was the only scorer of the six penalties taken as Spain avenged their defeat at Beijing 2008.

Football 7-a-side

Left: Eye on the prize. Ukraine's Ivan Dotsenko (left) vies for the ball with the Russian Federation's Ivan Potekhin. One goal for the Russian side decided the match.

Far left: Ivan Shkvarlo of Ukraine (left) is challenged by Viacheslav Larionov of the Russian Federation during the Football 7-a-side final. Ukraine, winners at Athens 2004 and Beijing 2008, lost their crown to the Russian side.

Ramonov goal seals Football 7-a-side victory for the Russian Federation

A goal from Eduard Ramonov in the 43rd minute clinched the gold medal for the Russian Federation, but the Beijing 2008 silver medallists had to work hard against Ukraine, the two-time defending champions, in the final at the Riverbank Arena.

Both teams had dominated the competition, so the last medal to be decided at the London 2012 Paralympic Games was always going to be a tough call. The deadlock was broken 13 minutes into the second half when Ramonov ran on to Zaurbek Pagaev's header. Despite pressure from Taras Dutko in pursuit, the striker hit the ball beyond the Ukraine goalkeeper Kostyantyn Symashko and into the net. The goal came as Ukraine, winners of two gold medals and two silvers from the last four Paralympic Games, had looked the more likely to score. They had soaked up a lot of the Russian Federation pressure in the first half, when 'keeper Symashko was especially busy. His best save came when he had to stretch to tip an Aleksandr Kuligin free kick over the bar.

At the other end, when Ukraine did venture from their own half, they were consistently denied by Vladislav Raretckii, the Russian Federation 'keeper.

There were chances for Ukraine to get back into the game, but not even Anatolii Shevchyk, the competition's top scorer with six goals, could find a way through. The Russian Federation could well have doubled their lead had Kuligin not lifted his shot over the bar after a pass from Viacheslav Larionov.

There was a late flurry from Ukraine, but it was the Russian Federation who held firm until the final whistle to win their their fifth consecutive Football 7-a-side medal at the Paralympic Games and their first gold since Sydney 2000.

Interestingly, the top five finishers at London 2012 were the same as they had been at Beijing 2008, with the gold and silver medallists being reversed. The Russian Federation, Ukraine, Iran and Brazil remained the dominant nations in the tournament.

Classification

C5 Athletes whose impairment causes the greatest disadvantage on the field of play and has a significant impact when walking and running.
C6 Athletes with an impairment that affects their arms and legs, especially when running.
C7 Athletes with an impairment that affects one arm and one leg on the same side of the body.
C8 Athletes whose impairments cause the least disadvantage on the field of play; they often have involuntary muscle contractions as well as a tightness in their muscles.

Each team must have at least one C5 or C6 classification player and no more than two C8 players are allowed to play at the same time.

Finland celebrate winning the men's Goalball final against Brazil. They completed a remarkable comeback in the competition to take home the gold medal.

'For us this is a special moment. Second place is special for Brazilian Goalball ... for players back home and for our supporters.'

Diego Goncalves Colletes, Brazilian Goalball coach

Men's event

Fabulous Finland defeat Brazil for Goalball gold 8–1

Finland had a remarkable road to the gold medal in the men's Goalball tournament, securing a victory that epitomised the inspirational spirit of the Paralympic Games.

The European champions looked to be down and out after they struggled in the early rounds, suffering three defeats in succession. They never gave up, however, battling on to just make the knockout rounds in which they began to display their true championship form.

Finland dominated the final with an emphatic victory over Brazil, who, having conceded only one goal in the knockout stages, appeared overawed by the occasion. Finland's goals came from Petri Posio (4), Jarno Mattila (3) and Erkki Miinala (1), with Brazil's consolation goal, scored by 19-year-old Leoman Moreno da Silva, coming 85 seconds from the final whistle.

Mattila, 27, described his team's gold medal as an incredible achievement. 'It's a great, great feeling. We did a good job. It was a difficult start, but we got stronger and stronger,' he said. 'We knew that we could beat Brazil.'

In the bronze medal match Turkey beat world champions Lithuania 4–1 to claim the nation's first Paralympic Goalball medal. Turkey's Huseyin Alkan became the crowd's favourite after mimicking their 'oohs and aahs' and even singing Beyonce's 'All The Single Ladies'.

The tournament captivated all those who witnessed the sport for the first time at these Paralympic Games. It included early exits for the defending champions, China, who lost to Lithuania in the quarter-finals.

Women's event

Japan defeat China to claim Goalball gold

The spectacle of watching top-class sporting action in total silence proved irresistible to the fans who visited the Copper Box to watch the Goalball tournament. In this sport unsighted players have to sense the ball in defence, listening intently for the sound of the bells inside the ball.

In the gold medal match Japan were the 1–0 victors over world champions China. They displayed a mastery of the art of defence, mounting an unbreakable barrier to protect their first-half lead when Adachi Akiko hit the back of the net. Throughout the competition Japan had been a difficult team to break down, and even China, who had scored an impressive 37 goals heading into the final, could not penetrate their stubborn defence.

The Japanese coach Eguro Naoki said that his team had anticipated an encounter with China and had trained specifically to beat the Chinese. 'Our dream came true and we got the gold medal,' he explained. 'Strong defence is our characteristic, so we made sure to reduce our mistakes and then to quickly go on the attack.' In the all-Scandinavian bronze medal match Sweden, who had defeated ParalympicsGB with a golden goal in the quarter-finals, beat Finland 5–1 to clinch their first Goalball medal for 12 years. Sofia Naesstrom marked her retirement by scoring twice in the game.

Below left: Rie Urata and Akiko Adachi of Japan block the ball during their Goalball gold medal match against China. Japan's strong defensive strategy proved too much for the Chinese side.

Below: The ecstatic Japanese team enjoy their celebrations after they beat China to win the women's Goalball gold medal. China's Ruixue Wang noted: 'Nothing really went wrong. Japan's defence was just too good.'

Olympic Stadium, Orbit,
Aquatics Centre and Water
Polo Arena at twilight.

Powerlifting

World record moment. Yakubu Adesokan of Nigeria takes in the cheers of the crowd after he broke the world record during the men's –48kg competition. He broke the record twice in the course of the competition to take home the gold.

Classification

Athletes must meet minimum criteria that show they have an impairment in their legs or hips.

'Thank you very much to the crowd for their support. It helped me no end.'

Anthony Peddle, ParalympicsGB athlete in the –48kg category

Siamand Rahman of Iran celebrates a successful lift during the men's +100kg competition. On his Paralympic debut, Rahman lifted 280kg for the gold medal, nearly 40kg more than his nearest rival.

Men's events

Adesokan takes –48kg gold with two improved world records

Yakubu Adesokan of Nigeria twice improved his own world record to win the gold medal in the men's –48kg category, on a day that saw one of Great Britain's star Paralympians bow out.

Adesokan, 33, came to the London 2012 Paralympic Games as the overwhelming favourite after setting the world record at 177kg in Dubai earlier in the year. He began by breaking his compatriot Ruel Ishaku's Paralympic record of 169kg, set at Beijing 2008, with his first lift.

Roared on by a capacity crowd at ExCeL, Adesokan broke his own world record with 178kg in his second lift before improving it to 180kg to secure the gold medal. 'I feel overjoyed,' the new champion said. 'I have been training for two months, there was no way I was going to fail. I can definitely lift more.'

A lift of 170kg, which also improved on the previous Paralympic Games record, was enough to give Vladimir Balynetc of the Russian Federation the silver medal, while Taha Abdelmagid of Egypt took bronze with 165kg.

The competition saw the retirement of Great Britain's Anthony Peddle after his seventh Paralympic Games. The 41-year-old won gold and set the world record at Sydney 2000. At London 2012 he finished eighth after lifting 140kg.

Rahman's record-breaking pace wins +100kg gold

When it came to the heavyweights, there was no stopping the powerful 24-year-old Siamand Rahman, making his Paralympic Games debut for Iran. He broke the Paralympic record with his first lift of 270kg, delighting the cheering Iranian supporters who packed the crowd. Already the world record holder, Rahman improved his Paralympic record to 280kg with his second lift, but failed to go beyond the magical 300kg barrier when he could not control the bar at 301kg.

His opponents were left to battle it out for silver and bronze. Faris Al-Ajeeli of Iraq picked up the silver medal with his second lift of 242kg, while Keun Bae Chun of Korea took bronze with 232kg.

Women's events

Magnificent Muslu triumphs in –40kg

Nazmiye Muslu of Turkey took the gold medal with a Paralympic record 106kg lift in her final attempt. The 33-year-old then celebrated by going on to break her own world record with a fourth lift of 109kg.

The competition was tense till the end, with Zhe Cui attempting 104kg in her final lift in a bid to put pressure on Muslu. She did not succeed, however, so took the silver medal.

Great Britain, who finished out of the medals at Beijing 2008, celebrated a first-day success with

Home grown success. Zoe Newson of Great Britain secures the bronze medal in the women's –40kg category with a 88kg lift. She won the medal on the first day of Paralympic competition.

'I would like to thank not just the Turkish fans but all of the fans today as they gave us the best support. I've never seen anything like it before.'

Nazmiye Muslu, gold medallist in the –40kg category

Zoe Newson. She claimed the bronze medal with a lift of 88kg in her final attempt of the competition. Already a world junior champion, the 20-year-old from Colchester drew rapturous applause from the enthusiastic crowd at ExCeL, touched by her smiles on the floor and tears on the podium.

The delighted Newson acknowledged that she came into the Paralympic Games thinking of a fourth- and fifth-place finish. 'I had to check with my coach that I had actually won bronze,' she admitted. 'I'm feeling quite emotional and can't stop crying. I'm usually really laid-back but this means a lot. I'll keep the medal round my neck always. It's absolutely amazing.'

Dramatic final lift wins –75kg gold for Fu

So intense was the rivalry for top honours in the women's –75kg category that the lifters continued beyond the official end of the competition with attempts on the world record. The gold medal went to Taoying Fu of China for the fourth successive Paralympic Games, but only after a thrilling tussle with 27-year-old Folashade Oluwafemiayo of Nigeria. She pushed the

eventual champion all the way with a Paralympic then a world record lift of 146kg to close.

Not to be outdone Fu, 44, took to the platform to match her rival's lift and then take the gold medal on weight advantage from the Nigerian. Both women then opted for extra lifts, beyond the competition, to improve on the world record. Fu took it to 147kg only for Oluwafemiayo to raise it again to 148kg. Tzu-Hui Lin of Taipei took the bronze medal with a 137kg lift.

Paralympic record for Ghazouani in –67.5kg

The world number one, Souhad Ghazouani of France, broke the Paralympic record as she won the gold medal in the women's –67.5kg category, achieving 146kg in her opening lift. She attempted to break the world record as well, but the 30-year-old failed at 148kg and 150kg. 'I hope to try again at Rio 2016,' she said.

Yuijao Tan of China tried to deprive Ghazouani of gold with an attempt at 147kg but did not succeed. She took the silver medal after her success at 139kg, while Nigeria's Victoria Nneji picked up the bronze at 125kg.

Nigeria top Powerlifting nation			
	G	S	B
NGR	6	5	1	12
EGY	4	3	4	11
IRI	4	1	1	6
CHN	3	6	6	15
TUR	1	1	1	3
MEX	1	0	1	2
FRA	1	0	0	1
RUS	0	3	1	4
IRQ	0	1	0	1
GBR	0	0	1	1
GRE	0	0	1	1
KOR	0	0	1	1
TPE	0	0	1	1
UKR	0	0	1	1

Paralympic Rowing

Classification

AS Impairments that mean an athlete can use only their arms and shoulders to accelerate the boat.
TA Impairments that mean an athlete can use their shoulders, trunk and arms to accelerate the boat.
LTA Athletes with an impairment that affects their ability to row but who are able to use their legs, trunk and arms to accelerate the boat. No more than two athletes in a crew may have a visual impairment.
AS and TA rowers may compete in LTA events, but an LTA athlete may not compete in AS or TA events.

Men's event

Upset for Aggar in the Single Sculls – ASM1x

The rising standard in arms-only single sculling was perfectly illustrated by the London 2012 Single Sculls – ASM1x event. In a surprise result, Cheng Huang of China raced to the gold medal and Tom Aggar of Great Britain lost for the first time since he took up the sport in 2007.

Huang had given notice that he was a force to be reckoned with by setting a world best time in the heats. He took the lead in the final after 250m and was never challenged, crossing the finish line on the 1000m course at Eton Dorney in 4:52.36. He was three seconds clear of Erik Horrie of Australia, who came from the back of the field to squeeze past the bronze medallist, Aleksey Chuvashev of the Russian Federation, by just 0.06. 'I followed my coaches' instructions,'

explained Huang. 'The first part, I went at normal speed. From 250m, I started using all my energy and I had good control.'

Aggar, meanwhile, appeared handily placed for the first half of the race, but his customary fast finish was not there when he needed it, leaving him to finish in fourth place. 'Going in I was the fastest on paper and my preparation was good, but when I asked for more today it just wasn't there,' he explained. 'The standard has moved on massively and I just wasn't myself today. I will be back though. I'm a fighter through and through.'

Women's event

Lysenko adds Paralympic gold to her collection in the Single Sculls – ASW1x

Alla Lysenko of Ukraine, the world and European champion, powered her way to victory in the women's Single Sculls – ASW1x final to take the gold medal in front of the renowned 'Dorney Roar'.

The 2010 world champion, Nathalie Benoit of France, made a strong start, but a race that went to form saw Lysenko in command before the scullers had passed 250m. She extended her lead throughout to finish in 5:35.29. Benoit held on for the silver medal in 5:43.56, while Liudmila Vauchok of Belarus, silver medallist at Beijing 2008, took the bronze in 5:47.54.

'I went into the race as the favourite, but felt no pressure,' Lysenko revealed. 'I like to keep it simple and be calm. I just start and finish. Now I am the world, European and Paralympic champion. This is the ultimate, but you can never have too many gold medals, so I will prepare for Rio 2016.'

China's Cheng Huang (centre) enjoys his gold medal win in the men's Single Sculls – ASM1x.

Mixed events

World champions triumph in the Double Sculls – TAMix2x

Tianming Fei and Xiaoxian Lou of China, the world champions, led from 300m and went on to win gold in the mixed Double Sculls – TAMix2x. Over the 1000m course at Eton Dorney they had established their superiority with a world best time in the heats.

The pair crossed the line in 3:57.63, almost six seconds ahead of Perle Bouge and Stephane Tardieu of France. 'The race was really open, but my hands hurt a lot because we have trained every morning and night to prepare,' commented Fei. 'Even if my body is exhausted, my mind is full of energy and excitement.'

The battle for the bronze medal resulted in Oksana Masters and Rob Jones of the USA edging out the fading British pair. It was a tight race, which Nicholas Beighton, a Captain in the Royal Engineers who was injured on duty in Afghanistan, and Samantha Scowen lost by less than half a second. Jones admitted that the effort that took the Americans to the line in 4:05.56 had left them drained. 'My body hurts. I couldn't really tell where we were at the end. We just sprinted and pulled out everything we had. I knew that was the time to empty the bank account of all the work we have been doing over the last year to get the bronze. Thankfully, that was enough.'

Home Nation gold in the Coxed Four – LTAMix4+

The golden glow returned to British Rowing at Eton Dorney when the mixed Coxed Four – LTAMix4+ triumphed in a pulsating race to close the Paralympic Games Rowing programme. For Pamela Relph, Naomi Riches, Dave Smith, James Roe and cox Lily van den Broecke, it was gold at last on a day when Great Britain's big hope, Tom Aggar,

Great Britain's (left to right) Pamela Relph, Naomi Riches, David Smith and James Roe celebrate winning the Coxed Four – LTAMix4+ gold medal with their cox Lily van den Broecke. The team reeled in an early lead from the German team to take to the front just before the grandstands at Eton Dorney.

had surprisingly finished out of the medals. It was also an improvement on the team's performance at Beijing 2008, when they took bronze.

The British crew that won the 2011 world title did not have the best of starts, however. In warm-up they suffered what van den Broecke called an 'equipment failure' when their speed coach, which shows the stroke rate, fell overboard. Added to this, Germany began the race well to take an early lead. Even after Great Britain had overtaken them just after halfway, they continued to press hard.

Despite tiring in the final 250m, the British boat held on to cross the line in 3:19.38, encouraged by the familiar 'Dorney Roar'. Germany, the pre-race favourites after their world best time in the heats, took the silver medal with 3:21.44 and Ukraine collected the bronze with 3:23.22, beating China by just 0.2 seconds.

The Great Britain cox van den Broecke explained that teamwork helped the crew overcome their pre-race mishap. 'This is the result of two years' work and it's incredible,' she added. 'We had a few interruptions on our way to the start, but kept our focus,' added her teammate Roe. 'We had confidence in what we could do.'

'We choose to be athletes, and now all the moments of pain and the hours of training have been worth it.'

Naomi Riches, member of ParalympicsGB's gold medal-winning Coxed Four – LTAMix4x

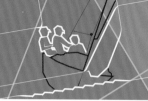

Paralympic Sailing

Gold for Australian pair in Two-Person Keelboat (SKUD18)

Just when the sailors needed a fair wind to complete their Paralympic Games races, the weather changed. The lack of wind in Britain's sudden Indian summer meant that the final day of competition had to be cancelled, with medals decided after 10 races instead of 11.

Ten races were more than enough for Liesl Tesch and Daniel Fitzgibbon of Australia, however. Skippered by the 36-year-old Fitzgibbon, four times voted Sailor of the Year with a Disability in Australia, the eventual champions had already moved out of their rivals' reach following four wins and five second places in the Weymouth and Portland waters. For Tesch, 43, the gold medal fullfilled an ambition she has held since Beijing

2008, when she switched from Wheelchair Basketball to Sailing. She sought to win at London 2012 as a tribute to her mother, who died of cancer on the opening weekend of the Paralympic Games. 'I was able to channel all of that emotion this week and we won the gold for Mum,' the Brisbane athlete explained.

Jen French and Jp Creignou of the USA took the silver medal. World champions Alexandra Rickham and Niki Birrell, denied the chance to push for silver in the final race by the lack of wind, had to settle for bronze, two points behind the French pair.

They were still proud, however. 'Alex and I will have medalled at every single Skud event on the planet,' Birrell observed. Theirs was among the first Paralympic Sailing medals awarded to Great Britain since the event was added to the Paralympic Games programme at Sydney 2000.

The Australian crew of Daniel Fitzgibbon and Liesl Tesch sailing in the Two-Person Keelboat (SKUD18) at Weymouth and Portland. With a lack of wind disrupting the final day of competition, they were awarded the gold medal after 10 races rather than the scheduled 11.

Lucas wins gold for Great Britain in the Single-Person Keelboat (2.4mR)

ParalympicsGB's Helena Lucas, the only woman in a competition of 15 men, had a nine-point lead before the final race was abandoned on the last day of Sailing. Her lead was enough to see Great Britain win its first gold medal since the sport entered the Paralympic Games programme.

Lucas, 37, who started sailing when she was eight years old, has won three bronze medals in the world championships and finished seventh at Beijing 2008. At Weymouth and Portland she won four of the 10 races completed in a week when some of her opponents thought the generally light winds might have favoured her. She denied this, however. 'I was consistent,' she explained. 'I had really good speed in all the conditions, which we have been working on really, really hard. I had great starts, which enabled me to use my speed and pull away from the competition.'

Heiko Kroger won the silver medal for Germany, with the bronze going to Thierry Schmitter of the Netherlands.

Reunited Dutch crew take Three-Person Keelboat (Sonar) gold

The Netherlands crew, reunited after taking silver at the Athens 2004 Paralympic Games, stepped up to a gold medal at London 2012 after the final day of competition was abandoned due to lack of wind.

Having quit the sport after Athens 2004, the Dutch crew, Udo Hessels, Marcel van de Veen and Mischa Rossen decided to regroup in 2012 for the world championships, held that year in Holland. Their success in taking a world title there inspired the trio to compete at London 2012, where they made an indifferent start to the Paralympic regatta. After taking the lead in the second day's racing, however, victory always seemed likely, despite some close encounters in the Weymouth and Portland waters. When the halt was called they held a 20-point lead over Jens Kroker, Siegmund Mainka and Robert Prem of Germany, so required no final race to secure the gold medal.

Aleksander Wang-Hansen, Marie Solberg and Per Eugen Kristiansen of Norway also had a sluggish start to the regatta, even surviving a disqualification on the third day's racing. They did enough over the ensuing days to secure the bronze medal, though, finishing just two points behind Germany.

The ParalympicsGB crew of John Robertson, Hannah Stodel and Stephen Thomas had been in the bronze medal position. They were relegated to fifth place after receiving a four-point penalty for unauthorised cleaning of their Sonar's keel. The boat had been taken out of the water for necessary repairs after the penultimate day's racing.

Left: Going it alone. Helena Lucas, the only woman in the Single-Person Keelboat (2.4mR) competition, races to a nine-point lead. She showed the men how it was done, winning Great Britain's first Paralympic Sailing gold medal.

'It's a sense of relief, something so, so special. It will hit me when it all settles down. My dad's cried more than me.'

Helena Lucas, Single-Person Keelboat (2.4mR) gold medallist

Below: The Japanese, French, Irish and Dutch crews race it out in the Three-Person Keelboat (Sonar). The Dutch crew (right) of Udo Hessels, Marcel van de Veen and Mischa Rossen, held a 20-point lead before the final day of competition was cancelled, taking home the gold medal.

Jakobsson finds his touch to win the R7–50m Rifle 3 Positions – SH1

The sport's most successful Paralympian, Jonas Jakobsson of Sweden, had not enjoyed the best of times going into his final competition at London 2012. He recovered his form, however, to secure his 17th gold medal from nine appearances at the Paralympic Games.

After a sluggish start, he scored 10s from his third shot to the end, taking the title with a total of 1,255.9 points.

Doron Shaziri of Israel reclaimed the silver he won at Beijing 2008 and Atlanta 1996 with 1,252.4 points. Chao Dong of China won bronze with 1,251.5, his second medal in London 2012.

Women's event

Zhang wins first gold of the Paralympic Games in the R2–10m Air Rifle Standing – SH1

The first of the 503 gold medals awarded at the Paralympic Games was claimed by Cuiping Zhang of China, who provided a masterclass in 10m Shooting. The 24-year-old missed the centre of the target only four times during the competition and her score of 500.9 points was a world record. She had also set a Paralympic record in qualifying, scoring 396 points. 'When I fired the last shot and it flashed up on the screen as a record, I didn't want to put the gun down,' she laughed. 'I just wanted to enjoy the moment.'

The silver medal was won by Manuela Schmermund of Germany, who scored a total of 493.6 points, while the bronze went to Natalie Smith of Australia on 492.4.

Men's events

Dong keeps cool to win R1–10m Air Rifle Standing – SH1

Chao Dong of China was the coolest man on the Shooting range at The Royal Artillery Barracks, on a day when more experienced athletes struggled in the unseasonable cold. Dong, 26, nicknamed 'the Hunter', opened up by marking a perfect 100 points in the third, fourth and fifth series. He qualified first for the final by equalling Swede Jonas Jakobsson's world and Paralympic record of 596 points, going on to take gold with 699.5 points.

Among those he beat was Jakobsson, the 47-year-old defending champion who was far from his best. 'I would have had to have been at the top of my game to be there with Dong,' he admitted after securing silver, his 29th Paralympic medal, with 696.5 points.

Josef Neumaier of Germany won bronze after a shoot-off with Seungchul Lee of Korea.

The Sport

Paralympic Shooting made its debut at Toronto 1976. At London 2012 the historic Royal Artillery Barracks in Woolwich, dating back to 1716, provided a magnificent Paralympic venue with its elegant architecture and 300m Georgian façade, the longest in the UK. Since 1980 Paralympic Shooting uses functional classification rather than disability classification, and there are now 12 medal events.

Classification

SH1 Athletes who can support their firearm without assistance
SH2 Athletes who require a stand to support their firearm

Mixed events

First title for Kovalchuk in the R5–10m Air Rifle Prone – SH2

Vasyl Kovalchuk of Ukraine emerged as the champion on his Paralympic debut. He proved the calmest in the final, securing the gold medal with his final shot after delaying to re-sight his aim. His final score was 106.4 for a total of 706.4 points, a Paralympic record. Raphael Voltz (FRA), the world number one, took silver after a shoot-off with Great Britain's James Bevis, who took bronze.

World record for Fevre wins the R3–10m Air Rifle Prone – SH1

Great Britain's Matthew Skelhon fought a close contest with Cedric Fevre of France, who finally claimed the gold medal with his last two shots. Both men scored perfect rounds of 600 points in qualifying, but it was Fevre, 28, who scored 10.7 and 10.6 to secure gold with a total of 706.7 points, setting a world and Paralympic record at his first Paralympic Games. Cuiping Zhang of

China finished in the bronze medal position on 705.8 points.

Skelhon, cheered on by an enthusiastic crowd at The Royal Artillery Barracks, hit a perfect 10.9 on his eighth shot to take silver medal with 706.4 points. It was a hugely popular medal for the defending champion, who made faces at the television camera and encouraged the crowd to give their support. 'My worst nightmare was messing up the qualifying,' said Skelhon. 'I've never seen eight guys shoot 600 before to get into the final.'

Alaryani stages upset in R6–50m Rifle Prone – SH1 final

There was an upset in the R6–50m Rifle Prone – SH1 final when Abdulla Sultan Alaryani won the United Arab Emirates' first gold medal in this event. Sweden's Jonas Jakobsson, the legendary defending champion, finished fourth as Alaryani scored 694.8 points. Spain's Juan Antonio Saavedra Reinaldo took the silver medal with 694.6 points, while Matthew Skelhon of Great Britain snatched bronze from Jakobsson with 693.2 points.

Opposite: Ice cool. Chao Dong of China keeps his cool during the men's R1–10m Air Rifle Standing – SH1 competition. He went on to win China's second Paralympic Shooting gold medal of London 2012 after qualifying for the final with a world and Paralympic record.

'I had to sacrifice something to become a champion. This is the result of what we have persisted in for the past four years, and what we aimed for.'

Vasyl Kovalchuk (UKR), R5–10m Air Rifle Prone – SH2 gold medallist

Vasyl Kovalchuk of Ukraine shoots for gold in the R5–10m Air Rifle Prone – SH2. The silver and bronze medals were decided with a shoot-off between France's Raphael Voltz and Great Britain's James Bevis, who took silver and bronze respectively.

The Aquatics Centre in Olympic Park
evokes a whale or stingray, with its
graceful, undulating shape.

Sitting Volleyball

Far right: China attempt to return a shot during the women's Sitting Volleyball final against the USA. The gold medal match ended with China taking their third Paralympic women's Sitting Volleyball gold medal in a row.

Right: Sadegh Bigdeli of Iran and teammates Davood Alipourian and Seyedsaeid Ebrahimibaladezaei block a ball during the men's Sitting Volleyball gold medal match. Bosnia and Herzegovina eventually overhauled Iran to take the gold medal.

The Sport

In Sitting Volleyball, a high-energy game of agility and skill, players aim to land the ball in their opponent's half. Three touches are permitted before the ball must cross the net and a part of the body between shoulders and bottom must be in contact with the court when a player plays or attempts to play the ball. The six-a-side game, developed by the Dutch in the 1950s, is a cross between the German game Sitzbal and Volleyball.

Classification

D Disabled
MD Minimally disabled
A squad of 11 is allowed two MD players, but only one may be on the court at any one time.

Men's event

Bosnia and Herzegovina beat old rivals to take Sitting Volleyball gold

The giants of the sport who contested gold and silver medals at Beijing 2008 were at it again at ExCeL. Four years ago Iran were the champions, but they had to give way to their old rivals as Bosnia and Herzegovina edged home 19–25, 25–21, 25–22, 25–15.

Both teams had been impressive at London 2012. For Bosnia and Herzegovina, Mirzet Duran and Safet Alibasic had scored freely, while Davood Alipourian and Isa Zirahi's spikes and blocks assisted Iran. The first set underlined how well the finalists were matched, with only Iran's accuracy taking them to a narrow 25–19 win.

From there, however, it was Bosnia and Herzegovina who held sway, their spikes levelling the match at 1–1. They took the third set and dominated the fourth to secure gold. Nizam Cancar and Zirahi finished the match as joint top scorers.

The bronze medal match, a five-set thriller, saw Germany, the number eight seeds, finally overhaul the Russian Federation 20–25, 26–24, 22–25, 25–22, 16–14.

Women's event

China completes gold medal hat-trick in Sitting Volleyball

Sell-out crowds enjoyed a thrilling climax to the women's Sitting Volleyball competition at ExCeL. China emerged as champions for the third Paralympic Games in a row with a 22–25, 15–25, 32–30, 25–15 victory over the USA.

With Yu Hong Sheng, one of the sport's best players, serving well and dominating at the net, China moved from a set down to take control. Just as the USA looked to be at their best, leading 10–9 in the second, the match turned. China took advantage as their opponents struggled.

At 1–1, the match moved into the longest set, 32 minutes. The two sides traded blows, with China losing five set points and the USA three. Having finally edged home in the fourth set 32–30, China won the final set in just 20 minutes. Ukraine took the bronze medal, defeating the Netherlands 3–0.

The Great Britain squad, making their first appearance at a Paralympic Games, were formed less than three years ago. They finished eighth without winning a set, but with performances that augured well for Rio 2016.

Paralympic Swimming

Classification

1-10 Athletes with physical impairments. Class 1 impairment has the greatest impact on the ability to perform strokes; class 10 has the least
11-13 Athletes with visual impairments. Class 11 have little or no sight; class 13 have limited sight
14 Athletes with intellectual impairments
S before the number represents the classification for Freestyle, Backstroke and Butterfly;
SB Breaststroke;
SM Individual Medley
Relays: contested by swimmers with classifications between S1 and S10. When the numbers of their classifications are added the total must not exceed 34.

Men's events

Zheng takes sensational gold in 100m Backstroke – S6

Tao Zheng (CHN) became the first Paralympic Swimming champion at London 2012 when he won the 100m Backstroke – S6 in world record time. Zheng, with a technique that brought rapturous applause from the capacity crowd in the Aquatics Centre, pulled away in the last 25m to touch in 1:13.56. His teammate, Hongguang Jia (CHN) took the silver medal while the fast-finishing Sebastian Iwanow of Germany snatched the bronze.

Fox opens Britain's medal account with gold in 100m Backstroke – S7

A world record of 1:09.86 in the heats served notice that Great Britain's Jonathan Fox was ready to improve on the silver medal he won at Beijing 2008 and the 21-year-old did not disappoint. Fox, from Newquay, was slower in the final but still too good for the rest, taking the gold medal with 1:10.46. The silver medallist, Yevheniy Bohodayko of Ukraine was more than half a second behind, while Mihovil Spanja of Croatia came third in 1:12.53.

Fox said, 'My plan was to go for the world

Powerhouse. Great Britain's Jonathan Fox swims in a 100m Freestyle – S7 heat. He went onto win gold in the 100m Backstroke – S7.

record in the final but it's all about trying to get that gold medal around your neck so I'm happy. I didn't know that it was Great Britain's first [Paralympic] gold medal in the Aquatics Centre. I am so focused on my own swim that I never know what's going on in the outside world.'

Wang denies the Hynd brothers to win the 400m Freestyle – S8

It happened at the Olympic Games and it happened again at the Paralympic Games: a young swimmer from China sprang a surprise in the Aquatics Centre.

On this occasion, it was the 22-year-old Yinan Wang who set a fast pace from the blocks that no one else was able to match. It meant that the Hynd brothers from Great Britain had to be content with silver and bronze medals.

Sam Hynd (GBR), the defending champion and world record holder, was the fastest qualifier from the morning's heats and the favourite for gold, while his younger brother, Oliver Hynd (GBR), went into the final as the Home Nation's hope for the silver.

Sam Hynd had the best start but it was Wang who assumed the lead just after the halfway point. Oliver had his time in the lead but Wang proved himself strongest of the three and pipped the Briton to the wall in 4:27.11. Oliver Hynd was second in 4:27.88 while his brother Sam took the bronze, his third Paralympic medal, in 4:32.93.

'Sharkman' wins bronze medal in 100m Butterfly – S10

Achmat Hassiem (RSA) was encouraged by South Africa's top swimmer, Natalie du Toit, to try Paralympic Swimming after he lost his right foot in a shark attack while lifeguard training. He finished ninth in the 100m Butterfly – S10 at Beijing 2008 but in the Aquatics Centre, the 30-year-old Hassiem, known as 'Sharkman', won the bronze medal in 57.76. Gold went to Andre Brasil of Brazil in a Paralympic record of 56.35 while the Russian Federation's Dmitry Grigorev touched the wall second in 56.89.

Yinan Wang (CHN) celebrates winning gold in the men's 400m Freestyle - S8.

Sharkman's in the water. (Left to right) David Levecq of Spain, Dmitry Grigorev (RUS) and Achmat Hassiem (RSA) in the men's 100m Butterfly – S10.

World record for Dias in 100m Breaststroke – SB4

Daniel Dias of Brazil broke the world record twice in a day as he powered to his third of six gold medals at London 2012, this time in the men's 100m Breaststroke – SB4, clocking 1:32.27. In the morning heats, the 24-year-old, who won nine medals at Beijing 2008, broke the record set by Ricardo Ten of Spain – for the first time.

The final saw Dias establish an unbeatable lead on his way to breaking the world record for the second time, and it was left to the 37-year-old Ten and Moises Fuentes Garcia (COL) to fight it out for the silver medal. That battle was won by Fuentes Garcia, who touched in 1:36.92 while Ten won bronze in 1:37.23.

Craig shocks even himself with gold in the 400m Freestyle – S7

Great Britain discovered a new superstar in the pool when 15-year-old Josef Craig twice broke the world record on his way to winning gold in the men's 400m Freestyle – S7. Tipped as a swimmer with enormous potential, not even Craig expected to reach such dizzy heights in his first Paralympic Games. He set a world record in the heats and then came from the middle of the pack to win the final in 4:42.81. Behind him in the silver medal position was Shiyun Pan (CHN) at 4:46.22. Bronze went to another 15-year-old, Andrey Gladkov of the Russian Federation in 4:46.76. Jonathan Fox (GBR), the 100m Backstroke champion and former world record holder, finished fourth.

Xu produces his best to win the 50m Butterfly – S6

Qing Xu produced another astonishing performance to win his third gold medal of the London 2012 Paralympic Games in a world record of 29.90. Still only 19, the swimmer, who won three gold medals at Beijing 2008, lost both

Amazing and amazed. Gold medallist Josef Craig of Great Britain poses on the podium during the Victory Ceremony.

forearms in a car accident in 1998. Xu, who won four gold medals at London 2012, said, 'This was the most important race because the 50m Butterfly is very challenging. New, good swimmers are coming up every year … I know I'm good, but I am surprised. My training over the past four years has not been wasted.'

Women's events

Du Toit resumes winning ways in the 100m Butterfly – S9

Natalie du Toit of South Africa confirmed that these would be her last Paralympic Games after winning the first of the three gold medals she would collect at the Aquatics Centre. The 28-year-old from Cape Town, who made history by competing in the 10km Marathon Swim at the Beijing 2008 Olympic Games, secured the win in the 100m Butterfly – S9

'It's very good to break records, but it's even better when you're not expecting it.'

Daniel Dias (BRA), 100m Breaststroke – SB4 gold medallist

Retiring champion Natalie du Toit (RSA) tears up the pool in the women's 200m Individual Medley – SM9 heat.

'I'm done – it's very official. It's sad, but I walk away knowing I gave it everything.'

Natalie du Toit (RSA) on her retirement from swimming

Right: Crowd favourite. An emotional Ellie Simmonds of Great Britain waves to spectators after winning gold in the women's 400m Freestyle – S6.

competing against myself and setting new goals for everyone. Records are made to be broken.'

Simmonds shows perfect timing in 400m Freestyle – S6

Ellie Simmonds (GBR) made her name by winning two gold medals in the pool at Beijing 2008 at just 13 years of age. At London 2012, she became an international heroine.

For 350m, Simmonds trailed her great rival, Victoria Arlen (USA), who had broken Simmonds' world record earlier in 2012. But the gap was never more than a few strokes and, at the final turn, the pair were level. Over the closing 50m, Simmonds' superior stamina helped her pull away to set a new world record of 5:19.17. Arlen clocked 5:20.18, which was inside her previous world record. Lingling Song claimed the bronze medal in 5:33.73 for China.

An exhausted Simmonds slapped the water in triumph when she turned and saw the winning

in 1:09.30, ahead of Sarai Gascon of Spain and Elizabeth Stone of the USA.

Du Toit, who won five gold medals at the Beijing 2008 and Athens 2004 Paralympic Games, went on to add two silver medals to her amazing collection.

Long dominates to win the 400m Freestyle – S8

Jessica Long (USA) is no stranger to winning gold medals and this, her ninth, came after what must rate as her most emphatic victory. The 20-year-old, who was born in Siberia and adopted from a Russian orphanage at 13 months, had already notched up one gold medal at London 2012, in the 100m Butterfly – S8, and won her second title at these Paralympic Games, breaking her own world record with 4:42.28. Long led from the start and finished more than 18 seconds ahead of the silver medallist, Heather Frederiksen of Great Britain. Maddison Elliott (AUS) took the bronze medal in 5:09.36.

It was a dominant performance by the swimmer who won three gold medals at Athens 2004 when she was just 12 years old. Long said, 'I swam my heart out and I gave it everything I had. That was the goal, to go in and break the world record. I set my goals very, very high and I feel like I'm always

Versatile Ellie Simmonds shows a champion's form in the women's 200m Individual Medley – SM6 final.

'That atmosphere, it's just unbelievable. I'm on a high all the time. I don't want it to end at all.'

Ellie Simmonds, double gold medallist

time. She grinned as she lapped up the rapturous applause from the capacity crowd in the Aquatics Centre. 'I can't believe I did it. It was so tough. I could see Arlen on the last 100m and I thought, "I've just got to put my head down and do it for all the people who have supported me". I knew Victoria was going to be on her game tonight. I just put my head down and went for it. I did it for myself. I did it for my family.'

Simmonds swims for gold in the 200m Individual Medley – SM6

Ellie Simmonds won her second gold medal at London 2012 and threw in a couple of world records just for good measure as the British success in the pool continued. She trailed during the butterfly, backstroke and breaststroke legs before launching her attack on the freestyle 50m. After a surprise world record in the heats, she improved her time to 3:05.39. Verena Schott of Germany was a long way back in second at 3:14.28 and Natalie Jones (GBR) earned the bronze in 3:14.29.

Frederikson retains her title in 100m Backstroke – S8

Five days after losing to Jessica Long (USA) in the 400m Freestyle – S8, Great Britain's Heather Frederiksen turned the tables on her rival by winning gold and retaining her title in the 100m Backstroke – S8. Her performance was all the more astonishing because illness at the start of the year had reduced Frederiksen's serious training for the Paralympic Games to just six weeks. 'That race meant absolutely everything to me,' she revealed. 'Yesterday, I was really, really nervous and I was nervous again tonight but I was determined I was going to fight and I was going to win it. And fight and win it I did.'

Olesya Vladykina (RUS) led from the start but Frederiksen began to assert her dominance at 50m. Frederiksen powered clear down the final 50m and won by a body length in 1:17.00, ahead of Long, who touched in 1:18.67 and Vladykina at 1:20.20.

History

Swimming has featured at every Paralympic Games since Rome 1960. Until 1990, swimmers with the same impairment competed against each other but in 1991 a sophisticated classification system was developed to allow swimmers to race one another regardless of their impairment.

A champion prepares. Ellie Cole of Australia makes final adjustments before going for gold in the 100m Backstroke – S9.

Gold for Cole and silver lining for Millward in 100m Backstroke – S9

Ellie Cole (AUS) won the gold medal in the women's 100m Backstroke – S9 and the race was also a triumph for the silver medallist, Stephanie Millward (GBR).

Millward, 30, was on the verge of international recognition as a non-disabled swimmer when she contracted multiple sclerosis at the age of 15. Her first of five medals at London 2012 came as the Swansea-based swimmer clocked 1:11.07 behind Cole's 1:09.42. The bronze medal went to Elizabeth Stone (USA) in 1:12.28.

World record victory for Freney in 200m Individual Medley – SM7

There was no stopping Australia's Jacqueline Freney in the Aquatics Centre. The 20-year-old student from New South Wales left London 2012 with a 100 per cent record, winning all six of her individual finals. She also took two gold medals as a member of Australia's 4 x 100m Freestyle Relay – 34 Points and 4 x 100 Medley Relay – 34 Points teams.

In the 200m Individual Medley – SM7, the three-time bronze medallist at Beijing 2008 led after the butterfly lap and increased her lead over the ensuing lengths. On the freestyle leg, she was 15m clear and going away, eventually touching for her third gold in 2:54.42 to break the world record. Brianna Nelson (CAN) won the silver medal in 3:04.60. Min Huang (CHN) took the bronze in 3:07.51.

'It's a great achievement ... My dad, grandparents, mum and sister are all here and they couldn't be prouder. It definitely makes a difference having them here and having my dad as coach. All his energies have gone into me.'

Jacqueline Freney (AUS), 200m Individual Medley – SM7 gold medallist

Opposite: Crystal blue persuasion. For a few moments, the Paralympic Swimming competitors can't hear the encouraging roar of spectators in the Aquatics Centre.

Paralympic Table Tennis

Eye on the ball. ParalympicsGB's Will Bayley serves during his men's Singles – Class 7 gold medal match against Germany's Jochen Wollmert.

Classification

1-5 Athletes with a physical impairment that affects their legs who compete in wheelchairs. The lower the number, the greater the impact the impairment has on an athlete's ability to compete.
6-10 Athletes with a physical impairment competing standing up. The lower the number, the greater the impact the impairment has on an athlete's ability to compete.
11 Athletes with an intellectual impairment.

Opposite: Great British success. Great Britain's Sara Head (left) and Jane Campbell celebrate winning a bronze medal in the women's Team – Class 1–3 competition.

Men's events

Wonderful Wollmert wins gold in Singles – Class 7

Germany's Jochen Wollmert won the gold medal in the men's Singles – Class 7 in an emotional contest that saw him defeat Great Britain's Will Bayley 3–1.

At the end of the action-packed match Bayley, 24, lay on the floor in tears. He seemed inconsolable in defeat until, in a fatherly gesture, 47-year-old Wollmert walked around the table, lifted the young player to his feet and raised his arm in salute to the cheering crowd. The German, whose lethal top-spin had bamboozled Bayley, had been expecting the silver medal after losing nine out of 10 encounters with the young British player. 'It was a big game and a fantastic crowd. My dream was to make the final against the local matador, Will,' he revealed.

Bayley gained hordes of new fans when images of him leaping into his coach's arms after the semi-final were shown on television across the world. His silver was Great Britain's first in the men's Paralympic Table Tennis Singles competition since Neil Robinson's at Atlanta 1996, and the first medal of any colour since Athens 2004. He apologised for not winning the gold medal, conceding 'I think I was too pumped up and maybe I wanted it a bit too much. The atmosphere was amazing … maybe I just went after it a bit too much. Jochen was very cool and calm.'

Mykhaylo Popov of the Ukraine took the bronze medal in a 3–2 win against compatriot Maxym Nikolenko.

Nikelis triumphs in quick-fire Singles – Class 1 final

Germany's Holger Nikelis defeated Jean-Francois Ducay of France 3–1 in a quick-fire final to win the gold medal in the Singles – Class 1.

The match for the bronze medal saw an upset when ParalympicsGB's Paul Davies beat world number four Chang Ho Lee of Korea, a player four places above him in the world rankings. The Welshman, 45, came from 2–1 down to level the fourth game, then surrendered two match points in the fifth game before securing victory. 'I've been playing for 21 years and now I'm a Paralympic bronze medallist,' said the delighted champion after the match.

Women's events

Powerful Partyka wins gold in Singles – Class 10

The gold medal in the women's Singles – Class 10 was won by the amazing Natalia Partyka of Poland, 23, who has never lost a match in 12 years

of Paralympic competition. Like Oscar Pistorious, she also participated in the London 2012 Olympic Games, where she finished in the last 32 of the Table Tennis competition.

Her 16-year-old opponent in the Paralympic event, Qian Yang of China, exploited Partyka's nerves as the burden of expectation weighed heavily on the champion, testing her skill and composure. But Partyka's powerfully strong play, mental toughness and light-footed action around the table ensured that she prevailed 3–2 over the teenager to claim her third consecutive gold medal. 'I'm very happy that I won,' said the relieved Partyka. 'It's not easy to play when everyone wants to beat you. That's pressure.'

Yang said that playing at London 2012 had improved her confidence. 'I feel really excited because this is my first international competition and also my first Paralympic Games. Experience is really important for me, especially as I am so young,' she explained. The bronze medal match saw Lei Fan of China beat Melissa Tapper of Australia 3–2.

Chebanika powers to gold in Singles – Class 6

Raisa Chebanika of the Russian Federation took the gold medal in the women's Singles – Class 6 less than a year after undergoing complex brain surgery. The 48-year-old defeated her tough Ukrainian opponent, Antonina Khodzynsk, 3–0

to complete a remarkable recovery by becoming Paralympic champion. Yuliya Klymenko, also of the Ukraine, beat Germany's Stephanie Grebe 3–1 to take the bronze.

Classy China retain title in Team – Class 1–3

China defended their Team – Class 1–3 Paralympic title, winning gold by defeating Korea 3–0.

The win meant double gold for Jing Liu, the Singles Class 1–2 champion, who won a thrilling five-set first match, while her teammate Qian Li won both her matches.

ParalympicsGB's Sara Head and Jane Campbell won the bronze medal, beating Italy 3–2 after a dramatic fight back from two sets down. Head said the home crowd had spurred the squad to play their best. 'The roar of the crowd, it was just phenomenal,' she revealed. 'To have everybody waving and cheering, what more can you ask for? They were helping me get the ball over. It was unbelievable.' Great Britain, who had failed to win any medals at Beijing 2008, took one silver and three bronze medals from the London 2102 Table Tennis tournament.

'For two weeks I was lying between life and death, unconscious. There were doubts about me playing here. I prayed to God to win and he answered my prayers.'

Raisa Chebanika, the Russian Federation's women's Singles – Class 6 gold medallist

Above left: Table Tennis star. Poland's Natalia Partyka serves during the women's Singles – Class 10 gold medal match. She continued her amazing run of never losing a match in 12 years of Paralympic competition with her win over Qian Yang of China.

Wheelchair Fencing

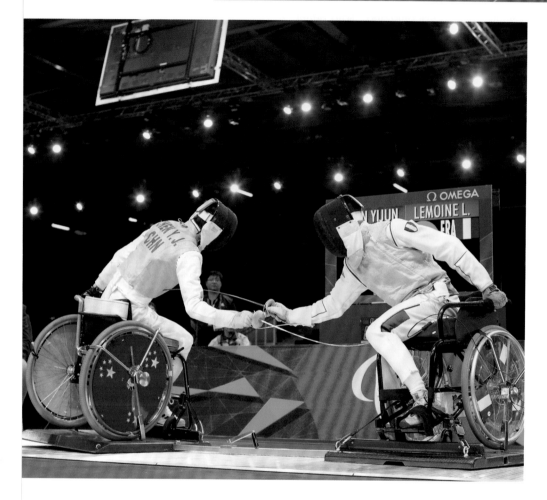

Above: Yijun Chen of China (left) and Ludovic Lemoine of France (right) compete in the Team – Open final at ExCeL. China, the world champions, added Olympic gold to their collection.

Classification

A Athletes with full trunk movement and good balance.
B Athletes with an impairment that affects either their trunk or fencing arm.

Men's event

China on top in the Team – Open

China went into these Paralympic Games as the world champions and their line-up included two gold medallists from the individual Foil categories at London 2012. Therefore, it was no surprise that the China equipe of Yijun Chen, Ruyi Ye and Daoliang Hu made it through to the final. The surprise lay in the fact that their opponents were not Hong Kong, China, as expected, but France.

In the final, China went into a 10–1 lead thanks to victories by Chen and Ye, but France responded well with wins for Damien Tokatlian and Ludovic Lemoine, who both beat Hu, a player from Category B, for those fencers with an impairment that affects either their trunk or fencing arm. China's lead was thereby reduced to 25–23.

Chen then won all three of his bouts and Hu beat Alim Latreche, France's Category B fencer. A drawn ninth and final bout between Ye and Lemoine assured China of a 45–32 victory and the gold medal. It was China's sixth Fencing gold and tenth Fencing medal of these Paralympic Games.

Hong Kong, China won the bronze medal after they beat Italy in a close 45–42 match.

Women's events

Yu beats Wu for gold in the Foil – Category A

The 28-year-old Chui Yee Yu of Hong Kong, China became a three-time Paralympic gold medallist after successfully defending the Foil – Category A title she won at Athens 2004 and Beijing 2008.

During the Paralympic Games, she was also successful in retaining her seat on the IPC's athletes' council and will be one of six athletes who will act for her fellow Paralympians in the run-up to Rio 2016.

In the final, she beat Baili Wu of China 15–13. Both women defeated Hungarians in their semi-finals, and in the bronze medal match, it was the world number one, Zsuzsanna Krajnyak, who prevailed over Veronika Juhasz.

China overcome determined Hungary to win Team – Open gold

Hungary's clever fencers offered stiff resistance, but it was China who took the gold medal in this absorbing final of the women's Team – Open 45–38.

After Veronika Juhasz opened Hungary's account with a defensive display that gave China a 1–0 lead, Zsuszanna Krajnyak took full advantage of being the Category A fencer by opening up a 10–2 lead in the second bout against her Category B opponent, Fang Yao.

The advantage was quickly wiped out, however, when the roles were reversed and Baili Wu claimed a 13–3 victory over Gyongyi Dani.

From then on, China scored consistently to win three of the remaining rounds, draw two of them and lose one by a single point, securing the gold medal.

The bronze medal match saw Hong Kong, China beat Poland 45–26.

Opposite: The champion. Yijun Chen celebrates winning the gold medal in the Sabre – Category A final. China won a total of 10 medals during the Wheelchair Fencing competition, six gold.

The Sport

Swashbuckling sword fighting is an ancient art but Wheelchair Fencing was developed in the 1940s at the Stoke Mandeville Hospital, the birthplace of the Paralympic Games. Fencers use three weapons – the epée, which is the heaviest, the lighter foil and the sabre, which is based on the cavalry sword. The sabre can only hit above the waist and the rule has its origins in the days when it was considered discourteous to hit a man's horse.

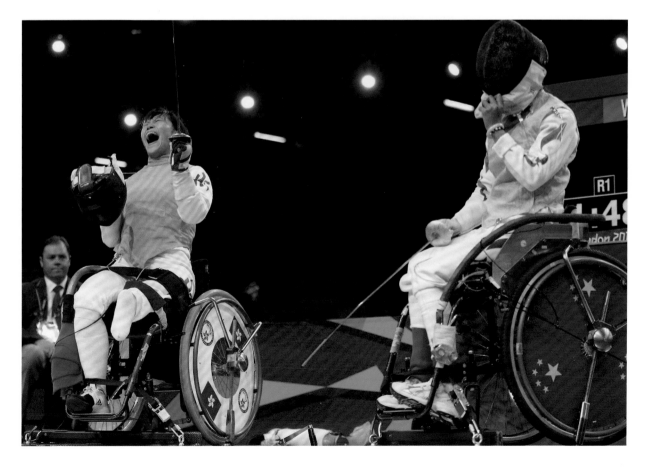

Left: Chui Yee Yu of Hong Kong, China is ecstatic after her win against Baili Wu of China. Yu defended her Foil – Category A title won at Athens 2004 and Beijing 2008.

Wheelchair Rugby

Catch me if you can. Australia's Wheelchair Rugby star Ryley Batt dodges the advancing Canadian side during their gold medal match. Batt was named Man of the Match at the end of the final.

Classification

Every player is assigned a point value – there are seven classes, from 0.5 to 3.5 – based on their physical function. The lower the number, the more severe the impairment. The total for the four players on the court at any time must not exceed 8; for each female player a team fields on court, the points maximum increases by 0.5.

'This has been a huge competition for Wheelchair Rugby. I played at Sydney 2000 and it has become hugely popular since. It has possibly even bypassed Wheelchair Basketball now.'

Brad Dubberley, Coach of the gold medal-winning Australian Wheelchair Rugby team

Batt stars as Australia take Wheelchair Rugby gold

The eagerly anticipated Wheelchair Rugby final saw an impressive performance by Ryley Batt secure the gold medal for Australia, who defeated Canada 66–51. The 23-year-old, named Man of the Match after the final on the last day of the Paralympic Games, ended the competition having scored a remarkable 161 points in the five matches he played.

The sport, originally called murderball and well known for its crashes and spills, did not disappoint at London 2012, attracting sell-out crowds to the Basketball Arena. However, the Paralympic Games matches proved that there was more to the game than that, with the crowds also coming to appreciate the level of skill involved.

Batt, from Port Macquarie in New South Wales, opened the scoring after only 30 seconds. He led from the front as Australia scored freely and displayed a defensive capability that stopped Canada doing the same. Numerous times Batt made his presence felt with defensive blocks and interceptions, as well as feeding telling passes to teammates Chris Bond and Naz Erdem. His speed on the court was often dazzling, as was his ability to spin on a sixpence to avoid trouble and so thwart Canada's attempts to find a way through.

Australia piled on the points through the second quarter as Canada, bronze medallists at Beijing 2008 and the team responsible for putting the USA, the defending champions, out of the final, found Batt too hot to handle.

By half-time the Australia lead was 34–21, and the result was rarely in doubt.

Ben Newton did score for Canada at the resumption of play, but, while both teams matched each other's efforts, Australia's lead was never reduced.

There were no complaints from Canada after the match. 'It's disappointing to not win, but the better team won on the day,' coach Kevin Orr observed.

As for Batt, he looked forward to celebrating with a beer and a meal after winning gold at his third Paralympic Games. 'Third time lucky,' he laughed. 'You can only go one better than silver and that's a gold … I know I've trained so hard over the last four years and so has the team to get to this point and it's finally paid off.'

The USA, who were beaten 50–49 by Canada, took the bronze medal after comfortably winning their play-off with Japan 53–43. The Great Britain team matched their world ranking by securing fifth place after defeating Sweden, the European champions, 59–47.

Above: Garett Hickling of Canada (centre) retains possession of the ball as the Australian team move to block him. However, the Canadian team could not reduce the lead that Australia held throughout.

Left: Third time lucky. Ryley Batt clashes with the Canadian team as Australia take control to win the gold medal. It was Batt's third Paralympic Games, and his first gold.

Wheelchair Tennis

Shingo Kunieda of Japan grimaces with exertion in the Wheelchair Tennis final against Stephane Houdet of France.

Classification

Open Athletes with an impairment of one or both legs that does not affect their arms or hands.

Quad Athletes with an impairment that affects their arms and legs, which limits their ability to handle the racket and to move their wheelchair compared with Open athletes.

Men's events

Kunieda wins Singles under golden sunset

Playing under a glorious sky illuminated by Eton Manor's floodlights, Japan's Shingo Kunieda became the first man to retain the men's Singles gold medal when he beat the top seed, Stephane Houdet of France, 6–4, 6–2.

Kunieda, 28, was at his tenacious best, chasing down Houdet's groundstrokes and easing ahead after converting his second set point. The high-quality match, played before a capacity 5,000-strong crowd, saw both players wheeling to all four corners of the court to retrieve seemingly lost causes and produce winners. In the end Kunieda, a Doubles gold medallist at Athens 2004, proved the stronger. The bronze medal match, between two players

from the Netherlands, was far closer. Ronald Vink eventually defeated Maikel Scheffers 4–6, 7–6, 6–4.

Sweden serve up Doubles surprise

Stefan Olsson and Peter Vikstrom came into the Paralympic Games seeded sixth, but defied the rankings to win gold in just over an hour.

The Beijing 2008 silver medallists beat both number three seeds from the Netherlands, Tom Egberink and Maikel Scheffers, in the quarter-finals and defending champions Stephane Houdet and Michael Jeremiasz of France in the semi-finals. In the final they defeated France's Frederic Cattaneo and Nicolas Peifer, seeded four, 6–1, 6–2.

The bronze medal match saw Houdet and Jeremiasz beat Robin Ammerlaan and Ronald Vink of the Netherlands 6–0, 6–0.

Women's events

Invincible Vergeer extends unbeaten run to another Singles gold

Esther Vergeer from the Netherlands won her 470th consecutive match in women's Wheelchair Tennis to take her fourth Paralympic Games gold medal. The 31-year-old was never in trouble in her 6–0, 6–3 defeat of compatriot Aniek van Koot, the only player to have tested her in recent years.

Blessed with warm sunshine, the crowd saw Vergeer at her best, spraying shots around the court and wrapping up the first set against a nervous van Koot in 23 minutes.

Jiske Griffioen completed a clean sweep of the medals for the Netherlands by beating Sabine Ellerbrock of Germany to claim bronze.

Vergeer adds Doubles gold in all-Netherlands final

The Netherlands domination of the Paralympic Games Tennis tournament continued in the women's Doubles final, where the all-conquering Esther Vergeer teamed up with Marjolein Buis to beat compatriots Jiske Griffioen and Aniek van Koot, 6–1, 6–3.

The women's competition also saw the Great British pairing of Lucy Shuker and Jordanne Whiley become the first British women to win a Wheelchair Tennis medal at the Paralympic Games. In an epic, three-set, three-hour match, supported by the crowd, they defeated the battling but tiring Sakhorn Khanthasit and Ratana Techameneewat of Thailand 6–7, 7–6, 6–3 to secure bronze.

Mixed events

Gershony wins Israel's first gold in the Quad Singles

A changing of the guard in the Quad Singles saw Great Britain's two-time defending champion Peter Norfolk go out in the quarter-finals, while a former helicopter pilot, Noam Gershony, won the title for Israel in his first Paralympic Games.

In less than an hour Gershony, 29, who only took up the sport seriously in 2008, beat the top seed, David Wagner of the USA, 6–3, 6–1. Wagner's Quad Doubles partner, Nick Taylor of the USA, took the Quad Singles bronze medal. The only player to use a power chair, Taylor threw the ball up with his feet and served underarm to defeat Shraga Weinberg of Israel 1–6, 6–3, 6–4.

USA hat-trick in Quad Doubles

A hat-trick of gold medals for the USA pair of David Wagner and Nick Taylor meant heartache for Great Britain's Peter Norfolk and Andy Lapthorne after an emotional Quad Doubles final.

The USA pairing's hard-fought 6–2, 5–7, 6–2 victory marked the first time a Wheelchair Doubles pair had won three consecutive Paralympic gold medals since the sport joined the programme at Athens 2004.

It was also the last Paralympic Games match for Norfolk, 51. Quad Singles champion at Athens 2004 and Beijing 2008, he had also won silver and bronze medals in the Doubles at both previous Games.

Above: Marjolein Buis (right) and Esther Vergeer (left) of the Netherlands celebrate winning the gold medal in their Doubles match against Jiske Griffioen and Aniek Van Koot, also of the Netherlands.

Below: Nicholas Taylor (USA) and his partner David Wagner take on Britain's Andy Lapthorne and Peter Norfolk in the Quad Doubles at Eton Manor.

Paralympic Games Closing Ceremony

At the Paralympic Games Closing Ceremony, Lord Coe found the perfect phrase to sum up London 2012: 'There are some famous words you can find stamped on the bottom of a product,' he told the 80,000 people in the Olympic Stadium and the millions watching on television. 'Words that, when you read them, you know mean high quality, mean skill, mean creativity. We have stamped those words on the Olympic and Paralympic Games of London 2012. "London 2012. Made in Britain."'

Entitled 'The Festival of the Flame', the Paralympic Games Closing Ceremony summoned the fire and energy that were present at every venue, at every event, in the heart of everyone there, by stoking the spirit of the Games. Director Kim Gavin chose the flame motif to mark the passing of the seasons, and fire – a universal symbol of beginnings and endings – was the dominant theme throughout.

To start the proceedings, Flagbearers of the 164 participating nations – including Great Britain's Sarah Storey and David Weir – gathered in the middle of the infield to create a heart shape around the central Sundial Stage. Captain Luke Sinnott, who lost both legs while serving in Afghanistan, climbed to the top of the flag pole to hang the Union flag. Lissa Hermans, who is blind and autistic, performed a moving rendition of the National Anthem.

'The stars, how they shine for you'

Central to the celebrations were Coldplay who were, in their own words, 'honoured' to be a part of the Paralympic Closing Ceremony. It was their rousing anthems, so suited to stadium concerts around the world, that filled the air as a cast of

Above: Head for heights. Captain Luke Sinnott climbs to hang the Union flag over the Olympic Stadium. He was chosen as part of a tribute to the armed forces and the work of forces charity Help for Heroes.

ParalympicsGB stars. Great Britain's Ellie Simmonds and Jonnie Peacock light their Torches from the Paralympic Flame. They extinguished the Flame to signal the end of London 2012.

Above: Prince Edward, Earl of Wessex (left) and Sir Philip Craven, President of the International Paralympic Committee, arrive at the Olympic Stadium. Their carriage was made out of second-hand cars.

Left: The Sun King burns spectacularly during the Paralympic Closing Ceremony. He symbolised death and rebirth, along with his counterpart, the Snow Queen.

1,336 volunteers, 120 children and more than 200 professional dancers, actors and acrobats performed around them.

The band performed many of their greatest hits, including *Us Against the World, Paradise, Clocks* and *Up in Flames* but it was their classic *Yellow* that allowed the real star of the show to shine. The array of lights in the Olympic Stadium bathed everything in yellow, and the pixels – dazzling LEDs attached to the back of the seats – illuminated the crowd. Adding to the warm glow inside the Olympic Stadium was a huge, flaming Sun King that rose from centre-stage as the 12 members of Candoco, a contemporary dance company for non-disabled and disabled performers, created the flame dance.

Fantastical trucks like the Clamposaurus, the Hellcopter and the Beast from the East – pieces of Soviet MiG21 fighter planes rescued from East Berlin welded onto the chassis of an East German all-terrain army vehicle, roared around the Olympic Stadium, surrounded by fireflies, flying motorbikes and crows on stilts. Mat Fraser, who was born with phocomelia, was on stage drumming with Coldplay. There were rousing tributes to the 70,000 volunteers and Games Makers, and it was only fitting that Jonnie Peacock and Ellie Simmonds, two home-grown Paralympic champions, took centre-stage to douse the Cauldron that had been lit from flames created on Britain's highest peaks.

Sir Phillip Craven, the President of the International Paralympic Committee, called the Paralympic Games 'an event absolutely no one wants to end'.

The final word, however, should lie with Lord Coe, Chair of LOCOG. 'In this country, we will never think of sport the same way and we will never think of disability the same way. The Paralympians have lifted the cloud of limitation.'

Overleaf: Bidding farewell. Athletes and spectators look on as the London 2012 Paralympic Games are brought to an impressive close with 'The Festival of the Flame'.

Chapter Five
The London 2012
Festival

The London 2012 Festival

'We're trying to put art back into the heart of the Games ... Pierre de Coubertin wanted art, education and sport to be the three pillars of the Games ... I hope that our artistic commissions will rest in peoples' hearts and souls, as well as remaining as a physical legacy.'

Ruth Mackenzie, Director of the Cultural Olympiad and London 2012 Festival

LOCOG were determined to rejuvenate the original concept of sport, art and education forming the 'three pillars' at the heart of the Games. They succeeded in a spectacular way, with the sporting festival inspiring the biggest explosion of cultural creativity in Britain since the 1960s. The London 2012 Festival ran for the four years leading up to the Games, offering thousands of performers and artists a focal point to display their skills and culminating in a blaze of artistic activity held over 12 weeks during the summer of 2012. Now regarded as the finest Cultural Olympiad of the modern era, its aim throughout was to attract new people, especially young people, into culture for the first time, all over the UK. Thousands of large and small events were staged across Britain during the four years, from festive trailblazers to the grand finale of the London 2012 Festival, which ran from 21 June to 9 September 2012.

Even as the Olympiad inspired some of the brightest lights from the arts, it also encouraged individuals to enjoy new opportunities on offer. LOCOG launched its programme with an Open Weekend in 2008 that drew out talent and creativity from hundreds of local events, from Cornwall to Inverness. Museums and galleries opened up their vaults to reveal hidden treasures; theatres and opera houses threw wide their doors to allow enthusiasts to take the stage; crowds of strangers came together to dance, sing, paint and retell age-old stories in famous venues. The event proved so successful that it was replicated for the next three summers, with participant numbers increasing every year. Over one million people flocked to the 2011 Open Weekend that marked 'one year to go'. 'We've always been clear that London 2012 is about more than just sport,'

commented Lord Coe, Chair of LOCOG. 'We created Open Weekend as part of the Cultural Olympiad, to enable people to share in the countdown celebrations towards London 2012, but also be inspired by the Games to discover new interests and develop their talents.'

At the heart of every event was the desire to inspire the next generation, with many projects offering young people their first taste of singing, animation, film-making and writing. One London 2012 Festival project set a Guinness World Record for the most individual contributions to an animated film, *The Itch of the Golden Nit*. More than 35,000 children contributed to the art, script, musical score and production of this remarkable film, organised by the Tate Movie Project. It drew upon material from over 250 workshops across the UK, transferred in tens of thousands of uploads to an online movie studio. The engaging plot tells the story of 11-year-old Beanie, who undertakes a mission to save his parents from Evil Stella and return the Golden Nit, the battery that powers the sun, to its rightful place in the solar core – and so save the universe from collapse. Sir Nicholas Serota, Director of Tate and Design Champion for the Olympic Delivery Authority (ODA) and LOCOG, praised the achievements of those who took part, noting that 'This project has provoked some astonishing work by children of all backgrounds, some of whom may well be the artists and creatives of the future.'

In another London 2012 Festival activity, the National Portrait Gallery in London launched the BP Portrait Award: Next Generation – an extension of its annual Portrait Award and exhibition. Hundreds of teenagers nationwide, many of whom had never set foot in an art gallery before, joined in a series

Compagnie Carabosse light up the World Heritage site of Stonehenge with a fire garden as part of the London 2012 Festival.

of free workshops that encouraged them to paint or draw portraits. They were guided by past winners of the Award. Londoner Bryan Lanas, aged 19, was one of those who participated. 'It was great being surrounded by like-minded young people and seeing the differences in style that each one of us had,' he said. 'It was a massive learning experience. I learned how to explore line shape and tone differently, and how to loosen up and be more expressive.' Lanas is now considering entering for next year's Award, and is looking at a career in the creative industry. 'I would definitely encourage young people to apply for a spot,' he added. 'It changes the way you think and may even change your life.'

The London 2012 Festival team also encouraged artists and performers to adopt Olympian aspirations on the field of play, urging participants to immerse themselves in their personal and artistic Olympic goals. Ruth Mackenzie, Director of the Cultural Olympiad and London 2012 Festival, described how her team approached potential artists, amateur and professional, to participate in this unique event. 'We encouraged ordinary community members, children and adults, to go beyond their personal best to learn a new creative skill. We commissioned great artists from around the world and we asked those great artists to try something new, dangerous, risky, extraordinary, to go beyond their personal best in Olympic terms, to come up with a once on a lifetime commission that would stand up to the once in a lifetime opportunity of the Games in this country in 2012.' It was a compelling invitation that struck a rich creative vein.

An innovative commission in the south east was the Boat Project, based upon an idea by artists Gary Winters and Gregg Whelan. The

'Made weak by time and fate but strong in will To strive, to seek, to find, and not to yield.'

The final lines of Alfred Lord Tennyson's poem *Ulysses*, engraved in stone in the Olympic Park

Collective Spirit. The result of the Boat Project which combined 1,200 pieces of wooden material donated by the public, takes to the water for the first time.

'It put us on our toes and taught us new tricks from cultures abroad and their different takes on Shakespeare.'

Michael Boyd applauds the Shakespeare Festival's impact on actors, directors and audiences

Above and right: Actors from the Iraqi Theatre Company rehearse a scene from Romeo and *Juliet in Baghdad.* Drawing on the country's rich traditions of music, poetry and ritual, the work was performed at the Swan Theatre in Stratford as part of the World Shakespeare Festival.

Boat, created by Olympic silver medallist Mark Covell and Simon Rogers, an international yacht designer, was built at Thornham Marina in West Sussex, in a process that took over a year. It was constructed from 1,200 pieces of wooden material donated by the public, full of personal associations and memories, which were then woven into the hull of the 9m yacht to create a living archive. They included pieces of wood from the Tudor warship *Mary Rose,* a fragment of Jimi Hendrix's guitar, a Victorian police truncheon, a plank from the London 2012 Velodrome and a section of Brighton's West Pier. 'The callout was for objects which had a significance and a story,' explained Winters, '… and we were given some lovely, lovely things, personal and emotional items.' The yacht, appropriately named *Collective Spirit,* took to the water on 7 May 2012. In July it sailed along the south coast to the Sailing venue in Weymouth and Portland, Dorset, where it proved a popular attraction for visitors during the Games.

'All the world's a stage'
One of the cornerstones of the London 2012 Festival was the World Shakespeare Festival. The biggest celebration of the Bard's work ever staged saw 70 productions performed at the home of the Royal Shakespeare Company in Stratford-upon-Avon and across the UK. The Globe Theatre, reconstructed on its original site by the Thames in London, held performances of all 37 of Shakespeare's plays in 37 languages. The Iraqi Theatre Company left the audience at Stratford's Swan Theatre spellbound by its emotionally charged production of *Romeo and Juliet,* set in present-day Baghdad.

The London 2012 Festival also brought new performers to Shakespeare, such as actress Meera Syal. She made her Shakespearean debut as Beatrice in *Much Ado About Nothing,* directed by Iqbal Khan and set in modern India. Syal observed that many of Shakespeare's plots could have come from a Bollywood film, and she believed many performers took the opportunity offered by the Olympiad to push their own artistic boundaries.

'I feel like I'm taking part in something historic,' she explained. 'I think people have used the Olympic and Paralympic Games to push the barriers. We want to show the world that we have artistic riches and a spirit of innovation. We're not just doing the safe stuff. We're doing the stuff that makes people go "wow, Britain is still cool".'

Michael Boyd, the outgoing Artistic Director of the Royal Shakespeare Company (RSC), described his involvement with the London 2012 Festival as, 'heartbreakingly wonderful'. He believed that it had been the most stimulating experience of his career, teaching him something new about Shakespeare. 'As with sport, you get better because of competitors, and there was a competitive element to this because there's the best work from all over the world and we've got to make sure that we're right up there.'

Commercially as well as creatively, the World Shakespeare Festival was an overwhelming success. Advance ticket sales from the Festival were larger than for the RSC's version of *Matilda*, the company's most popular musical production. Encouragingly 45 per cent of ticket buyers were new customers to the RSC, fulfilling one of the London 2012 Festival's core aims.

A musical celebration

London 2012 also produced a new wave of 'Cool Britannia' that reflected the celebratory mood. BT London Live mixed pop, rock and sport, with gold medal winners such as Bradley Wiggins, Jessica Ennis, Sir Chris Hoy and Laura Trott appearing on stage at live music gigs in central London during the Olympic Games. Bands performing there included Blur, Duran Duran, New Order, The Specials and the Noisettes, whose lead singer Shingai Shoniwa described the allure. 'It's part of history and it's fantastic to be doing something creative. Cheering people on is fantastic.' 'It's a chance of a life time and it's amazing to be involved,' added the band's guitarist Daniel Smith. 'All of our relations will be saying one day that their grandparents played at the Olympic and Paralympic Games.'

The BBC, the official London 2012 Olympic Games broadcaster, planned a series of special programmes, documentaries and events to complement the London 2012 Festival. Among them were its most ambitious outside event, Radio 1's Hackney Weekend – a free two-day music festival attended by 100,000 people and featuring headline artists such as Jay-Z and Rihanna. 'We wanted to make sure that we marked this in a fitting way, and in one that would give young people from London and beyond, who might not necessarily be engaged with the Games, a chance to celebrate,' explained Ben Cooper, controller of Radio 1 and

Above: Umbrella song. A girl brandishes a Union flag umbrella at the BT London Live Celebration concert in Hyde Park. Blur, Duran Duran, New Order, The Specials and the Noisettes were among the bands taking part.

Below: Midsummer magic. Rihanna brings the BBC Radio 1 Hackney Weekend to a close with her global number one hit, We Found Love.

Above: On the Africa stage at the BT River of Music, the music of French-speaking African countries comes to life. Muntu Valdo (left) and Mounira Mitchala (right) from Chad performed at the London 2012 Pleasure Gardens.

Above right: At the opening event of the London 2012 Festival, children from the Raploch Estate Big Noise orchestra play at The Big Concert on 21 June 2012. They performed outside Stirling Castle with the Simon Bolivar Orchestra from Venezuela and their conductor Gustavo Dudamel.

1Xtra. 'Hackney is the perfect fit for us: an Olympic borough with a vibrant music scene and a large young population, many of whom can often be overlooked and disengaged, so exactly the people that we wanted to reach and inspire.'

Even London's River Thames became a venue, hosting the BT River of Music – a global festival that reflected and embraced the huge diversity of countries participating at the Olympic and Paralympic Games. The festival included performances from a wide variety of international artists: Baaba Maal from Senegal; Benin's Angelique Kidjo; Zakir Hussain from India; and the inspirational Staff Benda Bilili from the Democratic Republic of Congo.

Eurostar presented a showcase of European talent at Granary Square, close to the company's transport hub at St Pancras Station. The extravaganza called *Traction* was produced by BBC Radio 6 Music DJ Gilles Peterson. 'It's a dream. If I could do anything else, I would be in sport and to be living here during the Olympic and Paralympic Games is exciting,' he revealed. 'I feel that I'm on a mission to show off my city.'

The London 2012 Festival ended in a crescendo

of music that reverberated around the UK in the Bandstand Marathon. The event saw more than 500 bandstands and open spaces welcome performing musicians and bands in a unique and tuneful climax to the Games.

The impossible comes alive

The London 2012 Festival was overseen by the Cultural Olympiad Board and chaired by Tony Hall, chief executive of the Royal Opera House and former director of news and current affairs at the BBC. For Hall, London 2012 represented a golden opportunity for imaginative teamwork that made the apparently impossible come to life. He was convinced that experience of working at London 2012 would foster a collective legacy and a knowledge bank for the arts in Britain in the future.

Hall passionately believes that the London 2012 Festival will inspire the next generation. He eloquently described his personal hope that the synthesis of sport and culture could spark people's creative awareness and imagination. 'I hope the Festival will have an impact on people's lives in many different ways ... that people see something that inspires them to go and do the same thing ... to make it their passion in life ... opera, painting, Morris dancing.' It was the enormous variety and nationwide accessibility that made the London 2012 Festival so great a hit. It managed a remarkable, and essentially British, juxtaposition of the professional beside the amateur; the amalgam of high art with a sense of fun and celebration, which combined to create an unforgettable summer of entertainment.

Children played a key role in many of the events. On the opening night of the London 2012 Festival an inspiring performance was held at Stirling Castle. It featured young people from the Raploch estate and Gustavo Dudamel's Simon Bolivar Orchestra, whose musicians come from shanty towns in Venezuela. This set the tone for the Festival. 'It was to be an inclusive arts event with an unpretentious, 'come and have a look' attitude.

One particularly moving evening of music took place at Coventry Cathedral when more than 200 young people and children from local schools, some as young as six, joined the City of Birmingham Symphony Orchestra. The celebratory concert marked the golden jubilee of the consecration of the Cathedral, rebuilt after being destroyed in the devastating bombing of the city during the Second World War.

The performance included the world premiere of composer James MacMillan's new setting of the *Gloria*, an ancient hymn of praise to the Trinity used since the second century. It proved a brilliant and beautiful piece by MacMillan, Britain's leading composer of religious music. Also an avid sports fan, he was thrilled to be involved with the London 2012 Festival. 'I'm a Celtic fan, so it's marvellous to see how the Olympic and Paralympic Games are making a connection between sport and culture,' he observed, adding 'A lot of sports people are inspired by the spiritual. The *Gloria* is a great hymn of joy, and that makes it appropriate for the Olympic Games.'

Theatre also played a key role in the London 2012 Festival, embracing a wide variety of forms. Stephen Beresford's powerful new play *The Last of*

the Haussmans saw actress Julie Walters return to the National Theatre for the first time in more than a decade. She played a 1960s hippy chick in the work, which she described as a 'funny, touching, uncomfortable, brilliant look at a dysfunctional family.' Walters declared that the London 2012 Festival was her own personal Olympic Games. 'It's team stuff, that competitive thing ... I hope we can inspire people to be more interested in the arts in the same way that the Olympic and Paralympic Games will inspire sport,' she explained. 'It's terribly moving to see people working so hard and it's not just about sport, it's also about celebrating the culture here.'

Comedy was represented with *Tall Tales from the Riverbank*, a comedy relay presented from a narrowboat by the Pleasance Theatre, Islington. Through the summer of 2012 the boat travelled from London to Edinburgh via Oxford, Birmingham, Manchester and Glasgow. British-based Australian comedian Tim Minchin appeared at the Eden Project in Cornwall, supported by young, up and coming artists from the south west. Singer-songwriter George Montague, who comes

'I hope that all sorts of people can say later on that they had their first idea of what they wanted to be in life at the London 2012 Festival.'

Tony Hall, Chair of the Cultural Olympiad Board

Tim Fitzhigham (left) and Andre Vincent (right) stand on the narrowboat during the launch of *Tall Tales from the Riverbank*. Fitzhigham was well qualified for the role of Master of Ceremonies during the trip, having once crossed the English Channel in a bathtub.

Top: Visitors enjoy Jeremy Deller's *Sacrilege* installation on the Greenwich Peninsula with the North Greenwich Arena beyond. The inflatable version of Stonehenge toured the capital and the UK as part of the London 2012 Festival.

Top right: Pupils from Burdett Coutts Primary School in south west London join in the Big Dance world record attempt with over half a million children in 53 countries. It was one of the many events that inspired Big Street Dance Day.

Above: Damon Albarn's opera *Dr Dee* is performed by The English National Opera at the London Coliseum. Albarn combined pop vocals with orchestral music played on 16th-century instruments.

Right: Don't look down. A dancer from Elizabeth Streb's Extreme Action dance group walks down City Hall. The group performed at iconic venues throughout the day with a finale on the London Eye.

from Gloucestershire, was delighted to contribute to the show. 'It was a great honour to be asked to perform my own music at the amazing Eden Project, as part of the London 2012 Festival, let alone playing on the same bill as the legend that is Mr Minchin: a truly memorable, uplifting and inspiring day.'

A flick through the London 2012 Festival programme reveals an eclectic mix of entertainment. The English National Opera offered Damon Albarn's fantastical opera *Dr Dee*, telling the story of Elizabethan alchemist Dr John Dee, who bestrode the worlds of science and magic. Claire Cunningham's striking dance piece, *Menage a Trois*, was staged at the South Bank Centre. Turner Prize winner Jeremy Deller undertook a nomadic tour of 25 locations across the country, inviting people to bounce on his *Sacrilege* installation, a life-sized blow-up replica of Stonehenge. Bouncers were invited to download Druid beards from the *Sacrilege* website. 'This is a way to get reacquainted with ancient Britain with your shoes off,' Deller laughed.

Activities for all

The London 2012 Festival was not all about huge productions and famous artists. Some of the most successful initiatives were small-scale events in local communities or at local libraries. Storylab, for example, drew children to attend their library and take part in educational activities linked to the Olympic Games, while adults and teenagers in the south west were offered a summer Reading Passport to encourage readers to discover world literature. As Mark Hawthorne, leader of Gloucestershire County Council, explained, 'As the world came to Britain, it was a great opportunity to find out more about the world. The Reading Passport was an incentive to read more and to try something different.'

Dancing has enjoyed a renaissance as a way to keep fit, fostered by the popularity of the BBC programme *Strictly Come Dancing* and the regular appearance of dancers on television talent shows. The Festival included a large element of dance-related activity, both on stage and in the street. Dancers at Cardiff Mela performed a world record breaking Bollywood dance, while a series of nationwide dance events aimed to get five million people up on their feet. Following the success of these initiatives 14 July was declared Big Street Dance Day, on which world famous choreographer Wayne McGregor marshalled 1,000 dancers from 35 dance groups to join in one huge performance in Trafalgar Square.

There was also an element of surprise and delight to the artistic endeavour at the London 2012 Festival. Spontaneity was encouraged, with pop-up performances and weird and wonderful happenings taking place across the UK. One of the most extraordinary sights in the summer of 2012 was acrobat Elizabeth Streb and her trapeze artists abseiling down the London Eye and City Hall. At Bexhill-on-Sea, Kent, Richard Wilson's full-scale replica of a coach dangling off the edge of a cliff, his homage to the classic scene from the film *The Italian Job*, appeared in glorious suspension on the roof of the De La Warr Pavilion. BMW cars with bodywork by Roy Lichtenstein, Andy Warhol and Jeff Koons raced around a car park in Shoreditch, and Berlin-based Argentinian dancer Constanza Macras performed in the woods of Wepre Park in Connah's Quay in North Wales.

The nationwide reach of the London 2012 Festival was embraced by enthusiastic audiences the length and breath of Britain. The events provoked debate about art and culture and evoked

Below and below left: Arthur's Seat in Edinburgh was one of the numerous British landmarks to take centre stage during the London 2012 Festival. Endurance runners and walkers using fluorescent lights created a choreographed public art piece to launch The Edinburgh International Festival with *Speed of Light*.

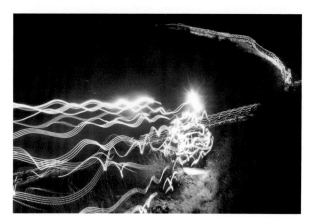

French pyrotechnic act Les Commandos Percu perform at Bowness-on-Windermere as part of Lakes Alive. The performance, coinciding with the opening night of the London 2012 Festival, helped to welcome the Olympic Flame to Windermere.

The London 2012 Festival in numbers

- 19.5 million people joined the UK wide London 2012 Festival
- 16.5 million free opportunities draw new audiences
- 9 out of 10 people attending events agree London was right to make culture a key part of the Games.

a sense of pride in the landmarks of Britain used to stage exciting and imaginative work. Runners in light suits raced around Arthur's Seat in Edinburgh, while Lake Windermere hosted fireworks, music and dance with Les Commandos Percu. Hans Peter Kuhn raised fluttering flags on the stunning Giants Causeway in Antrim, and Zachary Lieberman projected messages on to Hadrian's Wall, viewed digitally all over the world. Bristol hosted Europe's biggest urban arts festival and Newport staged the *Busk on the Usk* free festival. There was also activity in Ironbridge, Shropshire, birthplace of the Industrial Revolution that featured so prominently in the Opening Ceremony of the Olympic Games. Artist Kurt Hentschläger's *CORE* presented a series of mesmerising digital projections exploring weightlessness in one of the engine sheds at the Ironbridge Gorge Museum.

Art in the Park

Art was also brought to the heart of the sporting action with a stunning display of sculpture, architecture and street art in the Olympic Park itself. The most dramatic piece is the 115-metre high,

bright red, spiralling Orbit, designed by Anish Kapoor and Cecil Balmond. This helter-skelter style structure sitting beside the Olympic Stadium comprises the largest piece of public art in Britain, offering stunning views of the Park and the London skyline from its viewing platform.

Elsewhere in the Park Keith Wilson's huge boat moorings leap out of the River Lee like giant-sized coloured crayons. Monica Bonvicini's wonderful mirrored *RUN* sculpture urges people into action and provided sports fans with a fabulous photo opportunity outside the Copper Box. Waterfalls cascaded words from the night sky and clouds drifted along bridges; even the fingerprints of local people dotted the surface of a wall. Among the most simple and appealing of all the Art in the Park installations were the scores of pictures painted and drawn by local schoolchildren. They proudly decorated the walls of the Main Press Centre and welcomed the world to London.

In the end, the statistics were staggering. They showed that more than 19.5 million people attended the London 2012 Festival, with around 16.5 million people visiting free events. It was estimated that 3 million people visited paid-for events, for example the delightful Wallace and Grommit BBC Prom, *My concerto in Ee, Lad*, and art exhibitions such as David Hockney's A Bigger Picture at the Royal Academy.

The London 2012 Festival defied the doubters and the cynics to initiate the largest display of art and culture seen in the United Kingdom since the Festival of Britain that inspired the post-war generation in 1951. It proved so successful, and was so well received by the British public, that shortly after the Olympic Games ended the then Culture Secretary Jeremy Hunt announced the commissioning of a survey to explore the feasibility of staging a biennial culture festival. The London 2012 Festival illustrated that the British people have, as with sport, a huge thirst for art and culture, and the hope is that it will go on to inspire the post-Olympic generation.

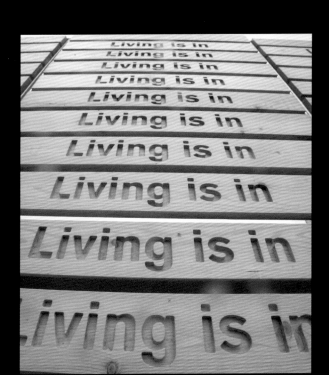

Above: Monica Bonvicini's mirrored glass sculpture *RUN* comes alive at night with its built-in LED lighting. During the day it acts as a mirror to visitors and their surroundings in its position outside the Copper Box.

Above left: One of three poems by Lemn Sissay that helped to bring poetry to the Olympic Park. This untitled work was etched into a wooden transformer enclosure to bring art to unexpected places.

Left: The massive and beautiful sculptured steel Orbit, a permanent installation in east London. Lit by 250 LED lights, it glows in the night sky, with the Olympic Stadium visible in the background.

Chapter Six
London 2012 Stats

Olympic Games – Medal Results by Country

Rank	Country	Gold	Silver	Bronze	TOTAL
1	United States of America (USA)	46	29	29	104
2	People's Republic of China (CHN)	38	27	23	88
3	Great Britain (GBR)	29	17	19	65
4	Russian Federation (RUS)	24	26	32	82
5	Republic of Korea (KOR)	13	8	7	28
6	Germany (GER)	11	19	14	44
7	France (FRA)	11	11	12	34
8	Italy (ITA)	8	9	11	28
9	Hungary (HUN)	8	4	5	17
10	Australia (AUS)	7	16	12	35
11	Japan (JPN)	7	14	17	38
12	Kazakhstan (KAZ)	7	1	5	13
13	Netherlands (NED)	6	6	8	20
14	Ukraine (UKR)	6	5	9	20
15	New Zealand (NZL)	6	2	5	13
16	Cuba (CUB)	5	3	6	14
17	Islamic Republic of Iran (IRI)	4	5	3	12
18	Jamaica (JAM)	4	4	4	12
19	Czech Republic (CZE)	4	3	3	10
20	Democratic People's Republic of Korea (PRK)	4	0	2	6
21	Spain (ESP)	3	10	4	17
22	Brazil (BRA)	3	5	9	17
23	South Africa (RSA)	3	2	1	6
24	Ethiopia (ETH)	3	1	3	7
25	Croatia (CRO)	3	1	2	6
26	Belarus (BLR)	2	5	5	12
27	Romania (ROU)	2	5	2	9
28	Kenya (KEN)	2	4	5	11
29	Denmark (DEN)	2	4	3	9
30	Azerbaijan (AZE)	2	2	6	10
30	Poland (POL)	2	2	6	10
32	Turkey (TUR)	2	2	1	5
33	Switzerland (SUI)	2	2	0	4
34	Lithuania (LTU)	2	1	2	5
35	Norway (NOR)	2	1	1	4
36	Canada (CAN)	1	5	12	18
37	Sweden (SWE)	1	4	3	8
38	Colombia (COL)	1	3	4	8
39	Georgia (GEO)	1	3	3	7
39	Mexico (MEX)	1	3	3	7
41	Ireland (IRL)	1	1	3	5
42	Argentina (ARG)	1	1	2	4
42	Slovenia (SLO)	1	1	2	4

Rank	Country	Gold	Silver	Bronze	TOTAL
42	Serbia (SRB)	1	1	2	4
45	Tunisia (TUN)	1	1	1	3
46	Dominican Republic (DOM)	1	1	0	2
47	Trinidad and Tobago (TRI)	1	0	3	4
47	Uzbekistan (UZB)	1	0	3	4
49	Latvia (LAT)	1	0	1	2
50	Algeria (ALG)	1	0	0	1
50	Bahamas (BAH)	1	0	0	1
50	Grenada (GRN)	1	0	0	1
50	Uganda (UGA)	1	0	0	1
50	Venezuela (VEN)	1	0	0	1
55	India (IND)	0	2	4	6
56	Mongolia (MGL)	0	2	3	5
57	Thailand (THA)	0	2	1	3
58	Egypt (EGY)	0	2	0	2
59	Slovakia (SVK)	0	1	3	4
60	Armenia (ARM)	0	1	2	3
60	Belgium (BEL)	0	1	2	3
60	Finland (FIN)	0	1	2	3
63	Bulgaria (BUL)	0	1	1	2
63	Estonia (EST)	0	1	1	2
63	Indonesia (INA)	0	1	1	2
63	Malaysia (MAS)	0	1	1	2
63	Puerto Rico (PUR)	0	1	1	2
63	Chinese Taipei (TPE)	0	1	1	2
69	Botswana (BOT)	0	1	0	1
69	Cyprus (CYP)	0	1	0	1
69	Gabon (GAB)	0	1	0	1
69	Guatemala (GUA)	0	1	0	1
69	Montenegro (MNE)	0	1	0	1
69	Portugal (POR)	0	1	0	1
75	Greece (GRE)	0	0	2	2
75	Republic of Moldova (MDA)	0	0	2	2
75	Qatar (QAT)	0	0	2	2
75	Singapore (SIN)	0	0	2	2
79	Afghanistan (AFG)	0	0	1	1
79	Bahrain (BRN)	0	0	1	1
79	Hong Kong, China (HGK)	0	0	1	1
79	Saudi Arabia (KSA)	0	0	1	1
79	Kuwait (KUW)	0	0	1	1
79	Morocco (MAR)	0	0	1	1
79	Tajikistan (TJK)	0	0	1	1

Paralympic Games — Medal Results by Country

Rank	Country	Gold	Silver	Bronze	TOTAL
1	People's Republic of China (CHN)	95	71	65	231
2	Russian Federation (RUS)	36	38	28	102
3	Great Britain (GBR)	34	43	43	120
4	Ukraine (UKR)	32	24	28	84
5	Australia (AUS)	32	23	30	85
6	United States of America (USA)	31	29	38	98
7	Brazil (BRA)	21	14	8	43
8	Germany (GER)	18	26	22	66
9	Poland (POL)	14	13	9	36
10	Netherlands (NED)	10	10	19	39
11	Islamic Republic of Iran (IRI)	10	7	7	24
12	Republic of Korea (KOR)	9	9	9	27
13	Italy (ITA)	9	8	11	28
14	Tunisia (TUN)	9	5	5	19
15	Cuba (CUB)	9	5	3	17
16	France (FRA)	8	19	18	45
17	Spain (ESP)	8	18	16	42
18	South Africa (RSA)	8	12	9	29
19	Ireland (IRL)	8	3	5	16
20	Canada (CAN)	7	15	9	31
21	New Zealand (NZL)	6	7	4	17
22	Nigeria (NGR)	6	5	2	13
23	Mexico (MEX)	6	4	11	21
24	Japan (JPN)	5	5	6	16
25	Belarus (BLR)	5	2	3	10
26	Algeria (ALG)	4	6	9	19
27	Azerbaijan (AZE)	4	5	3	12
28	Egypt (EGY)	4	4	7	15
29	Sweden (SWE)	4	4	4	12
30	Austria (AUT)	4	3	6	13
31	Thailand (THA)	4	2	2	8
32	Finland (FIN)	4	1	1	6
33	Switzerland (SUI)	3	6	4	13
34	Hong Kong, China (HKG)	3	3	6	12
35	Norway (NOR)	3	2	3	8
36	Belgium (BEL)	3	1	3	7
37	Morocco (MAR)	3	0	3	6
38	Hungary (HUN)	2	6	6	14

Rank	Country	Gold	Silver	Bronze	TOTAL
39	Serbia (SRB)	2	3	0	5
40	Kenya (KEN)	2	2	2	6
41	Slovakia (SVK)	2	1	3	6
42	Czech Republic (CZE)	1	6	4	11
43	Turkey (TUR)	1	5	4	10
44	Greece (GRE)	1	3	8	12
45	Israel (ISR)	1	2	5	8
46	United Arab Emirates (UAE)	1	1	1	3
47	Latvia (LAT)	1	1	0	2
47	Namibia (NAM)	1	1	0	2
47	Romania (ROU)	1	1	0	2
50	Denmark (DEN)	1	0	4	5
51	Angola (ANG)	1	0	1	2
52	Bosnia and Herzegovina (BIH)	1	0	0	1
52	Chile (CHI)	1	0	0	1
52	Fiji (FIJ)	1	0	0	1
52	Iceland (ISL)	1	0	0	1
52	Jamaica (JAM)	1	0	0	1
52	Former Yugoslav Republic of Macedonia (MKD)	1	0	0	1
58	Croatia (CRO)	0	2	3	5
59	Bulgaria (BUL)	0	2	1	3
59	Iraq (IRQ)	0	2	1	3
61	Colombia (COL)	0	2	0	2
62	Argentina (ARG)	0	1	4	5
63	Portugal (POR)	0	1	2	3
63	Taipei (Chinese Taipei)	0	1	2	3
65	Malaysia (MAS)	0	1	1	2
65	Singapore (SIN)	0	1	1	2
67	Cyprus (CYP)	0	1	0	1
67	Ethiopia (ETH)	0	1	0	1
67	India (IND)	0	1	0	1
67	Saudi Arabia (KSA)	0	1	0	1
67	Slovenia (SLO)	0	1	0	1
67	Uzbekistan (UZB)	0	1	0	1
73	Venezuela (VEN)	0	0	2	2
74	Indonesia (INA)	0	0	1	1
74	Sri Lanka (SRI)	0	0	1	1

Events Medal Listings

Olympic Games

AQUATICS – DIVING

MEN

3M SPRINGBOARD
1. Ilya Zakharov (RUS) 555.90 points
2. Kai Qin (CHN) 541.75 points
3. Chong He (CHN) 524.15 points

10M PLATFORM
1. David Boudia (USA) 568.65 points
2. Bo Qiu (CHN) 566.85 points
3. Thomas Daley (GBR) 556.95 points

SYNCHRONISED 3M SPRINGBOARD
1. CHN (Yutong Luo, Kai Qin) 477.00 points
2. RUS (Evgeny Kuznetsov, Ilya Zakharov) 459.63 points
3. USA (Troy Dumais, Kristian Ipsen) 446.70 points

SYNCHRONISED 10M PLATFORM
1. CHN (Yuan Cao, Yanquan Zhang) 486.78 points
2. MEX (Ivan Garcia Navarro, German Sanchez Sanchez) 468.90 points
3. USA (David Boudia, Nicholas McCrory) 463.47 points

WOMEN

3M SPRINGBOARD
1. Minxia Wu (CHN) 414.00 points
2. Zi He (CHN) 379.20 points
3. Laura Sanchez Soto (MEX) 362.40 points

10M PLATFORM
1. Ruolin Chen (CHN) 422.30 points
2. Brittany Broben (AUS) 366.50 points
3. Pandelela Rinong Pamg (MAS) 359.20 points

SYNCHRONISED 3M SPRINGBOARD
1. CHN (Zi He, Minxia Wu) 346.20 points
2. USA (Kelci Bryant, Abigail Johnston) 321.90 points
3. CAN (Jennifer Abel, Emilie Heymans) 316.80 points

SYNCHRONISED 10M PLATFORM
1. CHN (Ruolin Chen, Hao Wang) 368.40 points
2. MEX (Paola Espinosa Sanchez, Alejandra Orozco Loza) 343.32 points
3. CAN (Meaghan Benfeito, Roseline Filion) 337.62 points

AQUATICS – SWIMMING

MEN

100M BACKSTROKE
1. Matthew Grevers (USA) 52.16 OR
2. Nick Thoman (USA) 52.92
3. Ryosuke Irie (JPN) 52.97

200M BACKSTROKE
1. Tyler Clary (USA) 1:53.41 OR
2. Ryosuke Irie (JPN) 1:53.78
3. Ryan Lochte (USA) 1:53.94

100M BREASTSTROKE
1. Cameron van der Burgh (RSA) 58.46 WR
2. Christian Sprenger (AUS) 58.93
3. Brendan Hansen (USA) 59.49

200M BREASTSTROKE
1. Daniel Gyurta (HUN) 2:07.28 WR
2. Michael Jamieson (GBR) 2:07.43
3. Ryo Tateishi (JPN) 2:08.29

100M BUTTERFLY
1. Michael Phelps (USA) 51.21
=2. Chad le Clos (RSA) 51.44
=2. Evgeny Korotyshkin (RUS) 51.44

200M BUTTERFLY
1. Chad le Clos (RSA) 1:52.96
2. Michael Phelps (USA) 1:53.01
3. Takeshi Matsuda (JPN) 1:53.21

50M FREESTYLE
1. Florent Manaudou (FRA) 21.34
2. Cullen Jones (USA) 21.54
3. Cesar Cielo (BRA) 21.59

100M FREESTYLE
1. Nathan Adrian (USA) 47.52
2. James Magnussen (AUS) 47.53
3. Brent Hayden (CAN) 47.80

200M FREESTYLE
1. Yannick Agnel (FRA) 1:43.14
=2. Taehwan Park (KOR) 1:44.93
=2. Yang Sun (CHN) 1:44.93

400M FREESTYLE
1. Yang Sun (CHN) 3:40.14 OR
2. Taehwan Park (KOR) 3:42.06
3. Peter Vanderkaay (USA) 3:44.69

1500M FREESTYLE
1. Yang San (CHN) 14:31.02 WR
2. Ryan Cochrane (CAN) 14:39.63
3. Oussama Mellouli (TUN) 14:40.31

200M INDIVIDUAL MEDLEY
1. Michael Phelps (USA) 1:54.27
2. Ryan Lochte (USA) 1:54.90
3. Laszlo Cseh (HUN) 1:56.22

400M INDIVIDUAL MEDLEY
1. Ryan Lochte (USA) 4:05.18
2. Thiago Pereira (BRA) 4:08.86
3. Kosuke Hagino (JPN) 4:08.94

4 X 100M FREESTYLE RELAY
1. FRA (Amaury Leveaux, Fabien Gilot, Clement Lefert, Yannick Agnel, Alain Bernard, Jeremy Stravius) 3:09.93
2. USA (Nathan Adrian, Michael Phelps, Cullen Jones, Ryan Lochte, James Feigen, Matthew Grevers, Ricky Berens, Jason Lezak) 3:10.38
3. RUS (Andrey Grechin, Niki Lobintsev, Vladim Morozov, Danila Izotov, Evgeny Lagunove, Sergei Fesikov) 3:11.41

4 X 200M FREESTYLE RELAY
1. USA (Ryan, Lochte, Conor Dwyer, Ricky Berens, Michael Phelps) 6:59.70
2. FRA (Amaury Leveaux, Gregory Mallet, Clement Lefert, Yannick Agnel) 7:02.77
3. CHN (Yun Hao, Yunqi Li, Haiqi Jiang, Yang Sun) 7:06.30

4 X 100M MEDLEY RELAY
1. USA (Matthew Grevers, Brendan Hansen, Michael Phelps, Nathan Adrian) 3:29.35
2. JPN (Ryosuke Irie, Kosuke Kitajima, Takeshi Matsuda, Takuro Fujii) 3:31.26
3. AUS (Hayden Stoeckel, Christian Sprenger, Matt Targett, James Magnussen) 3:31.58

10KM MARATHON SWIM
1. Oussama Mellouli (TUN) 1:49:55.1
2. Thomas Lurz (GER) 1:49:58.5
3. Richard Weinberger (CAN) 1:50:00.3

WOMEN

100M BACKSTROKE
1. Missy Franklin (USA) 58.33
2. Emily Seebohm (AUS) 58.68
3. Aya Terakawa (JPN) 58.83

200M BACKSTROKE
1. Missy Franklin (USA) 2:04.06 WR
2. Anastasia Zueva (RUS) 2:05.92
3. Elizabeth Beisel (USA) 2:06.55

100M BREASTSTROKE
1. Ruta Meilutyte (LTU) 1:05.47
2. Rebecca Soni (USA) 1:05.55
3. Satomi Suzuki (JPN) 1:06.46

200M BREASTSTROKE
1. Rebecca Soni (USA) 2:19.59 WR
2. Satomi Suzuki (JPN) 2:20.72
3. Iuliia Efimova (RUS) 2:20.92

100M BUTTERFLY
1. Dana Vollmer (USA) 55.98 WR
2. Ying Lu (CHN) 56.87
3. Alicia Coutts (AUS) 56.94

200M BUTTERFLY
1. Liuyang Jiao (CHN) 2:04.06 OR
2. Mireia Belmonte Garcia (ESP) 2:05.25
3. Natsumi Hoshi (JPN) 2:05.48

50M FREESTYLE
1. Ranomi Kromowidjojo (NED) 24.05 OR
2. Aliaksandra Herasimenia (BLR) 53.38
3. Marleen Veldhuis (NED) 24.39

100M FREESTYLE
1. Ranomi Kromowidjojo (NED) 53.00 OR
2. Aliaksandra Herasimenia (BLR) 53.38
3. Yi Tang (CHN) 53.44

200M FREESTYLE
1. Allison Schmitt (USA) 1:53.61 OR
2. Camille Muffat (FRA) 1.55.58
3. Bronte Barratt (AUS) 1:55.81

400M FREESTYLE
1. Camille Muffat (FRA) 4:01.45 OR
2. Allison Schmitt (USA) 4:01.77
3. Rebecca Adlington (GBR) 4:03.01

800M FREESTYLE
1. Katie Ledecky (USA) 8:14.63
2. Mireia Belmonte Garcia (ESP) 8:18.76
3. Rebecca Adlington (GBR) 8:20.32

200M INDIVIDUAL MEDLEY
1. Shiwen Ye (CHN) 4:28.43 WR
2. Alicia Coutts (AUS) 2:08.15
3. Caitlin Leverenz (USA) 2:08.95

400M INDIVIDUAL MEDLEY
1. Shiwen Ye (CHN) 4:28.43 WR
2. Elizabeth Beisel (USA) 4:31.27
3. Xuanxu Li (CHN) 4:32.91

4 X 100M FREESTYLE RELAY
1. AUS (Alicia Coutts, Cate Campbell, Brittany Elmslie, Melanie Schlanger) 3:31.15 OR
2. NED (Inge Dekker, Marleen Veldhuis, Femke Heemskerk, Ranomi Kromowidjojo) 3:33.79
3. USA (Missy Franklin, Jessica Hardy, Lia Neal, Allison Schmitt) 3:34.24

4 X 100M MEDLEY RELAY
1. USA (Missy Franklin, Rebecca Soni, Dana Vollmer, Allison Schmitt) 3:52.05 WR
2. AUS (Emily Seebohm, Leisel Jones, Alicia Coutts, Melanie Schlanger) 3:54.02
3. JPN (Aya Terakawa, Satomi Suzuki, Yuka Kato Haruka Ueda) 3:55.73

4 X 200M FREESTYLE RELAY
1. USA (Missy Franklin, Dana Vollmer, Shannon Vreeland, Allison Schmitt) 7:42.92 OR
2. AUS (Bronte Barratt, Melanie Schlanger, Kylie Palmer, Alicia Coutts) 7:44.41
3. FRA (Camille Muffat, Charlotte Bonnet, Ophelie-Cyrielle Etienne, Coralie Balmy) 7:47.49

10KM MARATHON SWIM
1. Eva Risztov (HUN) 1:57:38.6
2. Haley Anderson (USA) 1:57:38.6
3. Martina Grimaldi (ITA) 1:57:41.8

AQUATICS – SYNCHRONISED SWIMMING

WOMEN

DUETS
1. RUS (Natalia Ishchenko, Svetlana Romashina) 197.100 points
2. ESP (Ona Carbonell Ballestero, Andrea Fuentes Fache) 192.900 points
3. CHN (Xuechen Huang, Ou Liu) 192.870 points

TEAMS
1. RUS (Anastasia Davydova, Maria Gromova, Natalia Ishchenko, Elvira Khasyanova, Daria Korobova, Alexandra Patskevich, Svetlana Romashina, Anzhelika Timanina, Alla Shishkina) 197.030 points
2. CHN (Si Chang, Xiaojun Chen, Xuechen Huang, Tingting Jiang, Wenwen Jiang, Ou Liu, Xi Luo, Yiwen Wu, Wenyan Sun) 194.010 points
3. ESP (Clara Basiana Canellas, Alba Cabello Rodilla, Ona Carbonella Ballestero, Margalida Crespi Jaume, Andrea Fuentes Fache, Thais Henriquez Torres, Paula Klamburg Roque, Irene Montrucchio Beaus, Laia Pons Arenas) 193.120 points

AQUATICS – WATER POLO

MEN

12-TEAM TOURNAMENT
1. CRO (Josip Pavic, Damir Buric, Miho Boskovic, Niksa Doloud, Maro Jokovic, Ivan Buljubasic, Petar Muslim, Andro Buslje, Sandro Sukno, Samir Barac, Igor Hinic, Paulo Obradovic, Frano Vican)
2. ITA (Srefano Tempesti, Amaurys Perez, Niccolo Gitto, Pietro Figlioli, Alex Giorgetti, Maurizio Felugo, Massimo Giacoppo, Valentino Gallo, Christian Presciutti, Deni Fiorentini, Matteo Aicardi, Danijel Premus, Giacomo Pastorino)
3. SRB (Slobodan Soro, Aleksa Saponjic, Zivko Gocic, Vanja Udovicic, Dusan Mandic, Dusco Pijetlovic, Slobodan Nikic, Milan Aleksic, Nikola raden, Filip Filipovic, Andrija Prlainovic, Stefan Mitrovic, Gojko Pijetlovic)

WOMEN

8-TEAM TOURNAMENT
1. USA (Betsey Armstrong, Heather Petri, Melissa Seidemann, Brenda Villa, Lauren Wenger, Maggie Steffens, Courtney Mathewson, Jessica Steffens, Elsie Windes, Kelly Rulon, Annika Dries, Kami Craig, Tumua Anae)
2. ESP (Laura Ester Ramos, Pascual Bach, Anni Espar Llaquet, Roser Tarrago Aymeri, Matilde Ortiz Reyes, Jennifer Pareja, Lorena Miranda Dorado, Pilar Pena Carrasco, Andrea Blas Martinez, Ona Meseguer Flaque, Maica Garcia, Laura Lopez Ventosa, Ana Copado Amoros)
3. AUS (Victoria Brown, Gemma Beadsworth, Sophie Smith, Holly Lincoln-Smith, Jane Moran, Bronwen Knox, Rowie Webster, Kate Gynther, Glencora Ralph, Ash Southern, Mel rippon, Nicola Zagame, Alicia McCormack)

ARCHERY

MEN

INDIVIDUAL COMPETITION
1. Jin Hyek Oh (KOR) 115 points
2. Takaharu Furukawa (JPN) 108 points
3. Xiaoxiang Dai (CHN) 136 points

TEAM COMPETITION
1. ITA (Michele Frangilli, Marco Galiazzo, Mauro Nespoli) 219 points
2. USA (Brady Ellison, Jake Kaminski, Jacob Wukie) 218 points
3. KOR (Bumbin Kim, Donghyun Im, Jin Hyek Oh) 224 points

WOMEN

INDIVIDUAL COMPETITION
1. Bo Bae Ki (KOR) 135 points
2. Aida Roman (MEX) 129 points
3. Mariana Avitia (MEX) 104 points

TEAM COMPETITION
1. KOR (Hyeonju Choi, Bo Bae Ki, Sung Jin Lee) 210 points
2. CHN (Ming Cheng, Yuting Fang, Jing Xu) 209 points
3. JPN (Ren Hayakawa, Miki Kanie, Kaori Kawanaka) 209 points

ATHLETICS

MEN

100M
1. Usain Bolt (JAM) 9.63 OR
2. Yohan Blake (JAM) 9.75
3. Justin Gatlin (USA) 9.79

200M
1. Usain Bolt (JAM) 19.32
2. Yohan Blake (JAM) 19.44
3. Warren Weir (JAM) 19.84

400M
1. Kirani James (GRN) 43.94
2. Lugelin Santos (DOM) 44.46
3. Lalonde Gordon (TRI) 44.52

800M
1. David Lekuta Rudisha (KEN) 1:40.91 WR
2. Nijel Amos (BOT) 1:41.73
3. Timothy Kitum (KEN) 1:42.53

1500M
1. Taoufik Makhloufi (ALG) 3:34.08
2. Leonel Manzano (USA) 3:34.79
3. Abdalaati Iguider (MAR) 3:35.13

5000M
1. Mohamed Farah (GBR) 13:41.66
2. Dejen Gebremeskel (ETH) 13:41.98
3. Thomas Pkemei Longosiwa (KEN) 13:42.36
10,000M
1. Mohamed Farah (GBR) 27:30.42
2. Galen Rupp (USA) 27:30.90
3. Tariku Bekele (ETH) 27:31.43
110M HURDLES
1. Aries Merritt (USA) 12.92
2. Jason Richardson (USA) 13.04
3. Hansle Parchment (JAM) 13.12
400M HURDLES
1. Felix Sanchez (DOM) 47.63
2. Michael Tinsley (USA) 47.91
3. Javier Culson (PUR) 48.10
3000M STEEPLECHASE
1. Ezekiel Kemboi (KEN) 8:18.56
2. Mahiedine Mekhissi-Benabbad (FRA) 8:19.08
3. Abel Kiprop Kipruto (KEN) 8:19.73
4 X 100M RELAY
1. JAM (Nesta Carter, Michael Frater, Yohan Blake, Usain Bolt, Kemar Bailey-Cole) 36.84 WR
2. USA (Trell Kimmons, Justin Gatlin, Tyson Gay, Ryan Bailey, Jeffery, Demps, Darvis Patton) 37.04
3. TRI (Keston Bledman, Marc Burns, Emmanuel Callender, Richard Thompson) 38.12
4 X 400M RELAY
1. BAH (Chris Brown, Demetrius Pinder, Michael Mathieu, Ramon Miller) 2:56.72
2. USA (Bryshon Nellum, Joshua Mance, Tony McQuay, Angelo Taylor, Manteo Mitchell) 2:57.05
3. TRI (Lalonde Gordon, Jarrin Solomon, Ade Alleyne-Forte, Deon Lendore) 2:59.40
DISCUS THROW
1. Robert Harting (GER) 68.27m
2. Ehsan Hadadi (IRI) 68.18m
3. Gerd Kanter (EST) 68.03m
HAMMER THROW
1. Krisztian Pars (HUN) 80.59m
2. Primoz Kozmus (SLO) 79.36m
3. Koji Murofushi (JPN) 78.71m
HIGH JUMP
1. Ivan Ukhov (RUS) 2.38m
2. Erik Kynard (USA) 2.33m
=3. Mutaz Essa Barshim (QAT) 2.29m
=3. Derek Drouin (CAN) 2.29m
=3. Robert Grabarz (GBR) 2.29m
JAVELIN THROW
1. Keshorn Walcott (TRI) 84.58m
2. Oleksandr Pyatnytsya (UKR) 84.51m
3. Antti Ruuskanen (FIN) 84.12m
LONG JUMP
1. Greg Rutherford (GBR) 8.31m
2. Mitchell Watt (AUS) 8.16m
3. Will Claye (USA) 8.12m
POLE VAULT
1. Renaud Lavillenie (FRA) 5.97m OR
2. Bjorn Otto (GER) 5.91m
3. Raphael Holzdeppe (GER) 5.91m
SHOT PUT
1. Tomasz Majewski (POL) 21.89m
2. David Storl (GER) 21.86m
3. Reese Hoffa (USA) 21.23m
TRIPLE JUMP
1. Christian Taylor (USA) 17.81m
2. Will Claye (USA) 17.62m
3. Fabrizio Donato (ITA) 17.48m
DECATHLON
1. Ashton Eaton (USA) 8869 points
2. Trey Hardee (USA) 8671 points
3. Leonel Suarez (CUB) 8523 points
20KM RACE WALK
1. Ding Chen (CHN) 1:18.46 OR
2. Erick Barrondo (GUA) 1:18.57
3. Zhen Wang (CHN) 1.19.25
50KM RACE WALK
1. Sergey Kirdyapkin (RUS) 3:35.59 OR
2. Jared Tallent (AUS) 3:36.53
3. Tianfeng Si (CHN) 3:37.16
MARATHON
1. Stephen Kiprotich (UGA) 2:08.01
2. Abel Kirui (KEN) 2:08.27
3. Wilson Kipsang Kiprotich (KEN) 2:09.37

WOMEN
100M
1. Shelly-Ann Fraser-Pryce (JAM) 10.75
2. Carmelita Jeter (USA) 10.78
3. Veronica Campbell-Brown (JAM) 10.81
200M
1. Allyson Felix (USA) 21.88
2. Shelly-Ann Fraser-Pryce (JAM) 22.09
3. Carmelita Jeter (USA) 22.14
400M
1. Sanya Richards-Ross (USA) 39.55
2. Christine Ohuruogu (GBR) 49.70
3. DeeDee Trotter (USA) 49.72
800M
1. Mariya Savinova (RUS) 1:56.19
2. Caster Semenya (RSA) 1:57.23
3. Ekaterina Poistogova (RUS) 1:57.53
1500M
1. Asli Cakir Alptekin (TUR) 4:10.23
2. Gamze Bulut (TUR) 4:10.40
3. Maryam Yusuf Jamal (BRN) 4:10.74
5000M
1. Meseret Defar (ETH) 15:04.25
2. Vivian Jepkemoi Cheruiyot (KEN) 15:04.73
3. Tirunesh Dibaba (ETH) 15:05.15
10,000M
1. Tirunesh Dibaba (ETH) 30:20.75
2. Sally Jepkosgei Kipyego (KEN) 30:26.37
3. Vivian Jepkemoi Cheruiyot (KEN) 30:30.44
100M HURDLES
1. Sally Pearson (AUS) 12.35 OR
2. Dawn Harper (USA) 12.37
3. Kellie Wells (USA) 12.48
400M HURDLES
1. Natalya Antyukh (RUS) 52.70
2. Lashinda Demus (USA) 52.77
3. Zuzana Hejnova (CZE) 53.38
3000M STEEPLECHASE
1. Yuliya Zaripova (RUS) 9:06.72
2. Habiba Ghribi (TUN) 9:08.37
3. Sofia Assefa (ETH) 9:09.84
4 X 100M RELAY
1. USA (Tianna Madison, Allyson Felix, Bianca Knight, Carmelita Jeter, Jeneba Tarmoh, Lauryn Williams) 40.82 WR
2. JAM (Shelly-Ann Fraser-Pryce, Sherone Simpson, Veronica Campbell-Brown, Kerron Stewart, Calvert Schillonie, Samantha Henry-Robinson) 41.41
3. UKR (Oleysa Povh, Hrystyna Stuy, Mariya Ryemyen, Elyzaveta Bryzgina) 42.04
4 X 400M RELAY
1. USA (DeeDee Trotter, Allyson Felix, Francena McCrory, Sanya Richards-Ross, Keshia Baker, Diamond Dixon) 3:16.87
2. RUS (Yulia Gushchina, Antonina Krivoshapka, Tatyana Firova, Natalya Antyyukh, Anastasiya Kapachinskaya, Natalya Nazarova) 3:20.23
3. JAM (Christine Day, Rosemarie Whyte, Shericka Williams, Novlene Williams-Mills, Shereefa Lloyd) 3:20.95
DISCUS THROW
1. Sandra Perkovic (CRO) 69.11m
2. Darya Pishchalnikova (RUS) 67.56m
3. Yanfeng Li (CHN) 67.22m
HAMMER THROW
1. Tatyana Lysenko (RUS) 78.18m OR
2. Anita Wlodarczyk (POL) 77.60m
3. Betty Heidler (GER) 77.12m
HIGH JUMP
1. Anna Chicherova (RUS) 2.05m
2. Brigetta Barrett (USA) 2.03m
3. Svetlana Shkolina (RUS) 2.03m
JAVELIN THROW
1. Barbora Spotakova (CZE) 69.55m
2. Christina Obergfoll (GER) 65.16m
3. Linda Stahl (GER) 64.91m
LONG JUMP
1. Brittney Reese (USA) 7.12m
2. Elena Sokolova (RUS) 7.07m
3. Janay Deloach (USA) 6.89m
POLE VAULT
1. Jennifer Suhr (USA) 4.75m
2. Yatisley Silva (CUB) 4.75m
3. Elena Isinbaeva (RUS) 4.70m
SHOT PUT
1. Valerie Adams (NZL) 20.70m
2. Evgeniia Kolodko (RUS) 20.48m
3. Lijiao Gong (CHN) 20.22m
TRIPLE JUMP
1. Olga Rypakova (KAZ) 14.98m
2. Caterine Ibarguen (COL) 14.80m
3. Olha Saladuha (UKR) 14.79m

HEPTATHLON
1. Jessica Ennis (GBR) 6955 points
2. Lilli Schwarzkopf (GER) 6649 points
3. Tatyana Chernova (RUS) 6628 points
20KM RACE WALK
1. Elena Lashmanova (RUS) 1:25.02 WR/OR
2. Olga Kaniskina (RUS) 1:25.09
3. Shenjie Qieyang (CHN) 1:25.16
MARATHON
1. Tiki Gelana (ETH) 2:23.07 OR
2. Priscah Jeptoo (KEN) 2:23.12
3. Tatyana Petrova Arkhipova (RUS) 2:23.29

BADMINTON

MEN
SINGLES
1. Dan Lin (CHN)
2. Chong Wei Lee (MAS)
3. Long Chen (CHN)
DOUBLES
1. CHN (Yun Cai, Haifeng Fu)
2. DEN (Mathias Boe, Carsten Morgensen)
3. KOR (Jae Sung Chung, Yong Dae Lee)

WOMEN
SINGLES
1. Xuerui Li (CHN)
2. Yihan Wang (CHN)
3. Saina Nehwal (IND)
DOUBLES
1. CHN (Yunlei Zhao, Qing Tian)
2. JPN (Mizuki Fujii, Reika Kakiwa)
3. RUS (Nina Vislova, Valeria Sorokina)

MIXED
DOUBLES
1. CHN (Nan Zhang, Yunlei Zhao)
2. CHN (Jin Ma, Chen Xu)
3. DEN (Joachim Fischer, Christinna Pedersen)

BASKETBALL

MEN
12-TEAM TOURNAMENT
1. USA (Tyson Chandler, Kevin Durant, Lebron James, Russell Westbrook, Deron Williams, Andrew Iguodala, Kobe Bryant, Kevin Love, James Harden, Chris Paul, Anthony Davis, Carmelo Anthony)
2. ESP (Pau Gasol, Rudy Fernandez, Sergio Rodriguez, Juan-Carlos Navarro, Jose Calderon, Felipe Reyes, Victor Claver, Fernando san Emeterio, Sergio Llull, Marc Gasol, Serge Ibaka, Victor Sada)
3. RUS (Alexey Shved, Timofey Mozgov, Sergey Karasev, Vitaliy Fridzon, Sasha Kaun, Evgeny Voronov, Victor Khryapa, Semen Antonov, Sergey Monya, Dmitry Khvostov, Anton Ponkrashov, Andrei Kirilenko)

WOMEN
12-TEAM TOURNAMENT
1. USA (Lindsay Whalen, Seimone Augustus, Sue Bird, Maya Moore, Angel McCoughtry, Asjha Jones, Tamika Catchings, Swin Cash, Diana Taurasi, Sylvia Fowles, Tina Charles, Candace Parker)
2. FRA (Isabelle Yacoubou, Endene Miyem, Clemence Beikes, Sandrine Gruda, Edwige Lawson-Wade, Celine Dumerc, Florence Lepron, Emilie Gomis, Marion Laborde, Elodie Godwin, Emmeline Ndongue, Jennifer Digbeu)
3. AUS (Jenna O'Hea, Samantha Richards, Jennifer Screen, Abby Bishop, Suzy Batkovic, Kathleen Macloed, Kristi Harrower, Laura Hodges, Belinda Snell, Rachel Jarry, Elizabeth Cambage, Lauren Jackson)

BOXING

MEN
LIGHT FLY WEIGHT (46–49KG)
1. Shiming Zou (CHN)
2. Kaeo Pongprayoon (THA)
=3. Paddy Barnes (IRL)
=3. David Ayrapetyan (RUS)
FLY WEIGHT (UP TO 52KG)
1. Robeisy Ramirez Carrazona (CUB)
2. Tugstsogt Nyambayar (MGL)
=3. Michael Conlan (IRL)
=3. Misha Aloian (RUS)
BANTAM WEIGHT (UP TO 56KG)
1. Luke Campbell (GBR)
2. Joe John Nevin (IRL)
=3. Satoshi Shimizu (JPN)
=3. Lazaro Alvarez-Estrada (CUB)
LIGHT WEIGHT (UP TO 60KG)
1. Vasyl Lomachenko (UKR)
2. Soonchul Han (KOR)
=3. Yasniel Toledo Lopez (CUB)
=3. Evaldas Petrauskas (LTU)
LIGHT WELTER WEIGHT (UP TO 64KG)
1. Roniel Iglesias Sotolongo (CUB)
2. Denys Berinchyk (UKR)
=3. Vincenzo Mangiacapre (ITA)
=3. Munkh-Erdene Uranchimeg (MGL)
WELTER WEIGHT (UP TO 69KG)
1. Serik Sapiyev (KAZ)
2. Freddie Evans (GBR)
3. Andrey Zamkovoy (RUS)
=3. Taras Shelestyuk (UKR)
MIDDLE WEIGHT (UP TO 75KG)
1. Ryota Murata (JPN)
2. Esquiva Falcao Florentino (BRA)
=3. Abbos Atoev (UZB)
=3. Anthony Ogogo (GBR)
LIGHT HEAVY WEIGHT (UP TO 81KG)
1. Egor Mekhontcev (RUS)
2. Adilbek Niyazymbetov (KAZ)
=3. Yamaguchi Falcao Florentino (BRA)
=3. Oleksandr Gvozdyk (UKR)
HEAVY WEIGHT (UP TO 91KG)
1. Oleksandr Usyk (UKR)
2. Clemente Russo (ITA)
=3. Tervel Pulev (BUL)
=3. Teymur Mammadov (AZE)
SUPER HEAVY WEIGHT (+91KG)
1. Anthony Joshua (GBR)
2. Roberto Cammarelle (ITA)
=3. Ivan Dychko (KAZ)
=3. Mago Medrasul Medzhidov (AZE)

WOMEN
FLY WEIGHT (48–51KG)
1. Nicola Adams (GBR)
2. Cancan Ren (CHN)
=3. Chungneijang Mery Kom Hmangte (IND)
=3. Marlen Esparza (USA)
LIGHT WEIGHT (57–60KG)
1. Katie Taylor (IRL)
2. Sofya Ochigava (RUS)
=3 Mavzuna Chorieva (TJK)
=3. Adriana Araujo (BRA)
MIDDLE WEIGHT (69–75KG)
1. Claressa Shields (USA)
2. Nadezda Torlopova (RUS)
=3. Marina Volnova (KAZ)
=3. Jinzi Li (CHN)

CANOE – CANOE SLALOM

MEN
CANOE SINGLE (C1)
1. Tony Estanguet (FRA) 97.06
2. Sideris Tasiadis (GER) 98.09
3. Michal Martikan (SVK) 98.31
CANOE DOUBLE (C2)
1. GBR (Tim Baillie, Etienne Stott) 106.41
2. GBR (David Florence, Richard Hounslow) 106.77
3. SVK (Pavol Hochschorner, Peter Hochschorner) 108.28
KAYAK SINGLE (K1)
1. Daniele Molmenti (ITA) 93.43
2. Vavrinec Hradilek (CZE) 94.78
3. Hannes Aigner (GER) 94.92

WOMEN
KAYAK SINGLE (K1)
1. Emilie Fer (FRA) 105.90
2. Jessica Fox (AUS) 106.51
3. Maialen Chourraut (ESP) 106.87

CANOE – CANOE SPRINT

MEN
CANOE SINGLE (C1) 200M
1. Yuri Cheban (UKR) 42.291
2. Jevgenij Shuklin (LTU) 42.792
3. Ivan Shtyl (RUS) 42.853

CANOE SINGLE (C1) 1000M
1. Sebastian Brendel (GER) 3:47.176
2. David Cal Figueroa (ESP) 3:48.053
3. Mark Oldershaw (CAN) 3:48.502

CANOE DOUBLE (C2) 1000M
1. GER (Peter Kretschmer, Kurt Kuschela) 3:33.804
2. BLR (Andrei Bahdanovich, Aliaksandr Bahdanovich) 3:35.206
3. RUS (Alexey Korovashkov, Ilya Pervukhin) 3:36.414

KAYAK SINGLE (K1) 200M
1. Ed McKeever (GBR) 36.246
2. Saul Craviotto Rivero (ESP) 36.540
3. Mark de Jonge (CAN) 36.657

KAYAK SINGLE (K1) 1000M
1. Eirik Larsen (NOR) 3:26.462
2. Adam van Koeverden (CAN) 3:27.170
3. Max Hoff (GER) 3:27.759

KAYAK DOUBLE (K2) 200M
1. RUS (Yury Postrigay, Alexander Dyachenko) 33.507
2. BLR (Raman Piatrushenka, Vadzim Makhneu) 34.266
3. GBR (Liam Heath, Jon Schofield) 34.421

KAYAK DOUBLE (K2) 1000M
1. HUN (Rudolf Dombi, Roland Kokeny) 3:09.646
2. POR (Fernando Pimenta, Emanuel Silva) 3:09.699
3. GER (Martin Hollstein, Andreas Ihle) 3:10.117

KAYAK FOUR (K4) 1000M
1. AUS (Tate Smith, Dave Smith, Murray Stewart, Jacob Clear) 2:55.085
2. HUN (Zoltan Kammerer, David Toth, Tamas Kulifai, Daniel Pauman) 2:55.699
3. CZE (Daniel Havel, Lukas Trefil, Josef Dostal, Jan Sterba) 2:55.850

WOMEN
KAYAK SINGLE (K1) 200M
1. Lisa Carrington (NZL) 44.638
2. Inna Osypenko-Radomska (UKR) 45.043
3. Natasa Douchev-Janics (HUN) 45.128

KAYAK SINGLE (K1) 500M
1. Danuta Kozak (HUN) 1:51.456
2. Inna Osypenko-Radomska (UKR) 1:52.685
3. Bridgitte Hartley (RSA) 1:52.923

KAYAK DOUBLE (K2) 500M
1. GER (Franziska Weber, Tina Dietze) 1:42.213
2. HUN (Katalin Kovacs, Natasha Douchev-Janics) 1:43.278
3. POL (Karolina Naja, Beata Mikolajczyk) 1:44.000

KAYAK FOUR (K4) 500M
1. HUN (Gabriella Szabo, Danuta Kozak, Katalin Kovacs, Krisztina Fazekas) 1:30.827
2. GER (Carolin Leonhardt, Franziska Weber, Katrin Wagner-Augustin, Tina Dietze) 1:31.298
3. BLR (Iryna Pamilova, Nadzeya Papok, Volha Khudzenka, Maryna Pautaran) 1:31.400

CYCLING – BMX RACING

MEN
1. Maris Strombergs (LAT)
2. Sam Willoughby (AUS)
3. Carlos Mario Oquendo Zabala (COL)

WOMEN
1. Mariana Pajon (COL)
2. Sarah Walker (NZL)
3. Laura Smulders (NED)

CYCLING – MOUNTAIN BIKE

MEN
CROSS-COUNTRY
1. Jaroslav Kulhavy (CZE)
2. Nino Schurter (SUI)
3. Marco Fontana (ITA)

WOMEN
CROSS-COUNTRY
1. Julie Bresset (FRA)
2. Sabine Sptiz (GER)
3. Georgia Gould (USA)

CYCLING – ROAD CYCLING

MEN
ROAD RACE (MASS START)
1. Alexandr Vinokurov (KAZ) 5:45:57
2. Rigoberto Uran Uran (COL) 5:45:57
3. Alexander Kristoff (NOR) 5:46:57

TIME TRIAL
1. Bradley Wiggins (GBR) 50:39.54

2. Tony Martin (GER) 51:21.54
3. Christopher Froome (GBR) 51:47.87

WOMEN
ROAD RACE (MASS START)
1. Marianne Vos (NED) 3:35:29
2. Elizabeth Armitstead (GBR) 3:35:29
3. Olga Zabelinskaya (RUS) 3:35:31

TIME TRIAL
1. Kristin Armstrong (USA) 37:34.82
2. Judith Arndt (GER) 37:50.29
3. Olga Zabelinskaya (RUS) 37:57.35

CYCLING – TRACK CYCLING

MEN
KEIRIN
1. Chris Hoy (GBR) 10.306
2. Maximilian Levy (GER) NM
=3. Simon van Velthooven (NZL) NM
=3.Teun Mulder (NED) NM

OMNIUM
1. Lasse Norman Hansen (DEN) 27 points
2. Bryan Coquard (FRA) 29 points
3. Edward Clancy (GBR) 30 points

SPRINT
1. Jason Kenny (GBR) NM
2. Gregory Bauge (FRA) NM
3. Shane Perkins (AUS) NM

TEAM PURSUIT
1. GBR (Steven Burke, Edward Clancy, Peter Kennaugh, Geraint Thomas) 3:51.659
2. AUS (Jack Bobridge, Rohan Dennis, Michael Hepburn, Glenn O'Shea) 3:54.581
3. NZL (Sam Bewley, Aaron Gate, Marc Ryan, Jesse Sergent) 3:55.952

TEAM SPRINT
1. GBR (Philip Hindes, Chris Hoy, Jason Kenny) 42.600
2. FRA (Gregory Bauge, Michael D'Almeida, Kevin Sireau) 43.013
3. GER (Rene Enders, Robert Forstemann, Maximilian Levy) 43.209

WOMEN
KEIRIN
1. Victoria Pendleton (GBR) 10.965
2. Shuang Guo (CHN) NM
3. Wai Sze Lee (HKG) NM

OMNIUM
1. Laura Trott (GBR) 18 points
2. Sarah Hammer (USA) 19 points
3. Annette Edmondson (AUS) 24 points

SPRINT
1. Anna Meares (AUS) NM
2. Victoria Pendleton (GBR) NM
3. Shuang Guo (CHN) NM

TEAM PURSUIT
1. GBR (Dani King, Joanna Rowsell, Laura Trott) 3:14.051 WR
2. USA (Dotsie Bausch, Sarah Hammer, Lauren Tamayo, Jennie Reed) 3:19.727
3. CAN (Gillian Carleton, Jasmin Glaesser, Tara Whitten) 3:17.915

TEAM SPRINT
1. GER (Kristina Vogel, Miriam Welte) 32.798
2. CHN (Jinjie Gong, Shuang Guo) REL
3. AUS (Kaarle McCulloch, Anna Meares) 32.727

EQUESTRIAN – DRESSAGE
INDIVIDUAL COMPETITION
1. Charlotte Dujardin on Valegro (GBR) 90.089 points
2. Adelinde Conrelissen on Parzival (NED) 88.196 points
3. Laura Bechtolsheimer on Mistral Hojris (GBR) 84.339 points

TEAM COMPETITION
1. GBR (Carl Hester, Laura Bechtolshheimer, Charlotte Dujardin) 79.979 points
2. GER (Dorothee Schneider, Kristina Sprehe, Helen Langehanenberg) 78.216 points
3. Ned (Anky van Grunsven, Edward Gal, Adelinde Cornelissen) 77.124 points

EQUESTRIAN – EVENTING
INDIVIDUAL COMPETITION
1. Michael Jung on Sam (GER) 40.60 penalties
2. Sara Ostholt Algotsson on Wega (SWE) 43.30 penalties

3. Sandra Auffarth on Opgun Louvo (GER) 44.80 penalties

TEAM COMPETITION
1. GER (Peter Thomsen on Barny, Dirk Schrade on King Artus, Sandra Auffarth on Opgun Louvo, Michael Jung on Sam, Ingrid Klimke on Butts Abraxxas) 133.70
2. GBR (William Fox-Pitt on Lionheart, Nicola Wilson on Opposition Buzz, Zara Phillips on High Kingdom, Mary King on Imperial Cavalier, Kristina Cook on Miners Frolic) 138.20
3. NZL (Jonelle Richards on Flintstar, Caroline Powell on Lenamore, Jonathan Paget on Clifton Promise, Andrew Nicholson on Nereo, Mark Todd on Campino) 144.40

EQUESTRIAN – JUMPING
INDIVIDUAL COMPETITION
1. Steve Guerdat on Nino des Buissonnets (SUI) NM
2. Gerco Schroder on London (NED) NM
3. Cian O'Connor on Blue Loyd 12 (IRL) NM

TEAM COMPETITION
1. GBR (Nick Skelton, Ben Maher, Scott Brash, Peter Charles) NM
2. NED (Jur Vrieling, Maikel van der Vleuten) Marc Houtzager, Gerco Schroder) NM
3. KSA (Prince Abdullah al Saud HRH, Kamal Bahamdan, Ramzy al Duhami, Abdullah Waleed Sharbatly) NM

FENCING

MEN
INDIVIDUAL EPÉE
1. Gascon Ruben Limardo (VEN)
2. Bartosz Piasecki (NOR)
3. Jinsun Jung (KOR)

INDIVIDUAL FOIL
1. Sheng Lei (CHN)
2. Alaaeldin Abouelkassem (EGY)
3. Byungchul Choi (KOR)

INDIVIDUAL SABRE
1. Aron Szilagyi (HUN)
2. Diego Occhiuzzi (ITA)
3. Nikolay Kovalev (RUS)

TEAM FOIL
1. ITA (Valerio Aspromonte, Andrea Baldini, Andrea Cassara, Giorgio Avola)
2. JPN (Kenta Chida, Ryo Miyaka, Yuki Ota, Suguru Awaji)
3. GER (Sebastian Bachmann, Peter Joppich, Benjamin Kleibrink, Andre Wessels)

TEAM SABRE
1. KOR (Junghwan Kim, Woo Young Won, Bongil Gu, Eunseok Oh)
2. ROM (Tiberiu Dolniceanu, Rares Dumitrescu, Alexandru Siriteanu, Florin Zalomir)
3. ITA (Aldo Montano, Diego Occhiuzzi, Luigi Tarantino, Luigi Samele)

WOMEN
INDIVIDUAL EPÉE
1. Yana Shemyakina (UKR)
2. Britta Heidemann (GER)
3. Yujie Sun (CHN)

INDIVIDUAL FOIL
1. Elisa Di Francisca (ITA)
2. Arianna Errigo (ITA)
3. Valentina Vezzali (ITA)

INDIVIDUAL SABRE
1. Jiyeon Kim (KOR)
2. Sofya Velikaya (RUS)
3. Olga Kharlan (UKR)

TEAM EPÉE
1. CHN (Na Li, Xiaojuan Luo, Yujie Sun, Anqi Xu)
2. KOR (Injeong Choi, Hyojung Jung, A Lam Shin, Eunsook Choi)
3. USA (Courtney Hurley, Maya Lawrence, Susie Scanlan, Kelley Hurley)

TEAM FOIL
1. ITA (Elisa Di Francisca, Arianna Errigo, Ilaria Salvatori, Valentina Vezzali)
2. RUS (Inna Deriglazova, Larisa Korobeynikova, Aida Shanaeva)
3. KOR (Hyun Hee Nam, Gil Ok Jung, Hee Sook Jeon, Ha Na Oh)

FOOTBALL

MEN
16-TEAM TOURNAMENT
1. MEX (Jose Corona, Israel Jimenez, Carlos Salcido, Hiram Mier, Darvin Chavez, Hector Herrera, Javier Cortes, Marco Fabian, Oribe Peralta, Giovani do Santos, Javier Aquino, Raul Jimenez, Diego Reyes, Jorge Enriquez, Nestor Vidrio, Miguel Ponce, Nestor Araujo Jose Rodriguez)
2. BRA (Gabriel, Rafael, Thiago Silva, Juan Jesus, Sandro, Marcelo, Lucas, Romulo, Leandro Damiao, Oscar, Neymar, Hulk, Bruno Uvini, Danilo, Alex Sandro, Ganso, Alexandre Pato, Neto)
3. KOR (Sungryong Jung, Jaesuk Oh, Sukyoung Yun, Younggwon Kim, Keehee Kim, Sungyeung Ki, Bokyung Kim, Sungdong Baek, Dongwon Ji, Chuyoung Park, Taehee Nam, Seokho Hwang, Jacheol Koo, Changsoo Kim, Jongwoo Park, Wooyoung Jung, Hyansung Kim, Bumyoung Lee)

WOMEN
12-TEAM TOURNAMENT
1. USA (Hope Solo, Heather Mitts, Christie Rampone, Becky Sauerbrunn, Kelley O'Hara, Amy le Peilbet, Shannon Boxx, Amy Rodriguez, Heather O'Reilly, Carli Llyod, Sydney Leroux, Lauren Cheney, Alex Morgan, Abby Wambach, Megan Rapinoe, Rachel Buehler, Tobin Heath, Nicole Barnhart)
2. JPN (Miho Fukumoto, Yukari Kinga, Azusa Iwashimizu, Saki Kumagai, Aya Sameshima, Mizuho Sakaguchi, Kozue Ando, Aya Miyama, Nahomi Kawasumi, Homare Sawa, Shinobu Ohno, Kyoko Yano, Karina Maruyama, Asuna tanaka, Megumi Takase, Mana Iwabuchi, Yuki Ogimi, Ayumi Kaihori)
3. CAN (Karina Leblanc, Emily Zurrer, Chelsea Stewart, Carmelina Moscato, Robyn Gayle, Kaylyn Kyle, Rhian Wilkinson, Diana Matheson, Candace Chapman, Lauren Sesselmann, Desiree Scott, Christine Sinclair, Sophie Schmidt, Melissa Tancredi, Kelly Parker, Jonelle Filigno, Brittany Timko, Erin McLeod, Melanie Booth, Marie-Eve Nault)

GYMNASTICS – ARTISTIC

MEN
FLOOR COMPETITION
1. Kai Zou (CHN) 15.933 points
2. Kohei Uchimura (JPN) 15.800 points
3. Denis Ablyazin (RUS) 15.800 points

HORIZONTAL BARS COMPETITION
1. Epke Zonderland (NED) 15.533 points
2. Fabian Hambuchen (GER) 16.400 points
3. Kai Zou (CHN) 16.366 points

INDIVIDUAL ALL-AROUND COMPETITION
1. Kohei Uchimura (JPN) 92.690 points
2. Marcel Nguyen (GER) 91.031 points
3. Danell Leyva (USA) 90.698 points

PARALLEL BARS COMPETITION
1. Zhe Feng (CHN) 15.966 points
2. Marcel Nguyen (GER) 15.800 points
3. Hamilton Sabot (FRA) 15.566 points

POMMEL HORSE COMPETITION
1. Krisztian Berki (HUN) 16.066 points
2. Louis Smith (GBR) 16.066 points
3. Max Whitlock (GBR) 15.600 points

RINGS COMPETITION
1. Arthur Nabrrete Zanetti (BRA) 15.900 points
2. Yibing Chen (CHN) 15.800 points
3. Matteo Morandi (ITA) 15.733

TEAM COMPETITION
1. CHN (Yibing Chen, Zhe Feng, Weiyang Guo, Chenglong Zhang, Kai Zou) 275.997 points
2. JPN (Ryohei Kato, Kazuhito Tanaka, Yusuke Tanaka, Kohei Uchimura, Koji Yamamuro) 271.952 points
3. GBR (Sam Oldham, Daniel Pruvis, Louis Smith, Kristian Thomas, Max Whitlock) 271.711 points

VAULT COMPETITION
1. Hak Seon Yang (KOR) 16.533 points
2. Denis Ablyazin (RUS) 16.399 points
3. Igor Radivlov (UKR) 16.316 points

WOMEN
BALANCE BEAM COMPETITION
1. Linlin Deng (CHN) 15.600 points
2. Lu Sui (CHN) 15.500 points
3. Alexandra Raisman (USA) 15.066 points

FLOOR COMPETITION
1. Alexandra Raisman (USA) 15.600 points
2. Catalina Ponor (ROU) 15.200 points
3. Aliya Mustafina (RUS) 14.900 points
INDIVIDUAL ALL-AROUND COMPETITION
1. Gabrielle Douglas (USA) 62.232 points
2. Victoria Komova (RUS) 61.973 points
3. Aliya Mustafina (RUS) 59.566 points
TEAM COMPETITION
1. USA (Gabrielle Douglas, Mc Kayla Maroney, Alexandra Raisman, Kyla Ross, Jordyn Wieber) 183.596 points
2. RUS (Kseniia Afanaseva, Anastasia Grishina, Victoria Komova, Aliya Mustafina, Maria Paseka) 178.530 points
3. ROU (Diana Laura Bulimar, Diana Maria Chelaru, Larisa Andreea Iordache, Sandra Raluca Izbasa, Catalina Ponor) 176.414 points
UNEVEN BARS COMPETITION
1. Aliya Mustafina (RUS) 16.133 points
2. Kexin He (CHN) 15.933 points
3. Elizabeth Tweddle (GBR) 15.916 points
VAULT COMPETITION
1. Sandra Raluca Izbasa (ROU) 15.191 points
2. Mc Kayla Maroney (USA) 15.083 points
3. Maria Paseka (RUS) 15.050 points

GYMNASTICS – RHYTHMIC
WOMEN
GROUP COMPETITION
1. RUS (Anastasia Bliznyuk, Uliana Donskova, Ksenia Dudkina, Alina Makarenko, Anastasia Nazarenko, Karolina Sevastyanova) 57.000 points
2. BLR (Maryna Hancharova, Anastasiya Ivankova, Nataliya Leshchyk, Aliaksandra Narkevich, Kseniya Sankovich, Alina Tumilovich) 55.500 points
3. ITA (Elisa Blanchi, Romina Laurito, Marta Pagnini, Elisa Santoni, Anzhelika Savrayuk, Andreea Stefanescu) 55.450 points
INDIVIDUAL ALL-AROUND COMPETITION
1. Evgeniya Kanaeva (RUS) 116.900 points
2. Daria Dmitrieva (RUS) 114.500 points
3. Liubou Charkashyna (BLR) 111.700 points

GYMNASTICS – TRAMPOLINE
MEN
INDIVIDUAL COMPETITION
1. Dong Dong (CHN) 62.990 points
2. Dmitry Ushakov (RUS) 61.769 points
3. Chunlong Lu (CHN) 61.319 points

WOMEN
INDIVIDUAL COMPETITION
1. Rosannagh Maclennan (CAN) 57.305 points
2. Shanshan Huang (CHN) 56.730 points
3. Wenna He (CHN) 55.950 points

HANDBALL
MEN
12-TEAM TOURNAMENT
1. FRA (Jerome Fernandez, Didier Dinart, Xavier Barachet, Guillaume Gille, Bertrand Gille, Daniel Narcisse, Guillaume Joli, Samuel Hornubia, Daouda Karaboue, Nikola Karabatic, Thierry Omeyer, William Accambray, Luc Abalo, Cedric Sorhaindo, Michael Guigou)
2. SWE (Mattias Andersson, Mattias Gustafsson, Kim Andersson, Jonas Kallman, Magnus Jernemyr, Niclas Ekberg, Dalibor Doder, Jonas Larholm, Tobias Karlsson, Johan Jakobsson, Johan Sjostrand, Fredrik Petersen, Kim Ekdahl du Rietz, Mattias Zakrisson, Andreas Nilsson)
3. CRO (Venio Losert, Ivano Balic, Domagoj Duvnjak, Blazenko Lackovic, Marko Kopljar, Igor Vori, Jakov Gojun, Zlatko Horvat, Drago Vukovic, Damir Bicanic, Denis Buntic, Mirko Alilovic, Manuel Strlek, Ivan Cupic, Ivan Nincevic)

WOMEN
12-TEAM TOURNAMENT
1. NOR (Kari Grimsbo, Ida Alstad, Heidi Loke, Tonje Nostvold, Karoline Dyhre Breivang, Kristine Lunde-Borgersen, Kari Johansen, Marit Malm Frafjord, Linn Sulland, Katrine Lunde Haraldsen, Linn-Kristin Koren, Goril Snorroeggen, Amanda Kurtovix, Camilla Herrem)

---

2. MNE (Marina Vukcevic, Radmila Miljanic, Jovanka Radicevic, Ana Dokic, Amrija Jovanovic, Ana Radovic, Andela Bulatovic, Sonja Barjaktarovic, Maja Savic, Bojana Popovic, Suzana Lazovic, Katarina Bulatovic, Majda Mehmedovic, Milena Knezevic)
3. ESP (Marta Lopez Herrero, Andrea Barno San Martin, Nely Alberto Francisca, Beatriz Fernandez Ibanez, Veronica Cuadrado Dehesa, Marta Mangue Gonzalez, Macarena Aguilar Diaz, Silvia Navarro Jimenez, Jessica Alonso Bernardo, Elisabeth Pinedo Saenz, Begona Fernandez Molinos, Vanessa Amoros Quiles, Patricia Elorza Equiara, Mihaela Ciobanu Ciobanu)

HOCKEY
MEN
12-TEAM TOURNAMENT
1. GER (Maxmillian Mueller, Martin Haener, Oskar Deecke, Christopher Wesley, Moritz Fuerste, Tobias Hauke, Jan Philipp Rabente, Benjamin Wess, Timo Wess, Oliver Korn, Christopher Zeller, Max Weinhold, Matthia Witthaus, Florian Fuchs, Philipp Zeller, Thilo Stralkowski)
2. NED (Jaap Stockmann, Tim Jenniskens, Klaas Vermeulen, Marcel Balkestein, Wouter Jolie, Billy Bakker, Roderick Weusthof, Robbert Kemperman, Sander Baart, Teun de Nooijer, Floris Evers, Bob de Voogd, Sander de Wijn, Rogier Hofman, Robert van der Horst, Valentin Verga, Mink van de Weerde)
3. AUS (Jamie Dwyer, Liam De Young, Simon Orchard, Glenn Turner, Christopher Giriello, Matthew Butturini, Mark Knowles, Russell Ford, Edward Ockenden, Joel Carroll, Matt Gohdes, Timothy Deavin, Matthew Swann, Nathan Burgers, Kieran Govers, Fergus Kavanagh)

WOMEN
12-TEAM TOURNAMENT
1. NED (Joyce Sombroek, Kitty van Male, Carlien Dirkse van den Heuvel, Kelly Jonker, Maartje Goderie, Lidewij Welten, Caia van Maasakker, Maartje Paumen, Naomi van AS, Ellen Hoog, Sophie Polkamp, Kim Lammers, Eva de Goede, Marilyn Agliotti, Merel de Blaeij, Margot van Geffen)
2. ARG (Laura del Colle, Rosario Luchetti, Macarena Rodriquez Perez, Martina Cavallero, Luciano Aymar, Carla Rebecchi, Delfina Merino, Florencia Habif, Rocio Sanchez Mocchia, Daniela Sruoga, Sofia Maccari, Mariella Scarone, Silvina D'elia, Noel Barrionuevo, Josefina Sruoga, Florencia Mutio)
3. GBR (Elizabeth Storry, Emily Maguire, Laura Unsworth, Crista Cullen, Hannah Macleod, Anne Panter, Helen Richardson, Kate Walsh, Chloe Rogers, Laura Bartlett, Alex Danson, Georgie Twigg, Ashleigh Ball, Sally Walton, Nicola White, Sarah Thomas)

JUDO
MEN
EXTRA LIGHTWEIGHT (UP TO 60KG)
1. Arsen Galstyan (RUS)
2. Hiroaki Hiraoka (JPN)
3. Felipe Kitadai (BRA)
3. Rishod Sobirov (UZB)
HALF-LIGHTWEIGHT (60–66KG)
1. Lasha Shavdatuashvili (GEO)
2. Miklos Ungvari (HUN)
3. Masashi Ebinuma (JPN)
3. Jun-Ho Cho (KOR)
LIGHTWEIGHT (66–73KG)
1. Mansur Isaev (RUS)
2. Riki Nakaya (JPN)
3. Nyam-Ochir Sainjargal (MGL)
3. Ugo Legrand (FRA)
HALF-MIDDLEWEIGHT (73–81KG)
1. Jae-Bum Kim (KOR)
2. Ole Bischof (GER)
3. Ivan Nifontov (RUS)
3. Antoine Valois-Fortier (CAN)
MIDDLEWEIGHT (81–90KG)
1. Dae-Nam Song (KOR)
2. Asley Gonzalez (CUB)
3. Ilias Iliadis (GRE)
3. Masashi Nishiyama (JPN)
HALF-HEAVYWEIGHT (90–100KG)
1. Tagir Khaibulaev (RUS)

---

2. Tuvshinbayer Naidan (MGL)
3. Henk Grol (NED)
3. Dimitri Peters (GER)
HEAVYWEIGHT (OVER 100KG)
1. Teddy Riner (FRA)
2. Alexander Mikhaylin (RUS)
3. Rafael Silva (BRA)
3. Andreas Toelzer (GER)

WOMEN
EXTRA LIGHTWEIGHT (UP TO 48KG)
1. Sarah Menezes (BRA)
2. Alina Dumitru (ROU)
3. Eva Csernoviczki (HUN)
3. Charline van Snick (BEL)
HALF-LIGHTWEIGHT (48C52KG)
1. Kum Ae An (PRK)
2. Yanet Bermoy Acosta (CUB)
3. Rosalba Forciniti (ITA)
3. Priscilla Gneto (FRA)
LIGHTWEIGHT (52–57KG)
1. Kaori Matsumoto (JPN)
2. Corina Caprioriu (ROU)
3. Marti Malloy (USA)
3. Automne Pavia (FRA)
HALF-MIDDLEWEIGHT (57–63KG)
1. Urska Zolnir (SLO)
2. Lili Xu (CHN)
3. Gevrise Emane (FRA)
3. Yoshie Ueno (JAP)
MIDDLEWEIGHT (63–70KG)
1. Lucie Decosse (FRA)
2. Kerstin Thiele (GER)
3. Yuri Alvear (COL)
3. Edith Bosch (NED)
HALF-HEAVYWEIGHT (70–78KG)
1. Kayla Harrison (USA)
2. Gemma Gibbons (GBR)
3. Mayra Aguiar (BRA)
3. Audrey Tcheumeo (FRA)
HEAVYWEIGHT (OVER 78KG)
1. Idalys Ortiz (CUB)
2. Mika Sugimoto (JPN)
3. Karina Bryant (GBR)
3. Wen Tong (CHN)

MODERN PENTATHLON
MEN
INDIVIDUAL COMPETITION
1. David Svoboda (CZE) 5928 points MPOR
2. Zhongrong Cao (CHN) 5904 points
3. Adam Marosi (HUN) 5836 points

WOMEN
INDIVIDUAL COMPETITION
1. Laura Asadauskaite (LTU) 5408 points MPOR
2. Samantha Murray (GBR) 5356 points
3. Yane Marques (BRA) 5340 points

ROWING
MEN
SINGLE SCULLS (1X)
1. Mahe Drysdale (NZL) 6:57.82
2. Ondrej Synek (CZE) 6:59.37
3. Alan Campbell (GBR) 7:03.28
PAIR (2-)
1. NZL (Eric Murray, Hamish Bond) 6:16.65
2. FRA (Germain Chardin, Dorian Mortelette) 6:21.11
3. GBR (George Nash, William Satch) 6:21.77
DOUBLE SCULLS (2X)
1. NZL (Nathan Cohen, Joseph Sullivan) 6:31.67
2. ITA (Alessio Sartori, Romano Battisti) 6:32.80
3. SLO (Luka Spik, Iztok Cop) 6:34.35
LIGHTWEIGHT DOUBLE SCULLS (2X)
1. DEN (Mads Rasmussen, Rasmus Quist) 6:37.17
2. GBR (Zac Purchase, Mark Hunter) 6:37.78
3. NZL (Storm Uru, Peter Taylor) 6:40.86
FOUR (4-)
1. GBR (Alex Gregory, Pete Reed, Tom James, Andrew Triggs Hodge) 6:03.97
2. AUS (William Lockwood, James Chapman, Drew Ginn, Joshua Dunkley-Smith) 6:05.19
3. USA (Glenn Ochal, Henrik Rummel, Charles Cole, Scott Gault) 6:07.20
LIGHTWEIGHT FOUR (4-)
1. RSA (James Thompson, Matthew Brittain, John Smith, Sizwe Ndlovu) 6:02.84

---

2. GBR (Peter Chambers, Rob Williams, Richard Chambers, Chris Bartley) 6:03.09
3. DEN (Kasper Winther, Morten Jorgensen, Jacob Barsoe, Eskild Ebbesen) 6:03.16
QUADRUPLE SCULLS (4X)
1. GER (Karl Schulze, Phillipp Wende, Lauritz Schoof, Tim Grohmann) 5:42.48
2. CRO (Daivd Sain, Martin Sinkovic, Damir Martin, Valent Sinkovic) 5:44.78
3. AUS (Christopher Morgan, Karsten Forsterling, James McRae, Daniel Noonan) 5:45.22
EIGHT (8+)
1. GER (Filip Adamski, Andreas Kuffner, Eric Johannesen, Maximilian Reinelt, Richard Schmidt, Lukas Mueller, Florian Mennigen, Kristof Wilke, Martin Sauer) 5:48.75
2. CAN (Gabriel Bergen, Douglas Csima, Rob Gibson, Conlin McCabe, Malcolm Howard, Andrew Byrnes, Jeremiah Brown, Will Crothers, Brian Price) 5:49.98
3. GBR (Alex Partridge, James Foad, Tom Ransley, Richard Egington, Mohamed Sbihi, Greg Searle, Matthew Langridge, Constantine Louloudis, Phelan Hill) 5:51.18

WOMEN
SINGLE SCULLS (1X)
1. Miroslava Knapkova (CZE) 7:54.37
2. Fie Erichsen (DEN) 7:57.72
3. Kim Crow (AUS) 7:58.04
PAIR (2-)
1. GBR (Helen Glover, Heather Stanning) 7:27.13
2. AUS (Kate Hornsey, Sarah Tait) 7:29.86
3. NZL (Juliette Haigh, Rebecca Scown) 7:30.19
DOUBLE SCULLS (2X)
1. GBR (Anna Watkins, Katherine Grainger) 6:55.82
2. AUS (Kim Crow, Brooke Pratley) 6:58.55
3. POL (Magdalena Fularczyk, Julia Michalska) 7:07.92
LIGHTWEIGHT DOUBLE SCULLS (2X)
1. GBR (Katherine Copeland, Sophie Hosking) 7:09.30
2. CHN (Dongxiang Xu, Wenyi Huang) 7:11.93
3. GRE (Christina Giazitzidou, Alexandra Tsiavou) 7:12.09
QUADRUPLE SCULLS (4X)
1. UKR (Kateryna Tarasenko, Nataliya Dovgodko, Anastasiia Kozhenkova, Yana Dementieva) 6:35.93
2. GER (Annekatrin Thiele, Carina Baer, Julia Richter, Britta Oppelt) 6:38.09
3. USA (Natalie Dell, Kara Kohler, Megan Kalmoe, Adrienne Martelli) 6:40.63
EIGHT (8+)
1. USA (Erin Cafaro, Zsuzsanna Francia, Esther Lofgren, Taylor Ritzel, Meghan Musnicki, Eleanor Logan, Caroline Lind, Caryn Davies, Mary Whipple) 6:10.59
2. CAN (Janine Hanson, Rachelle Vinberg, Krista Guloien, Lauren Wilkinson, Natalie Mastracci, Ashley Brzozowicz, Darcy Marquardt, Andreanne Morin, Lesley Thompson-Willie) 6:12.06
3. Ned (Jacobine Veenhoven, Nienke Kingma, Chantal Achterberg, Sytske de Groot, Roline Repelaer van Driel, Claudia Belderbos, Carline Bouw, Annemiek de Haan, Anne Schellekens) 6:13.12

SAILING
MEN
WINDSURFER (RS-X)
1. Dorian van Rijsselberge (NED) 15 points
2. Nick Dempsey (GBR) 41 points
3. Przemyslaw Miarczynski (POL) 60 points
ONE-PERSON DINGHY (LASER)
1. Tom Slingsby (AUS) 43 points
2. Pavlos Kontides (CYP) 59 points
3. Rasmus Myrgren (SWE) 72 points
ONE-PERSON DINGHY (HEAVYWEIGHT) (FINN)
1. Ben Ainslie (GBR) 46 points
2. Jonas Høgh-Christensen (DEN) 46 points
3. Jonathan Lobert (FRA) 49 points
TWO-PERSON DINGHY (470)
1. AUS (Mathew Belcher, Malcolm Page) 22 points
2. GBR (Luke Patience, Stuart Bithell) 30 points
3. ARG (Lucas Calabrese, Juan de la Fuente) 63 points
SKIFF (49ER)
1. AUS (Nathan Outteridge, Iain Jensen) 56 points
2. NZL (Peter Burling, Blair Tuke) 80 points
3. DEN (Allan Norregaard, Peter Lang) 114 points

KEELBOAT (STAR)
1. SWE (Fredrik Loof, Max Salminen) 32 points
2. GBR (Iain Percy, Andrew Simpson) 34 points
3. BRA (Robert Scheidt, Bruno Prada) 40 points

WOMEN
WINDSURFER (RS-X)
1. Marina Alabau Neira (ESP) 26 points
2. Tuuli Petaja (FIN) 46 points
3. Zofia Noceti-Klepacka (POL) 47 points
ONE-PERSON DINGHY (LASER RADIAL)
1. Lijia Xu (CHN) 35 points
2. Marit Bouwmeester (NED) 37 points
3. Evi Van Acker (BEL) 40 points
TWO-PERSON DINGHY (470)
1. NZL (Jo Aleh, Olivia Powrie) 35 points
2. GBR (Hannah Mills, Saskia Clark) 51 points
3. NED (Lisa Westerhof, Lobke Berkhout) 64 points
MATCH RACING (ELLIOTT 6M)
1. ESP (Tamara Echegoyen Dominguez, Sofia Toro Prieto Puga, Angela Pumariega Menendez)
2. AUS (Olivia Price, Nina Curtis, Lucinda Whitty)
3. FIN (Silja Lehtinen, Silja Kanerva, Mikaela Wulff)

SHOOTING
MEN
10M AIR RIFLE
1. Alin George Moldoveanu (ROU) 702.1 points
2. Niccolo Campriani (ITA) 701.5 points
3. Gagan Narang (IND) 701.1 points
50M RIFLE PRONE
1. Sergei Martynov (BLR) 705.5 points FWR
2. Lionel Cox (BEL) 701.2 points
3. Rajmond Debevec (SLO) 701.0 points
50M RIFLE 3 POSITIONS
1. Niccolo Campriani (ITA) 1278.5 points FOR
2. Jonghyun Kim (KOR) 1272.5 points
3. Matthew Emmons (USA) 1271.3 points
10M AIR PISTOL
1. Jongoh Jin (KOR) 688.2 points
2. Luca Tesconi (ITA) 685.8 points
3. Andrija Zlatic (SRB) 685.2 points
25M RAPID FIRE PISTOL
1. Leuris Pupo (CUB) 34 points
2. Vinay Kumar (IND) 30 points
3. Feng Ding (CHN) 27 points
50M PISTOL
1. Jongoh Jin (KOR) 662.0 points
2. Young Rae Choi (KOR) 661.5 points
3. Zhiwei Wang (CHN) 658.6 points
SKEET
1. Vincent Hancock (USA) 148 points FOR
2. Anders Golding (DEN) 146 points
3. Nasser Al-Attiya (QAT) 144 points
TRAP
1. Giovanni Cernogoraz (CRO) 146 points
2. Massimo Fabbrizi (ITA) 146 points
3. Fehaid Aldeehani (KUW) 145 points
DOUBLE TRAP
1. Peter Robert Russell Wilson (GBR) 188 points
2. Hakan Dahlby (SWE) 186 points
3. Vasily Mosin (RUS) 185 points

WOMEN
10M AIR RIFLE
1. Siling Yi (CHN) 502.9 points
2. Sylwia Bogacka (POL) 502.2 points
3. Dan Yu (CHN) 501.5 points
50M RIFLE 3 POSITIONS
1. Jamie Lynn Gray (USA) 691.9 points FOR
2. Ivana Maksimovic (SRB) 687.5 points
3. Adela Sykorova (CZE) 683.0 points
10M AIR PISTOL
1. Wenjun Guo (CHN) 488.1 points
2. Celine Goberville (FRA) 486.6 points
3. Olena Kostevych (UKR) 486.6 points
25M PISTOL
1. Jangmi Kim (KOR) 792.4 points
2. Ying Chen (CHN) 791.4 points
3. Olena Kostevych (UKR) 788.6 points
SKEET
1. Kimberly Rhode (USA) 99 points
2. Ning Wei (CHN) 91 points
3. Danka Bartekova (SVK) 90 points
TRAP
1. Jessica Rossi (ITA) 99 points FWR
2. Zuzana Stefecekova (SVK) 93 points

3. Delphine Reau (FRA) 93 points

TABLE TENNIS
MEN
SINGLES
1. Jike Zhang (CHN)
2. Hao Wang (CHN)
3. Dimitrij Ovtcharov (GER)
TEAM
1. CHN (Long Ma, Hao Wang, Jike Chang)
2. KOR (Saehyuk Joo, Sangeun Oh, Seungmin Ryu)
3. Ger (Timo Boll, Dimitrij Ovtcharov, Bastian Steger)

WOMEN
SINGLES
1. Xiaoxia Li (CHN)
2. Ning Ding (CHN)
3. Tianwei Feng (SIN)
TEAM
1. CHN (Ning Ding, Yue Guo, Xiaoxia Li)
2. JPN (Ai Fukuhara, Sayaka Hirano, Kasumi Ishikawa)
3. SIN (tianwei Feng, Jiawei Li, Yuegu Wang)

TAEKWONDO
MEN
UNDER 58KG
1. Joel Gonzalez Bonilla (ESP)
2. Daehoon Lee (KOR)
=3. Alexey Denisenko (RUS)
=3. Oscar Munoz Oviedo (COL)
UNDER 68KG
1. Servet Tazegul (TUR)
2. Mohammed Bagheri Motamed (IRI)
=3. Terrence Jennings (USA)
=3. Rohullah Nikpah (AFG)
UNDER 80KG
1. Sebastian Eduardo Crismanich (ARG)
2. Nicolas Garcia Hemme (ESP)
=3. Lutalo Muhammad (GBR)
=3. Mauro Sarmiento (ITA)
OVER 80KG
1. Carlo Molfetta (ITA)
2. Anthony Obame (GAB)
=3. Robelis Despaigne (CUB)
=3. Xiaobo Liu (CHN)

WOMEN
UNDER 49KG
1. Jingyu Wu (CHN)
2. Brigitte Yague Enrique (ESP)
=3. Chanatip Sonkham (THA)
=3. Lucija Zaninovic (CRO)
UNDER 57KG
1. Jade Jones (GBR)
2. Yuzhuo Hou (CHN)
=3. Marlene Harnois (FRA)
=3. Li-Cheng Tseng (TPE)
UNDER 67KG
1. Kyung Seon Hwang (KOR)
2. Nur Tatar (TUR)
=3. Paige McPherson (USA)
=3. Helena Fromm (GER)
OVER 67KG
1. Milica Mandic (SRB)
2. Anne-Caroline Graffe (FRA)
=3. Anastasia Baryshnikova (RUS)
=3. Maria del Rosario Espinoza (MEX)

TENNIS
MEN
SINGLES
1. Andy Murray (GBR)
2. Roger Federer (SUI)
3. Juan Martin del Potro (ARG)

DOUBLES
1. USA (Mike Bryan, Bob Bryan)
2. FRA (Michael Llodra, Jo-Wilfried Tsonga)
3. FRA (Julien Benneteau, Richard Gasquet)

WOMEN
SINGLES
1. Serena Williams (USA)
2. Maria Sharapova (RUS)
3. Victoria Azarenka (BLR)

DOUBLES
1. USA (Serena Williams, Venus Williams)
2. CZE (Andrea Hlavackova, Lucie Hradecka)
3. RUS (Maria Kirilenko, Nadia Petrova)

MIXED
DOUBLES
1. BLR (Victoria Azarenka, Max Mirnyi)
2. GBR (Laura Robson, Andy Murray)
3. USA (Lisa Raymond, Mike Bryan)

TRIATHLON
MEN
INDIVIDUAL
1. Alistair Brownlee (GBR) 1:46.25
2. Javier Gomez (ESP) 1:46.36
3. Jonathan Brownlee (GBR) 1:46.56

WOMEN
INDIVIDUAL
1. Nicola Spirig (SUI) 1:59.48
2. Lisa Norden (SWE) 1:59.48
3. Erin Densham (AUS) 1:59.50

VOLLEYBALL
MEN
12-TEAM TOURNAMENT
1. RUS (Nikolay Apalikov, Taras Khtey, Sergey Grankin, Sergey Tetyukhin, Alexander Sokolov, Yury Berezhko, Alexander Butko, Dmitriy Muserskiy, Dmitriy Ilinykh, Maxim Mikhhaylov, Alexander Volkov, Alexey Obmochaev)
2. BRA (Bruno Rezende, Wallace de Souza, Sidnei dos Santos Junior, Leandro Vissotto Neves, Gilberto Godoy Filho, Murilo Endres, Sergio Santos, Thiago Alves, Rodrigo Santana, Lucas Saatkamp, Ricardo Garcia, Dante Amaral)
3. ITA (Luigi Mastrangelo, Simone Parodi, Samuele Papi, Michal Lasko, Ivan Zaytsev, Dante Boninfante, Cristian Savani, Dragan Travica, Alessandro Fei, Emanuele Birarelli, Andrea Bari, Andrea Giovi)

WOMEN
12-TEAM TOURNAMENT
1. BRA (Fabiana Claudino, Danielle Lins, Paula Pequeno, Adenizia Silva, Thaisa Menezes, Jaqueline Carvalho, Fernanda Ferreira, Tandara Caixeta, Natalia Pereira, Sheilla Castro, Fabiana Oliveira, Fernanda Rodrigues)
2. USA (Danielle Scott-Arruda, Tayyiba Haneef-Park, Lindsey Berg, Tamari Miyashiro, Nicole Davis, Jordan Larson, Megan Hodge, Christa Harmotto, Logan Tom, Foluke Akinradewo, Courtney Thompson, Destinee Hooker)
3. JPN (Hitomi Nakamichi, Yoshie Takeshita, Mai Yamaguchi, Erika Araki, Kaori Inoue, Maiko Kano, Yuko Sano, Ai Otomo, Risa Shinnabe, Saori Sakoda, Yukiko Ebata, Saori Kimura)

VOLLEYBALL – BEACH VOLLEYBALL
MEN
24-TEAM TOURNAMENT
1. GER (Julius Brink, Jonas Reckermann)
2. BRA (Alsion Cerutti, Emanuel Rego)
3. LAT (Martins Plavins, Janis Smedins)

WOMEN
24-TEAM TOURNAMENT
1. USA (Kerri Walsh Jennings, Misty May-Treanor)
2. USA (April Ross, Jennifer Kessy)
3. BRA (Juliana Silva, Larissa Franca)

WEIGHTLIFTING
MEN
56KG
1. Yun Chol Om (PRK) 293kg
2. Jingbiao Wu (CHN) 289kg
3. Valentin Hristov (AZE) 286kg
62KG
1. Un Guk Kim (PRK) 327kg WR
2. Oscar Albeiro Figueroa Mosquera (COL) 317kg
3. Irawan Eko Yuli (INA) 317kg
69KG
1. Qingfeng Lin (CHN) 344kg
2. Triyatno Triyatno (INA) 333kg
3. Razvan Constantin Martin (ROU) 332kg

77KG
1. Xiaojun Lu (CHN) 379kg WR
2. Haojie Lu (CHN) 360kg
3. Ivan Cambar Rodriguez (CUB) 349kg
85KG
1. Adrian Edward Zielinski (POL) 385kg
2. Apti Aukhadov (RUS) 385kg
3. Kianoush Rostami (IRI) 380kg
94KG
1. Ilya Ilyin (KAZ) 418kg WR
2. Alexander Ivanov (RUS) 409kg
3. Anatoli Ciricu (MDA) 407kg
105KG
1. Oleksiy Torokhtiy (UKR) 412kg
2. Navab Nasirshelal (IRI) 411kg
3. Bartlomiej Wojciech Bonk (POL) 410kg
OVER 105KG
1. Behdad Salimikordasiabi (IRI) 455kg
2. Sajjad Anoushiravani Hamlabad (IRI) 449kg
3. Ruslan Albegov (RUS) 448kg

WOMEN
48KG
1. Mingjuan Wang (CHN) 205kg
2. Hiromi Miyake (JPN) 197kg
3. Chun Hwa Ryang (PRK) 192kg
53KG
1. Zulfiya Chinshanlo (KAZ) 226 OR
2. Shu-Ching Hsu (TPE) 219kg
3. Cristina Iovu (MDA) 219kg
58KG
1. Xueying Li (CHN) 246kg OR
2. Pimsiri Sirikaew (THA) 236kg
3. Yuliya Kalina (UKR) 235kg
63KG
1. Maiya Maneza (KAZ) 245kg OR
2. Svetlana Tsarukaeva (RUS) 237kg
3. Christine Girard (CAN) 236kg
69KG
1. Jong Sim Rim (PRK) 261kg
2. Roxana Daniela Cocos (ROU) 256kg
3. Maryna Shkermankova (BLR) 256kg
75KG
1. Svetlana Podobedova (KAZ) 291kg
2. Natalya Zablotnaya (RUS) 291kg OR
3. Iryna Kulesha (BLR) 269kg
OVER 75KG
1. Lulu Zhou (CHN) 333kg WR
2. Tatiana Kashirina (RUS) 332kg
3. Hripsime Khurshudyan (ARM) 294kg

WRESTLING – FREESTYLE
MEN
UP TO 55KG
1. Dzhamal Otarsultanov (RUS)
2. Vladimer Khinchegashvili (GEO)
=3. Kyong Il Yang (PRK)
=3. Shinichi Yumoto (JPN)
55–60KG
1. Toghrul Asgarov (AZE)
2. Besik Kudukhov (RUS)
=3. Coleman Scott (USA)
=3. Yogeshwar Dutt (IND)
60–66KG
1. Tatsuhiro Yonemitsu (JPN)
2. Sushil Kumar (IND)
=3. Akzhurek Tanatarov (KAZ)
=3. Livan Lopez Azcuy (CUB)
66–74KG
1. Jordan Ernest Burroughs (USA)
2. Sadegh Saeed Goudarzi (IRI)
=3. Soslan Tigiev (UZB)
=3. Denis Tsargush (RUS)
74–84KG
1. Sharif Sharifov (AZE)
2. Jaime Espinal (PUR)
=3. Dato Marsagishvili (GEO)
=3. Ehsan Naser Lashgari (IRI)
84–96KG
1. Jacob Varner (USA)
2. Valerii Adriitsev (UKR)
=3. George Goshelldze (GEO)
=3. Khetag Gazyumov (AZE)

96–120KG
1. Artur Taymazov (UZB)
2. Davit Modzmanashivil (GEO)
=3. Komeil Ghasemi (IRI)
=3. Bilyal Makhov (RUS)

WOMEN
UP TO 48KG
1. Hitomi Obara (JPN)
2. Mariya Stadnyk (AZE)
=3. Carol Huynh (CAN)
=3. Clarissa Chun (USA)
48–55KG
1. Saori Yoshida (JPN)
2. Tonya Verbeek (CAN)
=3. Jackeline Renteria Castillo (COL)
=3. Yuliya Ratkevich (AZE)
55–63KG
1. Kaori Icho (JPN)
2. Ruixue Jing (CHN)
=3. Battsetseg Soronzonbold (MGL)
=3. Lubov Volosolva (RUS)
63–72KG
1. Natalia Vorobleva (RUS)
2. Stanka Zlateva Hristova (BUL)
=3. Guzel Manyurova (KAZ)
=3. Maider Unda (ESP)

WRESTLING – GRECO-ROMAN
MEN
UP TO 55KG
1. Hamid Mohammad Soryan Reihanpour (IR)
2. Rovshan Bayramov (AZE)
=3. Peter Modos (HUN)
=3. Mingiyan Semenov (RUS)
55–60KG
1. Omid Noroozi (IRI)
2. Revaz Lashkhi (GEO)
=3. Zaur Kuramagomedov (RUS)
=3. Ryutaro Matsumoto (JPN)
60–66KG
1. Hyeonwoo Kim (KOR)
2. Tamas Lorincz (HUN)
=3. Manuchar Tskhadaia (GEO)
=3.Steeve Guenot (FRA)
66–74KG
1. Roman Vlasov (RUS)
2. Arsen Julfalakyan (ARM)
=3. Aleksandr Kazakevic (LUT)
=3. Emin Ahmadov (AZE)
74–84KG
1. Alan Khugaev (RUS)
2. Karam Ebrahim (EGY)
=3. Danyal Gajiyev (KAZ)
=3.Damian Janikowski (POL)
84–96KG
1. Ghasem Rezaei (IRI)
2. Rustam Totrov (RUS)
=3. Artur Aleksanyan (ARM)
=3.Jimmy Lidberg (SWE)
96–120KG
1. Mijain Lopez Nunez (CUB)
2. Heiki Nabi (EST)
=3. Riza Kayaalp (TUR)
=3. Johan Euren (SWE)

Paralympic Games

ARCHERY
MEN
INDIVIDUAL COMPOUND – OPEN
1. Jere Forsberg (FIN) 6 points
2. Matt Stutzman (USA) 4 points
3. Dogan Hanci (TUR) 6 points
INDIVIDUAL COMPOUND – W1
1. Jeff Fabry (USA) 6 points
2. David Drahoninsky (CZE) 2 points
3. Norbet Murphy (CAN) 7 points
INDIVIDUAL RECURVE – STANDING
1. Timur Tuchinov (RUS) 7 points
2. Oleg Shestakov (RUS) 3 points
3. Mikhail Oyun (RUS) 6 points
INDIVIDUAL RECURVE – W1/W2
1. Oscar de Pellegrin (ITA) 6 points

2. Hasihin Sanawi (MAS) 5 points
3. Lung Hui Tseng (TPE) 7 points
TEAM RECURVE – OPEN
1. RUS (Mikhail Oyun, Oleg Shestakov, Timur Tuchinov) 206 points
2. KOR (Young Joo Jung, Suk Ho Kim, Myeong-Gu Lee) 200 points
3. CHN (Changjie Cheng, Zhi Dong, Zongshan Li) 206 points
WOMEN
INDIVIDUAL COMPOUND – OPEN
1. Danielle Brown (GBR) 6 points
2. Mel Clarke (GBR) 4 points
3. Stepanida Artakhinova (RUS) 7 points
INDIVIDUAL RECURVE – STANDING
1. Huilian Yan (CHN) 6 points
2. Hwa Sook Lee (KOR) 4 points
3. Milena Olszewska (POL) 6 points
INDIVIDUAL RECURVE – W1/W2
1. Zahra Nemati (IRI) 7 points
2. Elisabetta Mijno (ITA) 3 points
3. Jinzhi Li (CHN) 6 points
TEAM RECURVE – OPEN
1. KOR (Ran Sook Kim, Hee Sook Ko, Hwa Sook Lee) 199 points
2. CHN (Fangxia Gao, Yanhong Xiao, Huilian Yan) 193 points
3. IRI (Zahra Javanmard, Zahra Nemati, Razieh Shir Mohammadi) 188 points

ATHLETICS
MEN
100M – T11
1. Lei Xue (CHN), Lin Wang (Guide) 11.17
2. Lucas Prado (BRA), Justino Barbosa dos Santos (Guide) 11.25
3. Felipe Gomes (BRA), Leonardo Souza Lopes (Guide) 11.27
100M – T12
1. Fedor Trikolich (RUS) 10.81
2. Mateusz Michalski (POL) 10.88
3. Yansong Li (CHN) 10.91
100M – T13
1. Jason Smyth (IRL) 10.46 WR
2. Luis Felipe Gutierrez (CUB) 11.02
3. Jonathan Ntutu (RSA) 11.03
100M – T34
1. Walid Ktila (TUN) 15.91 PR
2. Rheed McCracken (AUS) 16.30
3. Mohammed Hammadi (UAE) 16.41
100M – T35
1. Iurii Tsaruk (UKR) 12.62
2. Teboho Mokgalagadi (RSA) 13.10
3. Xinhan Fu (CHN) 13.12
100M – T36
1. Evgenii Shvetcov (RUS) 12.08 PR
2. Graeme Ballard (GBR) 12.24
3. Roman Pavlyk (UKR) 12.26
100M – T37
1. Fanie van der Merwe (RSA) 11.51 WR
2. Yongbin Liang (CHN) 11.51 WR
3. Roman Kapranov (RUS) 11.56
100M – T38
1. Evan O'Hanlon (AUS) 10.79 WR
2. Dyan Buis (RSA) 11.11
3. Wenjun Zhou (CHN) 11.22
100M – T42
1. Heinrich Popow (GER) 12.40
2. Scott Reardon (AUS) 12.43
3. Wojtek Czyz (GER) 12.52
100M – T44
1. Jonnie Peacock (GBR) 10.90 PR
2. Richard Browne (USA) 11.03
3. Arnu Fourie (RSA) 11.08
100M – T46
1. Xu Zhao (CHN) 11.05
2. Raciel Gonzalez Isidoria (CUB) 11.08
3. Ola Abidogun (GBR) 11.23
100M – T51
1. Toni Piispanen (FIN) 21.72 PR
2. Alvise de Vidi (ITA) 22.60
3. Mohamed Berrahal (ALG) 22.97
100M – T52
1. Raymond Martin (USA) 17.02
2. Salvador Hernandez Mondragon (MEX) 17.64
3. Paul Nitz (USA) 17.99

100M – T53
1. Mickey Bushell (GBR) 14.75 PR
2. Yufei Zhao (CHN) 15.09
3. Shiran Yu (CHN) 15.20
100M – T54
1. Leo Pekka Tahti (FIN) 13.79
2. Yang Liu (CHN) 13.92
3. Saichon Konjen (THA) 14.10
200M – T11
1. Felipe Gomes (BRA), Leonardo Souza Lopes (Guide) 22.97
2. Daniel Silva (BRA), Heitor de Oliveira Sales (Guide) 22.99
3. Jose Sayovo Armando (ANG), Nicolau Palanca (Guide) 23.10
200M – T12
1. Mateusz Michalski (POL) 21.56 WR
2. Fedor Trikolich (RUS) 21.81
3. Yansong Li (CHN) 22.04
200M – T13
1. Jason Smyth (IRL) 21.05 WR
2. Alexey Labzin (RUS) 21.95
3. Artem Loginov (RUS) 22.03
200M – T34
1. Walid Ktila (TUN) 27.98 WR
2. Mohamed Hammadi (UAE) 28.95
3. Rheed McCracken (AUS) 29.08
200M – T35
1. Iurii Tsaruk (UKR) 25.86 WR
2. Xinhan Fu (CHN) 26.21
3. Hernan Barreto (ARG) 26.59
200M – T36
1. Roman Pavlyk (UKR) 24.70
2. Wa Wai So (HKG) 24.77
3. Ben Rushgrove (GBR) 24.83
200M – T37
1. Roman Kapranov (RUS) 23.10 =WR
2. Guangxu Shang (CHN) 23.15
3. Omar Monterola (VEN) 23.34
200M – T38
1. Evan O'Hanlon (AUS) 21.82 WR
2. Dyan Buis (RSA) 22.51
3. Wenjun Zhou (CHN) 22.65
200M – T42
1. Richard Whitehead (GBR) 24.38 WR
2. Shaquille Vance (USA) 25.55
3. Heinrich Popow (GER) 25.90
200M – T44
1. Alan Fonteles Cardoso Oliveira (BRA) 21.45
2. Oscar Pistorius (RSA) 21.52
3. Blake Leeper (USA) 22.46
200M – T46
1. Yohansson Nascimento (BRA) 22.05 WR
2. Raciel Gonzalez Isidoria (CUB) 22.15
3. Simon Patmore (AUS) 22.36
200M – T52
1. Raymond Martin (USA) 30.25 PR
2. Tomoya Ito (JPN) 31.60
3. Salvador Hernandez Mondragon (MEX) 31.81
200M – T53
1. Huzhao Li (CHN) 25.61 PR
2. Brent Lakatos (CAN) 25.85
3. Yufei Zhao (CHN) 26.00
400M – T11
1. Jose Sayovo Armando (ANG), Nicolau Palanca (Guide) 50.75
2. Lucas Prado (BRA), Laercio Alves Martins (Guide) 51.44
3. Gauthier Tresor Makunda (FRA), Antoine Laneyrie (Guide) 52.45
400M – T12
1. Mahmoud Khaldi (TUN) 48.52 WR
2. Hilton Langenhoven (RSA) 49.04
3. Jorge Benjamin Gonzalez Sauceda (MEX) 50.41
400M – T13
1. Alexey Labzin (RUS) 48.59 PR
2. Alexander Zverev (RUS) 48.83
3. Mohamed Amguoun (MAR) 49.45
400M – T36
1. Evengii Shvetcov (RUS) 53.31 WR
2. Paul Blake (GBR) 54.22
3. Roman Pavlyk (UKR) 55.18
400M – T38
1. Mohamed Farhat Chida (TUN) 50.43
2. Wenjun Zhou (CHN) 51.56
3. Union Sekailwe (RSA) 51.97

400M – T44
1. Oscar Pistorius (RSA) 46.68 PR
2. Blake Leeper (USA) 50.14
3. David Prince (USA) 50.61
400M – T46
1. Gunther Matzinger (AUT) 48.45
2. Yohansson Nascimento (BRA) 49.21 WR
3. Pradeep Sanjaya Uggl Dena Pathirannehelag (SRI) 49.28
400M – T52
1. Raymond Martin (USA) 58.54
2. Tomoya Ito (JPN) 1:00.40
3. Thomas Geierspichler (AUT) 1:04.64
400M – T53
1. Huzhao Li (CHN) 49.70
2. Brent Lakatos (CAN) 50.17
3. Richard Colman (AUS) 50.24
400M – T54
1. Lixin Zhang (CHN) 46.88
2. Kenny van Weeghel (NED) 47.12
3. Chengming Liu (CHN) 47.36
800M – T12
1. Abderrahim Zhiou (TUN) 1:56.42
2. Egor Sharov (RUS) 1:56.65
3. David Devine (GBR) 1:58.72
800M – T13
1. Abdellatif Baka (ALG) 1:50.31 PR
2. David Korir (KEN) 1:53.16
3. Abdelillah Mame (MAR) 1:53.40
800M – T36
1. Evengii Shvetcov (RUS) 2:05.32 PR
2. Artem Arefyev (RUS) 2:06.13
3. Paul Blake (GBR) 2:08.24
800M – T37
1. Michael McKillop (IRL) 1:57.22 WR
2. Mohamed Charmi (TUN) 2:01.45
3. Brad Scott (AUS) 2:02.04
800M – T46
1. Gunther Matzinger (AUT) 1:51.82 WR
2. Samir Nouioua (ALG) 1:52.33
3. Abraham Tarbei (KEN) 1:53.03
800M – T52
1. Raymond Martin (USA) 2:00.34
2. Tomoya Ito (JPN) 2:00.62
3. Leonardo De Jesus Perez Juarez (MEX) 2:01.18
800M – T53
1. Richard Colman (AUS) 1:41.13
2. Brent Lakatos (CAN) 1:41.24
3. Joshua George (USA) 1:41.50
800M – T54
1. David Weir (GBR) 1:37.63
2. Marcel Hug (SUI) 1:37.84
3. Saichon Konjen (THA) 1:38.51
1500M – T11
1. Samwel Mushai Kimani (KEN), James Boit (Guide) 3:58.37 WR
2. Odair Santos (BRA), Carlos Antonio dos Santos (Guide) 4:03.66
3. Jason Joseph Dunkerley (CAN), Josh Karanja (Guide) 4:07.56
1500M – T13
1. Abderrahim Zhiou (TUN) 3:48.31 WR
2. David Korir (KEN) 3:48.84 WR
3. David Devine (GBR) 3:49.79
1500M – T20
1. Peyman Nasiri Bazanjani (IRI) 3:58.49
2. Daniel Pek (POL) 3:59.45
3. Rafal Korc (POL) 3:59.53
1500M – T37
1. Michael McKillop (IRL) 4:08.11 PR
2. Brad Scott (AUS) 4:14.47
3. Mohamed Charmi (TUN) 4:14.90
1500M – T46
1. Abraham Tarbei (KEN) 3:50.15 WR
2. Wondiye Fikre Indelbu (ETH) 3:50.87
3. Samir Nouioua (ALG) 3:51.80
1500M – T54
1. David Weir (GBR) 3:12.09
2. Prawat Wahoram (THA) 3:12.32
3. Gyu Dae Kim (KOR) 3:12.57
5000M – T11
1. Cristian Valenzuela (CHI), Cristopher Guajardo (Guide) 15:26.26
2. Jason Joseph Dunkerley (CAN), Josh Karanja (Guide) 15:34.07
3. Shinya Wada (JPN), Jun Shida (Guide), Takashi Nakata (Guide) 15:55.26

5000M – T12
1. Amin Chentouf Ei (MAR) 13:53.76 WR
2. Abderrahim Zhiou (TUN) 14:19.97
3. Henry Kirwa (KEN) 14:20.76

5000M – T54
1. David Weir (GBR) 11:07.65
2. Kurt Fearnley (AUS) 11:07.90
3. Julien Casoli (FRA) 11:08.07

4 X 100M RELAY – T11-13
1. RUS (Evgeny Kegelev, Alexey Labzin, Fedor Trikolich, Andrey Koptev, Sergey Petrichenko - Guide) 42.66 PR
2. CHN (Lei Xue, Yizhi Yuan, Yuqing Yang, Yangsong Li, Lin Wang - Guide) 42.68
3. AZE (Elchin Muradov, Rza Osmanov, Oleg Panyutin, Vladimir Zayets, Pavel Setin - Guide) 43.92

4 X 100M RELAY – T42-46
1. RSA (Samkelo Radebe, Zivan Smith, Arnu Fourie, Oscar Pistorius) 41.78 WR
2. CHN (Zhiming Liu, Fuliang Liu, Hexing Xie, Xu Zhao) 42.98
3. GER (Markus Rehm, Heinrich Popow, David Behre, Wojtek Czyz) 45.23

4 X 400M RELAY – T53/54
1. CHN (Yang Liu, Chengming Liu, Huzhao Li, Lixin Zhang) 3:05.46 WR
2. THA (Supachai Koysub, Saichon Konjen, Sopa Intasen, Prawat Wahoram) 3:13.28
3. AUS (Richard Nicholson, Natheniel Arkley, Matthew Cameron, Richard Colman) 3:13.42

CLUB THROW – F31/32/51
1. Zeljko Dimitrijevic (SRB) 26.88m WR
2. Radim Beles (CZE) 26.67m
3. Lahouari Bahlaz (ALG) 36.31m PR

DISCUS THROW – F11
1. David Casino (ESP) 38.41m
2. Vasyl Lishchynskyi (UKR) 35.66m
3. Bil Marinkovic (AUT) 34.59m

DISCUS THROW – F32/33/34
1. Yanzhang Wang (CHN) 49.03m WR
2. Hani Alnakhli (KSA) 34.65m WR
3. Lahouari Bahlaz (ALG) 22.30m WR

DISCUS THROW – F35/36
1. Sebastian Ernst Klaus Dietz (GER) 38.54m
2. Oleksii Pashkov (UKR) 37.89m
3. Wenbo Wang (CHN) 37.87m

DISCUS THROW – F37/38
1. Javad Hardani (IRI) 52.91m WR
2. Dong Xia (CHN) 55.81m WR
3. Tomasz Blatkiewicz (POL) 54.02m

DISCUS THROW – F40
1. Zhiming Wang (CHN) 45.78m WR
2. Paschalis Stathelakos (GRE) 44.11m
3. Jonathan De Souza Santos (Brazil) 40.49m

DISCUS THROW – F42
1. Aled Davies (GBR) 46.14m
2. Mehrdad Karam Zadeh (IRI) 44.62m
3. Lezheng Wang (CHN) 42.81m

DISCUS THROW – F44
1. Jeremy Campbell (USA) 60.05m PR
2. Dan Greaves (GBR) 59.01m
3. Farzad Sepahvand (IRI) 58.39m

DISCUS THROW – F51/52/53
1. Mohamed Berrahal (ALG) 12.37m WR
2. Aigars Apinis (LAT) 21.00m
3. Mohamed Zemzemi (TUN) 11.34m

DISCUS THROW – F54/55/56
1. Leonardo Diaz (CUB) 44.63m WR
2. Drazenko Mitrovic (SRB) 32.97m WR
3. Ali Mohammad Yari (IRI) 41.98m

DISCUS THROW – F57/58
1. Alexey Ashapatov (RUS) 60.72m WR
2. Rostislav (CZE) 46.89m
3. Metawa Abouelkhir (EGY) 64.19m

HIGH JUMP – F42
1. Iliesa Delana (FIJ) 1.74m
2. Girisha Hosanagara Nagarajegowda (IND) 1.74m
3. Lukasz Mamczarz (POL) 1.74m

HIGH JUMP – F46
1. Maciej Lepiato (POL) 2.12m WR
2. Jeff Skiba (USA) 2.04m
3. Hongjie Chen (CHN) 2.01m PR

JAVELIN THROW – F12/13
1. Pengkai Zhu (CHN) 64.38m WR
2. Sajad Nikparast (IRI) 63.15m
3. Branimir Budetic (CRO) 56.78m

JAVELIN THROW – F33/34
1. Mohsen Kaedi (IRI) 38.30m WR
2. Yanzhang Wang (CHN) 38.23m
3. Kamel Kardjena (ALG) 36.40m WR

JAVELIN THROW – F40
1. Zhiming Wang (CHN) 47.95m WR
2. Ahmed Naas (IRQ) 43.27m
3. Wildan Nukhailawi (IRQ) 42.31m

JAVELIN THROW – F42
1. Yanlong Fu (CHN) 52.79m WR
2. Kamran Steinstad (IRI) 52.06m
3. Runar Steinstad (NOR) 48.90m

JAVELIN THROW – F44
1. Mingjie Gao (CHN) 58.53m PR
2. Tony Falelavaki (FRA) 58.21m
3. Ronald Hertog (NED) 55.83m

JAVELIN THROW – F52/53
1. Alphanso Cunningham (JAM) 21.84m
2. Abdolreza Jokar (IRI) 20.72m
3. Mauro Maximo de Jesus (MEX) 20.14m

JAVELIN THROW – F54/55/56
1. Luis Alberto Zepeda Felix (MEX) 28.07m
2. Alexey Kuznetsov (RUS) 27.87m
3. Manolis Stefanoudakis (GRE) 27.37m

JAVELIN THROW – F57/58
1. Mohammad Khalvandi (IRI) 50.98m WR
2. Claudiney Batista dos Santos (BRA) 45.38m WR
3. Raed Salem (EGY) 47.90m

LONG JUMP – F11
1. Ruslan Katyshev (UKR) 6.46m
2. Elexis Gillette (USA) 6.34m
3. Duan Li (CHN) 6.31m

LONG JUMP – F13
1. Luis Felipe Gutierrez (CUB) 7.54m PR
2. Angel Jimenez Cabeza (CUB) 7.14m
3. Radoslav Zlatanov (BUL) 6.81m

LONG JUMP – F20
1. Jose Antonio Exposito Pineiro (ESP) 7.25m PR
2. Zoran Talic (CRO) 7.09m
3. Lenine Cunha (POR) 6.95m

LONG JUMP – F36
1. Roman Pavlyk (UKR) 5.23m
2. Mariusz Sobczak (POL) 5.14m
3. Vladimir Sviridov (RUS) 5.08m

LONG JUMP – F37/38
1. Gocha Khugaev (RUS) 6.31m WR
2. Yuxi Ma (CHN) 6.26m
3. Dyan Buis (RSA) 6.48m

LONG JUMP – F42/44
1. Markus Rehm (GER) 7.35m WR
2. Wojtek Czyz (GER) 6.33m
3. Daniel Jorgensen (DEN) 6.11m

LONG JUMP – F46
1. Fuliang Liu (CHN) 7.15m
2. Arnaud Assoumani (FRA) 7.13m
3. Huseyn Hasanov (AZE) 6.53m

SHOT PUT – F11/12
1. Andrii Holivets (UKR) 16.25m
2. Vladimir Andryushchenko (RUS) 15.21m
3. Russell Short (AUS) 14.73m

SHOT PUT – F20
1. Todd Hodgetts (AUS) 16.29m WR
2. Jeffrey Ige (SWE) 15.50m
3. Muhammad Ziyad Zolkefli (MAS) 15.21m

SHOT PUT – F32/33
1. Kamel Kardjena (ALG) 12.41m PR
2. Karim Betina (ALG) 10.37m
3. Mounir Bakiri (ALG) 9.49m

SHOT PUT – F34
1. Azeddine Nouiri (MAR) 13.10m WR
2. Mohsen Kaedi (IRI) 12.94m
3. Thierry Cibone (FRA) 12.86m

SHOT PUT – F37/38
1. Dong Xia (CHN) 17.52m WR
2. Ibrahim Ahmed Abdelwareth (EGY) 15.53m PR
3. Javad Hardani (IRI) 15.43m

SHOT PUT – F40
1. Zhiming Wang (CHN) 14.46m WR
2. Hocine Gherzouli (ALG) 12.91m
3. Paschalis Stathelakos (GRE) 12.78m

SHOT PUT – F42/44
1. Jackie Christiansen (DEN) 18.16m PR
2. Darko Kralj (CRO) 14.21m
3. Aled Davies (GBR) 13.78m

SHOT PUT – F46
1. Nikita Prokhorov (RUS) 15.68m WR
2. Zhanbio Hou (CHN) 15.57m

3. Tomasz Rebisz (POL) 15.01m

SHOT PUT – F52/53
1. Aigars Apinis (LAT) 10.23m WR
2. Mauro Maximo de Jesus (MEX) 8.68m
3. Scot Severn (USA) 8.26m

SHOT PUT – F54/55/56
1. Jalil Bagheri Jeddi (IRI) 11.63m PR
2. Karol Kozun (POL) 11.36m
3. Robin Womack (GBR) 11.34m

SHOT PUT – F57/58
1. Alexey Ashapatov (RUS) 16.20m PR
2. Janusz Rokicki (POL) 15.68m
3. Michael Louwrens (RSA) 13.64m

TRIPLE JUMP – F11
1. Denis Gulin (RUS) 12.91m
2. Duan Li (CHN) 12.75m
3. Ruslan Katyshev (UKR) 12.50m

TRIPLE JUMP – F12
1. Oleg Panyutin (AZE) 15.02m
2. Vladimir Zayets (AZE) 15.01m
3. Hewei Dong (CHN) 14.20m

TRIPLE JUMP – F46
1. Fuliang Liu (CHN) 15.20m WR
2. Arnuad Assoumani (FRA) 14.28m
3. Aliaksandr Subota (BLR) 14.00m

MARATHON – T12
1. Alberto Suarez Laso (ESP) 2:24:50 WR
2. Elkin Alonso Serna Moreno (COL), German Naranjo Jaramillo (GUIDE) 2:26:39
3. Abderrahim Zhiou (TUN) 2:26:56

MARATHON – T46
1. Tito Sena (BRA) 2:30:40
2. Abderrahman Ait Khamouch (ESP) 2:31:04
3. Frederic van den Heede (BEL) 2:31:38

MARATHON – T54
1. David Weir (GBR) 1:30:20
2. Marcel Hug (SUI) 1:30:21
3. Kurt Fearnley (AUS) 1:30:21

WOMEN

100M – T11
1. Terezinha Guilhermina (BRA) Guilherme Soares de Santana (Guide) 12.01 WR
2. Jerusa Geber Santos (BRA) Luiz Henrique Barboza da Silva (Guide) 12.75
3. Jhulia Santos (BRA) Fabio Dias de Oliveira Silva (Guide) 12.76

100M – T12
1. Guohua Zhou (CHN) Jie Li (Guide) 12.05
2. Libby Clegg (GBR) Mikail Huggins (Guide) 12.13
3. Oxana Boturchuk (UKR) 12.18

100M – T13
1. Omara Durand (CUB) 12.00 PR
2. Ilse Hayes (RSA) 12.41
3. Nantenin Keita (FRA) 12.47

100M – T34
1. Hannah Cockroft (GBR) 18.06 PR
2. Amy Siemons (NED) 19.49
3. Rosemary Little (AUS) 19.95

100M – T35
1. Ping Liu (CHN) 15.44 WR
2. Oxana Corso (ITA) 15.94
3. Virginia McLachlan (CAN) 16.42

100M – T36
1. Elena Ivanova (RUS) 14.44
2. Min Jae Jeon (KOR) 14.70
3. Claudia Nicoleitzik (GER) 14.88

100M – T37
1. Mandy Francois-Elie (FRA) 14.08
2. Johanna Benson (NAM) 14.23
3. Neda Bahi (TUN) 14.36

100M – T38
1. Margarita Goncharova (RUS) 13.45
2. Junfei Chen (CHN) 13.53
3. Inna Stryzhak (UKR) 13.64

100M – T42
1. Martina Caironi (ITA) 15.87 WR
2. Kelly Cartwright (AUS) 16.14
3. Jana Schmidt (GER) 16.19

100M – T44
1. Marie-Amelie le Fur (FRA) 13.26
2. Marlou van Rhijn (NED) 13.32
3. April Holmes (USA) 13.33

100M – T46
1. Yunidis Castillo (CUB) 12.01
2. Nikol Rodomakina (RUS) 12.49
3. Yanping Wang (CHN) 12.89

100M – T52
1. Marieke Vervoort (BEL) 19.69 PR
2. Michelle Stilwell (CAN) 19.80
3. Kerry Morgan (USA) 20.68

100M – T53
1. Lisha Huang (CHN) 16.42
2. Hongzhuan Zhou (CHN) 16.90
3. Angela Ballard (AUS) 17.14

100M – T54
1. Wenjun Liu (CHN) 15.82 WR
2. Hongjiao Dong (CHN) 15.86
3. Tatyana McFadden (USA) 16.15

200M – T11
1. Terezinha Guilhermina (BRA) Guilherme Soares de Santana (Guide) 24.82 PR
2. Jerusa Geber Santos (BRA) Luiz Henrique Barboza Da Silva (Guide) 26.32
3. Juntingxian Jia (CHN) Donglin Xu (Guide) 26.33

200M – T12
1. Assia El Hannouni (FRA) Gautier Simounet (Guide) 24.46 WR
2. Guohua Zhou (CHN) Jie Li (Guide) 24.66
3. Daqing Zhu (CHN) Hui Zhang (Guide) 24.88

200M – T34
1. Hannah Cockroft (GBR) 31.90 WR
2. Amy Siemons (NED) 34.16
3. Desiree Vranken (NED) 34.85

200M – T35
1. Ping Liu (CHN) 32.72
2. Oxana Corso (ITA) 33.68
3. Virginia McLachlan (CAN) 34.31

200M – T36
1. Elena Ivanova (RUS) 30.25
2. Min Jae Jeon (KOR) 31.08
3. Claudia Nicoleitzik (GER) 32.08

200M – T37
1. Johanna Benson (NAM) 29.26
2. Bethany Woodward (GBR) 29.65
3. Maria Seifert (GER) 29.86

200M – T38
1. Junfei Chen (CHN) 27.39 WR
2. Margarita Goncharova (RUS) 27.82
3. Inna Stryzhak (UKR) 28.18

200M – T44
1. Marlou van Rhijn (NED) 26.18 WR
2. Marie-Amelie le Fur (FRA) 26.76 WR
3. Katrin Green (GER) 27.53

200M – T46
1. Yunidis Castillo (CUB) 24.45 WR
2. Alicja Fiodorow (POL) 25.49
3. Anrune Liebenberg (RSA) 25.55

200M – T52
1. Michelle Stilwell (CAN) 33.80 PR
2. Marieke Vervoort (BEL) 34.83
3. Kerry Morgan (USA) 36.49

200M – T53
1. Lisha Huang (CHN) 29.18
2. Angela Ballard (AUS) 29.35
3. Hongzhuan Zhou (CHN) 29.40

400M – T12
1. Assia El Hannouni (FRA) 55.39
2. Oxana Boturchuk (UKR) 55.69
3. Daniela E Velasco Maldonado (MEX) Jose Guadalupe Fuentes Ortiz (Guide) 58.51

400M – T13
1. Omara Durand (CUB) 55.12 PR
2. Somaya Bousaid (TUN) 56.83
3. Alexandra Dimoglou (GRE) 56.91

400M – T37
1. Neda Bahi (TUN) 1:05.86
2. Viktoriya Kravchenko (UKR) 1:07.32
3. Evgeniya Trushnikova (RUS) 1:07.35

400M – T46
1. Yunidis Castillo (CUB) 55.72 WR
2. Anrune Liebenberg (RSA) 56.65
3. Alicja Fiodorow (POL) 58.48

400M – T53
1. Hongzhuan Zhou (CHN) 55.47
2. Angela Ballard (AUS) 56.06
3. Lisha Huang (CHN) 56.87

400M – T54
1. Tatyana McFadden (USA) 52.97
2. Hongjiao Dong (CHN) 55.43
3. Edith Wolf (SUI) 56.25

800M – T53
1. Hongzhuan Zhou (CHN) 1:52.85 PR
2. Lisha Huang (CHN) 1:53.10
3. Jessica Galli (CHN) 1:53.12

800M – T54
1. Tatyana McFadden (USA) 1:47.01
2. Edith Wolf (SUI) 1:49.87
3. Lihong Zou (CHN) 1:50.31

1500M – T12
1. Elena Pautova (RUS) 4:37.65
2. Elena Congost (ESP) 4:45.53
3. Annalisa Minetti (ITA) Andrea Giocondi (Guide) 4:48.88 WR

1500M – T20
1. Barbara Niewiedzial (POL) 4:35.26
2. Arleta Meloch (POL) 4:39.04
3. Ilona Biacsi (ITA) 4:42.31

1500M – T54
1. Tatyana McFadden (USA) 3:36.42
2. Edith Wolf (SUI) 3:36.78
3. Shirley Reilly (USA) 3:37.03

5000M – T54
1. Edith Wolf (SUI) 12:27.87
2. Shirley Reilly (USA) 12:27.91
3. Christie Dawes (AUS) 12:28.24

4 X 100M RELAY – T35-38
1. RUS (Anastasiya Ovsyannikova, Svetlana Sergeeva, Elena Ivanova, Margarita Goncharova) 54.86
2. CHN (Dezhi Xiong, Yuanhang Cao, Ping Liu, Junfei Chen) 55.65
3. GBR (Olivia Breen, Bethany Woodward, Katrina Hart, Jenny McLoughlin) 56.08

CLUB THROW – F31/32/51
1. Maroua Ibrahmi (TUN) 23.43m WR
2. Mounia Gasmi (ALG) 22.51m
3. Gemma Prescott (GBR) 20.50m

DISCUS THROW – F11/12
1. Liangmin Zhang (CHN) 40.31m PR
2. Hongxia Tang (CHN) 39.91m
3. Claire Williams (GBR) 39.63m

DISCUS THROW – F35/36
1. Qing Wu (CHN) 28.01m WR
2. Mariia Pomazan (UKR) 30.12m WR
3. Katherine Proudfoot (AUS) 25.22m

DISCUS THROW – F37
1. Na Mi (CHN) 35.35m WR
2. Quiping Xu (CHN) 32.08m
3. Beverley Jones (GBR) 30.99m

DISCUS THROW – F40
1. Najat El Garraa (MAR) 32.37m WR
2. Raoua Tlili (TUN) 31.16m
3. Genjimisu Meng (CHN) 30.44m

DISCUS THROW – F51/52/53
1. Josie Pearson (GBR) 6.58m WR
2. Catherine O Neill (IRL) 5.66m
3. Zena Cole (USA) 5.25m

DISCUS THROW – F57/58
1. Nassima Saifi (ALG) 40.34m PR
2. Stela Eneva (BUL) 36.56m
3. Orla Barry (IRL) 28.12m

JAVELIN THROW – F12/13
1. Tanja Dragic (SRB) 42.51m WR
2. Anna Sorokina (RUS) 38.79m
3. Natalija Eder (AUT) 38.03m

JAVELIN THROW – F37/38
1. Shirlene Coelho (BRA) 37.86m WR
2. Qianqian Jia (CHN) 31.62m
3. Georgia Beikoff (AUS) 29.84m

JAVELIN THROW – F46
1. Katarzyna Piekart (POL) 41.15m WR
2. Nataliya Gudkova (RUS) 41.08m
3. Madeleine Hogan (AUS) 38.85m

JAVELIN THROW – F33/34/52/53
1. Birgit Kober (GER) 27.03m WR
2. Marie Braemer-Skowronek (GER) 20.43m
3. Marjaana Huovinen (FIN) 19.47

JAVELIN THROW – F54/55/56
1. Liwan Yang (CHN) 17.89m WR
2. Hania Aidi (TUN) 17.40m
3. Martina Willing (GER) 23.12m

JAVELIN THROW – F57/58
1. Ming Liu (CHN) 23.48m
2. Safia Djelal (ALG) 28.87m
3. Larisa Volik (RUS) 21.95m

LONG JUMP – F11/12
1. Oksana Zubkovska (UKR) 6.60m WR
2. Juntingxian Jia (CHN) 4.73m

3. Anna Kaniuk (BLR) 5.83m

LONG JUMP – F13
1. Ilse Hayes (RSA) 5.70m
2. Lynda Hamri (ALG) 5.31m
3. Anthi Karagianni (GRE) 5.16m

LONG JUMP – F20
1. Karolina Kucharczyk (POL) 6.00m WR
2. Krestina Zhukova (RUS) 5.38m
3. Mikela Ristoski (CRO) 5.28m

LONG JUMP – F37/38
1. Margarita Goncharova (RUS) 4.84m PR
2. Inna Stryzhak (UKR) 4.97m
3. Yuanhang Cao (CHN) 4.40m PR

LONG JUMP – F42/44
1. Kelly Cartwright (AUS) 4.38m WR
2. Stef Reid (GBR) 5.28m PR
3. Marie-Amelie le Fur (FRA) 5.14m

LONG JUMP – F46
1. Nikol Rodomakina (RUS) 5.63m
2. Carlee Beattie (AUS) 5.57m
3. Jingling Ouyang (CHN) 5.41m

SHOT PUT – F11/12
1. Assunta Legnante (ITA) 16.74m WR
2. Hongxia Tang (CHN) 12.47m
3. Liangmin Zhang (CHN) 11.07m

SHOT PUT – F20
1. Ewa Durska (POL) 13.80m PR
2. Anastasiia Mysnyk (UKR) 12.67m
3. Svitlana Kudelya (UKR) 12.24m

SHOT PUT – F32/33/34
1. Birgit Kober (GER) 10.25m WR
2. Louise Ellery (AUS) 5.90m
3. Maroua Ibrahmi (TUN) 5.75m

SHOT PUT – F35/36
1. Mariia Pomazan (UKR) 12.22m WR
2. Jun Wang (CHN) 12.07m
3. Qing Wu (CHN) 10.64m WR

SHOT PUT – F37
1. Na Mi (CHN) 12.20m WR
2. Qiuping Xu (CHN) 11.04m
3. Eva Berna (CZE) 11.00m

SHOT PUT – F40
1. Raoua Tlili (TUN) 9.86m WR
2. Genjimisu Meng (CHN) 9.13m
3. Najat El Garraa (MAR) 8.62m

SHOT PUT – F42/44
1. Juan Yao (CHN) 13.05m WR
2. Yue Yang (CHN) 12.22m
3. Michaela Floeth (GER) 12.21m

SHOT PUT – F54/55/56
1. Liwan Yang (CHN) 7.50m WR
2. Marianne Buggenhagen (GER) 8.32m
3. Angela Madsen (USA) 8.88m PR

SHOT PUT – F57/58
1. Angeles Ortiz Hernandez (MEX) 11.43m WR
2. Stela Eneva (BUL) 11.38m
3. Eucharia Iyiazi (NGR) 11.11m

MARATHON – T54
1. Shirley Reilly (USA) 1:46:33
2. Shelly Woods (GBR) 1:46:34
3. Sandra Graf (SUI) 1:46:35

BOCCIA

INDIVIDUAL – BC1
1. Pattaya Tadtong (THA)
2. David Smith (GBR)
3. Roger Aandalen (NOR)

INDIVIDUAL – BC2
1. Maciel Sousa Santos (BRA)
2. Zhiqiang Yan (CHN)
3. So-Yeong Jeong (KOR)

INDIVIDUAL – BC3
1. Ye-Jin Choi (KOR)
2. Ho-Won Jeong (KOR)
3. Jose Macedo (POR)

INDIVIDUAL – BC4
1. Dirceu Jose Pinto (BRA)
2. Yuansen Zheng (CHN)
3. Eliseu dos Santos (BRA)

PAIRS – BC3
1. GRE (Maria-Eleni Kordali, Nikolaos Pananos, Grigorios Polychronidis)
2. POR (Armando Costa, Jose Macedo, Luis Silva)
3. BEL (Pieter Cilissen, Kirsten de Laender, Pieter Verlinden)

PAIRS – BC4
1. BRA (Eliseu dos Santos, Dirceu Jose Pinto)

2. CZE (Leo Lacina, Radek Prochazka)
3. CAN (Marco Dispaltro, Josh vander Vies)

TEAM – BC1/BC2
1. THA (Witsanu Huadpradit, Mongkol Jitsa-Ngiem, Pattaya Tadtong, Watcharaphon Vongsa)
2. CHN (Zhiqiang Yan, Weibo Yuan, Qi Zhang, Kai Zhong)
3. GBR (Daniel Bentley, Nigel Murray, Zoe Robinson, David Smith)

CYCLING – ROAD

MEN
ROAD RACE – B
1. Ivano Pizzi (ITA), Lucca Pizzi (Guide) 2:26:52
2. Krzysztof Kosikowski (POL), Artur Korc (Guide) 2:26:57
3. Vladislav Janovjak (SVK), Robert Mitosinka (Guide) 2:26:59

ROAD RACE – C1/2/3
1. Roberto Bargna (ITA) 1:42:51
2. Steffen Warias (GER) 1:42:51
3. David Nicholas (AUS) 1:42:51

ROAD RACE – C4/5
1. Yegor Dementyev (UKR) 1:55:38
2. Xinyang Liu (CHN) 1:55:48
3. Michele Pittacolo (ITA) 1:55:51

ROAD RACE – H1
1. Mark Rohan (IRL) 1:53:09
2. Tobias Fankhauser (SUI) 1:53:11
3. Name (country abbreviation) 1:53:24

ROAD RACE – H2
1. Walter Ablinger (AUT) 1:37:55
2. Jean-Marc Berset (SUI) 1:37:59
3. Vittorio Podesta (ITA) 1:38:02

ROAD RACE – H3
1. Rafal Wilk (POL) 1:50:05
2. Vico Merklein (GER) 1:51:34
3. Joel Jeannot (FRA) 1:53:37

ROAD RACE – H4
1. Alessandro Zanardi (ITA) 2:00:32
2. Ernst van Dyk (RSA) 2:00:33
3. Wim Decleir (BEL) 2:00:35

TIME TRIAL – B
1. Christian Venge (ESP), David Llaurado Caldero (Guide) 30:48.25
2. Ivano Pizzi (ITA), Lucca Pizzi (Guide) 30:50.41
3. James Brown (IRL), Damien Shaw (Guide) 31:13.00

TIME TRIAL – C1
1. Michael Teuber (GER) 25:16.43
2. Mark Colbourne (GBR) 25:29.37
3. Yu Li Zhang (CHN) 26:23.11

TIME TRIAL – C2
1. Tobias Graf (GER) 24:35.12
2. Guihua Liang (CHN) 24:40.33
3. Maurice Eckhard Tio (ESP) 24:40.76

TIME TRIAL – C3
1. David Nicholas (AUS) 23:22.13
2. Joseph Berenyi (USA) 23:31.73
3. Masaki Fujita (JPN) 23.55.54

TIME TRIAL – C4
1. Jiri Jezek (CZE) 32:59.92
2. Carol-Eduard Novak (ROU) 33:06.93
3. Jiri Bouska (CZE) 33:34.92

TIME TRIAL – C5
1. Yegor Dementyev (UKR) 32:12.98
2. Xinyang Liu (CHN) 32:21.03
3. Michael Gallagher (AUS) 33:12.03

TIME TRIAL – H1
1. Mark Rohan (IRL) 35:41.54
2. Koby Lion (ISR) 35:53.30
3. Wolfgang Schattauer (AUT) 38:02.35

TIME TRIAL – H2
1. Heinz Frei (SUI) 26:52.39
2. Walter Ablinger (AUT) 26:57.25
3. Vittorio Podesta (ITA) 27:01.98

TIME TRIAL – H3
1. Rafal Wilk (POL) 25:24.17
2. Nigel Barley (AUS) 26.18.34
3. Bernd Jeffre (GER) 27:00.90

TIME TRIAL – H4
1. Alessandro Zanardi (ITA) 24:50.22
2. Norbert Mosandl (GER) 25:17.40
3. Oscar Sanchez (USA) 25:35.26

WOMEN
ROAD RACE – B
1. Robbi Weldon (CAN), Lyne Bessette (Guide) 2:08:26

2. Josefa Benitez Guzman (ESP), Maria Noriega (Guide) 2:08:59
3. Kathrin Goeken (NED), Kim Van Dijk (Guide) 2:12.56

ROAD RACE – C1/2/3
1. Sini Zeng (CHN) 1:29:02
2. Denise Schindler (GER) 1:29:11
3. Allison Jones (USA) 1:29:11

ROAD RACE – C4/5
1. Sarah Storey (GBR) 1:40:36
2. Anna Harkowska (POL) 1:47:58
3. Kelly Crowley (USA) 1:48:34

ROAD RACE – H1/2/3
1. Marianna Davis (USA) 1:41.34
2. Monica Bascio (USA) 1:42.07
3. Rachel Morris (GBR) 1:43.08

ROAD RACE – H4
1. Andrea Eskau (GER) 1:31:05
2. Laura de Vaan (NED) 1:41:21
3. Dorothee Vieth (GER) 1:41:21

TIME TRIAL – B
1. Kathrin Goeken (NED), Kim Van Dijk (Guide) 35:02.73
2. Phillipa Gray (NZL), Laura Thompson (Guide) 35:07.68
3. Catherine Walsh (IRL), Francine Meehan (Guide) 35:29.56

TIME TRIAL – C1/2/3
1. Alison Jones (USA) 26:58.54
2. Tereza Diepoldova (CZE) 27:47.91
3. Sini Zeng (CHN) 27:57.16

TIME TRIAL – C4
1. Megan Fisher (USA) 26:04.39
2. Susan Powell (AUS) 26:31.30
3. Marie-Claude Molnar (CAN) 26:48.52

TIME TRIAL – C5
1. Sarah Storey (GBR) 22:40.66
2. Anna Harkowska (POL) 24:14.94
3. Kelly Crowley (USA) 25:14.51

TIME TRIAL – H1/2
1. Marianna Davis (USA) 31:06.39
2. Karen Darke (GBR) 33:16.09
3. Ursula Schwaller (SUI) 34:56.55

TIME TRIAL – H3
1. Sandra Graf (SUI) 33:21.61
2. Monica Bascio (USA) 33:39.26
3. Svetlana Moshkovich (RUS) 34.08.48

TIME TRIAL – H4
1. Andrea Eskau (GER) 28:18.09
2. Dorothee Vieth (GER) 30:00.27
3. Laura de Vaan (NED) 30:24.82

MIXED
ROAD RACE – T1/2
1. David Stone (GBR) 45:17
2. Giorgio Farroni (ITA) 45:24
3. David Vondracek (CZE) 48:34

TEAM RELAY – H1-H4
1. USA (Matthew Updike, Oscar Sanchez, Marianna Davis) 30:07.00
2. ITA (Vittorio Podesta, Alessandro Zanardi, Francesca Fenocchio) 30:50.00
3. SUI (Heinz Frei, Ursula Schwaller, Jean-Marc Berset) 30:58.00

TIME TRIAL – T1/2
1. David Stone (GBR) 45:17
2. Giorgio Farroni (ITA) 45.24
3. David Vondracek (CZE) 48.34

CYCLING – TRACK

MEN
KILO – B
1. Neil Fachie (GBR) Barney Storey (Guide/Pilot) 1:01.351 WR
2. Jose Enrique Porto Lareo (ESP) Jose Antonio Villanueva Trinidad (Guide/Pilot) 1:02.707
3. Rinne Oost (NED) Patrick Bos (Guide/Pilot) 1:03.052

KILO – C1/2/3
1. Zhang Yu Li (CHN) 1:05.021 WR
2. Mark Lee Colbourne (GBR) 1:08.471
3. Tobias Graf (GER) 1:09.979 WR

KILO – C4/5
1. Alfonso Cabello (ESP) 1:05.947 WR
2. Jon-Allan Butterworth (GBR) 1:05.985
3. Xinyang Liu (CHN) 1:07.638

PURSUIT – B
1. Kieran Modra (AUS) Scott McPhee (Guide/Pilot) 4:17.756 WR
2. Bryce Lindores (AUS) Sean Finning (Guide/Pilot) 4:22.269
3. Miguel Angel Clemente Solano (ESP) Diego Javier Munoz (Guide/Pilot) 4:24.015
PURSUIT – C1
1. Mark Lee Colbourne (GBR) 3:53.881 WR
2. Zhang Yu Li (CHN) 4:01.826
3. Rodrigo Fernando Lopez (ARG) 4:04.559
PURSUIT – C2
1. Guihua Liang (CHN) 3:45.243 WR
2. Tobias Graf (GER) 3:48.248
3. Laurent Thirionet (FRA) 3:53.547
PURSUIT – C3
1. Joseph Berenyi (USA) 3:37.912
2. Shaun McKeown (GBR) 3:38.637
3. Darren Kenny (GBR) 3:35.257
PURSUIT – C4
1. Carol-Eduard Novak (ROU) 4:42.00
2. Jiri Jezek (CZE) 4:45.232
3. Jody Cundy (GBR)
PURSUIT – C5
1. Michael Gallagher (AUS) 4:35.927
2. Jon-Allan Butterworth (GBR) 4:39.586
3. Xinyang Liu (CHN) 4:38.443
SPRINT – B
1. Anthony Kappes (GBR), Craig MacLean (Guide) NM
2. Neil Fachie (GBR), Barney Storey (Guide) NM
3. Jose Enrique Porto Lareo (ESP), Jose Antonio Villanueva Trinidad (Guide) NM

WOMEN
500M – C1/2/3
1. Yin He (CHN) 39.158 WR
2. Alyda Norbruis (NED) 39.174
3. Jyame Paris (AUS) 40.476 WR
500M – C4/5
1. Sarah Storey (GBR) 36.997
2. Jennifer Schuble (USA) 37.941
3. Jianping Ruan (CHN) 38.194 WR
KILO – B
1. Felicity Johnson (AUS) Stephanie Morton (Guide) 1:08.919 PR
2. Aileen McGlynn (GBR) Helen Scott (Guide) 1:09.469
3. Phillipa Gray (NZL) Laura Thompson (Guide) 1:11.245
PURSUIT – B
1. Phillipa Gray (NZL) Laura Thompson (Guide) 3:32.243
2. Catherine Walsh (IRL), Francine Meehan (Guide) 3:36.360
3. Aileen McGlynn (GBR), Helen Scott (Guide) 3:40.138
PURSUIT – C1/2/3
1. Sini Zeng (CHN) 4:20.820
2. Simone Kennedy (AUS) 4:24.893
3. Allison Jones (USA) 4:27.793
PURSUIT – C4
1. Susan Powell (AUS) 4:05.200
2. Megan Fisher (USA) 4:07.147
3. Alexandra Green (AUS) 4:07.921
PURSUIT – C5
1. Sarah Storey (GBR) -
2. Anna Harkowska (POL) OVL
3. Fiona Southorn (NZL) 3:55.867

MIXED
TEAM SPRINT – C1-C5
1. CHN (Xiaofei Ji, Xinyang Liu, Hao Xie) 49.804
2. GBR (Jon-Allan Butterworth, Darren Kenny, Richard Waddon) 49.808
3. USA (Joseph Berenyi, Sam Kavanagh, Jennifer Schuble) 53.174

EQUESTRIAN
CHAMPIONSHIP TEST: INDIVIDUAL – GRADE IA
1. Sophie Christiansen & Janeiro 6 (GBR)
2. Helen Kearney & Mister Cool (IRL)
3. Laurentia Tan & Ruben James 2 (SIN)
CHAMPIONSHIP TEST: INDIVIDUAL – GRADE IB
1. Joann Formosa & Worldwide PB (AUS)
2. Lee Pearson & Gentleman (GBR)
3. Pepo Puch & Fine Feeling (AUT)
CHAMPIONSHIP TEST: INDIVIDUAL – GRADE II
1. Natasha Baker & Cabral (GBR)
2. Britta Napel & Aquilina 3 (GER)

3. Angelika Trabert & Ariva Avanti (GER)
CHAMPIONSHIP TEST: INDIVIDUAL – GRADE III
1. Hannelore Brenner & Women of the World (GER)
2. Deborah Criddle & LJT Akilles (GBR)
3. Annika Dalskov & Aros A Fenris (DEN)
CHAMPIONSHIP TEST: INDIVIDUAL – GRADE IV
1. Michele George & Rainman (BEL)
2. Sophie Wells & Pinocchio (GBR)
3. Frank Hosmar & Alphaville (NED)
FREESTYLE TEST: INDIVIDUAL – GRADE IA
1. Sophie Christiansen & Janeiro 6 (GBR)
2. Laurentia Tan & Ruben James 2 (SIN)
3. Helen Kearney & Mister Cool (IRL)
FREESTYLE TEST: INDIVIDUAL – GRADE IB
1. Pepo Puch & Fine Feeling (AUT)
2. Katja Karalainen & Rosie (FIN)
3. Lee Pearson & Gentleman (GBR)
FREESTYLE TEST: INDIVIDUAL – GRADE II
1. Natasha Baker & Cabral (GBR)
2. Britta Napel & Aquilina 3 (GER)
3. Angelika Trabert & Ariva-Avanti (GER)
FREESTYLE TEST: INDIVIDUAL – GRADE III
1. Hannelore Brenner & Women of the World (GER)
2. Deborah Criddle & LJT Akilles (GBR)
3. Annika Dalskov & Aros A Fenris (DEN)
FREESTYLE TEST: INDIVIDUAL – GRADE IV
1. Michele George & Rainman (BEL)
2. Sophie Wells & Pinocchio (GBR)
3. Frank Hosmar & Alphaville (NED)
TEAM TEST – OPEN
1. GBR (Lee Pearson, Sophie Wells, Deborah Criddle, Sophie Christiansen)
2. GER (Angelika Trabert, Britta Napel, Steffen Zeibig, Hannelore Brenner)
3. IRL (Eilish Byrne, James Dwyer, Geraldine Savage, Helen Kearney)

FOOTBALL 5-A-SIDE

MEN
8-TEAM TOURNAMENT B1
1. BRA (Fabio Luiz Ribeiro de Vasconcelos, Emerson de Carvalho, Gledson da Paixao Barros, Cassio Lopes do Reis, Marcos Jose Alves Felipe, Jeferson da Conceicao Goncalves, Raimundo Nonato Alves Mendes, Severino Gabriel da Silva, Ricardo Steinmetz Alves, Daniel Dantas da Silva)
2. FRA (Jonathan Grangier, Gael Riviere, Hakim Arezki, Martin Baron, Abderrahim, David Labarre, Arnaud Ayax, Frederic Villeroux, Yvan Wouandji Kepmegni, Frederic Jannas)
3. ESP (Alvaro Gonzalez Alcaraz, Jose Luis Giera Tejuelo, Francisco Munoz Perez, Adolfo Acosta Rodriguez, Jose Lopez Ramirez, Alfredo Cuadrado Freire, Antonio Martin Gaitan, Youssef El Haddaoui Rabii, Marcelo Rosado Carrasco, Raul Diaz Ortin)

FOOTBALL 7-A-SIDE

MEN
8-TEAM TOURNAMENT
1. RUS (Aslanbek Sapiev, Alexey Tumakov, Aleksei Chesmin, Ivan Potekhin, Eduard Ramonov, Andrei Kuvaev, Aleksandr Lekov, Lasha Murvanadze, Viacheslav Larionov, Vladislav Raretckii, Zaurbek Pagaev, Aleksandr Kuligin)
2. UKR (Kostyantyn Symashko, Vitaliy Trushev, Yevhen Zinoviev, Taras Dutko, Anatolii Shevchyk, Ivan Shkvarlo, Ivan Dotsenko, Denys Ponomaryov, Oleksiy Hetun, Oleksandr Devlysh, Volodymyr Antoniuk, Igor Kosenko)
3. IRI (Mehran Nikooe Majd, Hashem Rastegarimobin, Sadegh Hassani Baghi, Farzad Mehri, Jasem Bakhshi, Ehsan Gholamhosseinpour Bousheh, Morteza Heidari, Bahman Ansari, Rasoul Atashafrouz, Moslem Akbari, Abdolreza, Moselm Khazaeipirsarabi)

GOALBALL

MEN
12-TEAM TOURNAMENT
1. FIN (Jarno Mattila, Ville Montonen, Erkki Miinala, Toni Alenius, Tuomas Nousu, Petri Posio)
2. BRA (Jose Ferreira de Oliveira, Alexsander Almeida Maciel Celente, Leoman Moreno da Silva, Romario Diego Marques, Filppe Santos Silvestre, Leandro Moreno da Silva)

3. TUR (Tekin Okan Duzgun, Huseyin Alkan, Mehmet Cesur, Yusuf Ucar, Abdullah Aydogdu, Tuncay Karakaya)
WOMEN
10-TEAM TOURNAMENT
1. JPN (Masae Komiya, Rie Urata, Akane Nakashima, Eiko Kakehata, Haruka Wakasugi, Akiko Adachi)
2. CHN (Ruixue Wang, Fengqing Chen, Shan Lin, Shasha Wang, Zhen Ju)
3. SWE (Viktoria Andersson, Sofia Naesstrom, Anna Dahlberg, Malin Gustavsson, Maria Waglund, Josefine Jalmestal)

JUDO

MEN
EXTRA LIGHTWEIGHT (UP TO 60KG)
1. Ramin Ibrahimov (AZE)
2. Xiaodong Li (CHN)
3. Ben Quilter (GBR)
3. Mouloud Noura (ALG)
HALF-LIGHTWEIGHT (60–66KG)
1. Davyd Khorava (UKR)
2. Xu Zhao (CHN)
3. Marcos Falcon (VEN)
3. Sid Ali Lamri (ALG)
LIGHTWEIGHT (66–73KG)
1. Dmytro Solovey (UKR)
2. Sharif Khalilov (UZB)
3. Eduardo Avila Sanchez (MEX)
3. Shakhban Kurbanov (RUS)
HALF-MIDDLEWEIGHT (73–81KG)
1. Olexandr Kosinov (UKR)
2. Jose Effron (ARG)
3. Isao Cruz Alonso (CUB)
3. Matthias Krieger (RUS)
MIDDLEWEIGHT (81–90KG)
1. Jorge Hierrezuelo Marcillis (CUB)
2. Samuel Ingram (GBR)
3. Jorge Lencina (ARG)
3. Dartanyon Crockett (USA)
HALF-HEAVYWEIGHT (90–100KG)
1. Gwang-Guen Choi (KOR)
2. Myles Porter (USA)
3. Antonio Tenorio (BRA)
3. Vladimir Fedin (RUS)
HEAVYWEIGHT (OVER 100KG)
1. Kento Masaki (JPN)
2. Song Wang (CHN)
3. Yangaliny Jimenez Dominguez (CUB)
3. Ilham Zakiyev (AZE)
WOMEN
EXTRA LIGHTWEIGHT (UP TO 48KG)
1. Carmen Brussig (GER)
2. Kai-Lin Lee (TPE)
3. Victoria Potapova (RUS)
3. Yuliya Halinska (UKR)
HALF-LIGHTWEIGHT (48–52KG)
1. Romona Brussig (GER)
2. Lijing Wang (CHN)
3. Michele Ferreira (BRA)
3. Nataliya Nikolaychyk (UKR)
LIGHTWEIGHT (52–57KG)
1. Afag Sultanova (AZE)
2. Lucia da Silva Teixeira (BRA)
3. Monica Merenciano Herrero (ESP)
3. Duygu Cete (TUR)
HALF-MIDDLEWEIGHT (57–63KG)
1. Dalidaivis Rodriguez Clark (CUB)
2. Tong Zhou (CHN)
3. Daniele Bernardes Milan (BRA)
3. Marta Arce Payno (ESP)
MIDDLEWEIGHT (63–70KG)
1. Maria del Carmen Herrera Gomez (ESP)
2. Tatiana Savostyanova (RUS)
3. Qian Zhou (CHN)
3. Nikolett Szabo (HUN)
HEAVYWEIGHT (OVER 70KG)
1. Yangping Yuan (CHN)
2. Nazan Akin (TUR)
3. Zoubida Bouazoug (ALG)
3. Irina Kalyanova (RUS)

POWERLIFTING

MEN
UP TO 48.00KG
1. Yakubu Adesokan (NGR) 180kg WR
2. Vladimir Balynetc (RUS) 170kg

3. Taha Abdelmagid (EGY) 165kg
UP TO 52.00KG
1. Qi Feng (CHN) 176kg
2. Ikechukwu Obichukwu (NGR) 175kg
3. Vladimir Krivulya (RUS) 175kg
UP TO 56.00KG
1. Sherif Othman (EGY) 197kg
2. Anthony Ulonnam (NGR) 188kg
3. Jian Wang (CHN) 185kg
UP TO 60.00KG
1. Nader Moradi (IRI) 196kg
2. Ifeanyi Nnajiofor (NGR) 188kg
3. Quanxi Yang (CHN) 185kg
UP TO 67.50KG
1. Lei Liu (CHN) 218kg
2. Roohallah Rostami (IRI) 208kg
3. Shaaban Ibrahim (EGY) 202kg
UP TO 75.00KG
1. Ali Hosseini (IRI) 225kg
2. Mohamed Elelfat (EGY) 219kg
3. Peng Hu (CHN) 213 kg
UP TO 82.50KG
1. Majid Farzin (IRI) 237kg
2. Xiao Fei Gu (CHN) 228kg
3. Metwaly Mathana (EGY) 227kg
UP TO 90.00KG
1. Hany Abdelhady (EGY) 241kg PR
2. Huichao Cai (CHN) 233kg
3. Pavlos Mamalos (GRE) 232kg
UP TO 100.00KG
1. Mohamed Eldib (EGY) 249kg WR
2. Dong Qi (CHN) 242kg
3. Ali Sadehzadehsalmani (IRI) 235kg
OVER 100.00KG
1. Siamand Rahman (IRI) 280kg PR
2. Faris Al-Ajeeli (IRQ) 242kg
3. Keun Bae Chun (KOR) 232kg
WOMEN
UP TO 40.00KG
1. Nazmiye Muslu (TUR) 106kg
2. Zhe Cui (CHN) 97kg
3. Zoe Newson (GBR) 88kg
UP TO 44.00KG
1. Ivory Nwokorie (NGR) 109kg
2. Cigdem Dede (TUR) 105kg
3. Lidiia Soloviova (UKR) 100kg
UP TO 48.00KG
1. Esther Oyema (NGR) 135kg WR
2. Olesya Lafina (RUS) 120kg
3. Shanshan Shi (CHN) 114kg
UP TO 52.00KG
1. Joy Onaolapo (NGR) 131kg WR
2. Tamara Podpalnaya (RUS) 119kg
3. Cuijuan Xiao (CHN) 118kg
UP TO 56.00KG
1. Fatma Omar (EGY) 142kg
2. Lucy Ejike (NGR) 135kg
3. Ozlem Becerikli (TUR) 118kg
UP TO 60.00KG
1. Amalia Perez (MEX) 135kg PR
2. Yan Yang (CHN) 125kg
3. Amal Mahmoud (EGY) 118kg
UP TO 67.50KG
1. Souhad Ghazouani (FRA) 146kg PR
2. Yuijiao Tan (CHN) 139kg
3. Victoria Nneji (NGR) 125kg
UP TO 75.00KG
1. Taoying Fu (CHN) 146kg
2. Folashade Oluwafemiayo (NGR) 146kg
3. Tzu-Hui Lin (TPE) 137kg
UP TO 82.50KG
1. Loveline Obiji (NGR) 145kg
2. Randa Mahmoud (EGY) 140kg
3. Yanmei Xu (CHN) 129kg
OVER 82.50KG
1. Grace Anozie (NGR) 162kg
2. Heba Ahmed (EGY) 140kg
3. Perla Barcenas (MEX) 135kg

ROWING

MEN
SINGLE SCULLS – ASM1X
1. Cheng Huang (CHN) 4:52.36
2. Erik Horrie (AUS) 4:55.85
3. Aleksey Chuvashev (RUS) 4:55.91

WOMEN
SINGLE SCULLS – ASW1X
1. Alla Lysenko (UKR) 5.35.29
2. Nathalie Benoit (FRA) 5:43.56
3. Liudmila Vauchok (BLR) 5:47.54

MIXED
DOUBLE SCULLS – TAMIX2X
1. CHN (Xiaoxian Lou, Tianming Fei) 3:57.63
2. FRA (Perle Bouge, Stephane Tardieu) 4:03.06
3. USA (Oksana Masters, Rob Jones) 4:05.56

COXED FOUR – LTAMIX4+
1. GBR (Pamela Relph, Nicholas Riches, David Smith, James Roe, Lily Van Den Broecke) 3:19.38
2. GER (Anke Molkenthin, Astrid Hengsbach, Tino Kolitscher, Kai Kruse, Katrin Splitt) 3:21.44
3. UKR (Andrii Stelmakh, K Morozova, Olena Pukhaieva, Denys Sobol, Volodymyr Kozlov) 3:23.22

SAILING
MIXED
SINGLE-PERSON KEELBOAT (2.4mR)
1. Helena Lucas (GBR) 37pts
2. Heiko Kroger (GER) 46pts
3. Thierry Schmitter (NED) 46pts

TWO-PERSON KEELBOAT (SKUD18)
1. AUS (Daniel Fitzgibbon, Liesl Tesch) 17pts
2. USA (Jen French, JP Creignou) 25pts
3. GBR (Alexandra Rickham, Niki Birrell) 27pts

THREE-PERSON KEELBOAT (SONAR)
1. NED (Udo Hessels. Marcel van de Veen, Mischa Rossen) 28pts
2. GER (Jens Kroker, Siegmund Mainka, Robert Prem) 49pts
3. NOR (Aleksander Wang-Hansen, Marie Solberg, Per Eugen Kristiansen) 57pts

SHOOTING
MEN
P1 – 10M AIR PISTOL – SH1
1. Seakyun Park (KOR) 664.7pts (Shoot off: 10.8)
2. M Korhan Yamac (TUR) 664.7pts (Shoot off: 9.9)
3. Juhee Lee (KOR) 662.7pts

R1 – 10M AIR RIFLE STANDING – SH1
1. Chao Dong (CHN) 699.5pts
2. Jonas Jakobsson (SWE) 696.5pts
3. Josef Neumaier (GER) 693.4pts

R7 – 50M RIFLE 3 POSITIONS – SH1
1. Jonas Jakobsson (SWE) 1255.9pts
2. Doron Shaziri (ISR) 1252.4pts
3. Chao Dong (CHN) 1251.5pts

WOMEN
P2 – 10M AIR PISTOL – SH1
1. Olivera Nakovska-Bikova (MKD) 475.7pts FPR
2. Marina Klimenchenko (RUS) 469.6pts
3. Sareh Javanmardidodmani (IRI) 469.0pts

R2 – 10M AIR RIFLE STANDING – SH1
1. Cuiping Zhang (CHN) 500.9pts FWR
2. Manuela Schmermund (GER) 493.6pts
3. Natalie Smith (AUS) 492.4pts

R8 – 50M RIFLE 3 POSITIONS – SH1
1. Cuiping Zhang (CHN) 676.6pts
2. Shibei Dang (CHN) 671.7pts
3. Veronkia Vadovicova (SVK) 669.6pts

MIXED
P3 – 25M PISTOL – SH1
1. Jianfei Li (CHN) 770.3pts
2. Sergey Malyshev (RUS) 765.5pts
3. Valery Ponomarenko (RUS) 764.9pts

P4 – 50M PISTOL – SH1
1. Seakyun Park (KOR) 642.4pts
2. Valery Ponomarenko (RUS) 633.2pts
3. Hedong Ni (CHN) 625.3pts

R3 – 10M AIR RIFLE PRONE – SH1
1. Cedric Fevre (FRA) 706.7pts FWR
2. Matthew Skelhon (GBR) 706.4pts
3. Cuiping Zhang (CHN) 705.8pts

R4 – 10M AIR RIFLE STANDING – SH2
1. Juyoung Kang (KOR) 705.5 PR
2. Gorazd Francek Tirsek (SLO) 704.7pts (Shoot off: 10.8)
3. Michael Johnson (NZL) 704.7pts (Shoot off: 10.3)

R5 – 10M AIR RIFLE PRONE – SH2
1. Vasyl Kovalchuk (UKR) 706.4pts FPR
2. Raphael Voltz (FRA) 705.9pts (Shoot off: 10.5)
3. James Bevis (GBR) 705.9pts (Shoot off: 10.4)

R6 – 50M FREE RIFLE PRONE – SH1
1. Abdulla Sultan (UAE) 694.8pts
2. Juan Antonio Saavedra Reinaldo (ESP) 694.6pts
3. Matthew Skelhon (GBR) 693.2pts

SITTING VOLLEYBALL
MEN
10-TEAM TOURNAMENT
1. BIH (Ismet Godinjak, Adnan Manko, Adnan Kesmer, Asim Medic, Mirzet Duran, Nizam Cancar, Dzavad Hamzic, Benis Kadric, Safet Alibasic, Sabahudin Delalic, Ermin Jusufovic)
2. IRI (Majid Lashgarisanami, Reza Peidayesh, Davood Alipourian, Ahmad Eiri, Naser Hassanpour Alinazari, Sadegh Bigdeli, Jalil Eimery, Seyedsaeid Ebrahimibaladezaei, Isa Zirahi, Ramezan Salehi Hajikolaei, Mohammad Khaleghi)
3. GER (Alexander Schiffler, Thomas Renger, Stefan Haehnlein, Sebastian Czpakowski, Heiko Wiesenthal, Peter Schlorf, Jurgen Schrapp, Christoph Herzog, Barbaros Sayilir, Torben Schiewe)

WOMEN
8-TEAM TOURNAMENT
1. CHN (Xue Mei Tang, Hong Qin Lu, Yanhua Tan, Li Mei Su, Xiong Ying Zheng, Yanan Wang, Liping Li, Xu Fei Zhang, Yan Ling Yang, Lijun Zhang, Yu Hong Sheng)
2. USA (Lora Webster, Brenda Maymon, Michelle Gerlosky, Kathryn Holloway, Heather Erickson, Monique Burkland, Kari Miller, Allison Aldrich, Nichole Millage, Kaleo Kanahele, Kendra Lancaster)
3. UKR (Margaryta Pryvalykhina, Anzhelika Churkina, Larysa Sinchuk, Galyna Kuznetsova, Olena Manakova, Ilona Yudina, Larysa Klochkova, Inna Osetynka, Olga Shatylo, Larysa Ponomarenko, Valentyna Brik)

SWIMMING
MEN
50M BACKSTROKE – S1
1. Hennadii Boiko (UKR) 1:04.29 WR
2. Christos Tampaxis (GRE) 1:20.76
3. Oleksandr Golovko (UKR) 1:32.44

50M BACKSTROKE – S2
1. Yang Yang (CHN) 1:00.90 WR
2. Aristeidis Makrodimitris (GRE) 1:04.71
3. Dmitrii Kokarev (RUS) 1:05.70

50M BACKSTROKE – S3
1. Byeong-Eon Min (KOR) 42.51
2. Dmytro Vynohradets (UKR) 46.26
3. Jianping Du (CHN) 46.48

50M BACKSTROKE – S4
1. Juan Reyes (MEX) 45.75
2. Aleksei Lyzhikhin (RUS) 46.73
3. Gustavo Sanchez Martinez (MEX) 47.17

50M BACKSTROKE – S5
1. Daniel Dias (BRA) 34.99 WR
2. Junquan He (CHN) 36.41
3. Zsolt Vereczkei (HUN) 38.92

100M BACKSTROKE – S6
1. Tao Zheng (CHN) 1:13.56 WR
2. Hongguang (CHN) 1:14.64
3. Sebastian Iwanow (GER) 1:15.95

100M BACKSTROKE – S7
1. Jonathan Fox (GBR) 1:10.46
2. Yevheniy Bohodayko (UKR) 1:11.31
3. Mihovil Spanja (CRO) 1:12.53

100M BACKSTROKE – S8
1. Konstantin Lisenkov (RUS) 1:05.43 PR
2. Denis Tarasov (RUS) 1:06.93
3. Oliver Hynd (GBR) 1:08.35

100M BACKSTROKE – S9
1. Matthew Cowdrey (AUS) 1:02.39 PR
2. James Crisp (GBR) 1:03.62
3. Xiaobing Liu (CHN) 1:03.73

100M BACKSTROKE – S10
1. Justin Zook (USA) 1:00.01 WR
2. Andre Brasil (BRA) 1:00.11
3. Benoit Huot (CAN) 1:00.73

100M BACKSTROKE – S11
1. Dmytro Zavlevskyy (UKR) 1:07.81
2. Bozun Yang (CHN) 1:08.07
3. Viktor Smyrnov (UKR) 1:08.22

100M BACKSTROKE – S12
1. Aleksandr Nevolin-Svetov (RUS) 59.35 WR
2. Tucker Dupree (USA) 1:01.36
3. Sergii Klippert (UKR) 1:01.55

100M BACKSTROKE – S13
1. Ihar Boki (BLR) 56.97 WR
2. Charles Bouwer (RSA) 59.92
3. Charalampos Taiganidis (GRE) 1:01.10

100M BACKSTROKE – S14
1. Marc Evers (NED) 1:01.85
2. Aaron Moores (GBR) 1:04.44
3. Kai Lun Au (HKG) 1:04.53

50M BREASTSTROKE – SB2
1. Jianping Du (CHN) 57.50
2. Arnulfo Castorena (MEX) 58.23
3. Dmytro Vynohradets (UKR) 58.51

50M BREASTSTROKE – SB3
1. Michael Schoenmaker (NED) 50.00
2. Miguel Luque (ESP) 50.18
3. Takayuki Suzuki (JPN) 50.26

100M BREASTSTROKE – SB4
1. Daniel Dias (BRA) 1:32.27 WR
2. Moises Fuentes Garcia (COL) 1:36.92
3. Ricardo Ten (ESP) 1:37.23

100M BREASTSTROKE – SB5
1. Woo-Guen LIM (KOR) 1:34.06
2. Niels Grunenberg (GER) 1:34.98
3. Pedro Rangel (MEX) 1:36.85

100M BREASTSTROKE – SB6
1. Yevheniy Bohodayko (UKR) 1:20.17 WR
2. Torben Schmidtke (GER) 1:25.23
3. Christoph Burkard (GER) 1:27.09

100M BREASTSTROKE – SB7
1. Blake Cochrane (AUS) 1:18.77 WR
2. Tomotaro Nakamura (JPN) 1:22.04
3. Matthew Levy (AUS) 1:22.62

100M BREASTSTROKE – SB8
1. Andriy Kalyna (UKR) 1:07.45
2. Matthew Cowdrey (AUS) 1:09.88
3. Maurice Deelen (NED) 1:11.09

100M BREASTSTROKE – SB9
1. Pavel Poltavtsev (RUS) 1:04.02 WR
2. Kevin Paul (RSA) 1:05.70
3. Furong Lin (CHN) 1:07.40

100M BREASTSTROKE – SB11
1. Bozun Yang (CHN) 1:10.11 WR
2. Keiichi Kimura (JPN) 1:14.00
3. Oleksandr Mashchenko (UKR) 1:14.43

100M BREASTSTROKE – SB12
1. Mikhail Zimin (RUS) 1:07.05 WR
2. Uladzimir Izotau (BLR) 1:07.28
3. Maksym Veraksa (UKR) 1:07.79

100M BREASTSTROKE – SB13
1. Oleksii Fedyna (UKR) 1:04.30 PR
2. Daniel Sharp (NZL) 1:06.72
3. Roman Dubovoy (RUS) 1:07.06

100M BREASTSTROKE – SB14
1. Yasuhiro Tanaka (JPN) 1:06.69 WR
2. Artem Pavlenko (RUS) 1:08.38
3. Marc Evers (NED) 1:08.43

50M BUTTERFLY – S5
1. Daniel Dias (BRA) 34.15 WR
2. Roy Perkins (USA) 34.57
3. Juanquan He (CHN) 37.20

50M BUTTERFLY – S6
1. Qing Xu (CHN) 29.90 WR
2. Tao Zheng (CHN) 30.27
3. Kyosuke Oyama (JPN) 31.43

50M BUTTERFLY – S7
1. Shiyun Pan (CHN) 29.49 WR
2. Yevheniy Bohodayko (UKR) 30.19
3. Jingang Wang (CHN) 30.75

100M BUTTERFLY – S8
1. Charles Rozoy (FRA) 1:01.24
2. Yanpeng Wei (CHN) 1:01.66
3. Maodang Song (CHN) 1:01.99

100M BUTTERFLY – S9
1. Tamas Sors (HUN) 59.54
2. Matthew Cowdrey (AUS) 59.91
3. Federico Morlacchi (ITA) 1:00.77

100M BUTTERFLY – S10
1. Andre Brasil (BRA) 56.35 PR
2. Dmitry Grigorev (RUS) 56.89
3. Achmat Hassiem (RSA) 57.76

100M BUTTERFLY – S11
1. Viktor Smyrnov (UKR) 1:03.32
2. Enhamed Enhamed (ESP) 1:03.93
3. Keiichi Kimura (JPN) 1:04.70

100M BUTTERFLY – S12
1. Roman Makarov (RUS) 57.21
2. Sergey Punko (RUS) 59.47

3. James Clegg (GBR) 1:00.00

100M BUTTERFLY – S13
1. Ihar Boki (BLR) 55.50 PR
2. Roman Dubovoy (RUS) 56.37
3. Timothy Antalfy (AUS) 56.48

50M FREESTYLE – S2
1. Yang Yang (CHN) 1:01.39
2. Dmitrii Kokarev (RUS) 1:02.47
3. Aristeidis Makrodimitris (GRE) 1:04.86

50M FREESTYLE – S4
1. Eskender Mustafaiev (UKR) 38.26
2. David Smetanine (FRA) 38.75
3. Jan Povysil (CZE) 39.47

50M FREESTYLE – S5
1. Daniel Dias (BRA) 32.05 WR
2. Sebastian Rodriguez (ESP) 33.44
3. Roy Perkins (USA) 33.69

50M FREESTYLE – S6
1. Qing Xu (CHN) 28.57 WR
2. Lorenzo Perez Escalona (CUB) 30.04
3. Tao Zheng (CHN) 30.06

50M FREESTYLE – S7
1. Lantz Lamback (USA) 27.84 PR
2. Shiyun Pan (CHN) 28.09
3. Matthew Walker (GBR) 28.47

50M FREESTYLE – S8
1. Denis Tarasov (RUS) 25.82 WR
2. Maurice Deelen (NED) 26.29
3. Yinan Wang (CHN) 26.31

50M FREESTYLE – S9
1. Matthew Cowdrey (AUS) 25.13 WR
2. Tamas Toth (HUN) 25.75
3. Jose Antonio Mari Alcaraz (ESP) 25.93

50M FREESTYLE – S10
1. Andre Brasil (BRA) 23.16 WR
2. Nathan Stein (CAN) 23.58
3. Andrew Pasterfield (AUS) 23.89

50M FREESTYLE – S11
1. Bozun Yang (CHN) 25.27 WR
2. Bradley Snyder (USA) 25.93
3. Enhamed Enhamed (ESP) 26.37

50M FREESTYLE – S12
1. Maksym Veraksa (UKR) 23.60
2. Aleksandr Nevolin-Svetov (RUS) 23.96
3. Tucker Dupree (USA) 24.37

50M FREESTYLE – S13
1. Charles Bouwer (RSA) 23.99
2. Ihar Boki (BLR) 24.07
3. Oleksii Fedyna (UKR) 24.09

100M FREESTYLE – S2
1. Yang Yang (CHN) 2:03.71 WR
2. Dmitrii Kokarev (RUS) 2:16.46
3. Aristeidis Makrodimitris (GRE) 2:21.04

100M FREESTYLE – S4
1. Gustavo Sanchez Martinez (MEX) 1:24.28
2. Richard Oribe (ESP) 1:25.33
3. David Smetanine (FRA) 1:25.76

100M FREESTYLE – S5
1. Daniel Dias (BRA) 1:09.35
2. Roy Perkins (USA) 1:14.78
3. Sebastian Rodriguez (ESP) 1:15.70

100M FREESTYLE – S6
1. Qing Xu (CHN) 1:05.82 PR
2. Sebastian Iwanow (GER) 1:07.34
3. Lorenzo Perez Escalona (CUB) 1:08.01

100M FREESTYLE – S7
1. Shiyun Pan (CHN) 1:00.57
2. Matthew Levy (AUS) 1:01.38
3. Lantz Lamback (USA) 1:01.50

100M FREESTYLE – S8
1. Yinan Wang (CHN) 56.58 WR
2. Denis Tarasov (RUS) 57.52
3. Konstantin Lisenkov (RUS) 58.33

100M FREESTYLE – S9
1. Matthew Cowdrey (AUS) 55.84
2. Tamas Toth (HUN) 56.46
3. Tamas Sors (HUN) 56.69

100M FREESTYLE – S10
1. Andre Brasil (BRA) 51.07 PR
2. Phelipe Andrews Melo Rodrigues (BRA) 52.42
3. Andrew Pasterfield (AUS) 52.77

100M FREESTYLE – S11
1. Bradley Snyder (USA) 57.43
2. Bozun Yang (CHN) 58.61
3. Hendri Herbst (RSA) 59.60

100M FREESTYLE – S12
1. Maksym Veraksa (UKR) 51.40 PR
2. Aleksandr Nevolin-Svetov (RUS) 51.70
3. Tucker Dupree (USA) 54.41

100M FREESTYLE – S13
1. Ikar Boki (BLR) 51.91 WR
2. Charles Bouwer (RSA) 52.97
3. Aleksandr Golintovskii (RUS) 53.45

200M FREESTYLE – S2
1. Yang Yang (CHN) 4:36.18 PR
2. Dmitrii Kokarev (RUS) 4:39.23
3. Itzhak Mamistvalov (ISR) 4:58.53

200M FREESTYLE – S4
1 Gustavo Sanchez Martinez (MEX) 2:58.09
2. David Smetanine (FRA) 3:01.38
3. Richard Oribe (ESP) 3:01.62

200M FREESTYLE – S5
1. Daniel Dias (BRA) 2:27.83 PR
2. Sebastian Rodriguez (ESP) 2:43.11
3. Roy Perkins (USA) 2:43.14

200M FREESTYLE – S14
1. Jon Margeir Sverrisson (ISL) 1:59.62 WR
2. Daniel Fox (AUS) 1:59.79
3. Wonsang Cho (KOR) 1:59.93

400M FREESTYLE – S6
1. Darragh McDonald (IRL) 4:55.56
2. Anders Olsson (SWE) 5:03.44
3. Matthew Whorwood (GBR) 5:11.59

400M FREESTYLE – S7
1. Josef Craig (GBR) 4:42.81 WR
2. Shiyun Pan (CHN) 4:46.22
3. Andrey Gladkov (RUS) 4:46.76

400M FREESTYLE – S8
1. Yinan Wang (CHN) 4:27.11
2. Oliver Hynd (GBR) 4:27.88
3. Sam Hynd (GBR) 4:32.93

400M FREESTYLE – S9
1. Brenden Hall (AUS) 4:10.88 WR
2. Thomas Sors (HUN) 4:17.95
3. Federico Morlacchi (ITA) 4:18.55

400M FREESTYLE – S10
1. Ian Jaryd Silverman (USA) 4:04.91 PR
2. Benoit Huot (CAN) 4:06.58
3. Robert Welbourn (GBR) 4:08.18

400M FREESTYLE – S11
1. Bradley Snyder (USA) 4:32.41
2. Enhamed Enhamed (ESP) 4:38.24
3. Bozun Yang (CHN) 4:41.73

400M FREESTYLE – S12
1. Sergey Punko (RUS) 4:10.26
2. Enrique Floriano (ESP) 4:14.77
3. Sergii Klippert (UKR) 4:17.12

400M FREESTYLE – S13
1. Ihar Boki (BLR) 3:58.78 WR
2. Danylo Chufarov (UKR) 4:05.85
3. Aleksandr Golintovskii (RUS) 4:11.13

150M INDIVIDUAL MEDLEY – SM3
1. Jianping Du (CHN) 2:43.72
2. Dmytro Vynohradets (UKR) 2:44.85
3. Hanhua Li (CHN) 3:01.16

150M INDIVIDUAL MEDLEY – SM4
1. Cameron Leslie (NZL) 2:25.98 WR
2. Gustavo Sanchez Martinez (MEX) 2:39.55
3. Takayuki Suzuki (JPN) 2:40.24

200M INDIVIDUAL MEDLEY – SM6
1. Qing Xu (CHN) 2:38.62 WR
2. Sascha Kindred (GBR) 2:41.50
3. Tao Zheng (CHN) 2:44.38

200M INDIVIDUAL MEDLEY – SM7
1. Yevheniy Bohodayko (UKR) 2:33.13 WR
2. Rudy Garcia-Tolson (USA) 2:33.94
3. Matthew Levy (AUS) 2:37.18

200M INDIVIDUAL MEDLEY – SM8
1. Oliver Hynd (GBR) 2:24.63
2. Jiachao Wang (CHN) 2:26.62
3. Maurice Deelen (NED) 2:27.17

200M INDIVIDUAL MEDLEY – SM9
1. Matthew Cowdrey (AUS) 2:15.95
2. Andriy Kalyna (UKR) 2:16.38
3. Federico Morlacchi (ITA) 2:20.28

200M INDIVIDUAL MEDLEY – SM10
1. Benoit Huot (CAN) 2:10.01 WR
2. Andre Brasil (BRA) 2:12.36
3. Rick Pendleton (AUS) 2:14.77

200M INDIVIDUAL MEDLEY – SM11
1. Bozun Yang (CHN) 2:22.40 WR
2. Viktor Smyrnov (UKR) 2:26.45

3. Oleksandr Mashchenko (UKR) 2:27.77

200M INDIVIDUAL MEDLEY – SM12
1. Maksym Veraksa (UKR) 2:12.42 PR
2. Aleksandr Nevolin-Svetov (RUS) 2:14.45
3. Sergey Punko (RUS) 2:14.83

200M INDIVIDUAL MEDLEY – SM13
1. Ihar Boki (BLR) 2:06.30 WR
2. Roman Dubovoy (RUS) 2:10.16
3. Danylo Chufarov (UKR) 2:10.22

4 X 100M FREESTYLE RELAY 34 POINTS
1. AUS (Andrew Pasterfield, Matthew Levy, Blake Cochrane, Matthew Cowdrey) 3:50.17 PR
2. CHN (Maodang Song, Jiachang Wang, Furong Lin, Yinan Wang) 3:51.68
3. RUS (Konstantin Lisenkov, Evgeny Zimin, Denis Tarasov, Dmitry Grigorev) 3:52.93

4 X 100M MEDLEY RELAY 34 POINTS
1. CHN (Xiaobing Liu, Furong Lin, Yanpeng Wei, Yinan Wang) 4:09.04 WR
2. RUS (Konstantin Lisenkov, Pavel Poltavtsev, Eduard Samarin, Denis Tarasov) 4:09.08
3. AUS (Michael Anderson, Matthew Cowdrey, Brendan Hall, Matthew Levy) 4:14.97

WOMEN

50M BACKSTROKE – S2
1. Yazhu Feng (CHN) 1:03.00 WR
2. Ganna Ielisavetska (UKR) 1:04.14
3. Iryna Sotska (UKR) 1:05.16

50M BACKSTROKE – S4
1. Lisette Teunissen (NED) 51.51
2. Edenia Garcia (BRA) 53.85
3. Juan Bai (CHN) 54.33

100M BACKSTROKE – S6
1. Dong Lu (CHN) 1:24.71 WR
2. Nyree Kindred (GBR) 1:26.23
3. Mirjam de Koning-Peper (NED) 1:29.04

100M BACKSTROKE – S7
1. Jacqueline Freney (AUS) 1:22.84 PR
2. Kirsten Bruhn (GER) 1:25.22
3. Cortney Jordan (USA) 1:25.33

100M BACKSTROKE – S8
1. Heather Frederiksen (GBR) 1:17.00
2. Jessica Long (USA) 1:18.67
3. Olesya Vladykina (RUS) 1:20.20

100M BACKSTROKE – S9
1. Ellie Cole (AUS) 1:09.42
2. Stephanie Millward (GBR) 1:11.07
3. Elizabeth Stone (USA) 1:12.28

100M BACKSTROKE – S10
1. Summer Ashley Mortimer (CAN) 1:05.90 WR
2. Sarah Pascoe (NZL) 1:06.69
3. Shireen Sapiro (RSA) 1:09.02

100M BACKSTROKE – S11
1. Rina Akiyama (JPN) 1:19.50 PR
2. Mary Fisher (NZL) 1:19.62
3. Cecilia Camellini (ITA) 1:19.91

100M BACKSTROKE – S12
1. Oxana Savchenko (RUS) 1:07.99 WR
2. Natali Pronina (AZE) 1:09.46
3. Hannah Russell (GBR) 1:10.15

100M BACKSTROKE – S14
1. Bethany Firth (IRL) 1:08.93 PR
2. Taylor Corry (AUS) 1:09.46
3. Marlou van der Kulk (NED) 1:09.50

100M BREASTSTROKE – SB4
1. Nataliia Prologaieva (UKR) 1:43.99 WR
2. Sarah Louise Rung (NOR) 1:45.68
3. Teresa Perales (ESP) 1:56.17

100M BREASTSTROKE – SB5
1. Kristen Bruhn (GER) 1:35.50
2. Linling Song (CHN) 1:47.19
3. Noga Nir-Kistler (USA) 1:50.76

100M BREASTSTROKE – SB6
1. Viktoriia Savtsova (UKR) 1:39.13 PR
2. Charlotte Henshaw (GBR) 1:39.16
3. Elizabeth Johnson (GBR) 1:40.90

100M BREASTSTROKE – SB7
1. Jessica Long (USA) 1:29.28 PR
2. Oksana Khrul (UKR) 1:35.68
3. Lisa den Braber (NED) 1:37.02

100M BREASTSTROKE – SB8
1. Olesya Vladykina (RUS) 1:17.17 WR
2. Claire Cashmore (GBR) 1:20.39
3. Paulina Wozniak (POL) 1:22.45

100M BREASTSTROKE – SB9
1. Khrystyna Yurchenko (UKR) 1:17.81
2. Sophie Pascoe (NZL) 1:18.38

3. Harriet Lee (GBR) 1:19.53

100M BREASTSTROKE – SB11
1. Maja Reichard (SWE) 1:27.98 WR
2. Yana Berezhna (UKR) 1:29.99
3. Nadia Baez (ARG) 1:31.21

100M BREASTSTROKE – SB12
1. Natali Pronina (AZE) 1:16.17 WR
2. Karolina Pelendritou (CYP) 1:16.38
3. Yaryna Matlo (UKR) 1:20.21

100M BREASTSTROKE – SB13
1. Prue Watt (AUS) 1:19.19
2. Elena Krawzow (GER) 1:20.31
3. Kelley Becherer (USA) 1:21.50

100M BREASTSTROKE – SB14
1. Michelle Alonso Morales (ESP) 1:16.85 WR
2. Magda Toeters (NED) 1:20.64
3. Shu Hang Leung (HKG) 1:21.21

50M BUTTERFLY – S5
1. Sarah Louise Rung (Norway) 41.76
2. Teresa Perales (ESP) 42.67
3. Joana Maria Silva (BRA) 46.62

50M BUTTERFLY – S5
1. Oksana Khrul (UKR) 36.05 WR
2. Dong Lu (CHN) 37.65
3. Fuying Jiang (CHN) 39.26

50M BUTTERFLY – S7
1. Jacqueline Freney (AUS) 35.16
2. Brianna Nelson (CAN) 36.03
3. Min Huang (CHN) 36.50

100M BUTTERFLY – S8
1. Jessica Long (USA) 1:10.32 PR
2. Kateryna Istomina (UKR) 1:11.53
3. Shengnan Jiang (CHN) 1:13.28

100M BUTTERFLY – S9
1. Natalie du Toit (RSA) 1:09.30
2. Sarai Gascon (ESP) 1:09.79
3. Elizabeth Stone (USA) 1:10.10

100M BUTTERFLY – S10
1. Sophie Pascoe (NZL) 1:04.43 WR
2. Oliwia Jablonska (POL) 1:08.55
3. Elodie Lorandi (FRA) 1:09.08

100M BUTTERFLY – S12
1. Joanna Mendak (POL) 1:06.16
2. Darya Stukalova (RUS) 1:06.27
3. Hannah Russell (GBR) 1:08.57

50M FREESTYLE – S3
1. Jiangbo Xia (CHN) 48.11 WR
2. Olga Sviderska (UKR) 48.39
3. Patricia Valle (MEX) 55.72

50M FREESTYLE – S5
1. Nataliia Prolongaieva (UKR) 35.88
2. Teresa Perales (ESP) 36.50
3. Inbal Roy Perkins (USA) 37.89

50M FREESTYLE – S6
1. Mirjam de Koning-Peper (NED) 34.77 PR
2. Victoria Arlen (USA) 35.32
3. Eleanor Simmonds (GBR) 36.11

50M FREESTYLE – S7
1. Jacqueline Freney (AUS) 32.63 PR
2. Cortney Jordan (USA) 33.18
3. Ani Palian (UKR) 33.30

50M FREESTYLE – S8
1. Mallory Weggemann (USA) 31.13 PR
2. Maddison Elliott (AUS) 31.44
3. Shengnan Jiang (CHN) 31.55

50M FREESTYLE – S9
1. Ping Lin (CHN) 29.12 PR
2. Louise Watkin (GBR) 29.21
3. Ellie Cole (AUS) 29.28

50M FREESTYLE – S10
1. Summer Ashley Mortimer (CAN) 28.10 WR
2. Sophie Pascoe (NZL) 28.24
3. Elodie Lorandi (FRA) 28.67

50M FREESTYLE – S11
1. Cecilia Camellini (ITA) 30.94 WR
2. Guizhi Li (CHN) 31.01
3. Mary Fisher (NZL) 31.67

50M FREESTYLE – S13
1. Kelley Becherer (USA) 27.46
2. Valerie Grand-Maison (CAN) 27.91
3. Prue Watt (AUS) 27.94

100M FREESTYLE – S3
1. Jiangbo Xia (CHN) 1:44.32 WR

2. Olga Sviderska (UKR) 1:52.91
3. Patricia Valle (MEX) 1:59.76

100M FREESTYLE – S5
1. Teresa Perales (ESP) 1:18.55
2. Nataliia Prolongaieva (UKR) 1:20.57
3. Inbal Pezaro (ISR) 1:22.56

100M FREESTYLE – S6
1. Victoria Arlen (USA) 1:13.33 WR
2. Eleanor Simmonds (GBR) 1:14.82
3. Tanja Groepper (GER) 1:16.83

100M FREESTYLE – S7
1. Jacqueline Freney (AUS) 1:09.39
2. Cortney Jordan (USA) 1:11.63
3. Susannah Rodgers (GBR) 1:12.61

100M FREESTYLE – S8
1 Jessica Long (USA) 1:05.63 WR
2. Heather Frederiksen (GBR) 1:08.07
3. Maddison Elliott (AUS) 1:08.37

100M FREESTYLE – S9
1. Ellie Cole (AUS) 1:02.77
2. Natalie du Toit (RSA) 1:03.45
3. Sarai Gascon (ESP) 1:03.62

100M FREESTYLE – S10
1. Sophie Pascoe (NZL) 1:00.89 PR
2. Elodie Lorandi (FRA) 1:01.09
3. Summer Ashley Mortimer (CAN) 1:01.58

100M FREESTYLE – S11
1. Cecilia Camellini (ITA) 1:07.29 WR
2. Mary Fisher (NZL) 1:09.83
3. Guizhi Li (CHN) 1:10.25

100M FREESTYLE – S12
1. Oxana Savchenko (RUS) 58.41 WR
2. Natali Pronina (AZE) 1:00.00
3. Darya Stukalova (RUS) 1:00.23

100M FREESTYLE – S13
1. Kelley Becherer (USA) 59.56
2. Valerie Grand-Maison (CAN) 1:00.07
3. Rebecca Anne Meyers (USA) 1:01.90

200M FREESTYLE – S5
1. Sarah Louise Rung (NOR) 2:49.74
2. Teresa Perales (ESP) 2:51.79
3. Inbal Pezaro (ISR) 2:56.11

200M FREESTYLE – S14
1. Jessica-Jane Applegate (GBR) 2:12.63 WR
2. Taylor Corry (AUS) 2:13.18
3. Marlou van der Kulk (NED) 2:14.80

400M FREESTYLE – S6
1. Eleanor Simmonds (GBR) 5:19.17 WR
2. Victoria Arlen (USA) 5:20.18
3. Lingling Song (CHN) 5:33.73

400M FREESTYLE – S7
1. Jacqueline Freney (AUS) 4:59.02 WR
2. Cortney Jordan (USA) 5:18.55
3. Susannah Rodgers (GBR) 5:18.93

400M FREESTYLE – S8
1. Jessica Long (USA) 4:42.28 WR
2. Heather Frederiksen (GBR) 5:00.50
3. Maddison Elliott (AUS) 5:09.36

400M FREESTYLE – S9
1. Natalie du Toit (RSA) 4:30.18
2. Stephanie Millward (GBR) 4:40.01
3. Ellie Cole (AUS) 4:42.87

400M FREESTYLE – S10
1. Elodie Lorandi (FRA) 4:34.55
2. Aurelie Rivard (CAN) 4:36.46
3. Susan Beth Scott (USA) 4:37.23

400M FREESTYLE – S11
1. Daniela Schulte (GER) 5:14.36
2. Amber Thomas (CAN) 5:15.48
3. Cecilia Camellini (ITA) 5:20.27

400M FREESTYLE – S12
1. Oxana Savchenko (RUS) 4:37.89
2. Hannah Russell (GBR) 4:38.60
3. Deborah Font (ESP) 4:39.75

200M INDIVIDUAL MEDLEY – SM5
1. Nataliia Prologaieva (UKR) 3:13.43 WR
2. Sarah Louise Rung (NOR) 3:15.89
3. Teresa Perales (ESP) 3:25.58

200M INDIVIDUAL MEDLEY – SM6
4. Eleanor Simmonds (GBR) 3:05.39 WR
5. Verena Schott (GER) 3:14.28
6. Natalie Jones (GBR) 3:14.29

200M INDIVIDUAL MEDLEY – SM7
1. Jacqueline Freney (AUS) 2:54.42 WR
2. Brianna Nelson (CAN) 3:04.60
3. Min Huang (CHN) 3:07.51

200M INDIVIDUAL MEDLEY – SM8
1. Jessica Long (USA) 2:37.09 PR
2. Olesya Vladykina (RUS) 2:41.79
3. Shengnan Jiang (CHN) 2:49.47

200M INDIVIDUAL MEDLEY – SM9
1. Natalie du Toit (RSA) 2:34.22
2. Stephanie Millward (GBR) 2:36.21
3. Louise Watkin (GBR) 2:37.79

200M INDIVIDUAL MEDLEY – SM10
1. Sophie Pascoe (NZL) 2:25.65 WR
2. Summer Ashley Mortimer (CAN) 2:32.08
3. Meng Zhang (CHN) 2:33.95

200M INDIVIDUAL MEDLEY – SM11
1. Mary Fisher (NZL) 2:46.91 WR
2. Daniela Schulte (GER) 2:49.57
3. Amber Thomas (CAN) 2:59.00

200M INDIVIDUAL MEDLEY – SM12
1. Oxana Savchenko (RUS) 2:28.00 WR
2. Natali Pronina (AZE) 2:28.45
3. Darya Stukalova (RUS) 2:28.73

200M INDIVIDUAL MEDLEY – SM13
1. Valerie Grand-Maison (CAN) 2:27.64 WR
2. Rebecca Anne Meyers (USA) 2:30.13
3. Kelley Becherer (USA) 2:30.36

4 X 100M FREESTYLE RELAY 34 POINTS
1. AUS (Ellie Cole, Maddison Elliott, Katherine Downie, Jacqueline Freney) 4:20.39 WR
2. USA (Susan Beth Scott, Victoria Arlen, Jessica Long, Anna Eames) 4:24.57
3. GBR (Stephanie Millward, Claire Cashmore, Susannah Rodgers, Louise Watkin) 4:24.71

4 X 100M MEDLEY RELAY 34 POINTS
1. AUS (Ellie Cole, Katherine Downie, Annabelle Williams, Jacqueline Freney) 4:53.95
2. GBR (Heather Frederiksen, Claire Cashmore, Stephanie Millward, Louise Watkin) 4:53.98
3. USA (Susan Beth Scott, Anna Johannes, Jessica Long, Mallory Weggemann) 4:54.13

TABLE TENNIS

MEN
SINGLES – CLASS 1
1. Holger Nikelis (GER)
2. Jean-Francois (FRA)
3. Paul Davies (GBR)

SINGLES – CLASS 2
1. Jan Riapos (SVK)
2. Kyung Mook Kim (KOR)
3. Fabien Lamirault (FRA)

SINGLES – CLASS 3
1. Panfeng Feng (CHN)
2. Zlatko Kesler (SRB)
3. Thomas Schmidberger (GER)

SINGLES – CLASS 4
1. Young Gun Kim (KOR)
2. Yan Zhang (CHN)
3. Sameh Saleh (EGY)

SINGLES – CLASS 5
1. Tommy Urhaug (NOR)
2. Ningning Cao (CHN)
3. Eun Chang Jung (KOR)

SINGLES – CLASS 6
1. Rungroj Thainyom (THA)
2. Alvaro Valera (ESP)
3. Peter Rosenmeier (DEN)

SINGLES – CLASS 7
1. Jochen Wollmert (GER)
2. William Bayley (GBR)
3. Mykhaylo Popov (UKR)

SINGLES – CLASS 8
1. Shuai Zhao (CHN)
2. Richard Csejtey (SVK)
3. Emil Andersson (SWE)

SINGLES – CLASS 9
1. Lin Ma (CHN)
2. Stanislaw Fraczyk (AUT)
3. Gerben Last (NED)

SINGLES – CLASS 10
1. Patryk Chojnowski (POL)
2. Yang Ge (CHN)
3. David Jacobs (INA)

SINGLES – CLASS 11
1. Peter Palos (HUN)
2. Byeongjun Son (KOR)
3. Pascal Pereira-Leal (FRA)

TEAM – CLASS 1-2
1. SVK (Martin Ludrovsky, Rastislav Revucky, Jan Riapos)
2. FRA (Vincent Boury, Fabien Lamirault, Stephane Molliens)
3. KOR (Kong Yong Kim, Kyung Mook Kim, Min Gyu Kim, Chang Ho Lee)

TEAM – CLASS 3
1. CHN (Pangfeng Feng, Yanming Gao, Ping Zhao)
2. GER (Thomas Bruechle, Jan Guertler, Holger Nikelis, Thomas Schmidberger)
3. FRA (Yann Guilhem, Florian Merrien, Jean-Philippe Robin)

TEAM – CLASS 4-5
1. CHN (Ningning Cao, Xinguan Guo, Yan Zhang)
2. KOR (Il Sang Choi, Eun Chang Jung, Jung Gil Kim, Young Gun Kim)
3. FRA (Emeric Martin, Gregory Rosec, Nicolas Saveant-Aira, Maxime Thomas)

TEAM – CLASS 6-8
1. POL (Alvaro Valera, Jordi Morales)
2. ESP (Piotr Grudzien, Marcin Skrzynecki)
3. GBR (William Bayley, Aaron McKibbin, Ross Wilson)

TEAM – CLASS 9-10
1. CHN (Yang Ge, Hao Lian, Xiaolei Lu, Lin Ma)
2. POL (Sebastian Powrozniak, Patryk Chojnowski)
3. ESP (Jorge Cardona, Jose Manuel Ruiz Reyes)

WOMEN
SINGLES – CLASS 1-2
1. Jin Liu (CHN)
2. Pamela Pezzutto (ITA)
3. Isabelle Lafaye Marziou (FRA)

SINGLES – CLASS 3
1. Anna-Carin Ahlquist (SWE)
2. Doris Mader (AUT)
3. Alena Kanova (SVK)

SINGLES – CLASS 4
1. Ying Zhou (CHN)
2. Borislava Peric-Rankovic (SRB)
3. Sung Hye Moon (KOR)

SINGLES – CLASS 5
1. Bian Zhang (CHN)
2. Gai Gu (CHN)
3. Ingela Lundback (SWE)

SINGLES – CLASS 6
1. Raisa Chebanika (RUS)
2. Antonina Khodzynska (UKR)
3. Yuliya Klymenko (UKR)

SINGLES – CLASS 7
1. Kelly van Zon (NED)
2. Yulia Ovsyannikova (RUS)
3. Viktoriia Safonova (UKR)

SINGLES – CLASS 8
1. Jingdian Mao (CHN)
2. Thu Kamsomphou (FRA)
3. Josefin Abrahamsson (SWE)

SINGLES – CLASS 9
1. Lina Lei (CHN)
2. Neslihan Kavas (TUR)
3. Meili Liu (CHN)

Singles – Class 10
1. Natalia Partyka (POL)
2. Qian Yang (CHN)
3. Lei Fan (CHN)

SINGLES – CLASS 11
1. Ka Man Wong (HKG)
2. Chi Ka Yeung (HKG)
3. Anzhelika Kosacheva (RUS)

TEAM – CLASS 1-3
1. CHN (Qian Li, Jing Liu)
2. KOR (Kyoung Hee Cho, Hyun Ja Choi, Sang Sook Jung)
3. GBR (Jane Campbell, Sara Head)

TEAM – CLASS 4-5
1. CHN (Gai Gu, Bian Zhang, Miao Zhang, Ying Zhou)
2. SWE (Anna-Carin Ahlquist, Ingela Lundback)
3. KOR (Ji Nam Jung, Young-A Jung, Sung Hye Moon)

TEAM – CLASS 6-10
1. CHN (Lei Fan, Lina Lei, Meili Liu, Qian Yang)
2. TUR (Umran Ertis, Neslihan Kavas, Kubra Ocsoy)
3. POL (Alicja Eigner, Malgorzata Jankowska, Natalia Partyka, Korolina Pek)

WHEELCHAIR BASKETBALL

MEN
12-TEAM TOURNAMENT
1. CAN (Dave Durepos, Yvon Rouillard, Bo Hedges, Richard Peter, Joey Johnson, Adam Lancia, Abdi Dini, Chad Jassman, Patrick Anderson, Brandon Wagner, Tyler Miller, David Eng)
2. AUS (Justin Eveson, Bill Latham, Brett Stibners, Shaun Norris, Michael Hartnett, Tristan Knowles, Jannik Blair, Tige Simmons, Grant Mizens, Dylan Alcott, Nick Taylor, Brad Ness)
3. USA (Eric Barber, Joseph Chambers, Jeremy Lade, Joshua Turek, Trevon Jenifer, William Waller, Matt Scott, Steven Serio, Jason Nelms, Ian Lynch, Paul Schulte, Nate Hinze)

WOMEN
10-TEAM TOURNAMENT
1. GER (Mareike Adermann, Johanna Welin, Britt Dillmann, Edina Mueller, Annika Zeyen, Maria Kuehn, Gesche Schuenemann, Maya Lindholm, Annabel Breuer, Annegret Briessmann, Marina Mohnen, Heike Friedrich)
2. AUS (Sarah Vinci, Cobi Crispin, Bridie Kean, Amanda Carter, Tina Mckenzie, Leanne del Toso, Clare Nott, Kylie Gauci, Shelley Chaplin, Sarah Stewart, Katie Hill, Amber Merritt)
3. NED (Inge Huitzing, Lucie Houwen, Jitske Visser, Roos Oosterbaan, Sanne Timmerman, Petra Garnier, Miranda Wevers, Cher Korver, Saskia Pronk, Barbara van Bergen, Carolina de Rooij-Versloot, Mariska Beijer)

WHEELCHAIR FENCING

MEN
EPÉE – CATEGORY A
1. Dariusz Pender (POL)
2. Romain Noble (FRA)
3. Matteo Betti (ITA)

EPÉE – CATEGORY B
1. Jovane Silva Guissone (BRA)
2. Chik Sum Tam (HKG)
3. Alim Latreche (FRA)

FOIL – CATEGORY A
1. Ruyi Ye (CHN)
2. Yijun Chen (CHN)
3. Richard Osvath (HUN)

FOIL – CATEGORY B
1. Daoliang Hu (CHN)
2. Anton Datsko (UKR)
3. Alim Latreche (FRA)

SABRE – CATEGORY A
1. Yijun Chen (CHN)
2. Jianquan Tian (CHN)
3. Wing Kin Chan (HKG)

SABRE – CATEGORY B
1. Grzegorz Pluta (POL)
2. Marc-Andre Cratere (FRA)
3. Alessio Sarri (ITA)

TEAM – OPEN
1. CHN (Yijun Chen, Ruyi Ye, Daoling Hu)
2. FRA (Ludovic Lemoine, Alim Latreche, Damien Tokatlian)
3. HKG (Tang Tat Wong, Wing Kin Chan, Ting Ching Chung)

WOMEN
EPÉE – CATEGORY A
1. Chui Yee Yu (HKG)
2. Zsuzsanna Krajnyak (HUN)
3. Baili Wu (CHN)

EPÉE – CATEGORY B
1. Saysunee Jana (THA)
2. Simone Briese-Baetke (GER)
3. Yui Chong Chan (HKG)

FOIL – CATEGORY A
1. Chui Yee Yu (HKG)
2. Baili Wu (CHN)
3. Zsuzsanna Krajnyak (HUN)

FOIL – CATEGORY B
1. Fang Yao (CHN)
2. Gyongyi Dani (HUN)
3. Marta Makowska (POL)

TEAM – OPEN
1. CHN (Jing Rong, Fang Yao, Baili Wu)
2. HUN (Veronika Juhasz, Zsuzsanna Krajnyak, Gyongyi Dani)
3. HKG (Pui Shan Fan, Chui Yee Tu, Yui Chong Chan)

WHEELCHAIR RUGBY

MIXED
8-TEAM TOURNAMENT
1. AUS (Ben Newton, Naz Erdem, Ryley Batt, Josh Hose, Jason Lees, Cody Meakin, Greg Smith, Chris Bond, Ryan Scott, Cameron Carr, Andrew Harrison)
2. CAN (Jason Crone, Patrice Dagenais, Garett Hickling, Ian Chan, Mike Whitehead, Trevor Hirschfield, Fabien Lavoie, Travis Murao, Jared Funk, David Willsie, Patrice Simard, Zak Madell)
3. USA (Chance Sumner, Seth McBride, Adam Scaturro, Chance Aoki, Jason Regier, Scott Hogsett, Nick Springer, Will Groulx, Andy Cohn, Chad Cohn, Derrick Helton, Joe Delagrave)

WHEELCHAIR TENNIS

MEN
SINGLES
1. Shingo Kunieda (JPN)
2. Stephane Houdet (FRA)
3. Ronald Vink (NED)

DOUBLES
1. SWE (Stefan Olsson, Peter Vikstrom)
2. FRA (Frederic Cattaneo, Nicolas Peifer)
3. FRA (Stephane Houdet, Michael Jeremiasz)

WOMEN
SINGLES
1. Esther Vergeer (NED)
2. Aniek Van Koot (NED)
3. Jiske Griffioen (NED)

DOUBLES
1. NED (Marjolein Buis, Esther Vergeer)
2. NED (Jiske Griffioen, Aniek Van Koot)
3. GBR (Lucy Shuker, Jordanne Whiley)

MIXED
SINGLES – QUAD
1. Noam Gershony (ISR)
2. David Wagner (USA)
3. Nicholas Taylor (USA)

DOUBLES – QUAD
1. USA (Nicholas Taylor, David Wagner)
2. GBR (Andy Lapthorne, Peter Norfolk)
3. ISR (Noam Gershony, Shraga Weinberg)

Olympic Competition Schedule

Sport	Venue	-2 Wed 25 Jul	-1 Thur 26 Jul	0 Fri 27 Jul	1 Sat 28 Jul	2 Sun 29 Jul	3 Mon 30 Jul	4 Tue 31 Jul	5 Wed 1 Aug	6 Thur 2 Aug	7 Fri 3 Aug	8 Sat 4 Aug	9 Sun 5 Aug	10 Mon 6 Aug	11 Tue 7 Aug	12 Wed 8 Aug	13 Thur 9 Aug	14 Fri 10 Aug	15 Sat 11 Aug	16 Sun 12 Aug
Archery	Lord's Cricket Ground			ranking round	M Team	W Team		M/W Indiv	M/W Indiv	W Indiv	M Indiv									
Athletics	The Mall											M 20km Walk, W Marathon							M/W Walks	M Marathon
	Olympic Stadium										M/W	M/W	M/W	M/W	M/W	M/W	M/W	M/W	M/W	M/W
Badminton	Wembley Arena				prelims	prelims	prelims	prelims	Ro16, QF	QF, SF	SF, MM (Mx)	SF, MM (W)	MM (M)							
Basketball	Basketball Arena				W prelims	M prelims	W prelims	W prelims	M prelims	W prelims	M prelims	W prelims	M prelims	W QF						
	North Greenwich Arena															•	•	•	•	•
Beach Volleyball	Horse Guards Parade				prelims	prelims	prelims	prelims	prelims	prelims	Ro16	Ro16	W QF	M QF	M/W SF	W MM	M MM			
Boxing	ExCeL				M Ro32	M Ro32	M Ro32	M Ro32	M Ro16	M Ro16	M Ro16	M Ro16	W Ro16, M QF	M/W QF	M QF	W SF, M QF	W F	M SF	M F	M F
Canoe Slalom	Lee Valley White Water Centre, Hertfordshire				M H	M/W H	M SF, F	M SF, F	M/W SF, F											
Canoe Sprint	Eton Dorney, Buckinghamshire												M/W, H, SF	M/W, H, SF	M/W, F	M/W, F	M/W, H, SF	M/W, F		
Cycling – BMX	BMX Track															M/W seeding	M QF	M/W SF, F		
Cycling – Mountain Bike	Hadleigh Farm, Essex																	W	M	
Cycling – Road	The Mall				M Road Race	W Road Race														
	Hampton Court Palace								M/W Time Trial											
Cycling – Track	Velodrome									M/W	M/W	M/W	M/W	M/W	M/W					
Diving	Aquatics Centre				W Sync 3m	M Sync 10m	W Sync 10m	M Sync 3m		W 3m prelims	W 3m SF	W 3m F	M 3m prelims	M 3m SF, F	W 10m prelims	W 10m SF, F	M 10m prelims	M 10m SF, F		
Equestrian – Dressage	Greenwich Park									day 1	day 2				Team F		Indiv F			
Equestrian – Eventing	Greenwich Park				dressage	dressage	cross-country	jumping												
Equestrian – Jumping	Greenwich Park										Indiv/Team	Indiv/Team	Team F		Indiv F					
Fencing	ExCeL				W Indiv Foil	M Indiv Sabre	W Indiv Epee	M Indiv Foil	M Epee, W Sab	W Team Foil	M Team Sabre	W Team Epee	M Team Foil							
Football	City of Coventry Stadium, Coventry	W prelims	M prelims		W prelims	M prelims		W prelims	M prelims	W QF							W MM			
	Hampden Park, Glasgow	W prelims	W prelims		W prelims				M prelims	W QF										
	Millennium Stadium, Cardiff	W prelims	M prelims		W prelims			W prelims	M prelims	W QF	M QF						M MM			
	Old Trafford, Manchester		M prelims			M prelims		W prelims	M prelims	M QF				W SF	M SF					
	St James' Park, Newcastle		M prelims			M prelims		W prelims	M prelims	W QF	M QF									
	Wembley Stadium					M prelims		W prelims	M prelims	M QF				W SF	M SF		W MM		M MM	
Gymnastics – Artistic	North Greenwich Arena				M Q	W Q	M Team F	W Team F	M All-Around	W All-Around		M/W F	M/W F	M/W F						
Gymnastics – Rhythmic	Wembley Arena																Q	Q	Indiv F	Group F
Gymnastics – Trampoline	North Greenwich Arena										M	W								

		-2 Wed 25 July	-1 Thur 26 July	0 Fri 27 July	1 Sat 28 July	2 Sun 29 July	3 Mon 30 July	4 Tue 31 July	5 Wed 1 Aug	6 Thur 2 Aug	7 Fri 3 Aug	8 Sat 4 Aug	9 Sun 5 Aug	10 Mon 6 Aug	11 Tue 7 Aug	12 Wed 8 Aug	13 Thur 9 Aug	14 Fri 10 Aug	15 Sat 11 Aug	16 Sun 12 Aug
Handball	Copper Box				W prelims	M prelims	W prelims	M prelims	W prelims	M prelims	W prelims	M prelims	W prelims	M prelims	W QF					
	Basketball Arena															M QF	W SF	M SF	W MM	M MM
Hockey	Riverbank Arena					W prelims	M prelims	W prelims	M prelims	W prelims	M prelims	W prelims	M prelims	W prelims	M prelims	W C, SF	M C, SF	W C, MM	M C, MM	
Judo	ExCeL				M/W	M/W	M/W	M/W	M/W	M/W	M/W									
Modern Pentathlon	Copper Box (Fencing) / Aquatics Centre (Swimming) / Greenwich Park (Riding and Combined Run/Shoot)																		M	W
Rowing	Eton Dorney, Buckinghamshire				H	H, rep	H, rep	rep, QF, SF	C, SF, F	C, SF, F	C, F	C, F								
Sailing	Weymouth and Portland, Dorset					M/W	M/W	M/W	M/W	M/W	M/W	M/W	M/W	M/W	M/W	M/W	W	W		
Shooting	The Royal Artillery Barracks				M/W Q, F	W Q, F	M Q, F	M Q, F	W Q, F	M Q, F	M Q, F	W Q, F	M Q, F	M Q, F						
Swimming	Aquatics Centre				H, SF, F	H, SF, F	H, SF, F	H, SF, F	H, SF, F	H, SF, F	H, SF, F	F								
	Hyde Park																W Marathon	M Marathon		
Synchronised Swimming	Aquatics Centre												Duets	Duets	Duets		Teams	Teams		
Table Tennis	ExCeL				prelims, R1, R2	R2, R3	R3, R4	M/W QF W SF	M QF, W MM	M SF, MM	Team	Team	Team M QF, W SF	M/W Team SF	W Team MM	M Team MM				
Taekwondo	ExCeL															M/W	M/W	M/W	M/W	
Tennis	Wimbledon				R1	R1	R2	R2, QF	R1 (Mx), R3	QF, SF	SF	MM	MM							
Triathlon	Hyde Park											W		M						
Volleyball	Earls Court				W prelims	M prelims	W prelims	M prelims	W prelims	M prelims	W prelims	M prelims	W prelims	M prelims	W QF	M QF	W SF	M SF	W MM	M MM
Water Polo	Water Polo Arena					M prelims	W prelims	M prelims	W prelims	M prelims	W prelims	M prelims	W QF	M prelims	W C, SF	M QF	W C, MM	M C, SF		M C, MM
Weightlifting	ExCeL				W	M/W	M/W	M/W	M/W		M/W	M	M	M						
Wrestling – Freestyle	ExCeL															W	W	M	M	M
Wrestling – Greco-Roman	ExCeL											M	M	M	M					

Key			
M	men	R1, R2, etc	round 1, round 2, etc
W	women	Ro32, Ro16	round of 32, round of 16
Mx	mixed	rep	repechages
Indiv	individual	C	classification(s)
Team	team	QF	quarterfinals
prelims	preliminaries	SF	semifinals
H	heats	F	final(s)
Q	qualification(s)	MM/MG	medal match(es)/game(s)
			gold medal(s) awarded

Paralympic Competition Schedule

Key
Gold medal session

Discipline	Venue	-2 Mon 27 Aug	-1 Tue 28 Aug	0 Wed 29 Aug	1 Thu 30 Aug	2 Fri 31 Aug	3 Sat 1 Sep	4 Sun 2 Sep	5 Mon 3 Sep	6 Tue 4 Sep	7 Wed 5 Sep	8 Thu 6 Sep	9 Fri 7 Sep	10 Sat 8 Sep	11 Sun 9 Sep
Olympic Park															
Swimming	Aquatics Centre				•	•	•	•	•	•	•	•	•	•	
Wheelchair Basketball	Basketball Arena				•			•				•			
Wheelchair Rugby									•		•		•	•	
Wheelchair Tennis	Eton Manor						•	•	•	•					
Goalball	Copper Box				•	•	•		•		•				
Football 5-a-side	Riverbank Arena				•		•		•					•	
Football 7-a-side						•		•		•		•		•	
Opening Ceremony	Olympic Stadium			•											
Closing Ceremony															•
Athletics						•	•	•	•	•	•	•	•	•	
Cycling Track	Velodrome				•	•	•	•							
Central London															
Athletics	The Mall														•
ExCeL															
Table Tennis	ExCeL – North Arena 1				•	•		•	•		•	•	•	•	
Judo	ExCeL – North Arena 2				•	•									
Wheelchair Fencing										•	•	•			
Boccia	ExCeL – South Arena 1									•		•		•	
Volleyball (sitting)	ExCeL – South Arena 2												•	•	
Powerlifting	ExCeL – South Arena 3				•	•	•	•	•	•	•				
Greenwich Park															
Equestrian	Greenwich Park				•	•	•	•	•	•					
Greenwich Peninsula															
Wheelchair Basketball	North Greenwich Arena				•	•	•	•	•	•	•				
UK Venues															
Cycling Road	Brands Hatch												•	•	•
Rowing	Eton Dorney					•	•	•							
Archery	Royal Artillery Barracks														
Shooting															
Sailing	Weymouth and Portland				•										

| | | -2 Mon 27 Aug | -1 Tue 28 Aug | 0 Wed 29 Aug | 1 Thu 30 Aug | 2 Fri 31 Aug | 3 Sat 1 Sep | 4 Sun 2 Sep | 5 Mon 3 Sep | 6 Tue 4 Sep | 7 Wed 5 Sep | 8 Thu 6 Sep | 9 Fri 7 Sep | 10 Sat 8 Sep | 11 Sun 9 Sep |

Index

Entries in italics refer to illustrations; entries in bold refer to text within a sidebar or box

Abbreviations: OG = Olympic Games; PG = Paralympic Games

Delivering a memorable Olympic Games to inspire a generation with the support of our Partners

Worldwide Olympic Partners

London 2012 Olympic Partners

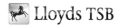

London 2012 Olympic Supporters

London 2012 Olympic Suppliers and Providers

Aggreko, Airwave, Atkins, The Boston Consulting Group, CBS Outdoor, Crystal CG, Eurostar, Freshfields Bruckhaus Deringer LLP, G4S, GlaxoSmithKline, Gymnova, Heathrow Airport, Heineken UK, Holiday Inn, John Lewis, McCann Worldgroup, Mondo, NATURE VALLEY, Next, Nielsen, Populous, Rapiscan Systems, Rio Tinto, Technogym, Thames Water, Ticketmaster, Trebor, Westfield.

Delivering a memorable Paralympic Games to inspire a generation with the support of our Partners

Worldwide Paralympic Partners

London 2012 Paralympic Partners

  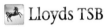

   Sainsbury's

London 2012 Paralympic Supporters

London 2012 Paralympic Suppliers and Providers

Aggreko, Airwave, Atkins, The Boston Consulting Group, CBS Outdoor, Crystal CG, Eurostar, Freshfields Bruckhaus Deringer LLP, G4S, GlaxoSmithKline, Gymnova, Heathrow Airport, Heineken UK, Holiday Inn, John Lewis, McCann Worldgroup, Mondo, NATURE VALLEY, Next, Nielsen, Otto Bock, Populous, Rapiscan Systems, Rio Tinto, Technogym, Thames Water, Ticketmaster, Trebor, Westfield.

LOTTERY FUNDED The London 2012 Paralympic Games also acknowledges the support of the National Lottery

The Victory Parade on 10 September through central London attracted an estimated million, wildly excited, spectators.

Authors' Acknowledgments

The authors would like to thank the following: Peter Cook, Keith, Sue, James and Spencer Davies, Ed, Dom and Garth Simpson, Billy Knight and Hazel Ruscoe, and the staff and Games Makers at the Main Press Centre in the Olympic Park.

Picture credits

The Publisher would like to thank the following for the use of their images:

All images © Getty Images except: p. 8: © ODA; p. 11: © Jason Orton; p. 12: © Wenlock Olympian Society; p. 14: © IOC; p. 19: © ODA; p. 20 ODA; p. 21: © Edmund Sumner; p. 22: © Wilkinson Eyre; p. 23 © Edmund Sumner; p. 24: © Mike King; p. 28 © Edmund Sumner; p. 29: © Corbis; pp. 30–31: © Mike King; p. 34 (both): © Press Association for LOCOG; p. 35: © Press Association for LOCOG; p. 42 (top): © Mike King; p. 44: © Mike King; p. 66: © Mike King; pp. 78–79: © Mike King; p. 82: © Mike King; p. 84: © Mike King; p. 85: © Mike King; p. 92: © Mike King; p. 93: © Mike King; pp. 118–119: © Mike King; p. 135 (right): © Edmund Sumner; p. 188 (both): © Mike King; p. 189: © Mike King; pp. 192-193: © Mike King; p. 198: © Mike King; p. 199: © Mike King; p. 203: © Mike King; pp. 210–211: © Mike King; p. 215: © Mike King; p. 253: © Mike King; p. 265: © Mike King; p. 271: © Boris Abalai; p. 275: © www.pleasanceahoy.com; p. 276: © Howard Barlow; p. 278: © Daniel Saint; p. 279: © London Legacy Development Corporation. Endpaper images © Mike King.